THE LEAVES
WE WRITE ON

James Cropper (1823-1900), founder and first chairman of the company that still bears his name. He began life as a paper-maker in July 1845.

THE LEAVES
WE WRITE ON

James Cropper: A history in paper-making

Mark Cropper

Ellergreen Press
LONDON
2004

Published by the Ellergreen Press 2004

British Library Cataloguing in Publication Data
A catalogue record for this book is available from the British Library.

ISBN 0 9549191 1 4

Printed by
Titus Wilson & Son, Kendal
2004

for Attosa and James

The paper: this book showcases a number of papers made by James Cropper plc at Burneside. The text is printed upon *Accent Natural* made for paper merchant G. F. Smith. Casebound copies feature *carbon free Ebony* endpapers from G. F. Smith's Colorplan range, while the bookcloth is a grade made for Winter & Company, *Wibalin Buckram 586.*

Contents

Foreword

WHEN James Cropper, my great-great grandfather, started marking paper in 1845, you would have been forgiven for thinking the prospects were not bright. He knew nothing about industry, even less about paper-making, and his motives were entirely unrelated. He decided to become a paper-maker, the career his family have pursued ever since, so that he could be nearer the love of his life, his cousin Fanny Alison Wakefield, whom he later married.

Given the circumstances, it was little surprise that he did not get off to a good start. In the first place he paid far too much for the two paper-mills he bought on Westmorland's river Kent, at Burneside and Cowan Head. Added to this he lost money on them year after year, and turning the situation around proved to be far more difficult than he had envisaged.

It was not the last time that the company he founded has faced an uphill struggle to survive. In the last one hundred and sixty years James Cropper plc has earned a reputation for itself as a great survivor in British paper-making by overcoming numerous threats, as this book reveals. Not least among these threats has been the extremely testing trading environment that I have witnessed in the course of my career. Indeed, when I succeeded Derek Willink as chairman of James Cropper plc over thirty years ago, the British paper industry was at a critical point in its history. Output was declining, many mills were beginning to close, and thousands of jobs were being lost.

At that time, James Cropper was one of many small provincial paper-mills, making traditional papers for long-standing markets within Britain. Its five machines, if not old in years, were ancient in design, dating back to the 1900s, and many aspects of the paper-making process had not changed since the nineteenth century, a fact shown by the extremely laborious nature of much of the work, and the large workforce that was needed to run the mills.

Not for the first time in its history, the firm reacted by reinventing itself. Today James Cropper plc is one of the leading suppliers of coloured and other specialist paper and board in the world. Its plant and machinery – which remain on one site at Burneside, on the fringes of the English Lake District – are some of the most up-to-date of their kind in the world. Its products are also worldwide leaders, a fact which is evident in the high percentage of turnover that is sold abroad every year. Thirty years ago hardly any Cropper paper was exported; today it is sold through a network of international agents to dozens of countries on all five continents.

Even more importantly, in the last twenty years the company has diversified into other areas for the first time in its history, first into Converting, and then into Technical Fibre Products, and lastly into retail with The Paper Mill Shop, an employee-driven initiative designed to use up surplus paper that continues to grow faster than expectations.

I have every hope that these changes have secured the future of the business for another generation and another century. And with a future secured, so it seems a good time to look back on the company's past. I was delighted when my son Mark agreed to write the history of the company, a project that we first contemplated on the occasion of our 150th Anniversary in 1995. He has devoted much time and effort to researching the history comprehensively, and I hope you find the results of his efforts as engaging as I have.

James Cropper, October 2004

Author's note and acknowledgement

WHEN I first agreed to write this book, longer ago than I care to remember, it appeared to be a relatively simple task. After all, the company in question had been making one product in one place with many of the same families involved for the duration of its history. All I had to do was cast my eyes over the records, speak to a few people, join up the dots, and the job would be done. At least that was what I thought.

As I delved into the material available, the situation changed dramatically. As I uncovered more and more, my appetite to dig even deeper only increased, as did the task of understanding the context and piecing everything together. Thus what started out as a relatively simple corporate history became much more: not only the portrayal of a company, but also a family, an industry, a region and much else besides. It has been a richly rewarding experience to weave a story out of the material I found, but one task has defeated me.

As I have charted the course of mills, machines and markets (to mention just three recurrent subjects), it has often been easy to forget that this history ultimately hinges upon lives. At times it has been difficult to emphasise the human dimension at the heart of this story; the tragedy, disappointment, hope and laughter that has animated the Cropper paper-mills for over a century and a half. Generations of friendships, falling-outs, fortunes and misfortunes have been lived out in its shadow, but to bring these to life I can only appeal to the reader's imagination.

This is also my only chance to acknowledge the many people who have helped me to research and write this book. First, I am particularly indebted to Janet Martin for her sustained guidance and support, and for reading the manuscript. My thanks also to Carlos Calvo and Danny Kruger for taking the time to read the manuscript in draft form.

Secondly, I would have made little progress without the huge input I received from the numerous people who have worked for James Cropper plc, past and present, who agreed to share their stories with me, including: Oliver Acland, Bernard Airey, Joe Carruthers, Peter Charlton, Maurice Crossley, May Dobson,

Robin Field, Philip Huck, John Larking, Tommy Pinch, George Quayle, Ronnie Reddish, Terry Robinson, Brian Scott, Harold Snowdon, Alan Sutton, Frank Thompson, Alf Whiteley, Albert Wilkinson, Mike Wilkinson, Nick Willink, Harry Wilson, Teddy Wilson, and Jenny Young. A special thanks to Mike Wilkinson, not only for giving so much of his time to talk to me but also for taking and preparing several of the pictures within this book.

I would also like to acknowledge the following for their help on many other important points: Chris Aspin, Steve Barber, Patrick Bogue, my grandmother Philippa Cropper, Mike Davies-Shiel, Percy Duff, John Gavin, Bobby Gibbs, Richard Hall and Kath Strickland of the Kendal Record Office, Richard Hills, Phillip Joyce, Nick Langdon of the Confederation of Paper Industries, Chris Martin, David Pointon and his team at Titus Wilson, Dosia Verney, Oliver Westall, Bill Willink, Charles Willink, and last and not least, Robert Woof.

Most of all I wish to thank my family, in particular my wife Attosa, whose continued support has been vital. Finally, I could not have contemplated writing this history without the encouragement and assistance of my father James Cropper.

Mark Cropper, November 2004

Fothergill Sc.

Fig. 1.1 – Our story unfolds in the foothills of the English Lake District. Burneside, home to the Cropper Mills and a site of industrial activity since the middle ages, is visible here in the middle distance.

Previous page: Burneside Mill, from an engraving of c.1835.

1

Early Mills: the Industrial Heritage, 1300-1845

Ingenious artists, ye, who daily make
The leaves we write on, may your labours fill
With wealth your coffers, while you propagate,
The means to eternise the wise and good!

(From "Cowan Head", by William Robinson, 1773)

OUR story begins with the river Kent, and the life it has given to generations of mills upon its rapid descent from the fells of the English Lake District to the Irish Sea. The earliest records of mills on the river date from the twelfth century, although records do not refer to a mill in the vicinity of Burneside and Cowan Head, the setting of the story that unfolds in these pages, until the late thirteenth century.[1] Its location remains unclear, although there was a manorial corn-mill at Burneside from medieval times, owned and controlled by the resident of Burneside Hall. Records of the hall date back to 1290, when it was occupied by Gilbert de Burneshead, and the manor subsequently descended through his only daughter, Margaret, to the Bellingham family of Northumberland, in whose ownership it remained until the sixteenth century. It then passed to the Braithwaite family of Ambleside.

By that time, corn-milling was not the only industry that was drawing power from the Kent at Burneside. Sheep pastures were, and still are, more characteristic of the landscape of the Kent valley than fields of corn, and medieval Kendal prospered from trade in wool rather than grain, as the town's motto – *Pannus mihi Panis* ("wool is my bread") – suggests. This led to the construction of dozens of water-powered mills carrying out a rather different industry: fulling, an essential stage in the process of cloth manufacture. "It was the custom to card, spin and weave the wool in the house", John Somervell explains –

> . . . but the woven cloth was so loose in texture that it really required "fulling", and this could only be efficiently done by power. The piece of cloth was put into a rounded trough, full of a special soapy mixture, into which a very heavy wooden beam about

eight feet long, with a heavy rounded foot [a fulling stock], came constantly down and pounded it . . . so that by very slow degrees the whole piece emerged "fulled", shrunk and ready to wear, after drying.[2]

By the mid-fifteenth century there was a fulling-mill at Burneside and probably one at Cowan Head as well, where records of a mill date back to the seventeenth century. As steep-sided fells give way to gentle foothills and pasture, the river Kent at Cowan Head falls twenty-three feet, the greatest drop on the river, and it is likely that such an abundance of natural power was exploited from medieval times.

Small corn-mills and fulling-mills typified the industrial landscape of the Kent until the mid-eighteenth century. Soon afterwards, however, the water power of the district began to be used for new and more specialised industries, making less vital and more luxurious commodities such as gunpowder, linen, paper and snuff.[3] In most cases this led to the construction of large new mills and changes in ownership. By the mid-eighteenth century Westmorland's mills were increasingly passing out of manorial control into the hands of a new and rising breed of man: the industrial entrepreneur.

One such entrepreneur was Thomas Ashburner, a Kendal stationer, printer, publisher, and bookseller. Exploiting the lapse of the Licensing Act in 1695 (which had restricted printing to London, Oxford, Cambridge and York), he had set up a printing press in the town's Fishmarket by 1734, when he began to publish a newspaper, *The Kendal Weekly Mercury* (Fig. 1.2). For a small town like Kendal this was a ground-breaking venture – in 1730 there were about twenty provincial newspapers in England – yet Thomas Ashburner, remarkably, established both press and paper in the face of existing competition. Thomas Cotton had set up

Fig. 1.2 – Thomas Ashburner's Kendal Weekly Mercury, *published from 1734 until 1749.*
(Source: Cumbria Record Office, Kendal)

Kendal's first printing press in 1730, and began publishing *The Kendal Weekly Courant*, the town's first newspaper, in 1731. He was understandably concerned when he informed his readers in January 1735 that "Mr Ashburner has erected a press, publish'd a News paper, and must naturally endeavour to enlarge his own trade, which may probably diminish mine".

His fears were not misplaced. Thomas Ashburner proved to be a more than effective competitor, and in 1736 Cotton shut down both press and paper and moved north to Whitehaven. *The Kendal Weekly Mercury* was more enduring. It continued to be published until 1749, when Thomas Ashburner replaced it with a weekly gazette, *The Agreeable Miscellany*.[4] The new periodical was not, however, such a success. It was discontinued in 1750 after thirty-nine issues, and Kendal had to wait until 1811 before a local paper was published again.

In common with other provincial newspapers of the time *The Kendal Weekly Mercury* did not provide its readers with local news. Articles of local interest were almost entirely absent from the publication, and most of its news was taken from London newspapers. It was, however, full of local advertising, including regular notices publicising Thomas Ashburner's own diverse range of goods and services. These included books and stationery, as well as more unexpected wares such as medicines. Like stationers nationwide he dispensed quack remedies, including "Daffy's Elixir", which was regularly promoted in the columns of his paper.*

By the 1740s Thomas Ashburner's various trades had earned him sufficient capital to invest elsewhere, and he began to build up a portfolio of small mills. In 1743 he purchased a tannery in Skelsmergh, called Stocks Mill, one of several in his possession by the middle of the eighteenth century.[5] Two years later he bought Henry Scarisbrick's north Kendal mills, informing the district of his new business by way of a handbill (Fig. 1.3). Significantly, this probably brought him into contact with paper-making for the first time. It is possible that paper was made there on a limited scale, although it is likely that most of the grades he advertised were made elsewhere, perhaps Milnthorpe.[6]

Thomas Ashburner's next purchase was the fulling-mill at Cowan Head, which he purchased in 1746 for £130.[7] This had come onto the market for the first time in its history owing to the decision of Thomas Shepherd, who had inherited Burneside Hall from his father, to break up the ancient manor and sell it off to various parties. At the time it seems to have been purchased as a going concern; a

---

* Daffy's Elixir was one of many opium-based syrups used as a tonic. It was invented by the vicar of Redmile in Leicestershire, first coming to public notice between 1660 and 1680. It was regularly bought in the 1720s and 1730s (perhaps from Ashburner) by Clement Taylor of Finsthwaite House, near Newby Bridge, who gave it to his maids. (*'The Account Book of Clement Taylor 1712-1753'*, Janet D. Martin (ed.), Record Society of Lancashire and Cheshire, Vol. CXXXV, 1997)

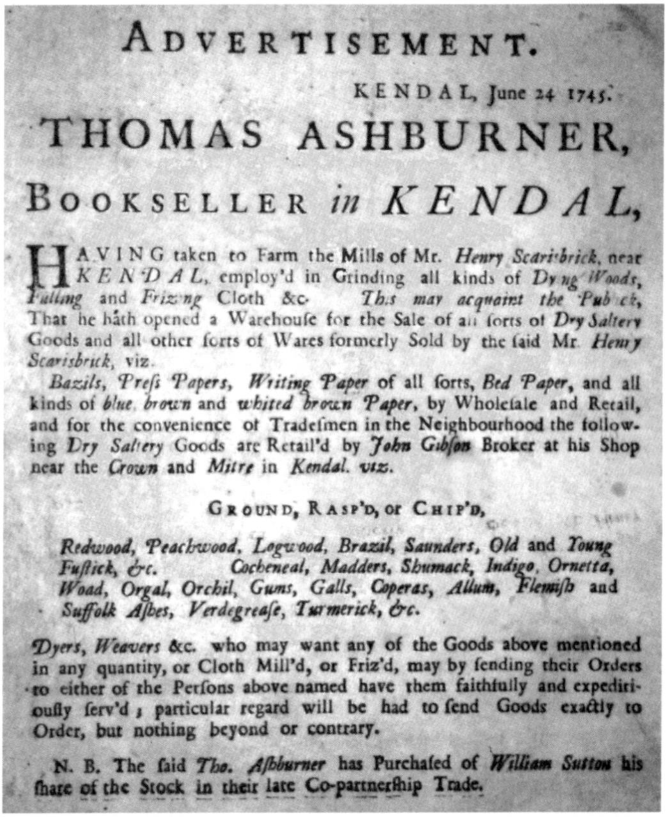

ADVERTISEMENT.

KENDAL, June 24 1745.

THOMAS ASHBURNER,

BOOKSELLER *in* *KENDAL*,

HAVING taken to Farm the Mills of Mr. *Henry Scarisbrick*, near *KENDAL*, employ'd in Grinding all kinds of *Dying Woods*, *Falling* and *Frizing* Cloth &c. *This may acquaint the Publick*, That he hath opened a Warehouſe for the Sale of all ſorts of *Dry Saltery* Goods and all other ſorts of Wares formerly Sold by the ſaid Mr. *Henry Scarisbrick*, viz.

Bazils, *Preſs Papers*, *Writing Paper* of all ſorts, *Bed Paper*, and all kinds of *blue*, *brown* and *whited brown Paper*, by Wholeſale and Retail, and for the convenience of Tradeſmen in the Neighbourhood the following *Dry Saltery* Goods are Retail'd by *John Gibſon* Broker at his Shop near the *Crown* and *Mitre* in *Kendal*. viz.

GROUND, RASP'D, or CHIP'D,

Redwood, *Peachwood*, *Logwood*, *Brazil*, *Saunders*, *Old* and *Young Fuſtick*, *&c.* *Cocheneal*, *Madders*, *Shumack*, *Indigo*, *Ornetta*, *Woad*, *Orgal*, *Orchil*, *Gums*, *Galls*, *Coperas*, *Allum*, *Flemiſh* and *Suffolk Aſhes*, *Verdegreaſe*, *Turmerick*, *&c.*

Dyers, *Weavers* &c. who may want any of the Goods above mentioned in any quantity, or Cloth Mill'd, or Friz'd, may by ſending their Orders to either of the Perſons above named have them faithfully and expeditiouſly ſerv'd; particular regard will be had to ſend Goods exactly to Order, but nothing beyond or contrary.

N. B. The ſaid *Tho. Aſhburner* has Purchaſed of *William Sutton* his ſhare of the Stock in their late Co-partnerſhip Trade.

Fig. 1.3 – Handbill announcing goods and services offered by Thomas Ashburner following his purchase of a Kendal mill, 1745. (Source: Cumbria Record Office, courtesy of the National Trust, Town End)

1749 document notes little change to the site, and it is probable that cloth continued to be processed there in the ancient way.[8] By the early 1750s, however, Ashburner began to draw up other plans for the site, and around 1753 started constructing a new mill there, especially for the manufacture of paper.

His new and substantial investment was both ambitious and pioneering. Since the first paper-mill in the Lakes region had been established at Cark-in-Cartmel in 1616, the local paper industry had been predominantly associated with the wool trade. Cark and the mills that followed it (notably those at Ambleside and Troutbeck) were almost wholly engaged in the manufacture of coarse brown paper used by the woollen industry for pressing and packing cloth.[9] In many cases the link with wool was physical. Most of Cumbria's early paper-mills were owned or worked by individuals involved in the wool trade, and in some cases paper-making and other textile related activities were carried on in a single mill.

Cowan Head was different. It was the first paper-mill in the area to be owned by a member of the book trade and the first to produce white paper in significant quantities. Its most important feature, however, was its size. Thomas Ashburner's new mill dwarfed the region's existing mills. Where paper manufacture had previously been confined to one or two rooms, Cowan Head possessed a whole range of rooms to serve different needs. By 1769 the site included two paper-mills, one glaze-mill, six warehouses and other rooms, all under one roof. In another building there were three drying rooms, two tenements, stables, hayhouse, carpenter's shop, kitchen and finishing room. The value of the premises also speaks of their supremacy. When Cowan Head was insured in 1769, the buildings alone were valued at £1,500, more than twice the value of the buildings at any other eighteenth century Cumbrian paper-mill.[10]

While there was much that was new about Cowan Head, one thing remained the same: the way in which the paper was made. True paper, as it was invented in China in the second century, is a matted material made from tiny cellulose fibres that are obtained from macerating or beating the raw material, plant or tree, into a fine pulp of fibres, called "stuff". This is then suspended evenly in water so that, when the water is drained off, a sheet of paper is created. Strength and cohesion are provided by the cellulose fibres, which bond with each other as the sheet is formed.

All plants contain the necessary cellulose, but few have proved to meet the specific requirements of the paper-manufacturer: to be available in large quantities, to contain a sufficient concentration of the necessary fibre, and (most importantly) for the fibre to be readily extractable. On this third count, before esparto and wood pulp became available in the latter half of the nineteenth century, western European paper-makers traditionally preferred a raw material which was partly processed when it entered the paper-mill. In this way brown paper was made from materials such as coloured rags, rope, canvas, netting and sacking. White paper, meanwhile, was made from better quality rags, mainly white linen and cotton.

Before a paper machine was installed at Cowan Head in 1835 every sheet of paper made there was made by hand, in a centuries-old process (Fig. 1.4). First of all, a large vat was filled with the solution of pulped fibres and water. Next, the paper-maker, or vatman, took a mould (a rectangular wooden framework covered with a fine wire mesh), and attached a narrow wooden frame (known as a deckle) to it. This was then dipped in the vat and then withdrawn, at which point the vatman shook the mould from side to side and back and forth as the water drained away, an action which interlocked the fibres in the sheet that was being formed, and gave it strength.

The vatman then removed the deckle from the mould and passed the mould to his assistant, the coucher, who removed the wet sheet of paper from the mould by

Fig. 1.4 – Making paper by hand.

turning it over and depositing it on a felt using a deft rocking motion. This was added to a stack of wet sheets and felts, known as a post, which was later put in a huge screw press to squeeze away most of the remaining water. Finally, the paper was taken to one of the three drying rooms, and hung up on lines to dry. Once dry the paper might be dispatched, or, if it was to be written or printed on, sealed with gelatine size so that it would not absorb the ink, and dried again. Lastly, if finer quality paper was being made, the paper would be taken to the finishing room and "finished" – pressed or smoothed, and sorted into grades.

So far as the preparation of raw materials was concerned, Cowan Head had access to more modern technology. By the 1740s the preparatory stage of paper-making was beginning to be transformed by the Hollander beater, named after the country where it had been invented some fifty years before (Fig. 1.5). Consisting of a large wooden tub with a rotating drum that churned and macerated the raw material, it was far more efficient that the primitive machine it replaced, the stamper.[11] Basically a huge pestle and mortar, these usually existed in rows – there were twenty at Cark in 1720 – but by the end of the eighteenth century they had largely disappeared.[12] By then one Hollander could process twelve times as much material as forty stampers.[13]

The scale of Cowan Head required that rags be gathered from near and far in order to ensure a sufficient supply, a practice that is recorded in the accounts of Abraham Dent, a Kirkby Stephen shopkeeper.[14] These document that he bought paper, magazines and books from Thomas Ashburner and his son James from 1759 until the 1770s. The paper was sold at prices ranging from 3d to 1s a quire, but was often exchanged, along with other goods, for rags collected by the Dents. In 1773 James Ashburner received about 770 stone of rags from the Dents, the white at 2s a stone, and the coarse at 9d. The Dent records further suggest that Thomas Ashburner maintained a widespread network of business contacts or agents. Kirkby Stephen is more then twenty miles from Kendal and there were undoubtedly many more contacts within that radius and perhaps some even further afield, forming a lucrative trading network.

Thomas Ashburner's success as a paper-maker also undoubtedly owed much to Cowan Head's proximity to Kendal. The town grew throughout the eighteenth century, in great part owing to its increasing importance as the hub of a network of turnpike roads. The building of the first of these began in 1753 (just at the moment that Thomas Ashburner began to develop Cowan Head) and within a few years Kendal was the epicentre of fourteen routes, and the meeting point for some nineteen packhorse teams per week. This made it an ideal place for distributing and collecting goods and materials and it soon became a regional centre of industry and trade. The number and wealth of its inhabitants rose accordingly. By the 1780s its population stood at 8,000, over three times the level of the 1730s.[15]

Fig. 1.5 – *The Hollander beater, from* The Useful Arts and Manufactures of Great Britain, *1861.*

The growth of Kendal benefited Cowan Head in a number of ways. Expanding trade ensured strong demand for brown paper, mainly used for wrapping an increasing spectrum of goods. This included glazed paper for pressing and packing woollen cloth, which was made in Cowan Head's glaze-mill. Here press-paper or mill-board was made by passing the paper through metal rollers (calenders) to give a shiny glazed surface to one or both sides. No doubt much was supplied to the large woollen mill at Burneside, which was built in 1761.[16] There was also a growing local market for white paper, not only for private and commercial correspondence but also for activities such as recording transactions, writing orders, issuing bills, and keeping accounts. It was also increasingly in demand as a medium for advertising, which, in the absence of a local newspaper between 1749 and 1811, usually took the form of handbills or posters. Several bearing Thomas Ashburner's imprint survive, and were no doubt printed on his own paper.

Demand for white paper, and indeed for all of Thomas Ashburner's products and services, was ultimately stimulated by the growth of literacy. In the seventeenth century reading was largely the preserve of the few, mainly scholars and the aristocracy. Books were very expensive, reading matter of any kind scarce – particularly in a provincial town like Kendal – and most people illiterate. During the eighteenth century, in contrast, people across all ranks of society and in all areas of the country began to learn and read and write. As printing, bookselling and paper-making spread across the provinces, more and more people were not only able to read and write, but also had the time, money and inclination to do so.

The cultural shift was huge, a significant step in the foundation of our own literate and literary culture, and, at a provincial level, one in which Thomas Ashburner played no small part. His various trades not only prospered from rising wealth and literacy, but also stimulated the advance of literacy and learning in the area. As a bookseller he keenly bought and sold libraries and stocked books on a vast array of subjects.[17] As a printer, his press gave Kendal the power to broadcast localised subjects, often religious; his imprint is found on several surviving sermons and hymnals.[18] The paper he made even gave those with creative aspirations a local source of writing material.

Befitting his position at the cultural heart of Kendal, Thomas Ashburner also supported other branches of the arts. In 1755 he was involved in the apprenticeship of the young George Romney to Christopher Steele, a Kendal artist, and in 1758 he established Kendal's first theatre, reconstructing premises behind the Football Inn in the town's Market Place.[19] All in all he was a significant figure in the history of the town, whose contribution deserves to be celebrated. A fitting epitaph, as it happens, is provided by one of his contemporaries, William Robinson, who wrote a poem about Cowan Head ("The property of Mr. Ashburner") in 1770.[20] "This paper mill adds beauty to the place", it reads –

. . . And renders Cowen-Head a scene of trade.
Let us step in, and view the various works,
Whence science is diffus'd thro' all the globe.
Thou, and thy sister, printing, noble arts.
Recorders of the genius' deathless fame;
Immortal arts! Why was your happy birth
Delay'd 'til Egypt, sacred wisdom's nurse,
And Rome and learned Athens were no more?
How many Homers, Shakespeares, Miltons, Popes,
Wanting your aid, are in oblivion lost!

Ingenious artists, ye, who daily make
The leaves we write on, may your labours fill
With wealth your coffers, while you propagate,
The means to eternise the wise and good!

It is a classic celebration of the art of the paper-maker, and the cultural value of
paper. Moreover, the eulogy was prophetic: a couple of decades later Cowan
Head's paper-makers furnished the young William Wordsworth with leaves to
write on. It is probable that the poet often wrote on Cowan Head paper, although
only one manuscript, the Windy Brow notebook of 1794, bears a Cowan Head
watermark (Fig. 1.6).[21]

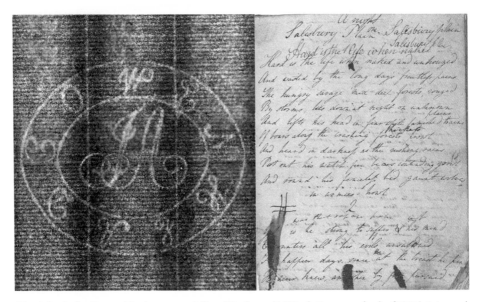

Fig. 1.6 – Left: *Cowan Head watermark from Wordsworth's Windy Brow notebook of 1794, J A stands
for James Ashburner.* Right: *Its contents include Wordsworth's* A night on Salisbury Plain. *(Source:
Wordsworth Trust)*

In the intervening years Cowan Head had passed to James Ashburner, the eldest son.[22] In contrast with his father, however, he made little mark. His trades made him a prominent and wealthy Kendal inhabitant, a member of the town's commercial élite, yet there are no records of his involvement in the social and political life of the town. Unlike his father, he never became a mayor or alderman, common positions for a man of his wealth and standing, nor did he show any signs of the entrepreneurial flair so evident in his father. Although neither bookshop nor mill failed under his ownership there are no indications that they expanded.

In his defence, James Ashburner was not favoured with the benign trading conditions that his father had enjoyed. After decades of steady growth the output of British paper-mills began to level off in the 1770s, a slow-down in part attributable to heavier excise duties.[23] At the same time the paper industry was affected by the widespread commercial recession precipitated by the War of American Independence (1775-83), which led to a spate of bankruptcies in all areas of commerce. Changes of ownership and mill closures suggest that Westmorland and Cumberland's paper industry followed the national trend. Backbarrow, for example, some fifteen miles from Cowan Head, went bankrupt in 1779 and became a cotton mill, and the paper-mills at Waterhouse and Milnthorpe were used as flax and cotton mills for a time.[24]

James Ashburner was also threatened by growing competition. Contemporary directories list him and William Pennington alone as Kendal's booksellers and printers in 1784.[25] Six years later, however, Kendal boasted four booksellers, with John Armstrong and W. Todhunter also trading in the town.[26] It was William Pennington (1745-1815), however, who really posed a threat. Apprenticed to Thomas Ashburner in 1761, he was not long out of his apprenticeship when he set up his own bookselling and printing business in Kendal, his first recorded publication dating from 1771.[27] Furthermore, in 1787, following the example of his master, he also began to make paper in partnership with his brother-in-law Richard Crampton, whose family made paper at Milnthorpe. Together they reconstructed the paper-mill at Starnthwaite, five miles west of Kendal.[28] His diverse activities suggest that he was more the spiritual successor of Thomas Ashburner than James. In particular, he was more active in publishing, issuing edition after edition of Thomas West's *Guide to the Lakes*, as well as several works published jointly with the London house of Richardson & Urquhart.

James Ashburner was not, however, without publications of his own. In 1777 he issued *The Kendal Diary* – a yearly almanac that survived until 1836 – and in 1790 he added to the growing tide of books on local subjects, publishing *The Westmorland Dialect, in three familiar dialogues in which an attempt is made to illustrate the Provincial Idiom*, printed on Cowan Head paper bearing the watermark JA.[29] In addition, like his father he printed sermons in small pamphlets, as well as numerous sale notices and handbills, including one advertising his own goods and services (Fig. 1.7).

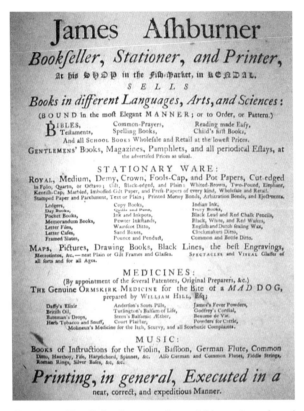

Fig. 1.7 – Handbill advertising James Ashburner's goods and services, c.1780. (Source: Cumbria Record Office, Kendal, courtesy of the National Trust, Town End)

Offering a great variety of wares, including paper, the bill shown in Fig. 1.7 is particularly notable for its reference to educational books, not only children's spelling and reading books – evidence of the contribution that the provincial bookseller made to literacy – but also instructive literature geared towards adults.[30] The rising middle classes were especially fond of such literature, which included guides to 'proper' language usage, a popular publishing genre that James Ashburner himself ventured into. In 1779 he published *The Accomplished Letter-writer; or Universal correspondent . . . To which is prefixed a compendious grammar of the English tongue.* It is a simple and practical instruction manual. Sample letters "to suit the most common occasions" form the bulk of the book, including, ". . .

books), catechisms, Watt's hymns, street songs, and chap-books.[36] These were pocket-sized story books, often carrying a Bewick-style woodcut on the front, and on subjects ranging from Arthurian legend to the confessions of condemned criminals. Several examples bearing the Branthwaite imprint are recorded, including the charmingly titled *The true history of the sailor who had both his legs shot off, with an account of his extraordinary Dream, and how remarkably it was fulfilled.*[37]

The Branthwaites also profited from jobbing printing and newspaper publishing work. In 1811 Michael Branthwaite was one of seven founding members of the *Westmorland Advertiser and Kendal Chronicle*, the first periodical published in the town since Thomas Ashburner's *Agreeable Miscellany* of 1750. The newspaper was printed and published on their Fishmarket premises and perhaps, given Michael Branthwaite's involvement, on Cowan Head paper. By 1813 Michael Branthwaite was also editing the paper, a position he occupied until 1818 when it passed to Richard Lough.[38]

Like Cowan Head, two miles upstream, the mills at Burneside changed dramatically from the mid-eighteenth century. The development was likewise led by a Kendal tradesman with industrial ambitions, but not, in this case, with links to the book trade. Roger Wakefield, who owned Burneside's corn, fulling, frizing, and sickle mills by the time of his death in 1756 was a shearman-dyer, a leading member of the district's lucrative woollen trade. In further contrast with Thomas Ashburner he was also, like many of his trade and status, a Quaker. His family had belonged to the Society of Friends for some time. This was important: Quakers were notoriously frugal folk, allowing them to accumulate the necessary capital to finance a move from trade into industry. This was certainly the case with the Wakefield family, as for a number of generations the family had even had sufficient funds to lend money to others.

The transformation of Burneside into an industrial site of some magnitude was in greatest part carried through by Roger's son, John Wakefield I (1738-1811). In 1761 he constructed a three-storey woollen mill on the banks of the Kent at Burneside, and by 1780 he had added an even larger cotton mill to the site (Fig. 1.8). Both developments are notable. The 1761 woollen mill was a remarkably early organisation of an industry for centuries practised on a domestic scale, and the cotton mill was one of the first in the world to take up cotton-spinning using machinery invented by Richard Arkwright. Both were also tremendously profitable. On a turnover of £13,000 in 1785 the woollen mill returned a profit of £4,200, and its profits from 1790 to 1803 remained at the same level. It continued to operate into the 1830s.[39]

In great part its prosperity was assured by John Wakefield's trading links with the New World, for he was not only a mill-owner but also a busy merchant,

Fig. 1.8 – Burneside, from an oil painting of c.1820. The woollen-mill is adjacent to the bridge; the cotton-mill is behind, with smoke coming out of the chimney.

operating a fleet of five ships from Liverpool. He used these to ship woollen cloth, probably made at Burneside, to the New World, and bring back sugar from Jamaica in return. His surviving accounts bear witness to these "adventures", as they were known at the time. Several voyages are recorded including an "Adventure to Barbados", and the more romantic-sounding "Adventure of the *Bella*".[40] Furthermore, while he was waiting for his ships to return, John Wakefield was busy expanding his business interests at home. In addition to his cotton and wool interests he owned a brewery and gunpowder mills, as well as investing in turnpike roads.

To cap it all, Wakefield was also a pioneering banker. In 1788 he established one of Kendal's first two banks – the other was opened on the same day – a sure indication, if any was needed, of his considerable wealth. At the time a bank could not be opened unless its owner possessed £10,000 or more of capital.[41] Like most of his projects, it was a resounding success. Over the next half-century John Wakefield & Sons showed remarkable resilience, remaining solvent in an age of foreign wars and numerous trade recessions. It was no doubt helped by its reputation for honesty and creditworthiness, virtues closely connected to the Quaker faith of its partners. Indeed, at one time this was so high that it was said that many preferred a "Jackie Wakefield" note to one of the Bank of England (Fig. 1.9).[42]

The success of the cotton mill, however, was less enduring. As the cotton industry became increasingly concentrated in Lancashire's towns, earlier mills in rural outposts such as Burneside became uneconomical and gradually began to close. By the 1820s, and perhaps earlier, cotton production had ceased in the Westmorland village, which was also an unfavourable location owing to its distance from the canal network that serviced most of Lancashire's mills.[43] The Wakefields' investment did not, however, go entirely to waste, for by the 1830s they had found a new use for the mill that has proved to be much more enduring: paper-making.

Fig. 1.9 – Wakefield bank-note, 1801.

In 1832 Burneside's cotton mill was leased to Hudson, Nicholson & Foster, a partnership of three local tradesmen. Like Thomas Ashburner over eighty years before, the new incumbents had all made their money in the book trade. Arthur Foster was a long-established bookseller and stationer in Kirkby Lonsdale, while John Hudson and Cornelius Nicholson had a long association with bookselling and printing in Kendal. The latter pair, who were the driving force behind the new venture, had both started out as apprentices of Richard Lough, who succeeded Michael Branthwaite as editor and publisher of the *Kendal Chronicle* in 1818.

Although younger than John Hudson, from an early age Cornelius Nicholson (Fig. 1.10) was the more prominent of the pair, evidently the more ambitious, and usually the instigator of their many ventures. The *Kendal Chronicle* apprenticeship fitted well his disposition. "His appetite for knowledge grew upon what it fed", his daughter Cornelia noted of his time there. "Literature and passing criticisms came to him in his daily work, and almost all his evenings were given to books, as many as he could buy or borrow."[44] Books were not, however, readily available to most young people in Kendal as there was no library, a deficiency that did not escape his

Fig. 1.10 – Cornelius Nicholson, 1804-89.

notice. In 1824 he proposed and led the establishment of a Mechanics' and Apprentices' Library and Institute in the town, an achievement which was not only notable for his age – he was still only nineteen – but also because the institution was one of the first of its kind in England.[45]

It was the first of many pioneering ventures in which he was involved. In 1832 he distinguished himself as Kendal's first historian, penning the *Annals of Kendal*. In later years he became an important figure in the town's history himself, foremost in its railways, reservoirs, gas and water works, not to mention papermaking. In 1835 he jointly founded Kendal's Natural History and Scientific Society, having secured the support of several prominent individuals including Lord Brougham, Wordsworth and Southey.[46] He was extraordinarily energetic: most of his diverse activities were conducted outside of the long hours he dedicated to his own businesses; the *Annals of Kendal*, for example, occupied the nights of two winters, only being worked on "after the compiler's day's work was over".[47]

The most important event in terms of his subsequent career was, however, the partnership he formed with John Hudson in 1825. In November of that year the pair began business as booksellers, stationers and printers in a small shop on

Kendal's Highgate. At the time Kendal had three other booksellers, and five other printers, a fiercely competitive market for a town of its size, but against the odds their business prospered.[48] Within a few years they had moved across the street into larger premises and also begun to operate as wholesalers from a warehouse nearby, a larger and more rewarding line of business.[49] They certainly proved more successful than one of their competitors, William Pennington, who went bankrupt in 1827.[50]

That failure had important consequences. The Starnthwaite paper-mill, set up by Pennington's father in 1787, became available, and Hudson and Nicholson quickly seized the opportunity to diversify into paper-making. In 1828 they leased it in partnership with John Roberts and George Taylor Eglin, and provided a third of the £1,200 capital, the firm taking the name Eglin, Roberts & Co.[51] It was a well considered arrangement, with designated roles for each party. Roberts, who took care of the paper-mill itself, belonged to a dynasty of paper-makers who had worked mills all over the North of England, including Milnthorpe and Starnthwaite. Eglin, in turn, who had commercial experience as a Kendal saddler and tanner, acted as book-keeper, cashier and traveller. Last and not least Hudson and Nicholson were responsible for the sale of paper and pasteboards, and stored rags and finished paper in their Kendal warehouse.[52]

The paper-making partnership did not, however, last long. Although it was set up to run for fourteen years, it was dissolved after four. Hudson and Nicholson's initial investment of £400 was refunded with £150 interest, plus a further sum of £250 to be paid within six months in cash or goods. It was a decent return, suggesting that the enterprise was in a healthy state and not, as might be expected, loss-making. Indeed, it is likely that the paper-making connection served Hudson and Nicholson well.[53] Nevertheless it was Nicholson who brought it to a premature end. The dissolution document is hastily scrawled in his own hand, and his intentions are clear. He was nurturing grander plans for his involvement with the paper industry: mechanisation.

In the 1830s the British paper industry was undergoing the most turbulent change in its history, being rapidly transformed by machines (Fig. 1.11). A machine for making paper had first been invented in the late 1790s by Nicolas Louis Robert, a clerk in a French paper-mill, but it was not until the 1820s that the new technology – which was developed and commercialised with British backing – really began to take off. By 1822 only forty-two Fourdrinier machines, which took the name of the wealthy London stationers who financed its development, had been sold.[54] By 1824, however, more paper was being made by machine than by hand, and thereafter the new process only gained momentum. The advent of machines pushed many hand-made mills out of business and by the late 1820s they were falling rapidly in number.[55] In the 1830s the trend continued: the number of

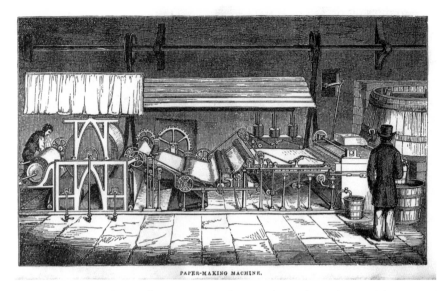

PAPER-MAKING MACHINE.

Fig. 1.11 – An early Fourdrinier paper-making machine, from The Useful Arts and Manufactures of Great Britain, *1861.*

paper machines in Britain jumped from 70 to 180, the sharpest increase in the history of the industry, while as many as 150 hand-made mills disappeared.[56]

According to his daughter, Cornelius Nicholson was urged to start making paper by machine when he saw one on the Isle of Man.[57] However, he must have also been persuaded that mechanisation was the way forward by the growing number of machines elsewhere, particularly in Lancashire, which was fast becoming a hotbed of the new industry. Lancashire took seven of the twenty-eight Fourdrinier machines erected between 1816 and 1822, and by 1832, when Nicholson looked to mechanisation, it is a distinct possibility that machine-made Lancashire paper was penetrating Westmorland markets, reaching Kendal via its canal, opened in 1819.

Nicholson's decision to make paper by machine undoubtedly prompted him to look for a new site. The Starnthwaite paper-mill was too small to convert and its water supply would have been insufficient. By the 1830s one Fourdrinier machine could produce five to seven times as much paper as a vat, but Starnthwaite had been reconstructed in the 1770s to service paper-making in two.[58] As a result he ended his partnership with Eglin and Roberts, and, accompanied by John Hudson, turned his attention to the Wakefield cotton-mill at Burneside.[59]

In contrast with Starnthwaite, the cotton-mill met the requirements of a mechanised paper-mill very well. Its long rooms (seventy-two by thirty feet) could handsomely accommodate a Fourdrinier paper-making machine, and would not more elegant Letters for Examples and Improvement of Style". Meanwhile, the book's various appendices include ". . . a Table of the Clerk-like Contraction of Words, for the Dispatch of Business, And the proper Mode of addressing Persons of All Ranks, either in Writing or Discourse".

When James Ashburner died without issue in 1794 at the age of fifty-seven, the paper-mill and Kendal shop were leased to his nephew, Isaac Wilson, and Michael Branthwaite, a native of Orton who had connections with Cark paper-mill.[31] Within two years, however, the concerns were entirely outside family hands. Isaac Wilson died in 1796 leaving the Ashburner empire in the hands of Michael Branthwaite, who was later joined in partnership by his younger brother Richard.

The few records relating to the Branthwaites largely refer to their publications, with little indication that significant changes or events occurred at Cowan Head. Indeed, mill inventories of 1769 and 1834 show that little changed in sixty-five years, paper continuing to be made by hand, sheet by sheet, in one of two vats. Plans of the mill, dating from 1787 and 1854, also reveal little change to the fabric of Cowan Head's buildings over an even longer period, and well into the era of the mechanised industry, testimony to the quality and scale of Thomas Ashburner's original development.[32]

The Branthwaites were, however, marketing and selling their paper and other goods further afield than their forebears. At the turn of the nineteenth century, for example, they were sending a wagon of paper and other Kendal goods weekly from Cowan Head to York.[33] Newcastle-upon-Tyne also fell within their catchment area. Michael Branthwaite regularly advertised in the Tyneside press, and there is evidence of contact with the famous Newcastle illustrator, Thomas Bewick.* The Branthwaites supplied him with paper in 1819 and 1825, and in 1822 they published *The Beauties of Aesop, and other Fabulists*, with a frontispiece by Bewick and twelve Bewick wood-cuts.[34] Further afield, the Branthwaites were possibly even involved in export trade: paper bearing Michael Branthwaite's watermark, M B 1799, has been found in the United States. Closer to home, meanwhile, the Branthwaites supplemented their trade with the continued sale of medicines, and by acting as agents for Norwich Union Insurance, promoting both vigorously in the local press.[35]

So far as their publishing work was concerned, the Branthwaites conducted a large wholesale trade in short, affordable publications, including battledores (ABC

---

* The *Newcastle Courant*, 15 September 1798, finds "Mr Branthwaite, Paper-Maker, Kendal", extolling the multifarious virtues of the "Cordial Balm of Gilead", evidence of the continuing vending of quack remedies by stationers.

have been difficult or costly to convert. Most importantly of all, however, the mill enjoyed one of the best water supplies in the area in the form of the river Kent, sufficiently large to power machinery as well as feed the paper-making process.

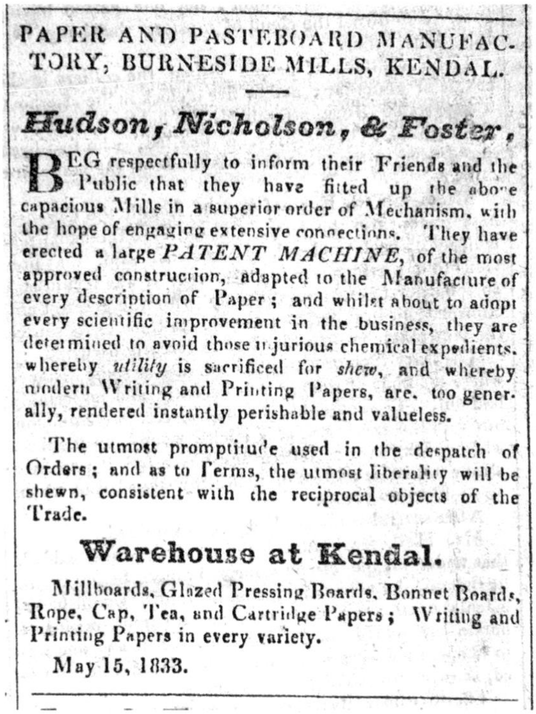

PAPER AND PASTEBOARD MANUFAC-
TORY, BURNESIDE MILLS, KENDAL.

Hudson, Nicholson, & Foster,

BEG respectfully to inform their Friends and the Public that they have fitted up the above capacious Mills in a superior order of Mechanism, with the hope of engaging extensive connections. They have erected a large *PATENT MACHINE*, of the most approved construction, adapted to the Manufacture of every description of Paper; and whilst about to adopt every scientific improvement in the business, they are determined to avoid those injurious chemical expedients, whereby *utility* is sacrificed for *shew*, and whereby modern Writing and Printing Papers, are. too generally, rendered instantly perishable and valueless.

The utmost promptitude used in the despatch of Orders; and as to Terms, the utmost liberality will be shewn, consistent with the reciprocal objects of the Trade.

Warehouse at Kendal.

Millboards, Glazed Pressing Boards, Bonnet Boards, Rope, Cap, Tea, and Cartridge Papers; Writing and Printing Papers in every variety.

May 15, 1833.

Fig. 1.12 – Hudson, Nicholson & Foster advertising the beginning of their new paper-making venture, West-morland Gazette, May 1833.

On 15 May 1833 a small advertisement in the *Westmorland Gazette* (Fig. 1.12) announced the commencement of Nicholson's new – and most importantly, mechanised – paper-making venture. Having fitted out the "capacious" Burneside Mills with a "large PATENT MACHINE . . . adapted to the Manufacture of every description of Paper", Hudson, Nicholson & Foster were ready to engage in trade. Little is known of Arthur Foster, the third partner in the enterprise, but he was no doubt a vital source of additional finance. It is known that the new partnership was short of funds – they even bought a second-hand machine to lower their set-up costs – but even then there was still a shortfall. "The difficulty was the want of working capital", recalled Cornelia Nicholson of the new concern. However, help was at hand in the form of John Wakefield III (1794-1866), the wealthy Kendal banker, who provided the necessary backing to get the new venture off the ground.[60]

At the outset Hudson, Nicholson & Foster did not only make paper by machine, as their opening advertisement suggests, but also by hand. According to Thomas Jones, who wrote a history of Burneside in 1912, the ground floor of the cotton mill was initially taken up by hand paper-makers, with the Fourdrinier machine upstairs.[61] This was almost certainly the case, as a number of moulds survive, dated 1838 and 1839 and carrying the initials of the three partners: H N F.[62]

Hudson, Nicholson & Foster's employment of vatmen and their teams was probably closely tied to their involvement with Cowan Head, where paper had been made by hand since the 1750s. The paper-mill had been advertised to let in March 1833 for entry in November, and on 11 November 1833 Hudson, Nicholson & Foster took out a twenty-one year lease on the mill, at £120 per year.[63] The closure of the Branthwaites' connection with the concern perhaps reflected Michael Branthwaite's age: he was sixty-four and seems to have always been more involved in managing the mill than his brother Richard.[64] The Branthwaites were also without a family successor. They had one son between them who proved to have more academic aspirations: he became a fellow of the Queen's College, Oxford, and Principal of St. Edmunds' Hall.

Many of Burneside's hand paper-makers must have been Cowan Head men, particularly since it was not long before the traditional process ceased altogether at the older mill. The 1833 lease included the provision that Hudson, Nicholson & Foster might "alter, enlarge, amend or improve machinery, fixtures, implements and utensils or alter the position of any of them", and by October 1834 it is evident that such alterations were afoot. An inventory of that date reveals that manual paper-making equipment was being removed to make way for the installation of a Fourdrinier machine.[65] This was ready in April 1835, when Hudson, Nicholson & Foster proudly announced in the Kendal press that Cowan Head too was mechanised, a new "Patent Paper Machine" having been "put in Operation . . . so that they are now enabled to Manufacture, on an extensive scale, and on the most improved principle, every particular kind of Paper in common use" (Fig. 1.13).[66]

The partners' investment in a second machine suggests that Burneside's machine was proving a success and that the sizeable risks entailed in such an unprecedented venture had paid off. It also, reveals the growing dominance of the machine over hand manufacture, a principal feature of the British paper industry in the 1830s. A measure of this is the impact that Hudson, Nicholson & Foster had on other local mills, where paper was, without exception, still being made by hand. Finding it impossible to compete with the new machines at Burneside and Cowan Head, several mills changed hands more than once, some paper-makers were bankrupted and a few mills ceased paper-making altogether. In 1835 Milnthorpe's Low Mills, where paper had been made since 1683, closed for good.

The nearby Waterhouse Mill at Beetham, meanwhile, where paper is still made by Billerud, experienced a succession of short-lived tenancies until a machine was eventually installed there in 1848.

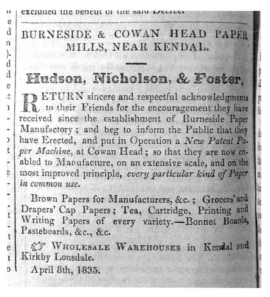

Fig. 1.13 – Advertisement announcing the installation of a paper-making machine at Cowan Head, Westmorland Gazette, *April 1835.*

The first and most directly affected, however, were Hudson and Nicholson's old partners, Eglin and Roberts. They stopped making paper at Starnthwaite (a paper-mill since 1708) in 1834, a matter of months after paper began to be made at Burneside. Their business was devastated by the withdrawal of Hudson and Nicholson from the partnership, not only because of the establishment of a new local competitor but also owing to the loss of their source of rags and their principal market, Kendal, both of which their former partners controlled. They did not, however, give up, moving westwards to Ellers Mill, Ulverston, and leasing Cark's ancient paper-mill. The new venture was not, however, a success. Roberts resisted Eglin's urge for mechanisation, and in 1837 it was taken over by another partnership, Inman & Ashburner, whose efforts were not long sustained either.[67] In 1841 Cark closed after more than two centuries of paper-making. Moreover, Wilcock, Teasdale & Turner, who took control of Ellers Mill from 1839 were similarly unsuccessful, even though they installed a paper machine in 1841 at a cost of £1,000. They were bankrupt within six months. Mechanisation, with the large sums of capital it demanded, was not without its risks.[68]

Hudson, Nicholson & Foster, in contrast, were more fortunate. There are no signs that the partnership experienced financial difficulties, though this perhaps reflected the support of John Wakefield III and his Kendal bank. Cornelius Nicholson knew him well, and the relationship perhaps assured the dominance and survival of the business at times when where other mills might have failed. The success of the venture was also perhaps due to Nicholson himself. He was the only one of the partners to live on site, first at Burneside and then in Thomas Ashburner's old house at Cowan Head, and the day-to-day management of the mills was his responsibility.

Little is recorded of his time there, although he is known to have promoted temperance, which is more important than it sounds. Sobriety was not only desirable for moral reasons. It was an especial virtue in the age of the machine, which demanded greater regularity, reliability and caution in the workplace.[69] The cause certainly proved popular. Temperance festivals were frequently held in the mills, events at which he "often presided, approved, and commended [their] efforts in the cause of sobriety".[70] The success of the mills was also perhaps helped by Nicholson's popularity as an employer. If the address given to him by his employees on his departure is to be believed, he enjoyed a good relationship with those in his employ. "Your general kindness to us on all occasions has commanded our highest respect and esteem", they informed him. "Our service in your employ has been a pleasure, we have laboured in peace, and we have been punctually rewarded by you for our labour."[71]

Cornelius Nicholson's management of Burneside and Cowan Head was not, however, entirely free from problems. In August 1843 the *Westmorland Gazette* reported that Richard Walker, aged thirteen, had lost both his hands, crushed between the cylinders of a glazing calender and later amputated.[72] It was a gruesome accident, emphasising the dangers of paper-mill work, although it did not prove to be Richard Walker's undoing. Supported by a subscription from Nicholson and his fellow employees, he subsequently enjoyed a successful career as a schoolmaster, and in later life even excelled as a cricketer and angler.[73]

Despite concentrating on paper-making more than his other partners Cornelius Nicholson continued to pursue many other interests outside the paper-mills. First and foremost, he remained a partner with John Hudson in the Kendal stationery, printing and bookselling business they had established together in 1825, a side of their partnership that had not been uneventful. In particular, they had increasingly profited from the growing market in Lake District topographical and travel literature, and from their connection with the area's most famous apostle, William Wordsworth. In 1835 they became the first local publishing house to issue a work by the poet, printing and publishing the fifth edition of his *Guide to the Lakes* (Fig.

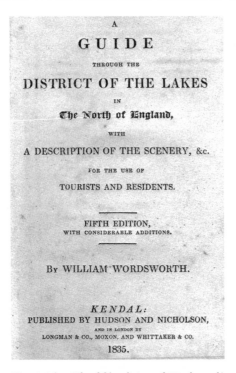

A

GUIDE

THROUGH THE

DISTRICT OF THE LAKES

IN

𝕿𝖍𝖊 𝕹𝖔𝖗𝖙𝖍 𝖔𝖋 𝕰𝖓𝖌𝖑𝖆𝖓𝖉,

WITH

A DESCRIPTION OF THE SCENERY, &c.

FOR THE USE OF

TOURISTS AND RESIDENTS.

FIFTH EDITION,
WITH CONSIDERABLE ADDITIONS.

BY WILLIAM WORDSWORTH.

KENDAL:
PUBLISHED BY HUDSON AND NICHOLSON,
AND IN LONDON BY
LONGMAN & CO., MOXON, AND WHITTAKER & CO.
1835.

Fig. 1.14 – The fifth edition of Wordsworth's Guide to the Lakes, *published by Hudson & Nicholson in 1835.*

1.14). The 1,500 copies were even printed on Hudson, Nicholson & Foster paper, some copies bearing their watermark HNF. It is a slim but important volume. First published anonymously in 1810 to introduce a folio of Lake District views by the Rev. Joseph Wilkinson, this fifth edition, with its "considerable additions", is generally considered the definitive version of Wordsworth's work. Subsequent editions were also published by Hudson & Nicholson, appearing within *A Complete Guide to the Lakes*, which they edited themselves. This first appeared in 1842 and went through five editions up to 1859.[74]*

From 1843, however, the *Complete Guide* appeared under Hudson's name alone. This reflected the end of Hudson & Nicholson's eighteen-year partnership, each going their separate ways to take charge of the concern that had long been their individual responsibility. At the same time Arthur Foster also withdrew from

---

* Nicholson himself knew Wordsworth from an early age. His parents were accustomed to frequent visits from the poet in their Ambleside post office. His admiration for the poet is evident in his purchase of Haydon's portrait of the poet on Helvellyn in later life. He was also a friend of Coleridge's son, Hartley. (Nicholson, 1890, pp. 2-3, 107)

the paper-making partnership, leaving Cornelius Nicholson as sole owner of Burneside and Cowan Head mills.[75]

In spite of the greater concentration on paper-making Nicholson did not diminish his interests elsewhere. He continued to pour his energies into a wide range of activities, more often than not leading the way.[76] In 1844 he became involved in plans to construct a reservoir at the head of the Kent valley to regulate the river Kent's flow. Summer droughts and winter floods were regularly causing many mills, including Burneside and Cowan Head, to stand still, a problem blamed on recent agricultural drainage which led to water draining downstream too quickly. By virtue of their milling interests on the Kent, Cornelius Nicholson and John Wakefield III – whose assistance was again sought and given – were both commissioners of the project (completed in 1848), although as ever Nicholson was at the forefront of the scheme. At the first public meeting relating to the reservoir it was reported by the *Westmorland Gazette* that "the scheme was explained by that tireless supporter of new commercial ventures, Cornelius Nicholson".[77]

In particular, Cornelius Nicholson had proved tireless in his support of that greatest commercial development of his age, the railway. "The enterprise which called forth most prominently the energy and persistence of my father's mind", his daughter recalled, "was the introduction of Railways through Westmorland", and in his obituaries, she adds, he was "almost invariably styled one of the pioneers of Railways in the North". At the earliest meeting relating to a line through Kendal in 1837 Nicholson was reported to have been the "great gun" of the gathering, further promoting the project through a pamphlet he had written and published.[78] He was subsequently appointed secretary and later a director (as was John Wakefield III) of the Lancaster to Carlisle line, became involved in raising the necessary capital of £1,200,000, and was one of two witnesses to address Parliament before the Bill giving consent for the railway was passed in 1844.[79]

Nicholson became further involved with railways in his promotion of the Kendal and Windermere Railway, a project he first suggested in the summer of 1844.[80] In its final form the Lancaster to Carlisle Railway passed a mile and a half east of Kendal, and the smaller line was proposed to link the trunk route with Kendal and extend the connection into the Lake District, to Windermere. In this Nicholson clashed with Wordsworth, who vigorously denounced the scheme in lengthy letters to the *Morning Post* as well as in a impassioned sonnet. "Is there no nook of English ground secure/From rash assault?", he enquired –

> . . . Plead for thy peace, thou beautiful romance
> Of Nature! And if human hearts be dead –
> Speak passing winds – ye torrents, with pure, strong,
> And constant voice protest against the wrong.

Neither Nature, not its winds, nor Wordsworth himself, however, could halt the railway's advance, though in the end the line did not advance up Windermere's banks to Ambleside nor through his beloved vales of Rydal and Grasmere as the elderly poet had feared. The Bill passed through Parliament without opposition, and on the 30 June 1845 it received the royal assent.[81]

On Wednesday 16 July 1845 Nicholson cut the first sod of the Kendal and Windermere Railway, marking the beginning of the project that he had first suggested a year before. The occasion further marked the opening of a new chapter in his own life, and one in which railways superseded paper-making. Only a few days before, he had sold his paper-mills, and he subsequently moved to Lancashire to take charge of the East Lancashire Railway.[82]

A few hours earlier, on the Tuesday evening, he had played host to two hundred employees and friends at a tea-party to mark his retirement from paper-making. The event, held in an upper room of Burneside Mill, did not escape the attentions of the Kendal press, who commented at length on the "most interesting and lively scene" that was presented in the "rural little village" of Burneside. After tea, noted the *Kendal Mercury*, "Mr Nicholson, labouring under great emotion, addressed the company in a very pleasing manner, saying farewell to his assembled work-people." "At the same time", the report continues, "he introduced to them his successor, Mr James Cropper."[83]

Fig. 2.1 – The document that changed it all: James Cropper's apprenticeship with Liverpool merchants Rathbone & Benson in 1790 marked the beginning of the family's association with trade and industry.

2

Yeomen to Philanthropists: Early Croppers, 1600-1845

"I am fully persuaded that a life of useful activity is likely
to be most consistent with the design of our Creator".
(James Cropper 1773-1840)

IN the summer of 1790, almost fifty-five years to the day before James Cropper
began life as a paper-maker, his grandfather and namesake faced his future
employers in an office on the edge of the river Mersey in Liverpool. This James
Cropper was also young – seventeen to his grandson's twenty-two years – and
likewise at the very beginning of his career. He was in the office of the Liverpool
merchants, Rathbone & Benson, to sign an apprenticeship document. Grandfather and grandson had still more in common. Each was embarking on a career
that was contrary to his family's background and experience, yet both were
accompanied by their fathers, who endorsed and supported their actions.

Their positions, however, were very different. On 1 August 1790 the elder
James, with his father's consent, was appointed to spend four years as an
apprentice to learn the "art and trade" of his masters (Fig. 2.1). For this he was to
receive £20 per year, with his father agreeing to provide him with "good and
sufficient Meat, Drink, Washing & Lodging & suitable Cloths and apparel of all
sorts".[1] Fifty-five years later, on 15 July 1845, the younger James stood at the brink
of a career as an industrialist, an owner of two mills and manager of a sizeable
workforce. The position had cost him over £13,000, a considerable sum that he
had not earned himself. Indeed, the younger James chiefly owed his new-found
position to the forebear after whom he was named. His grandfather had amassed a
considerable fortune during his lifetime, and it was this wealth that elevated James
to the career the family have pursued ever since. Furthermore, the elder James also
determined the direction followed by his descendants, laying a path that eventually
led his grandson to Westmorland and into paper-making. And so it is with his
career, and with his life and times, that this story begins.

The elder James Cropper was born in 1773 at Winstanley, near Wigan, Lancashire, into a family of yeoman farmers. It was a profession to which the early Croppers had long proved faithful. For generations they had been cultivating lands within a small area of the plain that stretches between the rivers Ribble and Mersey. The earliest record of the surname Cropper, dating from the mid-sixteenth century, is inscribed in a parish register at Ormskirk, and in the early 1600s James Cropper's ancestors were farming their own smallholding at Bickerstaffe. Here they continued to live and work for several generations, the limits of their world rarely extending further than the markets they frequented, at Ormskirk and Wigan, and sometimes Preston, Warrington and Bolton. They never ventured far, even in marriage.

Peter Cropper's marriage in 1696 was characteristically local. His bride, Sarah, was the daughter of a neighbouring yeoman farmer, Richard Cubham. Yet although he had not had to look far for a suitable partner, the union brought with it the membership of a community of much broader horizons.[2] Richard Cubham was a Quaker, an early follower of the Society of Friends, the nonconformist sect founded by George Fox in 1652. A Bickerstaffe Quaker congregation or "Meeting" had been set up only a year later, and proved popular with local yeoman farmers, although there was a price to pay for membership.[3] Quakers were, for many years, severely persecuted for their radical beliefs.* Such persecution drove them into a closed and self-supporting brotherhood, which in turn was reinforced by their beliefs regarding marriage. Owing to their refusal to recognise appointed clergy, marriage outside the Society – which called for the ministry of a paid priest – was forbidden. Hence Friends married amongst themselves, and in order to marry Sarah Cubham, Peter Cropper was obliged to become a Quaker.

At first the Cropper family proved to be less than angelic adherents to the Quaker way of life. Peter Cropper was reprimanded by his Quaker brethren on several occasions, while his first son, Edmund, was expelled for "quarrelsomeness, swearing, and disorderly conduct".† In addition, his second son Thomas (James's grandfather) was also for a time disowned for committing a "flagrant offence".[5] In time, however, adherence to Quaker values (particularly truth in all matters) proved to be a strong and long-lasting influence on the character of the family. Membership of the Society of Friends also, importantly, determined the paths trodden by future generations of the family, for it brought them into contact with a community of individuals far beyond the narrow bounds of the Bickerstaffe farmer's world.

---

* Richard Cubham was imprisoned for his beliefs on a number of occasions and is several times mentioned in Besse, *A Collection of the Sufferings of the People called Quakers*, (London, 1753).
† Peter Cropper was "one of a wild race", according to one source, "with the failings and vices of a remote agricultural district".

As Quakers, Peter and Sarah Cropper were joined to a well organised network arranged around a structure of intermittent Meetings, bringing Friends together from near and far. First, the Bickerstaffe Meeting, where Croppers, Cubhams and others might gather once or more a week, was annexed to a larger congregation – the Hardshaw Meeting – at which Friends met monthly. In turn these monthly congregations converged at a still larger quarterly assembly, covering the whole of Lancashire. Finally, there were annual meetings at a provincial and national level that saw Quakers gathering together from still further afield.

Meetings were not just an opportunity for worship, but also existed to administer the affairs of Friends. At the Monthly Meeting, for example, a whole range of matters were discussed, including questions of discipline, reviewing membership, monitoring marriages, recording sufferings, and assisting Friends in need. As a secular event these meetings were also important as points of contact between distant communities. The Hardshaw Monthly Meeting, for example, brought Bickerstaffe Quakers into contact with Quakers from Liverpool, Manchester, and Warrington.

When Thomas Cropper (Peter's grandson and the elder James's father) left home as a boy for the village of Winstanley, ten miles east, it was probably discussed and perhaps even arranged at the Hardshaw Meeting. It is also likely that he was entrusted to the care of fellow Quakers in his new home, which fell within the bounds of the Monthly Meeting.[6] His move there was further cemented by his marriage to a local Quaker girl, Rebecca Winstanley, in 1768. The new surroundings did not, however, result in a change of career. Although Thomas later took over his uncle-in-law's malting business, for the most part he remained, like his forebears, a yeoman, owning and farming his own land.[7]

It was a profession he expected his son to pursue, and in line with his father's wishes James Cropper first worked on the family farm. "But he had little taste for it", his daughter-in-law Anne Cropper later recalled. "And I have heard him say that at the close of a hard days work at the plough, he came to the conclusion that he would much rather work with his head than his hands." It was a conclusion of substantial consequence. "He immediately resolved, with his father's permission, to try his fortune in Liverpool."[8]

Again the Quaker network proved invaluable. William Rathbone and Robert Benson, the merchants to whom James Cropper was apprenticed, were prominent Liverpool Quakers, as was James's uncle, Jonathan Binns, who secured the opening. Rathbone and Benson were also acquainted with James's father, Thomas. Robert's wife and William's sister, Sarah, was present at his wedding in 1768, and he supplied the merchant house with barley and malt, a typical instance of Quakers conducting trade amongst themselves.[9]

Without fellow Quakers into whose care he could entrust his son it is

inconceivable that Thomas Cropper would have allowed his teenage son to depart
for Liverpool. In turning to the town James Cropper was relinquishing a stable,
quiet and close-knit environment for a fast-moving, noisy and dangerous world. In
the late eighteenth century Liverpool remained a perilous and unsanitary place,
with brothels, taverns and narrow and dirty streets roamed by raucous mobs, even
press-gangs. "Scarcely a town by the margin of the ocean would have more salt in
its people than the men of Liverpool", one resident recalled, ". . . so barbarous
were they in their amusements, bull-baiting, and cock and dog fighting, and
pugilistic encounters."[10] James Cropper's mother was understandably concerned. "I
believe it is not possible for any one to have more anxious desires for the welfare of
a child than I have for thee", she wrote to her son soon after he had left home for
Liverpool. "I pray that thou mightst be preserved from the many evils that are in
the world."[11]

In commercial terms, however, Liverpool was less hostile. James Cropper
entered the port at a time of great prosperity, the culmination of a century of
growth during which Liverpool had risen to dominate the surrounding region.[12] In
1720, with one dock and a population of 11,000, the town was beginning to make
its mark as a port, although it still handled a fraction of Britain's seagoing and
overseas trade.[13] By the 1790s, in contrast, it was one of the most important ports
in the kingdom, a key beneficiary of the huge expansion in trade in the previous
decades.[14] It boasted acres of docks and numerous wharves and warehouses, and by
1800 its population had exceeded 74,000.[15] Much of the port's wealth was
founded on slavery – it remained the key British port in the slave trade until its
abolition in 1807 – although by 1790 it was also beginning to prosper from the
dramatic growth of mechanised industry. Linked by canals to England's industrial
heartland from the 1770s, Liverpool became the port of choice for the new
mechanised mills in Lancashire and the Midlands, a vital link in the import of raw
materials and the export of finished goods.

The growth of the merchant house that James Cropper joined had coincided
with the rise of Liverpool. Starting out as a sawyer in Liverpool in the 1720s,
William Rathbone II (1696-1746), a yeoman farmer's son, had built up a
prosperous timber business, supplying wood for the construction of ships, shops,
warehouses and homes. His son, William III (1726-89), then diversified from
timber (which was bought from a network of agents in Europe and the Americas)
into ship-building and trade in other commodities. By the 1790s, by which time
the business had passed into the hands of William IV (1757-1809) and his
brother-in-law Robert Benson (1749-1802), a general merchanting business had
evolved, specialising in trade with the newly independent United States of
America. By then the timber side of the business was in decline, largely owing to
the merchants' refusal to supply wood to anyone connected with slavery.[16]

For James Cropper the opening with Rathbone & Benson was an opportunity not to be missed. Merchanting was the bedrock of Liverpool's power and wealth, and an apprenticeship with a merchant house the first rung in one of the best careers of the day. Nevertheless, at first the work was hard and unrewarding. "A clerk in a Liverpool merchant's office, when we were young", recalled Henry Chorley, an apprentice under James Cropper a few years later, "was expected to be a mere machine . . . It was a terrible subjection . . . a slavery ill-compensated for by any indulgence or hope of advancement".[17]

Tasks assigned to apprentices included transcribing letters, documenting ship's cargoes, updating lists of commodity prices, and filling out numerous ledgers and invoices.[18] James Cropper could still recall his fear that he would make a mistake nearly forty years later, ". . . which far exceeded anything I have felt since I was my own master".[19] He did not, however, find the work difficult, as he was a gifted mathematician, and found figure work easy.[20] He was also blessed with considerate employers, who gave him time off to go home, and rewarded him for his hard work. "He possessed more than ordinary energy and talent, strict integrity and good feeling, and they did not remain unnoticed, or unappreciated," wrote Anne Cropper. "A friendship was formed between him and his employers".[21] Robert Benson, for one, had complete confidence in his protégé. "I care nothing as to the price that or any other Article ought to obtain with you," he wrote to James Cropper on one occasion, "and leave it wholly to your judgement". James Cropper's abilities more than justified his employer's confidence, and in 1795, only a year out of his apprenticeship, he was made a partner at the age of twenty-two.[22]

By then Britain was at war with France, ushering in a more uncertain time for overseas trading, which could not be conducted with the safety and confidence of the preceding decade. Rathbone & Benson, however, only went from strength to strength after war broke out, becoming the second biggest shipbuilders in Liverpool and maintaining the large trade with America. Nevertheless, the war years were not without problems for the merchants, although they were of the personal rather than commercial kind. Not least, James Cropper's employers opposed the conflict – Quakers were against war of any kind – and for their political sympathies they were branded "Jacobins", the hated French revolutionaries who murdered Louis XVI.[23] More seriously, the business was threatened by the health of its partners. For years Robert Benson had been afflicted by poor health – perhaps one reason for James Cropper's rapid promotion – and in 1796 it forced him to withdraw from the day-to-day management of the business. Unfortunately for William Rathbone, James Cropper was also bedridden by an unknown illness and withdrew from the business at the same time. As a result Rathbone, Benson & Cropper was dissolved in October 1796 after only a year in partnership.[24]

By 1797, however, James Cropper was sufficiently well to return to the fold, setting up business as an importer of American grain and flour. His recuperation – we are told – had owed much to the attention of his landlady, Mary Brinsden. She nursed him back to health so well, recalls one family member, "that when he recovered he felt and said that the least he could do was to marry her".[25] Although fourteen years her junior, James Cropper married her in 1796, and a year later their first child, John, was born.

It was proving to be a busy year for the young merchant, still only twenty-four. Embarking in business on his own was particularly demanding. "You can be very little aware of the care, the anxiety and the exertion involved", he later told his sons. "When I commenced . . . I knew not one individual in the World to whom I could look for business and I had a very small capital to begin with".[26] He was further hindered by the economic climate, as 1797 was another year of crisis, with trade in recession and banks withholding payments.[27] In his favour, however, he did have numerous American contacts from his time with Rathbone & Benson, and though he was to a degree competing with them, he remained in close contact with his former partners.

The preservation of that relationship – no doubt helped by their common Quaker ties – was important. In 1799 Robert Benson suggested that James Cropper go into partnership with his nephew, Thomas Benson. It was a logical suggestion: more capital would be brought into the concern, and the risk and the stress of managing the business shared. In due course James Cropper accepted the offer and with Robert Benson's financial assistance a new firm was born: Cropper, Benson of No1 Graving Dock by Salthouse gates, Liverpool, active in the American trade.[28]

The concentration on trade with America benefited the new firm beyond measure. For while the Napoleonic Wars jeopardised overseas trade with Europe, and indeed with Asia and Africa, until the mid-1800s trade with America was scarcely affected. In contrast with many trade routes the transatlantic passage remained open and free from hostile privateers, a reflection of Britain's dominance at sea, which in turn was assured by several naval victories, including Trafalgar in 1805. Furthermore, by the turn of the century Liverpool was fast becoming the leading British port in the American trade, with more ships leaving the port for American destinations, including Philadelphia, New York and Baltimore, than from all the other ports of Britain and Ireland put together.[29]

Cropper, Benson exploited the favourable conditions to the full. The firm became the leading merchant house in Liverpool to specialise in trade with America, earning it enormous profits at a time when many British merchants were sorely tested to stay solvent. Indeed, it achieved such a primacy in the American trade that, according to one source, it even acted as a kind of unofficial consular service for the American government. It also, befitting its status, played a leading part in the foundation of an American Chamber of Commerce in Liverpool in 1801. First presided over by an American, James Maury, who later became Liverpool's first official American consul, the institution was also twice headed by James Cropper, in 1806 and 1816.[30]

In spite of its notable success the early years of the Cropper, Benson partnership were not without problems. Thomas Benson died in 1801 aged twenty-three and his brother William, who replaced him, did not live long either, dying in 1805, aged twenty-nine. His death did not, however, mark the end of the firm. Before Robert Benson (James Cropper's first employer) died in 1802 he had bought a share in the merchant house for his teenage son Robert Rathbone Benson (1785-1846), who joined Cropper, Benson in 1805.[31] At about the same time Thomas Cropper (1786-1819) followed his elder brother to Liverpool and also joined the merchant house (Fig. 2.2).

Fig. 2.2 – Thomas Cropper, 1786-1819.

The assistance of the new (and longer-lived) recruits was much needed, as the Napoleonic wars were finally beginning to make life more difficult for the merchants. In 1806 Napoleon closed continental ports to British vessels, severing trade between Britain and every country in Europe except Sweden. In response Britain, which was already blockading the French coast, barred trade (by any country) with any territory belonging to Napoleon or his allies. This affected Britain's American merchants like everyone else: even though transatlantic trade remained open they were prevented from re-exporting materials and goods to Europe.

Cropper, Benson, however, survived the crisis almost unscathed. While Liverpool lost almost a quarter of its entire trade in 1807, the Quaker merchant house remained buoyant. "It is a serious business to be doing so much business in such times as the present", wrote James Cropper in 1807. "Our payments for the last four months have considerably exceeded £1,000 per day on average."[32]

By the end of 1807, however, events finally began to take their toll on the merchant house. The French and British blockades greatly damaged the trade of neutral countries and America was incensed by France and Britain's refusal to permit neutral territories to trade with their respective enemies. The upshot was that America's Congress, after months of failed negotiation, placed an embargo on trade with Britain in December 1807. To make matters worse, in 1808 Britain passed Orders in Council that aggravated America still more, and although the embargo only lasted until March 1809 it was years before the two countries finally reached settlement.

The American embargo was potentially ruinous for Cropper, Benson. The firm was, however, better positioned than most to brave the loss of its most important market, for it was already diversifying into other areas, and with some success. Not least, it had recently begun trading with Russia, sending ships through the Arctic seas to Archangel as the Baltic ports were closed by Napoleon's blockades. Using Russian-built ships manned by Russian and Prussian sailors, the merchants transported cargoes of fine white sugar bought in Cuba at 30s, "a very low price owing to [Cuba] having no American trade".[33] Demand for sugar in Russia was high – "Archangel alone takes off *two thousand tons*", reported Thomas Cropper in 1807 – and if their ships docked safely there, the trade reaped tremendous profits.[34]

Cropper, Benson also compensated for its American losses through trade with Brazil, which was opened to Britain in November 1807 when the Portuguese royal family fled there to escape the clutches of Napoleon. It was swift to exploit the new market, quickly dispatching ships to Pernambuco for supplies of Brazilian cotton, a much-demanded commodity in the absence of American grown materials.[35]

Such alternative markets remained important for Cropper, Benson for many years, and long after the American embargo was lifted in March 1809. Anglo-American relations remained tense for years, compounded by the continuing seizure by Britain of American ships that contravened their blockades. By 1812 more than 1,000 American vessels were impounded in British ports.[36] And when the British orders that hindered American commerce were finally suspended, in June 1812, it was too late. News that America had declared war on Britain arrived two days later, and it was three weeks before news of the British suspension could reach America by sea.[37]

Trade with America again ceased, and Cropper, Benson was further hit by soaring overheads. Insurance premiums rocketed and merchants also had to pay a tax for the protection of their ships by the navy. This was no guarantee, however, that ships were safe from attack or capture. Even though British maritime power was superior, the Americans inflicted enormous damage on Britain's merchant fleet, as Cropper, Benson discovered to its own cost. In the summer of 1813 its *Eliza Ann* was captured by the celebrated American brig *Yankee* and taken into Boston.[38]

Once again Cropper, Benson offset its losses by seeking trade elsewhere. By the end of the Anglo-American war in December 1814, they had added yet another important overseas destination to their portfolio: India. Trade with the subcontinent had been the sole preserve of the East India Company until the renewal of its charter in 1813, when its longstanding monopoly was revoked. Although the company retained the exclusive rights to the China trade for another twenty-one years, this was something of a victory for merchants such as James Cropper. He and his circle had long campaigned against the company's monopoly, not least because it limited the Far East trade to the port of London alone.

One of the first firms to obtain a licence to send ships to India, Cropper, Benson and Rathbone joined forces to quickly commission a new vessel to engage in the trade. Built on the Clyde, the 410 ton *Bengal* was the second ship to reach India from Liverpool following the lapse of the monopoly. James Cropper and his partners were undoubtedly proud of their new connection and to commemorate the event they commissioned Robert Salmon, an emerging maritime artist who subsequently found fame and fortune in America, to portray the *Bengal* before she set sail (Fig. 2.3). Shown at Greenock on the Clyde, she looks, to all intents and purposes, like a normal ship of her time, down to the line of cannon which were present to ward off attacks from privateers and the French. Being staunch Quakers, however, Cropper, Benson would not allow the ship to be armed, so a compromise was reached. Fake wooden cannon were installed instead, a tactic that proved successful. In the following years the *Bengal* safely made its way to India and back three times, in subsequent seasons accompanied by other Cropper, Benson vessels, no doubt armed in the same way.[39] In total the merchant house financed nine voyages to the subcontinent up to 1818.[40]

By then Cropper, Benson had added yet another venture to its portfolio, this time involving America, where trade had swiftly resumed on the restoration of peace in 1814. Through Quaker contacts the merchants were acquainted with Jeremiah Thompson, a Friend who had settled in New York to co-ordinate the sale of the woollens his family manufactured in Yorkshire, and in 1817 he asked them to join him in his latest commercial venture. Thompson had first-hand experience of the frustrating irregularity of overseas trading – merchants would often delay the departure of a ship for days or weeks if its hold was not full – which prompted

Fig. 2.3 – The Bengal, *built by Cropper, Benson and Rathbone to engage in trade with India; before setting off she was depicted by Robert Salmon off Greenock on the Clyde, where she was built.*

him to come up with a simple but brilliant solution. He decided to start a regular shuttle service between Liverpool and New York, with ships sailing to a schedule of fixed departure dates, and subsequently asked Cropper, Benson (again joined by Rathbone) to organise the Liverpool end of the operation. Under the name of the Black Ball Line, the commencement of the venture was announced on 5 December 1817 in the *Liverpool Mercury*. Its four vessels would "positively sail, full or not full from Liverpool on the 1st and from New York on the 5th of every month, throughout the year", and on the 1 January 1818 the service was inaugurated when the *Courier* set sail from Liverpool.[41]

The line was a success from the start. By removing the uncertainty of departure dates, it attracted custom that more than offset the chief risk of the venture: that ships would lose money by sailing before they were full.* Indeed, demand for space was so great that the Black Ball fleet was soon doubled from four to eight ships – including the 495 ton *James Cropper* launched in 1821 – with sailings

---

* The other great risk – that adverse winds would prevent the ships sailing and thus undermine the regularity of the service – was also effectively removed. In the event of bad weather Cropper, Benson employed steam boats to tow their ships out to sea, a canny exploitation of new technology. The first steam boat on the Mersey had appeared in 1815. (Aspin, 1995, p.11)

twice a month between Liverpool and New York, and in a few years dozens of lines were sending ships across the Atlantic, all in the wake of Thompson's simple, yet revolutionary, idea.[42] For Cropper, Benson the line not only earned its partners excellent returns but also strengthened the firm's position as one of Liverpool's premier American merchant houses. In addition, they benefited from the venture by using the line to transport their own goods, in particular cotton.

By the 1820s American grown cotton was the mainstay of the Cropper, Benson operation. By then the merchant house (together with Rathbone) numbered amongst the most important and longest established importers of American cotton in Liverpool. Rathbone, for example, sometimes had as many as twenty-five ships consigned to the trade in dock at the same time, and Cropper, Benson was equally dominant.[43] Furthermore, James Cropper, noted one of his descendants, did everything in his power to promote the manufacture of cotton goods. "He met all warnings against over-production", she remarked, "by saying that of this there was no danger till it became cheaper for a man to burn his shirt than to wash it".[44]

Liverpool and its American merchants had not always, however, had such a dominant position in the cotton trade. Before the late eighteenth century nearly all the cotton imported into Britain had come through London, and none of it from America. Until the 1780s America was an unheard of source of the material, Britain's cotton mills processing raw cotton from Turkey or the Spanish West Indies.[45] The first American-grown cotton to be landed on British shores arrived at Liverpool in 1784, imported by William Rathbone IV. Even then it had not proved especially popular. Although he only imported eight bags of the material, it was some time before he found a buyer, and several years later the number of bags of American cotton imported through Liverpool still only numbered 500.[46]

By 1800, however, the situation was very different. Liverpool had superseded London as the chief port of the British cotton industry, and America was fast becoming Britain's principal supplier of raw cotton, best meeting the demands of quality and quantity required by British manufacturers.[47] India, which Cropper, Benson had hoped would provide an alternative source, proved disappointing. As a result East Indian sugar became the chief commodity that they imported from the Orient.

After the end of the Napoleonic wars in 1815 demand for raw cotton rose exponentially, a consequence of the rapid advance of mechanised weaving looms. In 1813 it was estimated that 2,400 power-looms were operating in Britain; by 1820 there were about 14,000, and by 1833 about 100,000.[48] Liverpool was a chief beneficiary of the growth: 290,000 bags of American cotton were being shipped through the port by the early 1820s, and in 1823 eighty-five percent of the raw cotton imported into Britain was landed in Liverpool, of which seventy-two percent (412,000 bags) was American-grown. In 1825 cotton became Britain's biggest import, the first time a raw material rather than a luxury foodstuff or beverage had topped the list.[49]

Cropper, Benson not only profited from the cotton industry by importing raw cotton but also by exporting finished cotton goods. In the Napoleonic era exports of cotton manufactures grew four times faster than any other and by the 1820s accounted for forty-five percent of British exports.[50] It was a remarkably lucrative commodity for merchants, filling holds on outward and inbound voyages. On its second voyage, for example, the *Bengal* returned to India laden with Lancashire printed cottons, having only recently brought back raw cotton from the subcontinent.[51]

Cropper, Benson further made money from cotton as speculators, betting on future demand for the material and buying or selling accordingly.[52] This reached a height in the early 1820s, when the merchants joined a loose syndicate of individuals and concerns to speculate in the commodity, united in the belief that the consumption of cotton was overtaking production and that prices would rise. "The Quaker confederation", as the group was termed by one member, says much of the international scope of Cropper, Benson's business and their position in the cotton trade: Rathbone, as ever, was involved, as well as Isaac Cooke of Cooke & Comer, Liverpool's foremost cotton brokers; Daniel Willink, Liverpool's Dutch Consul; Hottinguer & Cie of Paris and Le Havre; Jeremiah and Francis Thompson of New York; and Vincent Nolte of New Orleans.

At first the results were promising. In 1824 the group's members reaped prodigious returns on their speculations.[53] A year later, however, they were less fortunate. In 1825 the cotton market collapsed when a small Scottish merchant house burst the bubble of high prices by importing 5,000 bales below the market price. Many members of the Quaker confederation were bankrupted, including Nolte, Willink and Jeremiah Thompson. Cropper, Benson survived, but nevertheless sustained considerable losses, not least as major creditors of Nolte's. Even worse, it lost one of its most profitable ventures. Thompson's bankruptcy forced him to sell the Black Ball line, and the new owners did not retain Cropper, Benson as Liverpool agents.[54]

The outlook was also bleak in general. The downturn in the cotton market mirrored a national recession in trade that severely affected merchants on all fronts. By the end of 1825 Great Britain was "one scene of confusion, dismay and bankruptcy", a state of affairs that persisted for some time. John Gladstone, one of Liverpool's leading merchants and father of the future prime minister, had never known anything like it. "In all my experience for above forty years as a man of business", he declared in August 1826, "I never could look forward with less satisfaction and more dread".[55]

James Cropper and his partners did, however, have one thing to look forward to. By 1825 their attention was beginning to be diverted away from merchanting by an altogether novel involvement: the Liverpool & Manchester Railway. By the 1820s the power and wealth of the port of Liverpool and its merchants principally depended on its links with its industrial hinterland, in particular with Manchester, which grew famous as "Cottonopolis". The transport links between the two great towns, however, were poor. The road was slow, rough and expensive, and canal links were not much better.[56] A handful of canal companies together exercised a virtual monopoly of the route, charging excessive tolls for a slow and uncertain means of transport. The Bridgewater Canal, for example, the chosen route of Liverpool merchants, carried goods at 12s 6d per ton, when it could have charged 5s and still made a profit.[57]

This prompted Liverpool's merchants – who were fervently opposed to the monopoly of the canals – to back a scheme to connect Liverpool and Manchester by rail. The first survey of the route in 1821 was financed by a Liverpool corn merchant, Joseph Sandars, and befitting their prominence in the cotton trade, James Cropper and Robert Benson were soon involved. James Cropper was one of the earliest promoters of the scheme, and both were later directors; each provided five percent of the original capital (Fig. 2.4).[58]

Fig. 2.4 – As a director of the Liverpool & Manchester Railway, James Cropper received a special ticket in the form of an engraved ivory tablet; his name is inscribed on the reverse.

In doing so, they involved themselves in one of key events of the Industrial Revolution. Although railway lines and steam locomotives were not new inventions, the Liverpool & Manchester Railway revolutionised transport (Fig. 2.5). It was the first railway in the world to connect two industrial cities, the first line open to the public for the transport of passengers and goods alike, and the first to use steam locomotives as the sole means of propulsion. And as well as

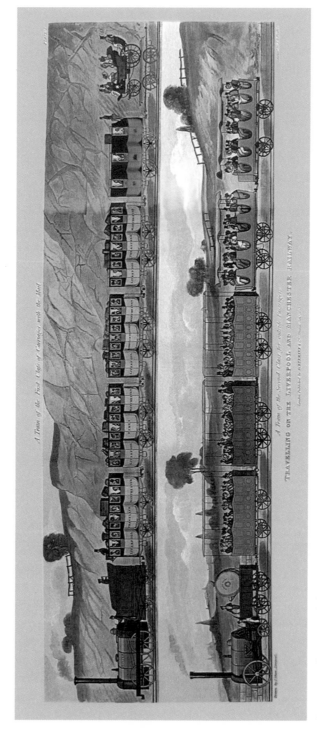

Fig. 2.5 – The Liverpool & Manchester Railway, opened in 1831, from a print published by Ackermann shortly afterwards. As James Cropper noted, on its opening it revealed a quite unexpected market for passengers.

providing the blueprint for future railway design, it also provided the catalyst. Its success sparked a spectacular era of railway development that transformed Britain and later the world. Within twenty years Britain was traversed by a network of over 6,000 miles of railway lines.[59]

The railway was also a spectacular commercial success, although not in the way its promoters had intended. Men like James Cropper had backed the line because it offered a cheap and efficient means of transporting goods in and out of Lancashire, but on its opening the railway revealed a quite unexpected market for passengers. Four hundred thousand people travelled on it in its first year, and in 1832, noted James Cropper, the weekly revenue from passengers was more than three times that for goods, at £3,600 compared to £1,000.[60] Such revenues assured him substantial returns on the capital he invested in the venture. In 1832 he estimated that his income for the year from dividend payments alone was set to be £2,800.[61] In railways, as in shipping, he had proved to be an eminently successful capitalist.

Although James Cropper's success owed much to the fortunate circumstances of his career, it was also undoubtedly underpinned by his character. He was, for instance, remarkably energetic, with a mind of "much energy & vigour", noted Anne Cropper, his daughter-in-law. "He entered into every thing which occupied him with his whole heart . . . every thing was full of thought, experiment, curious theory, and deductions from facts; which, though mostly correct, and often important, had rarely presented themselves to others".[62] He was also very persuasive. At a single meeting in 1825, for example, he managed to sell shares to the amount of £175,000 in a scheme to cultivate sugar in India, prompting Zachary Macaulay, who was present, to observe that his "powers of persuasion and of influencing the opinions of those who listened to him were very remarkable . . . it was commonly said of him, 'Give him pen and ink and he will demonstrate that black is white' ".[63] In this way the secrets of his success in commerce begin to be revealed. He had the analytical powers, confidence, energy, and eye for opportunity of a business pioneer; and he was, remarks one historian, "a prototype of the self-made entrepreneurs who were transforming the British economy".[64]

James Cropper's success in commerce is also informed by his Quaker inheritance. Although he left home at seventeen, he remained an active member of the Quaker community frequented by his forebears, and in later years was active as a Friend on a national and international level, regularly attending the London Yearly Meeting, and corresponding with fellow Quakers nationwide and abroad.[65] He was also identifiably Quaker in manner and appearance (Fig 2.6). True to the Quaker insistence on equality he dressed in plain and sombre clothes and addressed all alike: "thou" and "thee".[66] His faith also caused him to denote the

Fig. 2.6 – James Cropper, 1773-1840.

days of the week and the months with numbers rather than call them by their pagan names.

Far from conflicting with his career, James Cropper's membership of the Society of Friends encouraged him to be successful in trade. Indeed, since their earliest days Quakers had considered trade a medium through which they might show forth the truth in the world, and demonstrate their integrity and trustworthiness. "Be diligent in business", James Cropper's mother cautioned him in 1790, "but remember to be fervent in spirit serving the Lord", and although her concern is evident, the message is clear. Activity in commerce *and* religion was desirable. They were not incompatible concerns.[67]

In an age when commerce was usually conducted through partnerships or family firms, as a Quaker James Cropper was advantaged in many ways. Helped by the Meeting network and intermarriage, the Society of Friends was a wellspring of contacts, a source of employees, partners and capital, agents, correspondents and customers.[68] Such contacts were also, importantly, more reliable and trustworthy than most. Quakers were explicitly "Friends of Truth", and their beliefs served them well in business. They were hard-working, active people, and luxury and idleness were vices they were bidden to avoid. James Cropper's noted activity, for example, owed much to his religious convictions: "I am fully persuaded", he commented on one occasion, "that a life of useful activity is likely to be most consistent with the design of our Creator."[69]

James Cropper's Quaker inheritance was not, however, entirely in accord with his career in business. Much as it helped him, it also invited his withdrawal. As early as 1808 he was keen to leave Liverpool for the country, and for expressly religious reasons: "My mind is strongly inclined to the country", he remarked, "and agriculture is an employment that has less than any other to do with administering to the follies and vices of mankind, and as such most consistent for a true Quaker".[70] His retirement was not, however, forthcoming, principally because his partners were against it. They argued, reported James, that ". . . the house could not be supported if I left" (a measure of the central role he played in its management) and he felt compelled to consent to their wishes. In consequence it was a number of years before he began to scale down his Liverpool business commitments.[71] In recompense, he did move away from the centre of Liverpool in 1811, to Lodge Lane in Everton, a leafy suburb of fields and farmsteads overlooking Liverpool Bay, a mile below.[72]

When James Cropper did finally begin to devote less time to merchanting in the 1820s, he did not, however, retreat into a life of quiet devotion. Nevertheless, the reasons for his withdrawal were tied to his religious convictions, as the new involvement that drew on his time – promoting the abolition of slavery – was a popular cause with Quakers. They had been foremost in promoting the abolition of the slave trade, as James Cropper was well aware. His uncle Jonathan Binns (who secured him his apprenticeship) and his first employers, William Rathbone IV and Robert Benson, had campaigned for abolition alongside Roscoe, Clarkson and Wilberforce at a time when the commercial prosperity of Liverpool largely rested on the slave trade.[73] "If our slave trade had gone there's an end to our lives", proclaimed an election jingle of 1790 –

> . . . Beggars all we must be, our children and wives
> No ships from our ports their proud sails e'er would spread
> And our streets grown with grass, where the cows might be fed.

In the late eighteenth century Liverpool was the centre of the British slave trade – 134 slave ships were sent out from Liverpool in 1797, while London dispatched seventeen and Bristol only five – and in opposing slavery Rathbone and Benson were opposing the majority of Liverpudlians.[74] Their efforts were not, however, in vain. Slave trading was abolished in the British dominions in 1807, and the abolitionists hoped that slavery itself would die out as a result.

Slavery did not, however, decline, and James Cropper in spite of his convictions, long continued to profit from slave-grown produce, not least as a leading importer of American cotton. It was a clash of principle and practice that he was sorely vexed to resolve. "It is a very difficult thing to keep from touching in any shape slave produce", he wrote to Joseph Sturge in 1827.

. . . We have nearly one million of persons employed in this country in the manufacture of cotton which is the produce of slave labour, and some of our best and warmest friends are engaged in this business. Should we propose that they should shut up their works and turn off their workmen?[75]

In spite of the difficulties of the situation, however, James Cropper was convinced there was room for action. He was not seeking to excuse himself. "There are points in almost every case in which it is difficult to draw the line between right and wrong", he continued, "but surely this is no reason why we should go on doing wrong, where the distinction is clearly to be seen."[76]

He practised as he preached. From 1821, when he first made his opposition to slavery public in a series of open letters to William Wilberforce published in the columns of the *Liverpool Mercury*, he devoted a great part of his life to campaigning against slavery. In particular, he made it clear to his peers that slavery was not, as had been hoped, dying out, and that further action was necessary. It was a significant observation, and one that assured him a place in the annals of abolition. "He was instrumental in shifting national attention from the African slave trade to West Indian slavery", explains David Brion Davis, "in organising the first British society specifically dedicated to slave emancipation; in raising funds, mostly from Quaker sources, to finance the activities and publications of the Liverpool and London societies; and in establishing communication with various American anti-slavery groups."[77]

As the 1820s progressed anti-slavery work became James Cropper's principal employment. He gathered and distributed evidence of the cruelties of slavery, promoting abolition through newspaper articles, pamphlets and public meetings. He also helped to plan and fund Thomas Clarkson's six-thousand mile tour of 1823-4 (which stirred up anti-slavery sentiment nationwide), and in 1825 he took to the road himself, addressing audiences in towns across the nation, from Plymouth to Hull.[78] Furthermore, he tried to encourage Britain to support the cultivation of sugar in India by free labour rather than depending on the West Indies where slavery persisted. The cause engaged his heart, mind, pen and pocket for the rest of his life, and his efforts were not without success. Slavery was abolished in the British dominions on 1 August 1834.

Already distanced from merchanting by his anti-slavery work, James Cropper's attitude towards wealth further encouraged him to devote less time to commerce. While he felt that making money and being a true Christian were not conflicting concerns, he fervently believed that being wealthy incurred responsibility.[79] Like George Fox he believed that rich men were stewards of what they possessed, and should use their wealth in good works. "The accumulation of wealth" he declared to the London Yearly Meeting of Quakers in 1831, "without sufficiently using it as the property of Him to whom all belongs" was "what all admitted to be the greatest evil we had."[80]

True to his own declaration, from the 1820s he increasingly put philanthropy before commerce. In 1824, for example, he set off on a two-month tour of Ireland accompanied by his daughter Eliza, concerned by the condition of the country and its peasantry. This resulted in a fifty-nine page pamphlet, "The present state of Ireland, with a plan for improving the position of the people", which was published in 1825. In it James Cropper noted the "Providential" abundance of water power and cheap labour in the country and proposed that Ireland should have its own cotton industry. He even tried to get the ball rolling himself by investing in a cotton mill in Limerick.[81] Nearer home, meanwhile, he established an agricultural school at Fearnhead near Warrington, a farm he had inherited from his father. Believing that the principal cause of misery and crime among the working classes was the lack of work and education, his school combined manual and agricultural labour with useful learning. He also gave evening classes for local inhabitants and their families.[82] One of his main objectives was, not surprisingly, to spread the Christian message. "We that are blessed with abundance, and have time to spare", he remarked on one occasion "should take more pains by example to those amongst whom we live to Christ."[83]

Significantly, James Cropper also urged his sons, John and Edward, to consider devoting their lives to philanthropy rather than commerce. Both had followed him into Cropper, Benson – they were partners by 1820 – yet by the 1830s he was more than keen that they, like him, should withdraw from the merchant house. "An investigation into your affairs has now proved the ample sufficiency of your property", he wrote to them both in a seminal letter in 1830 –

> . . . and it behoves you to consider the dangers and responsibilities attached to your situation. "It is easier for a camel to pass through the eye of a needle, than for a rich man to enter into the kingdom of God" was the awful language of our blessed Saviour, and though this is possible with God, yet how few are there who do not trust in these possessions . . . We have been peculiarly blessed – blessed with an abundance in the things of this life . . . If then we fall short, we have no excuse. We must give account for what we have received.[84]

Although it was not until 1836 that the decision was taken to wind up Cropper, Benson, John and Edward seem to have agreed with their father. They were chiefly responsible for the break up of the partnership, and it seems likely (certainly in John's case) that they were motivated by similar feelings.[85] In addition, Robert Benson was not averse to ending the partnership for himself. Increasingly lame with gout, he was likewise disposed to pursue other interests.[86] It was eighteen months, however, before the partnership was disbanded, the delay reflecting the considerable size of the Cropper, Benson operation. In 1836 the merchant house owned thirty-two ships, and was still taking delivery of cargoes from around the world. This included tea from Canton, a valuable trade which had begun in 1833 with the ending of the East India Company's monopoly of trade with China.[87]

So it was that the younger James, John and Anne Cropper's first son, entered a world in which he was never really secured a place. He was born in 1823 and from his earliest years his family were beginning to withdraw from merchanting; only a year after his birth, in 1824, they had retreated, to a degree, from Liverpool itself. His childhood home, Dingle Bank, was two miles upstream from the centre of Liverpool (Fig. 2.7). Then "quite in the country", this was worlds away from Duke Street, his birthplace, a thoroughfare in the heart of the bustling port.[88] "It is a fair scene", wrote one relation of Dingle Bank as it was in 1824. "The gently undulating meadow slopes rapidly down, some quarter of a mile, to the glittering waves of the broad Mersey about a hundred feet below". Beyond this, "fringing the southern sky, rises a distant range of Welsh mountains, and in the furthest south-east, the isolated rock crowned with Beeston Castle".[89]

For all the splendour of the young James Cropper's surroundings, his upbringing was singularly unworldly. Although his family's new home was in

Fig. 2.7 – Dingle Bank, built on the banks of the river Mersey, was the idyllic home of the Cropper family from 1824.

many ways a *nouveau riche* residence – it was typical of self-made men to withdraw from the source of their wealth, deserting a town's centre for a villa on its fringes – the atmosphere of the household was little softened by wealth. John and Anne Cropper (Fig. 2.8) were almost single-minded in their insistence on religious, unworldly living. This remained the case despite their decision to leave the Society

Fig. 2.8 – John and Anne Cropper, c.1870; Anne still wears a bonnet in Quaker fashion.

of Friends around 1836, at a time when the previously peaceful world of English Quakerism was shattered by the wave of evangelicalism sweeping through Britain. They continued to be dissenting in their faith (becoming Baptists) and in many respects were still Quaker in spirit. Both continued to dress soberly – Anne covering her hair with a cap – and the whole family continued to address each other as "thee" and "thou".

In Quaker fashion, John Cropper also continued to think of himself as a "steward" of his wealth, practically making philanthropy his profession. In this he was peculiarly favoured by the new medium of railway investment, which yielded him a substantial income without demanding much of his time. Although he was for a while director of the Grand Junction Railway, it was a role he did not relish – "I find the burden and responsibility in the Railway very distressing", he commented on one occasion – and he was more than happy to devote less time to making money and more to giving it away.[90] He was involved in philanthropic work in Liverpool at every level: he gave money to hospitals, reformatories, missions and penitentiaries, founded an Orphan School in 1830, campaigned against drinking and prostitution, and entertained chimney sweeps and juvenile delinquents at Dingle Bank. He became famous in Liverpool for such work. "Someone addressed a begging letter to 'The most generous man in Liverpool, c/o the General Post Office", recalled Alfred Willink. "It was delivered without hesitation to John Cropper."[91]

As parents John and Anne Cropper were similarly motivated by Quaker values. Their "heartfelt, prayerful desire" for their children, recalled one relation, was "that they be true servants of God, and give up their lives to His service. . . . True religion was all in all". Anne Cropper's "one desire" in bringing up her son James "was to keep him 'unspotted from the world'".[92] A journal she kept of his conduct from his sixth to ninth years reveals more: "James was a little thoughtless and rude once or twice this evening", she reported a few days after his ninth birthday, "I hope he closed his eyes desiring to become one of the lambs of Christ's fold." A month later she again set pen to paper: "He is in general tractable and obedient to my wishes. The principal thing I could wish different is that James would take more decided pleasure in religion – in studying the bible and in endeavouring to live according to its holy precepts."[93]

James Cropper's upbringing continued to be dominated by spiritual considerations into his teenage years. He was educated at home, growing up in an environment of religion and philanthropy. Amusement and self-indulgence were strictly discouraged. "My training rather forbade pleasure as an object", he later recalled. "My grandfather expressed his view plainly that play was unnecessary and that diversity of occupation was all that boys needed."[94] Life at Dingle Bank was correspondingly puritan. "The Quaker idea of economy and restraint in ornament or indulgence ruled with us and our meals", he noted, "and my sisters' dresses were always of the plainest".[95] Mealtimes were further influenced by the family's anti-slavery associations: they ate off specially made crockery, each piece depicting a slave in chains holding up his hands and exclaiming: "Am I not a man and a brother?" (Fig. 2.9)[96]*

---

* This emblem was copied from medallions produced by Joshua Wedgwood for the Anti-slavery Society.

Fig. 2.9 – The last surviving piece of a dinner service made for the Cropper family depicting slaves in chains.

The young James, however, coped well in the strict and repressive atmosphere, and was not only a favourite with his mother but also his grandfather, after whom he was named. "I cannot help attaching a pre-eminent importance to dear James", commented the elder James, who had long shown a marked interest in what career his grandson might pursue, hopeful that the younger James might take up his own philanthropic plans.[97] "Often when I look at the uncertainty of time to me", he wrote in 1834, "the thought of this dear boy being likely to carry on my plans does indeed rejoice my heart." And with such hopes in mind, he had already furnished his grandson with substantial sums of capital, even though the younger James had yet to enter his teens. "When my property was considerably increased by Railways", he wrote to Joseph Sturge in 1836, "I determined . . . to appropriate a considerable part of that increase to my Grandson James in the belief that he was likely to apply it as I wished."[98]

As time wore on, however, it became increasingly unclear what the younger James might do. In 1838 his parents decided to broaden his education – on turning fifteen he became a pupil at Liverpool's Royal Institution, a day-school of moderate expense – but a question mark continued to hang over his career.[99] By the autumn of 1839 this had become a matter of some urgency. It was "a vastly momentous concern", according to the elder James, who corresponded at length with John and Anne on the subject. In due course a conclusion was reached: "I quite agree that you can do nothing to induce him to take any particular course", he wrote to John in September 1839. Their shared verdict was characteristically unworldly: "Our united wishes and prayers will be *that God will direct his paths*".[100]

Divine direction was not, however, forthcoming. A few months later the elder James died at Fearnhead, aged sixty-six, and when the younger James departed for Edinburgh University in 1840, he and his family were still unsure what career he might pursue. The extension to his education temporarily postponed the issue, but it did not leave him or his parents any the wiser. Three years later, by which time he was back in Liverpool, the issue was still unresolved. His father was even continuing to seek divine guidance about the matter. "I trust I may still as earnestly seek direction for James," John Cropper confided in his journal on March 1843, "and unreservedly commit all to the care of my dearest Lord."[101]

As his family awaited a response, James Cropper eventually took matters into his own hands. It was an unusual course of action for a young man of his time, even more so given that his eventual decision – to become a paper-maker in Westmorland – was a far from obvious choice. Indeed, when he took control of Burneside and Cowan Head paper-mills in July 1845, only halfway through his twenty-second year, he had little experience of business let alone a new and rapidly changing industry. His knowledge of the paper industry was limited to a few weeks spent with the Scottish paper-makers Alexander Cowan & Sons in May 1845, and while this might have been valuable – the Cowan mills were among the largest and most advanced in the country at the time – it was hardly sufficient preparation for managing two paper-mills and more than sixty men, women, girls and boys.[102] Even more surprising, he had elected to take on the business alone, operating as a sole trader without partners or any other experienced individual to advise him while he learnt the ropes. "I had not one trustworthy agent to rely on in the works", he later remarked, "nor anybody to take counsel with outside them."[103]

James Cropper's eventual choice of career thus seems all the more extraordinary, yet some sense can be made of his decision. For one, the opportunity had come his way through relatives. Burneside was one of a number of mills that belonged to the Quaker Wakefield family, to whom he was connected via a series of marriages and business partnership that dated back to the 1760s (see Appendix III). These had culminated in the marriage of his father to Anne Wakefield in 1820, and without doubt it was his mother's family (probably his two uncles) that first drew attention to the opening at Burneside and Cowan Head.

Furthermore, it is clear that his decision to become a paper-maker had not been taken lightly. The two paper-mills set him back over £13,000, and while there was no doubt that he could afford the position – he had inherited sufficient capital from his grandfather to cover the cost – he was careful to seek the counsel of various parties before he completed the transaction. Naturally his family were consulted but also, more importantly, he sought the advice of Charles Cowan, the head of the Cowan paper-mills, who accompanied him on a visit to Burneside and Cowan Head in March 1845.[104] Cowan was one of the leading lights of the industry in the mid-nineteenth century, and it seems likely that he supported James's choice of workplace, whatever reservations he might have had about the young man's lack of experience.[105]

Fig. 3.1 – James and Fanny Cropper, c.1860; their love for one another was ultimately responsible for drawing James to Westmorland and into paper-making.

3

Love, Loss, Profit and God:
James Cropper, 1845-80

"How I did hate the whole thing and myself for blundering into it".
(James Cropper on his early years in paper-making)

WHEN James Cropper started life as a paper manufacturer on 5 July 1845, one thought was foremost in his mind. It was not, however, an interest in paper-making, nor in fact a wish to pursue a career of any kind, commercial or philanthropic. Indeed the twenty-two year old's strongest motive was entirely different. He had loved his cousin, Fanny Alison Wakefield, since his teenage years. "In truth the whole aim of my life, since I was seventeen", he later told his grandchildren, "was to win your Grandmother's love and to make her my wife."[1]

Two years later he had made considerable progress. The pair were engaged in 1842, when James was nineteen. At the same time he joined the Church of England, to which Fanny and her family belonged. It was a revealing move as his parents opposed the established church, suggesting that by then it was Fanny Alison, not they, who had the greater hold on his affections. Indeed, as James acknowledged himself, his relationship with her was "the turning point of my whole career", not least the chief motive behind his decision to go into paper-making in 1845. "We exchanged long letters once a month", James later remarked of his long engagement, "and we read and learnt, and thought about each other all the intervening days. And when the time came I fixed upon this Westmorland home and business, simply because it seemed to make a fixture in my life, and to point to our union and our home."[2]

And so it did. On 25 November 1845, almost five months after he started out as a paper manufacturer, James Cropper married Fanny Alison Wakefield at Heversham Church, five miles south of Kendal. Afterwards celebrated at Sedgwick, the Wakefield family home, the wedding was also, appropriately, celebrated at Burneside and Cowan Head. "There were rejoicings at Mr Cropper's Paper Mills on an equally liberal scale", reported the *Kendal Mercury*, "every man being presented with a new hat, and half a crown given to his wife, in addition to their being treated to a large and well supplied tea party, which afforded them an evening of great enjoyment."[3]

Two weeks later, when James Cropper returned home to Cowan Head with his new bride, his workforce returned the hospitality, treating him and Fanny Alison to a rapturous welcome. "On the arrival of the happy pair at Junction Cottages, Burneside, where a handsome evergreen arch was thrown over the way, they were greeted with loud huzzas," reported the *Kendal Mercury*.

> The carriage was stopped – the horses taken from it – and about thirty of his workmen yoked themselves, and dragged it to Cowan Head. On their arrival there, a novel and highly exhilarating scene presented itself. The house, mill, and cottages were brilliantly illuminated, and another evergreen arch, with the motto Welcome! thrice happy pair! was placed over the entrance gate.[4]

It was an auspicious reception – "a pleasing demonstration of the high esteem in which Mr Cropper is held by his work people", the *Kendal Mercury* told its readers – suggesting that in spite of his youth and inexperience, James Cropper was faring well as an employer. So far it seems he had won the respect and approval of the workforce he had only recently taken charge of. "We feel thankful", one employee wrote to him the day after his wedding, "for your very kind treat & present and more especially so when we consider the very kind feeling shown towards us by you since we have stood in the relationship of Master and Servant. It gave me heartfelt pleasure to find that we had gained your confidence and I sincerely trust that we shall each show by our conduct that this confidence is not misplaced."[5]

By the end of 1845 James Cropper's new life seemed thus in place. Accepted and respected by his workforce, he was also, by virtue of his connection with the Wakefields, quickly accorded a place in local society. His domestic life was an even greater source of happiness and support: "I have never passed a day", he fondly declared in old age, "without rejoicing in the love and help of the most remarkable woman whom I have ever known."[6] To add to this there was soon a family on the way: Frances Anne was born in June 1847, Mary Wakefield in May 1849, and Charles James in July 1852.

There was also the excitement of a new home. In 1847, at Fanny's prompting, James began building a new house on a site just above Burneside which commanded panoramic views across the surrounding countryside. Named Ellergreen owing to its proximity to Green Farm and a profusion of alder trees (known locally as 'ellers'), in total it cost James Cropper almost three thousand pounds, a sure expression, if any were needed, of the strength of his commitment to his new life, and of the hopes he had for his family and his career.[7] The family moved there from the mill-house at Cowan Head in 1849 (Fig. 3.2).

Fig. 3.2 – Ellergreen, the family home built by James Cropper in 1848.

Ellergreen was not, however, an expression of the prosperity of his early years in paper-making. The new house and the fourteen acre site it occupied were not financed with profits from his two paper-mills on the River Kent, winding through the valley floor below. Far from it: in spite of the apparent good nature of his workforce, the mills were losing money. Added to this there was the dreadful realisation that Cornelius Nicholson had charged him far too much for the business in the first place.[8] John Cropper was incensed by this: "We were shamefully deceived and cheated", he lamented in his journal.[9] For James Cropper it was one regretful circumstance among many. "I knew I had been hasty and impulsive in buying the works", he wrote to his son Charles in 1882, "and that I had been overreached in the bargain by their previous occupant. I lost money on them year by year. . . . People did not hesitate to comment on my taking such a trade . . . How I did hate the whole thing and myself for blundering into it."[10]

In part the poor performance of the mills probably reflected the fluctuating economic climate. 1845 and 1846 were good years for trade, but in 1847 and 1848 there was a severe economic depression. "We have passed thro' the most sad times of commercial suffering ever known", wrote John Cropper of the period, "and the consequence has been the most unlooked for reverses, and the change in the value of money and property is extraordinary."[11]

James Cropper's initial difficulties also, however, owed much to his own lack of experience. As he noted himself, running a paper-mill profitably could not be learnt overnight. "Until you know by experience it is almost impossible to conceive the many points which affect the profit in this trade", he informed his cousin William Wakefield in 1847. "There is no uniform manufacture & no uniform material, each sort of rag & waste has a different price & much depends on the combination of them in the right quantities, so that you do not make the stuff too dear, & yet do not injure the colour of the manufactured article."[12]

His resolve, however, remained strong. Indeed, despite the fact that he was the sole investor in a business that was losing money and which he had paid too much for, he remained committed. "And yet even then", he remarked of his problematic early years as a paper-maker, "and still more when the tide turned and the whole began to work satisfactorily, I knew I had more of what I aimed at in life here, than I should have had in another position. I loved the country, I was fond of mechanics . . . I had a reason for having constant dealings with men."[13]

The turnaround was far from immediate. It took James Cropper several years to bring the paper-mills back into the black. "For years it was uphill work", reported Frances, his daughter, "and he had to work hard, both at machinery and trade, to get the place into businesslike order."[14] In 1853, for example, the first year for which a result is recorded, the mills were still losing money, although the outlook was brighter. The loss of £405 was followed by a profit of £1,274 in 1854, and profits soared in the next two decades. The mills did not lose money again until 1922.

The reversal of James Cropper's paper-making fortunes was achieved in a number of ways. Preventing stoppages helped: "I find [the result] so much better than usual", James Cropper noted in 1852, "owing to the Mills having run regularly."[15] In this he was favoured by improvements made to the water supply of both mills. In 1845 Cowan Head and Burneside were wholly dependent on the river Kent for power and process, yet the river was prone to extremes of high and low water that regularly brought the mills to a standstill.[16] By 1848, however, such problems were largely confined to the past. The reservoir at the head of the Kent (proposed in 1844 by, among others, Cornelius Nicholson and John Wakefield) had been completed.[17] It was soon performing its function: "So low is the water in the river", reported the *Kendal Mercury* on 13 May 1848, "that the mills on the Kent are said to be chiefly dependent on the water supplied by the new reservoir."

The operation was further improved by changes inside the mills themselves. There was a wealth of detail to attend to, both large and small. "When he took it over", noted his daughter Frances, "the whole place needed remodelling."[18] His response, however, was far from immediate. With the exception of a couple of improvements at Burneside until 1852 the mills were hardly altered at all.[19] From 1853, in contrast, machinery was updated, buildings enlarged and replaced, and power-generating equipment improved. In particular, large sums of money were sunk into Cowan Head, which was closed for several months in 1855 while alterations were carried out.[20] A new machine was installed at a cost of £911 (replacing Hudson, Nicholson & Foster's machine of 1835) a new building put up

(£654), and a new salle constructed (£103).[21] The salle, an airy well-lit room, was the part of a paper-mill where finished paper was checked and sorted, usually by girls.

Fig. 3.3 – Thomson patent vortex water-wheel, installed at Cowan Head in 1855.

At the same time the mill's power supply was also improved. Taking advantage of the abundant water supply, James Cropper invested in an improved mill-race (£369), and a water turbine (£577) (Fig. 3.3).[22] This was something of a novelty at the time, and was granted a mention in the local press. "It is 3ft 4ins in diameter, 1 ft broad, with a fall of 20ft, taking a very moderate supply of water and yielding about forty horse-power," noted the *Westmorland Gazette* on 24 November 1855, "and it bids fair to supersede the ordinary waterwheel as to saving expense and economising the water."[23]

Such improvements did not come cheaply. Between 1853 and 1856 James Cropper spent more than £5,000 on the mills.[24] The capital expended came from a number of sources, including Wakefield & Crewdson, the Kendal bank headed by his uncle (his debts with them rose to £4,915 in 1856) as well as his own pockets, which remained deep owing to considerable sums still tied up in railways. James Cropper did not, however, place all his eggs in one basket. He also raised the necessary capital by recruiting partners to invest in the concern. In 1852 he ceased business as a sole trader and transferred the mills into a private company owned by three partners: himself, George McCorquodale and William Blacklock. Each took a third share.

Like his predecessors at Burneside and Cowan Head, the new incumbents were both involved in the printing and stationery trades. This time, however, they were not provincial but national tradesmen. George McCorquodale (Fig. 3.4) had started out as a Liverpool printer and stationer in 1837, but by the 1850s was expanding his business in a manner "seldom witnessed even in Liverpool". In a few years he had extensive printing works in Liverpool, London, Leeds, Glasgow, and Newton-le-Willows.[25] William Blacklock, meanwhile, had risen from humble origins to a position of some eminence. Apprenticed to George Bradshaw, a Manchester map engraver, in 1831, within five years he had advanced to the position of partner. Meanwhile Bradshaw had decided to diversify into printing, and the new trade soon won both of them wealth and renown. Bradshaw & Blacklock became the country's foremost publishers of railway guides and timetables, an altogether new and extremely lucrative trade (more of which later).[26]

James Cropper owed his partnership with both men to his Liverpool

Fig. 3.4 (left) – George McCorquodale, James Cropper's partner from 1852; the McCorquodale family remained major customers, shareholders and non-executive directors until the 1970s. Fig. 3.5 (right) – John Dewar, Burneside foreman 1854-87.

connections. The McCorquodales numbered among a sizeable Scottish presence in the port, having been resident there at least since 1800, and several records indicate that they were familiar with the Cropper family.[27] On 18 September 1844, for example, James Cropper and George McCorquodale were both present at a breakfast gathering at Dingle Bank, the Cropper family home, an occasion which is also notable for the presence of Charles Cowan, the Scottish paper-maker under whom James Cropper had trained for a few weeks in 1845.[28] Cowan had probably been introduced to James Cropper by the Liverpool McCorquodales: the Cowans and McCorquodales were relations and were in close contact with one another. Blacklock, likewise, was a McCorquodale contact: although a Manchester man by trade and residence, he was a partner in George McCorquodale's printing business, a position he held until his death in 1870.[29]

Going into partnership with George McCorquodale and William Blacklock was an extremely shrewd move. Both men not only brought extra capital into the concern, but also brought large new outlets for paper. Each was a wellspring of contacts in his native city, Liverpool or Manchester, as well as a lucrative customer in his own right. Indeed, George McCorquodale and his descendants, remained one of James Cropper & Co.'s most important customers for over a hundred years. Partnership did not in itself, however, bring new faces to Burneside and Cowan Head. With sizeable commitments elsewhere McCorquodale and Blacklock were both sleeping partners, leaving the day-to-day management of the concern to James Cropper.

James Cropper was by no means, however, running his paper-mills alone. With the future of his business assured by his move into partnership, he began to recruit new personnel to help him turn it around. In 1854, for example, Burneside gained a new and experienced foreman, John Dewar (Fig. 3.5), whom James Cropper recruited from Alexander Cowan & Sons.[30] Dewar was well qualified to take on one of the most important jobs in the mill: he had spent years working in the Cowan's Valleyfield Mill, one of the largest and most modern paper-mills in Great Britain.[31] He remained Burneside foreman until 1887, and eventually retired in 1892, aged seventy, having spent five years in charge of the salle.[32]

1854 was also a notable year for the arrival of James Savage and his son James, paper-making engineers from Lancashire. Each took care of one mill: James senior was Burneside's first chief engineer, while James junior took up residence at Cowan Head on his arrival, where he was soon busy overseeing an extensive programme of modernisation. He later succeeded his father at Burneside, and remained James Cropper & Co.'s chief engineer until his death in 1887.[33]

The most important arrival of the era, however, was that of John Bryce (Fig. 3.6), who also came from Cowan in 1853. Although only twenty-one at the time, he had more years of paper-making experience behind him than James Cropper.

Fig. 3.6 – John Bryce, 1832-96.

His father James was a vatman, making paper by hand at Cowan's Bank Mill, and it was under him that John began his career aged twelve in 1844, first as a "parter" – separating the freshly made sheets of paper after they had gone through the wet press – and then as a "layer", the third member of the hand paper-making team.[34] In time he also gained experience of mechanised paper-making (a machine was installed at Bank Mill in 1847) and, most importantly, of the office as well as the shop-floor. He finished his apprenticeship as a clerk in Alexander Cowan & Son's offices.[35]

At Burneside, where he also began work as a clerk, John Bryce soon made his mark. "By straight forwardness, punctuality and keen attention to duty, he rapidly advanced", noted the *Westmorland Gazette* many years later. The newspaper was not mistaken. Within two years John Bryce had so far gained the confidence of his employer that he was sent out as traveller for the firm.[36] By 1860, however, he was back at Burneside, where he became James Cropper's right-hand man and a key player in the management of the firm. This was rightly reflected by his position. In 1859, only six years after he had joined James Cropper & Co., he was made a partner.[37]

It was not a nominal position. On his promotion John Bryce was allocated a quarter share of all profits over £1,500, and in the following years the mills consistently returned a profit well in excess of his earnings threshold. The average profit from 1859 to 1871 was over £4,500. His share of profits in this period was little, however, compared with the sums he earned after his promotion to full partner in 1871 (from which point he was granted a quarter share of all profits). From 1871 to 1880 profits averaged over £11,800, leaping from £4,570 in 1871 to a high of £16,740 in 1874, and John Bryce's income soared almost tenfold (from £450 in 1870 to £4,070 in 1874).[38] In possession of such a handsome income, he soon did what most men in his position would, building himself and his wife a large new house in Burneside, named Gowan Lea (now Melmore, James Cropper plc offices).[39]

Since 1854, when James Cropper & Co. had first returned a profit, the company had advanced enormously. In part this reflected the continuing development of the mills themselves. Over £30,000 was invested in Burneside and Cowan Head between 1854 and 1880.[40] Additional paper-making machines were installed (a second at Cowan Head in 1860 and second and third machines at Burneside in 1863 and 1871) pushing up output from a modest 380 tons in 1854 to 2,249 tons by 1880. At the same time preparation, finishing and storage facilities were enlarged to deal with the greater volumes of raw materials and finished paper, and the power plants at both mills improved. By 1865, for example, Burneside Mill (Fig. 3.7) accommodated two paper-machines and eight beating engines, powered by a 4hp water-turbine, a 25hp steam engine (installed in 1859 at a cost of £584),

Fig. 3.7 – Burneside Mill, c.1855. The outside of the mill had changed little since its construction as a cotton-mill, but inside many changes were afoot. (Source: Margaret Duff collection)

a water wheel generating 25hp (powering the preparation plant), and a 25hp water-turbine.[41]

The profitability of the mills, although subject to periodic fluctuations, also advanced dramatically. The business yielded an average annual return of profit on capital of fifteen percent in the 1850s, twenty percent in the 1860s, and thirty percent in the 1870s, not least owing to the exceptional profitability of 1874 to 1877, in which years the return exceeded forty percent.[42]

Such exceptional returns not only reflected the hard work and money that was invested in the business, but also the economic climate of the age. In the 1850s and 1860s Great Britain experienced a boom the like of which the world had never seen before. ". . . This double decade of the world's short span", proclaimed one contemporary poet –

> Is richer than two centuries of old:
> Richer in helps, advantages, and pleasures,
> In all things richer – even down to gold . . .[43]

He was not mistaken. The great gold discoveries of California, Australia and elsewhere saw a dramatic increase in the amount of gold coinage in circulation, which lowered interest rates and encouraged the expansion of credit.[44] At the same time (and in marked contrast with most of the nineteenth century) businessmen were favoured by buoyant prices.[45]

The strength of the economy in greatest part reflected the strength of British industry. While other nations were rocked by wars and revolutions during the early and mid-nineteenth century, Britain had developed and extended a lead in manufacturing that no other nation could challenge. Evident in the triumphant display of products and machinery at the Great Exhibition of 1851, for the next two decades and more Britain was the undisputed "workshop of the world". It was a golden age for her manufacturers: with a lead in technology and infrastructure, British industrialists were way ahead of their competitors at home and abroad. Exports tell the tale well: they nearly doubled from £72 million to £150 million between 1850 and the early 1860s, and by 1870 the foreign trade of the United Kingdom was more than that of France, Germany, and Italy put together, and nearly four times that of the United States.[46]

The fortunes of the British paper industry followed the general pattern. By the mid-nineteenth century Britain was the greatest paper exporting country in the world, and the lead only grew as time went on. Exports grew threefold between 1850 and 1860.[47] Exports, were nothing, however, compared to the growing quantities of paper being consumed by domestic markets. In Britain itself demand for paper soared, stimulated by a range of developments including growing population, literacy and the general rise in prosperity.[48] Output rose accordingly, doubling between 1845 and 1859 from 49,000 to 97,000 tons, a rise in production that would have been impossible without the paper-making machine.[49] There were also many more types of paper on sale. A paper catalogue of 1860, for example, listed 681 different types of paper, varying in size, weight, colour, finish, use and much more besides.[50]

Paper prices followed the trend. Having fallen dramatically since the 1810s, they levelled out in the 1850s, even showing a slight upwards tendency. For instance, "Shops" made at Cowan Head, a thin paper probably used for wrapping in shops, advanced in price from 3d to 4d per lb between 1853 and 1860, an upwards trend that is evident in the sales prices of most of James Cropper & Co. grades.[51] Nevertheless, paper was more affordable than ever. In the decades leading up to 1850, the cost of paper had halved, not only because of the lesser expense of machine production but also owing to decreases in the amount of tax imposed on the material. In 1836 excise was reduced to 1d per lb payable on all grades of paper.[52] In 1861 excise duties were abolished altogether, part and parcel of the free trade reforms introduced by a succession of Liberal governments. This led to a further sharp fall in price.[53] At Burneside and Cowan Head James Cropper & Co. were able to reduce their prices by over a quarter, with immediate effect. For example, "Bag cap" paper made at Cowan Head, another wrapping paper, fell from 5d to 4d per lb.[54]

As well as lowering the price paid by consumers without reducing paper-makers' revenues, abolition of excise duties did away with a considerable amount of red tape. "Every step of the manufacture of paper must be conducted under the surveillance of the Excise", noted one commentator on the industry in 1855, "and the provisions as to entries, folding, weighing, sorting, labelling, removing, and so on, are not only exceedingly numerous and vexatious, but enforced under heavy penalties."[55] At Burneside and Cowan Head, for example, every ream of paper had to be labelled and then signed by an Excise Officer who came up from Kendal twice a week (Fig. 3.8).[56]

Free from the restrictions of excise, James Cropper & Co. exploited several growing markets for paper. At Cowan Head the machines produced several wrapping grades, which were sold to Britain's burgeoning retail sector. This included papers for wrapping groceries and other goods, named "shops" and "caps", as well as more specialised grades. "Self-blue", for example, was a wrapping paper chiefly used by chemists and druggists, while pink and blue "tobacco" was probably fancy packaging for the noxious weed. On one occasion the company even made "loaf paper Blue", no doubt used for wrapping bread.[57]

Burneside, meanwhile, produced wrapping papers of diverse types, albeit more expensive grades. In particular, the mill produced a growing range of coloured paper, a development which owed much to spectacular advances in the dye-stuffs

Fig. 3.8 – Ream label for Burneside Mill, classified as Mill 162; before 1861 a tax had to be paid on every ream of paper made, and the label signed by an Excise officer.

industry, which began with William Perkin's invention of mauve, the first synthetic dye, in 1856. In the succeeding years paper of every colour was made at Burneside – including mauve – an early and important precedent (if not the origin) of the mill's continuing specialisation in coloured paper and card in the twenty-first century.[58] In 1873, for example, the Edinburgh clock-makers, James Ritchie (who are still in business today) bought a selection of pink, blue, green and yellow paper in large "double crown" size sheets, perhaps as fancy packaging for pocket-watches.[59]

The company also made packaging of a different kind: the envelope. This was a relatively new market for paper: the development of the envelope largely resulted from Rowland Hill's reform of Britain's postal services in 1840, which revolutionised communication. Before then postage was extremely expensive, not only for the writer of a letter (who had to pay tax on it) but also for the recipient, who was charged the cost of delivery according to distance. It cost 1s 1d, for example, to send a letter from London to Edinburgh.[60] The Penny Post, in contrast, which Hill established in 1840, introduced a uniform charge of one penny, regardless of distance, for any letter posted in the United Kingdom. As a result the number of letters posted rose dramatically, from 75,000,000 in 1840 to 329,000,000 in 1849 and almost a billion by 1870.[61]

Importantly, the penny post also changed the way in which letters were sent.

Before 1840 postage rates were not only based on mileage but also on the number of sheets in a letter – if a letter contained two sheets the rate was doubled – so most letters consisted of a single sheet, folded in half with the message inside and the address on the outside.[62] The new postal rates, in contrast, were based on weight, and any number of sheets could be posted for 1d so long as the weight of the whole packet did not exceed half an ounce. This not only encouraged letter-writers to consume more paper by writing longer letters but also allowed them to enclose their message within a protective 'pocket', as they were first called, or envelope.[63]

By the mid-nineteenth century making envelope paper was one of James Cropper & Co.'s principal specialities.[64] And it was, perhaps surprisingly, a more specialised product than most. Envelopes had to be lightweight – to minimise the cost of postage – yet opaque and durable, and resistant to folding and wear and tear, as well as relatively waterproof in case of rain. James Cropper & Co. consequently made highly glazed papers for envelopes, including "buffs" and "casings" in various colours, even installing machinery especially suited to the task. The two paper machines installed at Burneside in 1863 and 1871 were both MG (machine glazed) machines, similar to a Fourdrinier machine except with a single large drying cylinder instead of several smaller ones. These produced lightweight paper ideal for envelopes. The smooth single cylinder imparted a high machine glaze to one side of the paper (ideal for writing upon and reasonably waterproof too), while the other side remained rough (ideal for taking the gum).[65]

James Cropper & Co. not only made envelope paper but also manufactured the envelopes itself. "Envelope making is carried on in these works", noted the *Kendal Times* in a description of Burneside Mills in February, 1865. "It is a simple process. A steel die acting on paper . . . cut out the shape of the envelope before its sides were gummed together; another machine made the folding grooves, gummed the edges, and stamped the part lapping over . . . and hand labour pressed the gummed parts together, with the greatest rapidity".[66]

Within a few years Burneside's envelope-makers had even more on their hands. In 1869 James Cropper & Co. secured a contract to supply the Stationery Office with orange envelopes for Britain's electric telegraph network. At the time this was something of a coup. Although development of the network had begun in the 1840s it was not until the late 1860s, when the network was nationalised under the control of the Post Office, that the cutting-edge technology really began to take off. The number of telegraphs sent per year rose from 6,500,000 in 1869 to 10,000,000 by 1871 and 20,000,000 by 1875, and with a contract to supply the envelopes in which telegraph messages were delivered the company was quick to profit from its success.[67] The trade certainly impressed the company's bankers, Wakefield & Crewdson. "James Cropper makes all the envelopes for the telegraphs, five tons per week", they noted in 1873 in a memorandum which commented on the profitability of the paper-mills. "His business realised last year £10,000 and this year will be £12,000, even though he writes off all he can to keep down the profit."[68]

While helped by such factors as the telegraph contract, the dramatic change in James Cropper's paper-making fortunes since the early 1850s was ultimately underpinned by the greatest development of the mid-nineteenth century: the railway. James Cropper's purchase of the paper-mills coincided with a great surge in railway investment, and by 1851 almost seven thousand miles of track were in operation in Britain, two-thirds of which had been constructed since 1845. In the following decades the total continued to grow, and by 1880 nearly every town in Britain was linked to a railway network eighteen thousand miles long.[69] The effect was overwhelming. Journeys suddenly became a matter of hours rather than days, and the increase in mobility – of men, materials and goods – transformed Britain's economy and culture beyond measure. "If there was a single image that symbolised to the Victorians the divide between the old world and the new, it was the train", remarks one historian of the period, and the mid-nineteenth century was, as he suggests, "the Railway Age".[70]

For James Cropper & Co., the impact of the railways was profound. Indeed, the whole history of the company in the nineteenth century is intimately linked with the advent of the new form of transport, starting with James Cropper's purchase of the mills in 1845. Cornelius Nicholson retired from paper-making in order to pursue a career in railways: he became Managing Director of a Lancashire line and later of the Great Indian Peninsula Railway.[71] James Cropper, meanwhile, moved in the opposite direction, into paper-making from a background which (financially at least) largely lay in railways.

By the 1840s they were his family's principal commercial involvement. Following on from his grandfather's connection with the pioneering Liverpool & Manchester line, his father John was a director of the Grand Junction Railway, which joined Birmingham with Lancashire and was another of England's pioneering lines. At the same time his uncle Edward was a director of the equally important London & Birmingham, and in time joined the board of the great London & North Western.[72] James Cropper was also, in time, a railway director himself, first with the Kendal & Windermere Railway (from 1846), and later with the Lancaster & Carlisle.

His family were also prolific investors in the new mode of transport. His grandfather had provided five percent of the capital for the Liverpool & Manchester, while his father and uncle prolonged the tide of investment into the 1840s and beyond. James also invested substantially himself. His ledger documents share dealings in twenty-seven different railways in Britain, France and the United States between 1844 and 1877, including the Dundee & Perth, Paris & Lyons, Cedar Falls & Minnesota and Illinois Central.[73]

Such investment was important. First and foremost, it was the chief source of the capital with which James Cropper bought Burneside and Cowan Head Mills in 1845.[74] His significant wealth was principally derived from the Liverpool & Manchester Railway, first in the form of profits (given to him in cash by his grandfather in 1836) and later in the form of shares (given to him by his grandfather on his death in 1840).[75] Secondly, railways were also an important source of finance for James Cropper after 1845. While his mills lost money in the late 1840s he continued to draw money from railway investments, not only to support himself and his family but also to prop up his business.

Railways also played a key part in James Cropper's entry into partnership with George McCorquodale and William Blacklock in 1852. Like James Cropper, William Blacklock's fortune was founded in railways, not only as a railway director and shareholder – he was involved with the East Lancashire and the Lancashire & Yorkshire – but also, equally importantly, as a printer. In partnership with George Bradshaw in Manchester, he was a pioneering printer and publisher of railway guides and timetables, which took Bradshaw's name.[76] These were the first to cover all the railways in Great Britain, and certainly the most successful. *Bradshaw's Railway Guide* (Fig. 3.9), which was first published by Bradshaw & Blacklock in

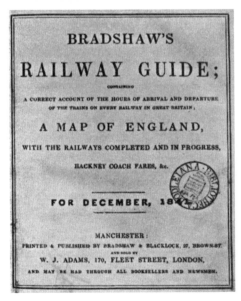

Fig. 3.9 – Bradshaw's Railway Guide, *first published in 1841 by George Bradshaw and William Blacklock, James Cropper's partner.*

1841 and incorporated timetables with a map of England's railways and other information, became the most famous and popular publication of its kind, sold by railway companies and booksellers everywhere.[77]

George McCorquodale had also capitalised on the huge new market that the railways opened up for printing and stationery firms. In 1846 he secured exclusive rights to the printing and stationery business of the London & North Western (perhaps, we might speculate, with the assistance of James Cropper's uncle Edward). This was a huge and expanding trade: within a few years the London & North Western's territories extended from London to Glasgow, with many places in between. George McCorquodale's business grew accordingly, soon comprising of offices and printing works in Liverpool, London, Leeds, Glasgow and Newton-le-Willows. And not surprisingly, all were situated close to mainline railway stations. The London premises, for example, were adjacent to Euston, the London & North Western terminus.[78]

For James Cropper & Co. Britain's new transport network was also an important market for paper. As well as McCorquodale & Co. and Bradshaw & Blacklock the company traded with numerous other concerns with railway connections. Waterlow & Sons of London, for example (a key customer for several decades), enjoyed "a good share of the large stationery and printing business of the railway companies" throughout the nineteenth century.[79] Bemrose & Sons of Derby, meanwhile, another major buyer of Cropper paper, were long-standing printers and stationers for the Midland Railway (which controlled lines stretching out from Derby to London, Bristol, Manchester and Leeds) and pioneering publishers of railway timetables, like Bradshaw & Blacklock.[80] In addition, James Cropper & Co. also dealt with railway companies direct. In 1869, for example, it was supplying paper to the Great Eastern, another of Britain's biggest railway companies, which it supplied again in 1875, this time through Wiggins Teape.[81]

The rise of steam locomotives also helped James Cropper & Co. in indirect ways, not least for the part they played in the development of postal services. Trains, which were entrusted with the post from 1838, were able to cope with a comparatively limitless volume of mail, as well as being a far quicker, regular and reliable mode of transport than the stage-coach.[82] Similarly, the development of Britain's telegraph network also owed much to railways. The earliest public telegraph line was laid from Paddington to Slough on the Great Western Railway in 1843, and was a precedent of all future development. The telegraph network that developed thereafter was built almost entirely along railway lines.[83]

For James Cropper & Co. railways were most important of all, however, for their primary function. In contrast with his predecessors, James Cropper could never depend on Kendal, nor on Westmorland, as a principal market for his paper. Kendal remained modest in size, possessing neither sufficient trade and industry nor population to consume the output of two mechanised paper mills. The small market town was only marginally more populous in the nineteenth century than it was in the eighteenth, never growing in the way that its Lancashire counterparts did. Its population only grew from about 8,000 in 1800 to 13,500 by the end of the century.[84] Westmorland, furthermore, was the most sparsely populated county in England as late as 1891, with only eighty-one inhabitants per square mile against a national average of 497.[85] As a result, James Cropper was obliged to dispatch paper beyond the confines of the county, where larger markets beckoned, and it was also outside Westmorland that he was compelled to look for raw materials.[86]

The success and survival of the paper mills was thus extremely dependent on transport links in and out of the area. In 1845, however, these were less than good. While James Cropper had journeyed to Westmorland and into paper-making on the back of railway profits, he had not travelled there by train. The West Coast main line only extended as far as Lancaster, and the last twenty-five miles had to be taken by coach or canal. His mills also depended on the canal to transport raw materials and finished goods. "The first consignments of paper when he took over the mills had to go by barges down the canal", noted James's grand-daughter Maisie Fletcher, who wrote at length about her family and home, Ellergreen. The canal, however, was a very slow mode of transport, and, even worse, the canal-head was in the centre of Kendal, two miles from Burneside and Cowan Head. This meant that all the necessary raw materials and finished goods had to be transported to and from it by horse and cart.[87]

Fortunately for James Cropper railways were not far away. Indeed, he started out in paper-making at exactly the moment that the age of steam arrived in the Lake District. The first steam boat in the Lakes, *Lady of the Lake*, took to the waters of Windermere on 23 July 1845, and two months later the Lancaster to Kendal section of the Lancaster & Carlisle Railway was opened.[88] More importantly, the construction of another local railway, the Kendal & Windermere, was also under way. Designed to connect the Lancaster & Carlisle Railway (which passed a mile and a half east of Kendal) with Kendal and Windermere, it had been given the go-ahead by Parliament on 30 June 1845, five days before James Cropper started life as a paper manufacturer. And two weeks later, on 16 July, it began to be built, when Cornelius Nicholson, its most energetic promoter, cut the first sod.[89]

Two years later, on 20 April 1847, the line was opened (Fig. 3.10). The Lake District was now more accessible than ever before. Within a few years a sizeable village had grown up around the end of the line at Windermere, and thousands of tourists began to pour into the area from Lancashire and elsewhere.[90] For James Cropper, however, the railway was far more important as a way of transporting

Fig. 3.10 – The opening of the Kendal & Windermere Railway, 1847.

goods in and out of the area.[91] The Kendal & Windermere Railway passed directly through Burneside, where a siding and goods shed were soon constructed for the use of the paper-mill, a stone's throw away.[92] In due course a horse-drawn tramway was built into the heart of Burneside Mill, and in 1875 this was extended to Cowan Head, a mile and a half upstream.[93]

The new transport link was, in every way, a lifeline for James Cropper & Co. Indeed, without it the mills could never have expanded in the way they did, and probably would not have survived. During the mid-nineteenth century many paper-mills in rural areas ceased trading, a decline which can be attributed to poor locations in relation to railways. By 1860, for example, all the mills in the rural county of Herefordshire had closed, as well as the majority of those in Shropshire and Monmouthshire.[94]

With a railway link at its disposal, however, the disadvantage of James Cropper & Co.'s rural location was significantly diminished. Within a few years (by which time a national railway network was largely in place) the new mode of transport enabled the company to sell paper the length and breadth of the country, an opportunity that was not overlooked. By the 1870s it was selling paper in almost every large town and city across the nation, from Aberdeen to Plymouth. A surviving order book from Cowan Head, which dates from 1870 to 1872, reveals more. Of the 170 customers listed in it only four were based in Kendal, compared to eighteen in Birmingham, and thirty in Glasgow to name just two other places: a sure measure, if any were needed, of the importance of distant rather than local markets.[95]

Railways were also fundamentally important to James Cropper & Co. as a

means of bringing in supplies. Following the completion of the Kendal &
Windermere Railway in 1847, raw materials could be brought to the mills within
a matter of hours rather than days, and in almost limitless bulk. This ensured the
survival of the business far beyond 1880, by which time output had reached 2,250
tons. Supplies continued to come to Burneside by rail until the early 1970s, when
output stood at over 20,000 tons. Trains also brought in coal (Fig. 3.11) and
chemicals, which were likewise required in large quantities. Bleaching powder, for
example, almost a ton of which was being consumed each day by the 1870s, came
by train from Flint in North Wales.[96]

*Fig. 3.11 – Cropper coal wagons, c.1960; coal was brought to Burneside by
rail until the early 1970s.*

Britain's railway network did not, however, advantage James Cropper & Co. in
every way. While it enabled the company to market and sell paper in national rather
than regional markets, it also radically increased competition. Hundreds of paper-
mills were now potential rivals, where competition had previously been much more
limited and local. This had one significant result: rather than manufacturing papers
of every grade to meet all the requirements of a local market, paper-makers began to
specialise in particular grades, making smaller ranges of paper.[97] This not only
reduced competition but also improved the efficiency of a paper-mill: as machines
became faster and more expensive to run it became impractical and inefficient to
make many different types of paper in small quantities.

At Burneside and Cowan Head such a tendency towards specialisation is clear to see. In 1835 James Cropper's predecessors, Hudson, Nicholson & Foster, had boasted that they were ". . . able to Manufacture on an extensive scale every particular kind of paper in Common use – Brown Papers for Manufacturers, etc., Grocers' and Drapers' Cap Papers, Tea, Cartridge, Printing & Writing Paper of every variety, Bonnet Boards, Paste Boards, etc."[98] By the 1860s, in contrast, James Cropper & Co. had chosen to make a far more limited range of papers. Between 1860 and 1874 *The Paper Mills Directory*, an annual guide to the British paper industry, records that Burneside produced colours, cartridges, and envelope papers, while Cowan Head made colours, cartridges, small hands and caps (Fig. 3.12). Such specialisation dramatically reduced the competition; in 1860, for example, *The Paper Mills Directory* noted that ten English paper manufacturers specialised in coloured paper, and nineteen in cartridges.[99]

Fig. 3.12 – Samples of coloured paper made by James Cropper & Co., nineteenth century.

James Cropper & Co.'s decision to specialise in certain grades did not, however, solve the greatest problem that British paper-makers were troubled by in the mid-nineteenth century: a severe shortage of raw material. In the 1850s most papers were still being made from cotton and linen rags, the traditional source of cellulose. Demand for rags, however, was beginning to outstrip supply. Throughout the 1850s rags became increasingly scarce, and between 1852 and 1860 most grades of rags increased in price by twenty to thirty percent.[100]

It was a worrying time for paper-makers, particularly as they were sorely vexed to find an alternative, despite their best efforts. By the 1850s the search for a substitute for rags had become frantic: of the 120 patents taken out on new raw materials for paper-making between 1800 and 1859, ninety-two were taken out after 1850.[101] Indeed, the problem not only exercised the minds of paper-makers but also those of publishers and politicians. In 1854 *The Times* offered a reward of £1,000 to anyone who could discover a perfect substitute for rags (Fig. 3.13), and in 1861 a Government Select Committee discussed the issue at length.[102]

Fig. 3.13 – In 1854 The Times *offered a £1,000 reward for anybody who developed a viable alternative to rags; it was never awarded.*

In spite of such efforts, however, the quest for a new raw material met with little success. Nearly every suggestion for a substitute for rags was rejected, either because the material proposed was too scarce, too difficult to prepare, too costly to transport, or a combination of these.[103] *The Times* never awarded its £1,000 prize and the Select Committee concluded that although "great efforts" had been made a substitute remained elusive.[104] "I think there is no probability of any substitute for rags being discovered", one prominent paper-maker pessimistically told the Committee in 1861, summing up well the prevailing view.[105]

At the outset James Cropper found it as difficult to secure sufficient material as everyone else. In 1853, the first full year of his partnership with George McCorquodale and William Blacklock, he was making paper out of almost anything he could get his hands on. Materials used included tow (the coarse or broken part of flax or hemp), waste paper, prints, bass-mats and fustians, ropes, black bagging, sacking, checks, and even dishcloths.[106] The results were not good. While using such a mixture of materials might have kept machines running, the mills failed to return a profit. In 1853 James Cropper & Co. sustained a loss of £405, a result which in part was no doubt due to the difficulties, expense and wastage involved in making decent paper out of so many different materials.

The 1853 loss also reflected the unsuccessful outcome of an experiment with straw at Burneside. Straw had long been proposed as a potential substitute for rags, but it was not, as James Cropper and his partners discovered, an especially economic replacement.[107] While straw was much cheaper (in 1853 it cost them 2s 2d per cwt) it was expensive to process and yielded little in the way of paper-making fibre. In the fortnight leading up to 3 December 1853 for example, when Burneside turned out paper made almost entirely from straw, a loss of £129 was sustained, mainly due to the large quantity of bleaching powder used (over 60 cwt was consumed, costing £37) and the huge loss on material of eighty-five percent.[108] Straw was not used again.

Thereafter, however, the company was more successful in its choice of raw materials. Indeed, while many paper manufacturers continued to be troubled by rag shortages, it managed to find alternative supplies that were not only available, but also economic. As a result, the company not only managed to increase production while it was falling at other paper-mills (output doubled from 380 tons in 1854 to over 800 tons by 1862) but also to improve profit margins.[109]

In the first instance, the company's success owed much to surat, a type of Indian grown cotton. Used in considerable quantities at Burneside from 1853 and at Cowan Head from 1854, it was the main material used at both mills into the 1860s.[110] James Cropper & Co. clearly recognised its merits: although coarser than conventional rags, it was an extremely cheap source of fibre. Between 1853 and 1856, for example, it cost the company an average 6s 6d per cwt, considerably less than the sums they paid for other materials: fustians, for example, cost 13s 6d per cwt and black bagging 19s.[111] Moreover, while other paper manufacturers struggled to secure regular supplies of rags, by all accounts James Cropper & Co. found in surat (at least for a while) a reliable source of paper-making fibre. Even though the firm's requirements grew and grew, it managed to secure sufficient quantities of the material from 1854 into the 1860s.[112]

Surat was not, however, an obvious choice of material. According to one contemporary source, only twenty spinners in Great Britain were using Indian cotton before the early 1860s.[113] Nor was it much used by paper-makers: there are no indications that other manufacturers depended on it in the 1850s to the degree that James Cropper & Co. did.[114] Its deployment at Burneside and Cowan Head can, however, be explained. It probably reflected James Cropper's background. Cropper, Benson, the Liverpool merchant house founded by his grandfather in 1799, had imported Indian cotton on occasion, and it is possible that James Cropper exploited his contacts in Liverpool and the Indian trade to procure surat with which to make paper. At the same time the choice of surat also perhaps reflected James Cropper's anti-slavery and Quaker links. Surat was the product of free labour, and James Cropper may have secured it through Quaker cotton merchants who declined to use slave-grown produce.

Supplies of surat were not, however, destined to last. In 1861 its availability was suddenly jeopardised by the outbreak of the American Civil War, which cut off supplies of American cotton. As a result demand for surat soared, as contemporary evidence suggests: "Recent circumstances have forced almost every spinner in Great Britain to work up East Indian cotton, often indiscriminately called Surat", noted the author of *Indian Cotton Supply – The only effectual and permanent measure for Relief in Lancashire* in 1863.[115] As a result prices rose from 8s per cwt in 1861 to 10s in 1862 and 11s in 1863.

Faced with the sudden loss of its principal raw material James Cropper & Co. did not hesitate to try an alternative which had only recently come to light: esparto, a type of grass grown in North Africa and southern Spain. This began to be touted as a paper-making material in 1860 owing to the invention of a commercially viable way of processing it pioneered by Thomas Routledge. Esparto was not, however, widely used in British paper-mills until after 1862, when Routledge won an award for his work at the International Exhibition. In this way the firm was perhaps one of the first paper manufacturers in the country to use it, experimenting with the material in the autumn of 1862, evidence indeed that it was vigorous and forward-thinking in its choice of raw materials.[116]

Peculiar to the British paper industry, esparto grass proved popular with paper-makers in Britain and did much to relieve raw material shortages.[117] Imports of the material tell the tale well, rising dramatically from 900 tons in 1862 to 20,000 tons in 1863, and almost 200,000 tons by 1880.[118] James Cropper & Co. was not, however, won over by the new material. Although it was cheap (at 5s per cwt it was under half the price of surat) the results of a trial at Cowan Head were disappointing. Processing costs were high (in November, 1862, for example, £48 worth of alkali was required to process £82 worth of esparto) and profit margins were accordingly slim. Taking into account several losses, profits averaged a lowly £26 per fortnight at Cowan Head in the twelve fortnights when esparto was used. This was well below the usual returns, and as a result James Cropper & Co. decided to stop using the material in March 1863 and start making paper from surat again.[119]

By then surat was not, however, as cheap or available as it had been. In 1863 the output of the mills began to fluctuate wildly as it had a decade before, suggesting that materials were in short supply. Fortunately, the firm was not without a solution to the problem. It once again sought an alternative, and by the summer of 1863 had discovered yet another new raw material which could supply most of its needs: jute.

Again it had looked to India as a source of paper-making fibre. Jute, like surat, was Indian grown, first imported from Bengal by the East India Company in 1791.[120] Chiefly made into coarse cloth and bagging, its potential as a raw material for paper was soon realised. In 1797 a pamphlet was published extolling its virtues as a paper-making material, and in 1801 the Royal Society for the Encouragement of Arts, Manufacture and Commerce awarded twenty guineas to Thomas Wilmott, a Kent paper-maker, for jute-made paper. Such publicity did not, however, make much impression on paper-makers. In the 1860s jute was still a relatively untapped source of paper-making fibre.[121]

This was not without reason: although cheap and strong, jute was difficult to process. "It would receive much more extensive application in the manufacture of paper", noted George Clapperton in his paper-making manual of 1894, "were it not for the almost insurmountable difficulties which lie in the way of producing from it, at a reasonable cost, a pulp of sufficient whiteness to be used in the making of fine papers."[122]

James Cropper & Co., however, made a great success of the material, as George Clapperton soon found out. Soon after the publication of his book he was appointed a foreman at Burneside, a post he held until 1901.[123] There he discovered that jute, while unsuitable for the manufacture of fine white papers, could easily be made into the coloured and off-white paper that his new employers specialised in. Indeed, while it was almost impossible to bleach jute white, the material took dyes readily.[124] Paper made from jute was perhaps, however, inferior in quality, if James Cropper & Co.'s deployment of clay is any indication. Used to add opacity and weight to a paper that might otherwise lack it, clay began to be used at exactly the moment the company switched to jute from surat in the summer of 1863.[125]

Whatever its shortcomings, jute successfully fulfilled the two other main criteria of a paper-making material: it was both cheap and available.[126] During the American Civil War spinners were forced to find new fibres to process and jute imports rose dramatically. By the end of the conflict in 1865, India, the main source of the material, was exporting over 2,600,000 tons per year, most of which was landed on British shores. This was double the pre-war average.[127]

For James Cropper & Co. the cheapness and availability of jute also perhaps owed something to the way in which it was bought. Rather than buying jute waste such as old sacking (which was what most paper-makers did if they used the material at all), James Cropper & Co. bought "Jute Cuttings" by the bale direct from abroad.[128] James Cropper's Liverpool connections again perhaps helped: for several years nearly all the jute used by his paper-mills was purchased straight off ships anchored in the docks there.[129] By the early 1870s, however, the company were beginning to use a more convenient source: in 1872 the Barrow Flax & Jute Company opened for business. A huge concern – it soon earned itself the distinction of being ". . . the largest jute spinning and manufacturing works in England" – it supplied Burneside and Cowan Head with jute into the 1880s.[130]

With such sources in place jute remained the company's principal source of paper-making fibre from the middle of 1863 into the 1880s, in which period the output of Burneside's and Cowan Head's machines increased from 850 tons to over 2,200 tons per year. In spite of its merits, however, James Cropper & Co. did continue to use surat on occasion as well as another raw material that entered paper-makers' vocabulary in the 1860s: wood pulp.

Again, James Cropper & Co. was quicker than most to recognise the potential of a new material. Although wood had long been touted as a potential source of paper-making fibre, it was not until the 1850s, when machinery to make mechanically ground wood pulp was invented in Germany, that an economical way to process it was developed.[131] This was used by German paper-makers from 1852, but in Britain the new source of paper-making fibre did not catch on so quickly. Indeed, it was hardly used at all before the 1870s.[132] In this way James Cropper & Co. seem to have numbered among the earliest paper manufacturers in the country to use the material: it first used wood pulp in 1864 and continued to use it for the rest of the decade, albeit in extremely small quantities.[133]

Indeed, although it was never rejected (as esparto had been) it was not until the 1890s that wood pulp became the firm's principal source of paper-making fibre. Nevertheless, its use from the 1860s was significant: it marked the end of the company's (and indeed the whole paper industry's) search for an alternative to rags, and the end of a chapter in the history of paper-making.

For all his initial inexperience James Cropper's decision to become a paper manufacturer had proved to be an excellent choice as his career progressed. Like many Quakers and their descendants, he proved to be a keen man of business, the world of commerce suiting well his character and temperament. Arresting in

Fig. 3.14 – James Cropper, 1823-1900.

appearance, with bright blue eyes and a thick head of hair that turned brilliant white in his later years (Fig 3.14), he was quick and decisive in movement and likewise sharp in mind. "He had a gift", recalled one relation, "for coming to instant decisions in business and social life."[134] He was also, like his grandfather and namesake, inclined to activity: "He was sometimes over-worked", remarked Frances, his daughter, "but he used to say his ideal of happiness was having a little too much to do."[135] Most importantly, he was interested in managing men and money (he had a penchant for statistical analysis, evident in many of his writings) as well as machinery.* "He took the keenest interest in all mechanical appliances", noted Frances, "and had a quick eye to detect any avoidable cause of waste or wear in machinery, material, or steam; and to the last would say, 'I do badly if I cannot save a sovereign every time I walk through the mill'."[136] At the same time he seems to have enjoyed the creative input that his business demanded. "Nearer home I have been working rather more at the Mills", he remarked on one occasion, "and always find a certain pleasure in the endless call for contrivance which this gives."[137]

---

* In 1871, for example, James Cropper noted in detail the technical specifications of the *Abyssinia*, the steam-ship on which he and his son Charles were travelling to New York. Later in the trip Charles explicitly refers to his father's love of statistics. "Very interesting", he wrote to his sister about one visit. "I didn't get many statistics, I left those to father." (Tolson MSS, 8/12)

For his employees, however, paper-mill work could be less pleasant. Hours were long: women and youngsters worked ten hours a day and a twelve hour day was normal for men (until 1919 the day was split into two shifts only).[138] By modern standards many employees were also extremely young. It was customary to take on paper-making apprentices at the age of fourteen, but there is evidence that boys and girls as young as twelve and thirteen were working in Burneside and Cowan Head mills.[139]* James Cropper did not, however, sanction child labour: "I prefer not to have such young ones", he wrote to his mother on one occasion, "and have to refuse them from their own parents."[140]

At the same time wages were low and holidays almost non-existent. Apprentices, for example, were paid three shillings a week in their first year and ten shillings by their final, seventh year, with little in the way of bargaining power to improve their lot. In the nineteenth century paper-making unions were small, weak and severely divided, and in general not disposed towards industrial action.[141] At Burneside and Cowan Head there was only one strike in the course of the century (in 1854), and if Thomas Jones, the Burneside schoolmaster, is to be believed, it was not exactly a success. "Mr. Cropper, with his usual foresight and tact, losing no time, accepted the situation", he later noted of the event, "and in about two days was able to bring them to reason. The kindly lesson was accepted, and all returned to work, sensible of their wrong, and grateful for the lenient treatment."[142]

In retrospect, the revolt was probably justified. Inside the mills working conditions were unpleasant and often dangerous. Raw material stores were "dirty and dusty and choking", according to the *Kendal Times* reporter who visited Burneside Mills in 1865.[143] Processing the raw materials was even more hazardous: it not only involved large quantities of corrosive chemicals (such as bleach and lime) but also rag boilers, huge cauldrons in which materials were digested.[144] Until the later nineteenth century these were open at the top and needed to be treated with great care. Safety measures and considerations, however, were few and far between, as one horrific accident suggests. In February 1866 two young girls were put to work tearing up waste paper and putting it into a rag boiler at Cowan Head. The results were tragic: on 4 March one of the two, Mary Raven, a fourteen year old paper-picker, fell into the boiler. Although quickly fished out by two labourers, she died a day later from the injuries sustained. She had been "standing on a plank across the boiler and pressing the paper down with a fork", Hannah Fuller, her work-mate, told the inquest. In due course a verdict of accidental death

---

* There is even one record of a child under ten working in the mills. Levi Keates is reported to have started working half days in the mills in 1873 at the age of nine. He retired sixty years later in 1933 but still had sufficient energy to enjoy twenty years of retirement; he died in 1953 aged ninety.

was returned, although the company was severely censured for letting the girls work in such a dangerous place.[145]

It was not the only fatal accident. In 1858 Kennedy Walker, who was responsible for looking after the gas-works at Burneside Mills, was killed by a gas explosion. "The lid of the gas purifier blew off", reported the *Kendal Mercury*, ". . . striking Kennedy Walker in the neck so as to cause instant death". He was sixty-two years old. "The deceased workman had been above twenty years employed at Burneside", continued the newspaper report, "and bore an excellent character. He was a tee-totaller of long-standing and his loss is deplored by all."[146] In 1868 Christopher Walker, a sixty year old labourer at Burneside Mills, also died from injuries sustained in the workplace. He fell through a trap door through which he was throwing jute bales to break them into pieces; a rope around a bale had caught his shoe-heel. "We have only made a practice of throwing down the jute since about Martinmas last," Frank Allan, a witness, informed the coroner's inquest. "It did not formerly come so hard packed."[147]

Other accidents were caused by machinery, and though not fatal, were gruesome all the same. In 1871 the *Kendal Mercury* reported that an unnamed Cowan Head employee had been ". . . caught up in the machinery, and whirled around the shaft several hundred times". He had been fitting a belt on a pulley while the shaft was still in motion. "When released from his dreadful position it was found that his leg and thigh had been broken. It proved necessary to amputate the limb".[148] In 1875 a sixteen-year-old apprentice was injured, at Burneside this time. "A poor boy Wilson Clark was hurt at the B.S. paper machine last Monday", noted James Cropper in his journal

> . . . and seems to me hopelessly sunk from the effects of the injury though at first it appeared but a stripping of the skin from the arm. I saw his arm dressed on Saturday and it was an awful wound, so much surface having been sloughed off all round the elbow . . . God bless him poor little fellow.[149]

Wilson Clark, fortunately, recovered; in 1880 he finished his apprenticeship "creditably".[150]

In spite of such accidents, however, James Cropper was (by the standards of his day) a more enlightened employer than most. In contrast with many Victorian employers, his career as a capitalist was always moderated by his and his wife's strong religious beliefs, and he always felt as responsible for the welfare of the people of Burneside and Cowan Head as he did for the prosperity of his paper-mills.* "All that affects Burneside has a deep interest in me", he revealingly wrote on one occasion, and his concern was genuine.[151] "I have only seen a part of the people yet at Burneside", he wrote in 1861 on his return home after a long absence. "Most of them have got some story to say and I do like to have them feel sure that I shall care to hear that a son has got a good place, or that a brother's wife is dead, or a complaint mended, and I really do care too."[152]

Fanny, his wife, likewise took an interest in the well-being of the local community. "You could not know, as I have done", James Cropper wrote in an open letter to the people of Cowan Head and Burneside on her death in 1868, "the deep interest she took in your welfare, the anxiety she felt to improve your home comforts and advantages, the sorrow which instances of vice and sin caused her, or the great pleasure she had when she heard or knew that any one of you, old or young, were striving to serve God, or to show kindness to each other."[153] Her interest in Miles Walker, who came to Burneside at her behest in 1858, was characteristic. Hearing that he had been dismissed from the Lancaster and Carlisle Railway because he refused to work on Sundays, she felt that he must be "a man of worth and character", and persuaded her husband to offer him a position in the mills.[154]

As the examples cited suggest, there was a strong moralistic streak in James and Fanny Cropper's concern for others, a common trait amongst many Victorians of their class. Many of the addresses he gave to his employees were delivered like sermons and religious in tone and subject, emphasising the importance of godliness and church attendance.† He and his wife were not, however, only interested in the moral and spiritual welfare of the local community. There was also a more secular side to their concern, which is evident, for example, in their keenness to make education available to all. In 1845 Burneside had had a school for over a century, yet it was closed to most. It was carried on by the parson "who gave a limited education to a few", noted Thomas Jones, "leaving the majority to learn as they could".[155] To remedy the situation James Cropper established a school

---

* James and Fanny Cropper were fervent in their belief that they should be accountable to God in every word and deed. "You know well", James wrote to his grandson in 1895, "that the sense of God's knowledge of us and our doings is the true motive for conduct". Fanny, meanwhile, was – like James's mother Anne – singular in her desire that herself and her family live like true Christians, as a letter she wrote to James in 1848 suggests. "Dear dear James thou art indeed my joy and delight yet I do wish for thee and for myself more faithfulness and devotion to our heavenly Master". As a result she believed that charitable, Christian work was far more important than commerce. "I am very anxious James should not undertake any more purely business work", she informed his mother on one occasion. "Whatever he adds to his present employments I should like to be of a nature that one could fell distinctly Christian or benevolent". (JCII to JWC, 6 Mar. 1895, Tolson MSS, 12/1. FAC to AC, undated. Tolson MSS, 9/1)

† Interestingly, when James Cropper first arrived in Burneside, hardly anybody in the village went to church. In 1899 he noted that the first time he attended a Sunday service at Burneside, only four people were present: the vicar, the clerk, himself and a little girl. Over fifty years later he reported that the church was crowded at every service, perhaps not least owing to his own exertions. (*Kendal Mercury*, 4 Aug. 1899)

for girls and infants in 1847 – which later became his wife's responsibility – and in 1855 was involved in the foundation of a large new Burneside school, where Thomas Jones – the village's first certified and trained teacher – taught from 1859 until 1897. Constructed just across the River Kent from Burneside Mills (and now the James Cropper plc laboratory) it provided education for all school age children.[156] In addition he and John Bryce – who also gave much to the local community – took evening classes for employees, at the outset out of necessity as much as anything else. "In answer to many advertisements for workers who could read and write, there were no applicants", recalled Thomas Jones:

> . . . This state of things urged several residents to do what they could to educate the employees. Evening classes were opened in the old Reading Room. The Schoolmaster, Mr. Bryce and Mr. Cropper did the teaching. Very soon the value of this elementary knowledge affected the whole village. To vary the organisation, two nights per week were given to mutual improvement, such as short lectures on various subjects, games, reading etc., to inculcate sober habits . . . All this was gratuitous.[157]

Like many Victorian nonconformists and their liberal successors, James Cropper also believed in self-improvement and temperance. He often spoke at the Burneside Mutual Improvement Society and was a keen advocate of temperance, not least owing to his belief that the "drunkenness of the people is the chief cause of their frequent misery". He regularly lent his employees a room in which to hold temperance meetings, and on occasion he attended such events himself. At one such meeting in 1875, for example, he appealed for all in the parish ". . . to stem from the sin and shame of intoxication".[158] And such views were not unpopular: Burneside's inhabitants seem to have shared his outlook. "I venture to assert", wrote a correspondent to the *Kendal Mercury* in 1856, "there is not another village of equal population in the whole county that can boast of a more temperate people! In Mr Cropper's paper mills, there are one hundred workpeople, not one of whom has the character of being a tippler."[159]

James Cropper also seems to have been popular in the village, especially so if the welcome he received on his return home from a trip to Egypt in 1861 is any indication. He was greeted by a four hundred strong crowd of employees and their families, and presented with a bible as a token of their respect.[160] One mill worker even wrote a letter to the *Westmorland Gazette* to express his regard on the occasion:

> . . . by the affability of their manners, by the kindness of their dispositions, by being first and foremost in every good work, by the deep interest they ever manifest for the rising generation, and by their unwearied anxiety for the welfare and happiness of those around them . . . the Croppers have won the affections of the people.[161]

Such a tribute no doubt reflected James and Fanny's proximity to the workplace. While the location of their home Ellergreen (elevated above Burneside with a commanding outlook) symbolised well their patriarchal position in the parish, they remained in sight and earshot of the mills, and they did not strive to distance themselves from their employees, as many mill-owning families did. Indeed, the closeness of the Cropper family's involvement in village life is striking. It was a close-knit community in which family affairs, including births, marriages and deaths, were village affairs. The birthday of James's son Charles, for example, was regularly celebrated with parties at Ellergreen for employees and friends, and when Fanny Cropper died aged forty-two in 1868 it was likewise a communal affair.[162] The day after her death James Cropper, who was heartbroken by the loss, addressed "The People of Burneside and Cowan Head", in an open letter noteworthy for its personal and emotional tone.* "Before we meet to lay her in the grave", he wrote, "I wish to write a few words, which in my distress, I am not able to speak to all of you." In particular, he made known his wife's final wishes: "Ask all the people to my funeral", she had beseeched him on her deathbed, "and let them carry me to my grave".[163]

James and Fanny Cropper were also closely involved in the life of Kendal. The Kendal workhouse children were entertained nearly every Saturday at Ellergreen, and between 1852 and 1880 James Cropper was chairman of the Kendal Board of Poor Law Guardians, which took charge of the workhouse and looked after the poor in Kendal and surrounding parishes. It was a post he valued far above his appointment as High Sheriff of Westmorland in 1875. "The shrievalty is simply a name", he commented, comparing the two, ". . . its dignity is *conferred* not *earned*".[164]

James Cropper was also drawn to Kendal by several other appointments. He was president of the town's Mechanics' Institute and vice-president of its Natural History and Scientific Society, and delivered lectures to both institutions including one entitled "Young Men and Self Improvement", which was delivered to a crowd of four hundred at Castle Mills in 1854.[165] In 1851 he was elected a Kendal Councillor, a post he held until 1854, and at various times he was also president of the local Church Missionary Society; governor of Kendal Grammar School; chairman of the Kendal Education Committee and Justice of the Peace. Furthermore, in 1870 he founded Kendal's first hospital in memory of his wife,

---

* James Cropper mourned the loss of his wife for the rest of his life, and for several years thoughts of her dominated his mind, waking and sleeping. A journal entry of 1870 was typical: "The love I have from others, the comfort of my home, the occupations before me, what are they when I contrast them with the sound of her voice and the touch of her hand and the loving trusting glance of her eye?". (JCII's Journal, 9 Oct 1870, Tolson MSS 8/10)

while further afield he was governor of Sedbergh Grammar School and took a great interest in the new railway communities of Tebay and Lowgill, helping them in the foundation of churches, schools and co-operative stores.[166]

With such a range of activities calling upon James's time it is not surprising to find that paper-making only took up half his day. "I am going on with my mill work every morning", he wrote to his mother on one occasion, summing up well the pattern of his life, "and something away from home in Kendal or elsewhere usually occupies me in the afternoon."[167] Nevertheless, the mills still remained very much his responsibility, though by the 1870s it was becoming clear that he was not enjoying it so much. "My Burneside work is all detail", he confided in his journal in 1870, "and becoming too engrossing through my habit of managing all the details myself."[168]

Weary of paper-making, James Cropper wondered if he might not be more gainfully employed, and from the early 1870s began to consider alternative careers.[169] In 1874, on the death of his father, John, he thought about taking on his father's philanthropic interests in Liverpool, while in 1876 he considered becoming a director of the London & North Western Railway, a position he had twice declined already at his wife's wish. In the event, however, he decided against both courses of action, not least because he had another career on his mind: politics.[170]

James Cropper had played a part in the political life of Kendal since the early 1850s. In 1851, for example, he was vice-chairman of a Committee to promote Liberal sentiments in the town. It was not, however, until the 1870s that he began to consider the possibility of a political career. "I know I should like to be in Parliament", he noted in 1872, "and it seems as if some such claim on my powers would help me". By the end of the decade it was the only alternative he was considering: "Parliamentary life", he remarked in 1879, "would now be the only possible change". There was, however, one problem: Kendal's serving MP, John Whitwell, a carpet manufacturer, had no desire to retire, and James Cropper did not want to stand for Westmorland as a whole.[171]

In December 1880, however, the unforeseen occurred. John Whitwell died suddenly and James Cropper was selected as Kendal's Liberal candidate in the ensuing by-election. He won the contest with a majority of three hundred (out of an electorate of 1,500) and in the New Year of 1881, accompanied by his daughter Mary, left Westmorland and paper-making for London, to take his place in the House of Commons under William Gladstone.

Like many of the key events of James Cropper's life the election victory was marked with a party at Burneside Mills, where, as ever, he felt obliged to make a speech. "After modestly pointing out the work he had before him and stating his determination to do that well", reported the *Westmorland Gazette* of his address, "he gave a graphic description of the progress Burneside had made during the last thirty-five years, pointing to the many improvements in wages, machinery and locomotion". He also, importantly, looked forward. "He concluded", noted the newspaper, "by stating that those left in charge were quite capable of carrying on the concern to still greater things".[172]

In particular, James Cropper was thinking of his son, Charles, by then aged twenty-eight. "I know I shall have many rebuffs and many a sense of failure in Parliament", he wrote of his electoral success, "but it seems to me right to go forward and it will give Charlie the opportunity of taking my place while I can yet advise him".[173] Indeed, for many years it had been James Cropper's acknowledged wish ". . . to give Charlie more responsibility here, which my own constant Burneside supervision makes difficult – in my absence or Mr Bryce's he evidently feels himself more involved. This is important."[174]

Fig. 4.1 – Charles Cropper, 1852-1924.

4

Foreigners, Fire and the Fox: Charles Cropper, 1880-1914

"How will it all result? His life is to be so much
like mine, his training for it so different".
(James Cropper on his son Charles, 1876)[1]

I N contrast with his father, Charles Cropper never had to worry much about
what career he might pursue. While James Cropper had faced an increasingly
uncertain future as he grew up, Charles's prospects only became clearer. His
family's ties with Westmorland and Burneside, for example, grew from strength to
strength as he advanced in age. During the 1860s and 1870s his father began to
buy up tracts of land around Ellergreen, the family home, and within a few years
had laid the foundations of the agricultural estate that the family have lived upon
ever since.

The family's connection with paper-making also grew firmer as Charles
advanced from child to adulthood. Even though James Cropper began to consider
alternative careers for himself in the 1870s, he had no desire (as his forebears had)
to sever his and his family's business connections. Far from it: in 1870, following
the death of his partner William Blacklock, he not only increased his holding in
the paper-mills (from a third to a half) but also made Charles – who had just
turned eighteen and was still at school – a joint partner, evidently hopeful that his
son would follow him into the firm.[2]

Charles's appointment was premature to say the least. He did not begin
working full-time at Burneside and Cowan Head until 1874. Nevertheless, if his
mother is to be believed, he had already expressed a desire to follow in his father's
footsteps. "If it pleases GOD we live", she wrote to him in 1867, when he was
fifteen, "and you do marry and are still of the same mind in wishing to live near us
and carry on Papa's work at Burneside, we might then build you a house
somewhere near."[3]

Charles's entry into the family firm was not, however, a foregone conclusion.
Like many first generation industrialists, James Cropper felt that his own

education had been inadequate, particularly from a social point of view. "I have looked with perhaps undue envy all my life at Public School boys", he commented on one occasion. As a result he decided to educate his son away from home, starting with a preparatory school in Surrey, where Charles was dispatched in 1862 at the age of ten.[4] This was followed by Rugby (one of the leading public schools in Victorian England) where he remained a pupil until 1870, then by Cambridge University, where he studied History and Economics at Trinity College.

For many industrialists' sons, such an education did not result in them stepping into their fathers' shoes. "Too often the mill proved too bleak a destiny for those passing through the [public school and university] system", comments one historian, and as Charles Cropper would have found out a career in trade was, for most graduates, neither a desirable nor a respectable attainment.[5] Indeed, many of Charles's contemporaries frowned upon working in trade. He even discussed the problem with his father: "The feeling of objection to trade is no new one", James Cropper remarked to his son on one occasion:

> . . . A man's being in trade, rising from trading people and generally making money by buying and selling naturally gives a first impression in his disfavour among cultivated people. The presumption is that his association has been with money people, if not people recently raised by money from a different position, and that his ideas will be limited, if not ostentatious . . .

James Cropper was not, however, unduly worried by such associations. "I should say the disadvantage is a passing one and that when once found to be no bar to level intercourse, its influence is gone".[6] Nor does his son seem to have been much concerned: Charles's resolve to work for his father only strengthened as he grew older. By the end of his schooldays his mind was made up: "His own wish is in the end to settle here", James Cropper noted in 1870, "and take up my work and what may come of it to himself."[7]

As an undergraduate Charles's wish remained the same. He even began working inside the paper-mills, spending two months in the office at Cowan Head during his summer holidays in 1872. His tasks included filling in the order book, which still bears his distinctive handwriting.[8] He evidently enjoyed the experience: "Dear Charlie's readiness to take office work at the mills", noted James at the time, "has given quite a fresh impulse to my interest in paper-making, and I am thinking over a new Burneside extension which will be very useful."[9]

By 1873 there were no doubts whatsoever that Charles would follow his father into paper-making. On the occasion of his twenty-first birthday, which was celebrated at Ellergreen with a party for family, friends and mill employees, there were numerous references to his impending career, not least by John Bryce, who addressed the gathering on behalf of the workforce and presented Charles with an illuminated address (Fig. 4.2). "Occasionally we have been favoured with glimpses of his excellent character, when he has spent his holidays with us", he told the assembled crowd, "and it is with pleasure that we learn that he is going to stay among us."[10] And so he did: a year later, on the completion of his degree, Charles returned to Westmorland to begin life as a paper manufacturer. He was, as his father had been in 1845, twenty-two years old. "The impression in my mind all week", noted James Cropper in his journal on 12 July 1874, "has been the new sense of Charlie being here not to leave again. I am in constant thought about his employment and training."[11]

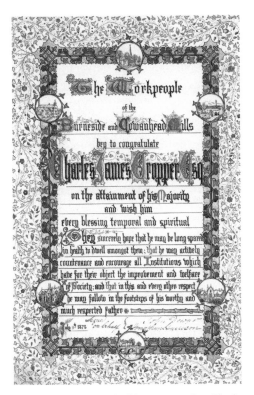

Fig. 4.2 – Illuminated address presented to Charles Cropper by the paper-mill workforce, on the occasion of his twenty-first birthday, 1873.

At first Charles spent most of his time in the office, helping to keep the books. At the close of 1874, for example, he compiled the half-yearly reports for Burneside and Cowan Head, and from the beginning of 1875 he began to keep the firm's fortnightly reports. This was an important and instructive task that involved breaking down the running costs of both mills and calculating their profitability and productivity every two weeks. It gave him a regular insight into the working and performance of the business, and one he evidently valued: he continued to compile the reports until 1890.[12]

Following his return to the mills for good, Charles rapidly rose through the ranks. Only six months after he had joined the firm his father was thinking about giving him more responsibility, and James's wish remained the same, even after Charles became a full partner in 1876.[13] "Sometimes I want to plan some other work for myself so that Charlie may have more claim upon him at Burneside", noted James in his journal shortly after his son's promotion. "When I am there it is so easy for me to settle matters in the Mills or village that they do not yet come to depend on him, and I do not like this to grow into a habit."[14] It was not until 1881, however, when he left Westmorland for London as Kendal's MP that James Cropper finally relinquished control of the mills in favour of his son, by then aged twenty-eight.

The passage of James Cropper & Co. from the first generation to the next was, compared to the course taken by many family businesses, a remarkably smooth affair, carried out with a minimum of fuss and no signs of friction or discord. In great part this reflected the firm friendship that existed between Charles and James. Although different in temperament and inclination, they enjoyed the first in a series of close and harmonious relationships between fathers and sons that have persisted for several generations, and ensured, perhaps above all other factors, the survival of the family's connection with paper-making to this day. "In the Ellergreen story", remarks Maisie Fletcher in her account of the Cropper home and its generations of occupants –

> . . . one thing that stands out so clearly is the wonderful relationship between father and son in successive generations. Although each generation produced such a different type of personality there was no breach at all in their deep affections. They counted on each other and the older generation delighted in the new ideas that came from the next one, while the younger felt a real pride in his elder's achievements.[15]

Initially Charles Cropper and his father were perhaps drawn together by the loss of his mother Fanny in 1868, when he was fifteen. James was truly shattered by his wife's premature death, and his son proved to be one of the only people who really lifted his forlorn spirits. In the aftermath Charles became the focus of his father's hope and affection. Not least this is evident in James's decision to tour the United States of America with him in 1871. "I am wishful to have a fair opportunity of being thrown together with him", noted James in his journal shortly before they set off by steam-ship for New York in March 1871, "and that our tastes and interests should not sever gradually more and more . . . I feel that life must to me be very dependent on him, and further that his character needs guidance and counsel." In addition, James hoped that the trip might be "good for us both and might renew for Charlie's manhood the loving fellowship which has so much marked his feeling for me during his youth".[16]

He was not disappointed. "I have been glad of my intercourse with Charlie on our tour", he wrote on their return from abroad. "It has made us each more to the other".[17] And so it did: for the rest of their lives the bond between father and son was never broken. James, for one, delighted in his son's companionship: "I enjoy his being at home", he declared in 1876, "more than I have enjoyed any other thing for years. I feel his tenderness extremely, and I see how much he thinks of me and is glad to carry out anything I wish him to do".[18] He was not mistaken: "If my influence was in any way for good at Cambridge", Charles told his fiancee Edith Holland shortly after their engagement in that year –

> . . . it was simply Father's doing, in fact every respectable action of my life has been all his wish. He has been all the conscience I ever had almost, I never feel God has any personal influence over me . . . I wish there was any chance of you finding me to be such a man as father is. You will have a good father-in-law at any rate.[19]

Charles's readiness to follow his father into paper-making also perhaps owed something to the location of his father's paper-mills in the foothills of the English Lake District. If the mills had been situated where most factories were – in the heart of a smoky industrial town, a world away from Westmorland's fells and lakes – it is unlikely that he would have been so willing to work in them. Indeed, he might well have followed in the footsteps of those hundreds of industrialists' sons who deserted their industrial roots for fairer climes. Roger Crompton, for example, on inheriting Stoneclough paper-mill from his brother in 1844, abandoned Lancashire for a house in Regent's Park, London, where he "kept an almost princely retinue of servants and entertained a lot".[20]

Burneside and Cowan Head, however, being a stone's throw from the heart of the Lake District were hardly situated in an environment from which it was desirable to escape. Far from it: they were in exactly the place that numerous Victorian and Edwardian industrialists chose to live once they had amassed a fortune, including Thomas Wrigley, a Manchester paper manufacturer and millionaire insurance broker who built himself a villa on the shores of Windermere.[21] There is an important distinction, however, between the Croppers and men such as Wrigley: for them the Lake District has been and remains a place to make money as much as spend it.

Closer to home, Charles Cropper was perhaps further encouraged to follow his father into paper-making by the good relationship he and his family enjoyed with their employees. Labour relations were good (but for the one short-lived instance of unrest in 1854) and from an early age Charles seems to have been popular and respected in the local community (perhaps not least due to the numerous parties his father gave in his honour). On his marriage to Edith Holland in London in 1876, for example, he came home to a reception every bit as enthusiastic as the welcome his parents had received thirty-one years before (Fig. 4.3). "As they had done for James and his bride", noted Maisie Fletcher, "the village people took out the horses when they reached the village and themselves drew the couple home".[22]

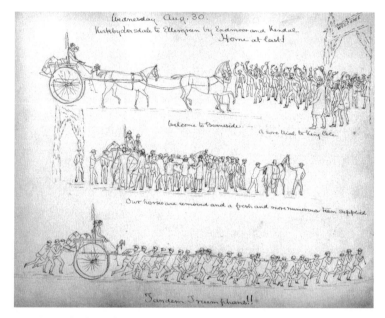

Fig. 4.3 – Charles and Edith Cropper's homecoming, following their marriage in August 1876, depicted by Charles in an album he kept of their "wedding tour".

Two days later their homecoming was further celebrated with a party at Ellergreen, at which John Bryce – "in the name of those employed in the Burneside and Cowan Head Mills" – extended Edith Cropper a warm welcome. "She may find our northern climate somewhat colder than that of the south, where she has lived", he told the assembled crowd, "but we trust she may never find our northern hearts less warm than those she has left behind."[23]

The outlook was promising. Over four years before his father left Westmorland for London as Kendal's MP, Charles Cropper's life and career was firmly in place. Soon after his marriage he and his bride moved into their own home, Tolson Hall, a quarter of a mile across a field from Ellergreen, and a family was not long in the coming. Eleanor Margaret, the first of five children, was born in May 1878, and fifteen months later, in August 1879, James Winstanley.

Their first (and again only) son, his birth was celebrated in customary style with a lavish party at Ellergreen for friends, family, and employees. The mills were even stopped for the event. "The workpeople attended *en masse* . . ." reported the *Kendal Times* in a lengthy account of the proceedings, which included dancing, games and sports, a Punch and Judy show, fireworks and a 100lb cake.[24] Hopes for the next generation clearly ran high. Charles Cropper, who spoke to the assembled crowd after tea, was especially optimistic: "He trusted that the little boy would love Westmorland, and especially Burneside", recounted the *Kendal Times*, "and that he would spend his life there."[25]

Inside the paper-mills, on the valley floor below, there were further grounds for optimism. The 1870s had proved to be an exceptionally prosperous period for James Cropper & Co. Between 1874 and 1877 Burneside and Cowan Head mills returned record results, and though profits began to dip as the decade drew to a close even then the business returned a profit on capital of twenty-five percent, a good result by any standards. Moreover, with good labour relations and the mills continuing to be developed year after year, James Cropper believed that the future would bring even greater prosperity. Following his election to Parliament in December 1880 he confidently declared that the paper-making concern he had founded in 1845 could be carried on ". . . to still greater things", even in his absence.[26]

Departing for London as Kendal's new MP in January 1881, James Cropper not only left his business in the hands of his son but also those of John Bryce, his able and trusted partner since the 1850s, who continued to work at Burneside into the 1890s. At the same time the day to day running of the mills was overseen by a range of experienced individuals including James Savage, the chief engineer, and John Dewar and Jonathan Harrison (the senior foremen at Burneside and Cowan Head respectively), all of whom had worked for the company for years.[27] James Cropper himself, meanwhile, continued to offer advice and guidance when it was needed, and not for long from afar. In the 1885 General Election the constituency of Kendal was abolished and he narrowly lost the contest for the county of Westmorland to the Tory candidate, Lord Bective.[28] Coming back to Ellergreen, he did not, however, return to full-time work in the paper-mills, instead dedicating the rest of his life to philanthropic and committee work, such as the chairmanship of the Westmorland County Council, a post he was appointed to in 1889.

By the end of the century, however, the company had lost its first generation of management. James Savage died in 1887 and John Bryce in 1896, aged sixty-four, while John Dewar retired in 1892, aged seventy. Furthermore, within a few years the company had also lost George McCorquodale, James Cropper's partner since 1852 (who died in 1895, aged seventy-eight) as well as James Cropper himself, who died in 1900. On a trip to Paris in October of that year he caught pneumonia, and died within a matter of days, aged seventy-seven. It was, in many respects, the end of an era, for before the winter was over the Queen too was dead, and Victorian Britain no more.

The places of the departed did not go unfilled. First, in 1889 Burneside Mill gained a new foreman, Daniel McNeill, a twenty-nine year old Scotsman who came from a long-established family of paper-makers, and had worked in several paper-mills in England and Scotland.[29] The tradition of recruitment north of the border was further perpetuated by the appointment of George Clapperton as Cowan Head's foreman in 1894. Arriving from Penicuik, a centre of the Scottish paper industry, he was again a man of considerable experience, and had only recently written a book on paper-making: *Practical Paper-Making, A Manual for Paper-Makers and Owners and Managers of Paper Mills*. He did not, however, stay long. Ambitious to further his career, he left the company in 1901 for greater things, and by the First World War was one of the leading lights of the British paper industry, controlling seven mills.[30]

Other arrivals at Burneside stayed longer, first and foremost being Alfred Willink, Charles Cropper's first cousin, who had joined James Cropper & Co. in 1879 (Fig. 4.4). Like his uncle James, who had arranged the opening, he had grown up at Dingle Bank, the Cropper homestead in Liverpool, before leaving the

Fig. 4.4 – Alfred Willink, 1860-1947.

port at the age of nineteen to pursue a career in paper-making.[31] His arrival encouraged James Cropper to build a new mill for the preparation of raw materials at Bowston (midway between Burneside and Cowan Head) work on which started in 1879 and cost £4,000 in total. "I trust it may be for his happiness and ours", commented James Cropper.[32]

He was not disappointed: "It is a pleasure and a great advantage to me to have you where you are", James Cropper wrote to Alfred two years later, "and I look forward to you being more and more important and useful at Burneside".[33] Promotion, perhaps not surprisingly, came quickly: Alfred Willink was appointed a partner in 1884 and a director in 1889 (by which time he was a major shareholder) and by the 1890s he was largely in charge of the day-to-day running of the mills.[34]

The renewed association of Willinks and Croppers in business proved to be much more fruitful than their previous foray into business together. Alfred's grandfather, Daniel Willink, the Liverpool Dutch consul, had been bankrupted in the 1820s when the cotton market in which he was speculating with Cropper, Benson collapsed (see Chapter Two). Fortunately, Alfred fared better. He remained an active and fully paid up director of James Cropper & Co. into his late eighties, only retiring a matter of months before his death in 1947, aged eighty-seven. Furthermore, through Alfred's nephew, Derek Willink, and in turn Derek's son and grandson, Nick and Patrick, the Willink family has remained involved in paper-making at Burneside until the present day.

Another cousin, Vincent Jones, son of the Burneside vicar, the Reverend William Jones and James Cropper's sister Margaret, further strengthened the ranks of family members within the firm. Starting work in 1893 aged nineteen, he became a shareholder on the death of John Bryce in 1896, an assistant director on James Cropper's death in 1900 and a full director in 1907.

The Croppers and their relatives were not, however, the only family whose commitment to paper-making ensured the survival of James Cropper & Co. Inside the mills themselves, there were many other dynasties in the making. By 1914 numerous families had worked inside Burneside or Cowan Head paper mills for two generations or more, their surnames including Daws, Davis, Dent, Dobson, Ellwood, Hutchinson, Lightley, Palmer, Pearson, Reed, Robinson, Shepherd, Snowdon, Thompson, Walker, Winskill, and Wightman (Fig. 4.5 (i, ii)).[35]

The workforce's commitment to the firm was extremely important. Throughout the late nineteenth and early twentieth century, the business enjoyed years of sustained expansion. In line with the British paper industry as a whole, the output of the Cropper mills grew from 2,200 tons in 1881 to 6,200 in 1900 and almost 12,000 by 1914. In part the growth was underpinned by the greater availability of raw materials, particularly wood pulp. Used in increasing quantities

Fig. 4.5 (i) – George Robinson (left) and a member of the Walker family, outside the Burneside stoke-hole, c.1890. Seven generations of the Robinson family have worked at Burneside, a record of service that continues today.

Fig. 4.5 (ii) – Group of mill employees and children outside the Cowan Head mill house, c.1885.

throughout the 1880s, by 1895 it had superseded jute and surat as the principal raw material used in the Cropper mills, the change in raw material usage coinciding with a sharp rise in output. By 1900 the company was manufacturing paper that was over seventy-five percent wood pulp, most of which was secured through a pulp agent in London.[36]

The continuing expansion of output was also underpinned by growing demand for paper. Stimulated by rising wealth, population and literacy, by 1890 Britain was consuming over 430 million pounds of paper per year, more paper per capita than any other country in the world. Much of this was newsprint, which James Cropper & Co. did not manufacture (by 1896 newspaper circulation had reached 174 million), but there was plenty of growth in other areas that did benefit them.[37] In particular the firm profited from the continuing expansion of Britain's postal and telegraph services. The number of letters posted per year in England and Wales increased from 700 million in 1870 to 2,800 million by 1913, while the number of telegraphs grew tenfold. James Cropper & Co. continued to supply both markets, making MG envelope papers and Orange Laid paper for telegraph envelopes, which was supplied to the Post Office through Waterlow & Sons.[38]

Britain's railway network, which grew in length from 13,500 to 20,000 miles in length between 1871 and 1913, continued to be another important source of demand.[39] Between 1880 and 1914 James Cropper & Co. supplied paper to nearly all the major railway companies, including the Great Western, South Eastern, Caledonian, Great Northern, and London & North Western, usually through railway stationers.[40] This included Waterlow & Sons and McCorquodale, the official printer and stationer for many of Britain's largest railway companies, including the London & North Western.[41]* Links with the firm remained strong, despite the death of George McCorquodale in 1895. His five sons (amongst whom his shareholding was split) all remained committed to James Cropper & Co., and one of them, Alick, was appointed an honorary director. It was a more than valuable connection. The McCorquodales were not only huge customers in their own right – in 1887, for example, they bought almost 1,000 tons of Cropper "buffs", over a third of the total output in that year – but also managed to secure contracts for James Cropper & Co. with other stationery houses.[42]

The relationship between the two firms, however, could be strained at times, as one meeting between Alfred Willink and George F. McCorquodale, the eldest son, suggests. "I have had the most miserable morning's work I ever experienced",

---

* Waterlow & Sons were particularly predominant in the production of railway tickets. "From this office," noted the *London, Provincial and Colonial Press News* in an April 1888 report on Messrs Waterlow & Sons, "more railway tickets are issued than from any other in England, and probably more than any single factory in the world".

Alfred informed Charles Cropper shortly after visiting McCorquodale & Co.'s London offices in 1902:

> George McCorquodale worked himself up into rage after rage . . . He cares nothing for his connection with Croppers. He said Croppers were fifty times more in McCorquodale's debt than McCorquodale & Co. to Croppers, and that we owed Waterlow's trade to him and Millington's and heaps of others and Dickinson's, and that he was ready to sell his shares in Croppers now at once rather than have the disadvantage of being influenced by them.[43]

Fortunately for James Cropper & Co. the spat passed and the McCorquodales remained important shareholders and customers up to the First World War and beyond. Moreover, George F. McCorquodale even continued to secure custom for Croppers with other stationery houses. In 1904, for example, he somehow ensured that Waterlow & Sons renewed their contract with James Cropper & Co. for telegraph envelope paper. "Simply quote the present price", Charles Cropper was covertly instructed by George's brother, Harold. "You'll see you'll get the Contract all right."[44]

James Cropper & Co. also entered new markets for paper in the years leading up to the First World War. These included paper for Guinness bottle labels (first made in 1899), MG Poster paper (first made in 1901) and cloth-lined paper for registered envelopes (more of which later).[45] The company even began to make paper for insulating cables, capitalising on the new and rapidly growing electrical industry.[46] Paper's potential as a material was, as James Cropper noted in 1895, far from exhausted. "Nothing seems to open out for itself", he wrote to Charles, "to so many uses and such constant development as paper".[47]

By the turn of the century the firm was also making duplex paper, a two-ply paper made of two different colours or qualities used for envelopes and packaging. Although this was not exactly a new grade (in origin duplex dated back to 1824, when John Dickinson patented a process for sticking two sheets of paper together) the way in which it was made was novel. It was developed by Silas Clarke, a fifty-three year old paper-maker who had been working for James Cropper & Co. since 1867.[48] Exactly what his innovation was remains unclear, although it was clearly valued by Charles Cropper and his fellow directors, who presented him with a large ebony and marble clock. "Presented to Silas Clarke by James Cropper & Co. Limited", the inscription on it reads, "in recognition of a valuable invention". And truly valuable it was, as James Cropper & Co. sold duplex paper for decades, not least to McCorquodales, who had previously bought the grade from abroad.[49]

James Cropper & Co.'s success with such papers did not, however, spell increased returns for the firm. Far from it: after James Cropper entrusted the concern to his son Charles and John Bryce in 1880, the company's results were more than disappointing. In 1881 profits plummeted from £9,400 to £3,300, the lowest level since 1863, and even though they picked up in the following years – rising to £7,000 in 1882 and £10,800 in 1883 – they never returned to the levels of the mid-1870s until the First World War, even though more and more capital was being invested in the concern and more and more paper being made.[50] Indeed, while the output of Burneside and Cowan Head mills grew steadily after 1880, profits fluctuated dramatically throughout the period, with little in the way of underlying growth.

At first glance, the company's lacklustre performance might be attributed to Charles Cropper. While he was committed to the family firm there are several indications that he was not quite "the keen man of business" that his father was.[51] "He begins again to go to the office", remarked James Cropper on Charles's return from abroad in 1875, "but I can not suppose he applies much to business and I hardly know how to make it interesting to him".[52] His education was perhaps to blame. Rugby was far more intent on turning out "Christian gentlemen" than competitive capitalists, and Cambridge University did not groom its students for careers in industry either, as Charles noted himself. "I should have made a much better business man if I had never gone to Cambridge", he commented on one occasion.[53] In addition, he was also perhaps less inclined to the serious matter of running a business owing to the freer upbringing his father had granted him. "I have taken an opposite course with him", James Cropper commented in 1876, contemplating his own upbringing. "I have made all the advantages of the world open to him, have helped him as far as I could to try its pleasures & judge them for himself. How will it all result?"[54]

The effects are plain to see. Where James Cropper (in his own words) "never quite lost the Puritan view", and was a sober, self-denying character in the Quaker mould, Charles Cropper embraced the world and its diversions with zeal, enjoying life without the sense of guilt and sinfulness that had checked the thoughts and actions of his forebears.[55] He was outgoing and sociable, fun-loving and light-hearted, more inclined to sing a song or tell a story at a gathering of people, for example, than deliver an earnest lecture. His father did not entirely approve ("My beloved Fanny and I", wrote James on one occasion, "had a like feeling against amusements and ordinary worldly enjoyments") and, like every parent, often worried that standards and ideas were being lowered in the next generation.[56] "Gaiety grew and grew", he noted in his journal after one visit of Charles's friends at Ellergreen, "and there was too much stir and publicity and worldliness . . . I have made sure it does not happen here again."[57]

From an early stage Charles Cropper's parents were also concerned by his great love of field sports. "I hope as the love of Christ grows stronger and stronger in your heart", his mother wrote to him shortly before her death, "the love of hunting and shooting will grow weaker – not that I think them wicked, but I think they harm our fellow creatures and lead us away from God too".[58] His father was similarly concerned: "I had a long talk with my dear son", he noted in his journal on one occasion, "on the need for his holding a higher standard for himself, socially, intellectually and religiously, than the young men whom he sees in Westmorland hunts."[59]

Their words, however, fell on deaf ears. For as long as he lived Charles Cropper hunted with an enthusiasm that verged on obsession. It was the love of his life, and the subject-matter of his most vivid legacy, *Hunting Scraps*, an album containing hundreds of drawings and water-colours. Drawn and painted by him over the course of forty-seven years of hunting with friends and family, it is a remarkable pictorial record of how he and his like spent their days (Fig. 4.6).*

Hunting was undoubtedly a distraction from paper-making, and arguably one reason for the relative decline of James Cropper & Co. after 1880. "Going to the dogs", remarks Neil McKendrick, "has acquired more than proverbial significance in English entrepreneurial history", and Charles Cropper, it is true, does seem to have been one of that breed of gentleman capitalists who chose "to pursue foxes rather than profits".[60] Between 1880 and 1914 he spent over 1,340 days away from the office hunting with packs nationwide, an average of almost forty days per season, and usually not at weekends. The most popular day for hunting was Friday.

It would be misleading, however, to attribute the poor performance of James Cropper & Co. after 1880 to hunting alone. While Charles's pursuit of the fox provides a convenient and diverting explanation for the faltering fortunes of the business, in reality it had less to do with the firm's management than with the wide range of problems that were encountered in the decades leading up to 1914. First, business was not as profitable for British tradesmen and industrialists as it had been. Even though industrial output and exports continued to grow, profits and prices fell and foreign competition grew increasingly severe.[61] Indeed, as the nineteenth century drew to a close, Britain began to lose her uncontested supremacy in manufacturing, and other countries were fast becoming fierce economic competitors, particularly Germany, which had only recently become a unified political entity under Bismarck in the 1860s.

---

* According to one obituarist, Charles Cropper hunted with over seventy-five packs in his lifetime. In his spare time he kept accounts of all his horses, tabulating the gains or losses he made on their sale and commenting on their handling. He also drew up charts of his hunting seasons in calendar form, remarking on the location and quality of the hunts in which he participated. Evidence of his enthusiasm for the sport is abundant. In the 1900 and 1901 season, for example, when hunting on horseback was periodically banned during the official period of mourning for Queen Victoria, he instead spent thirty-five days hunting on foot.

Fig. 4.6 – Detail from one of hundreds of drawings and watercolours from Charles Cropper's Hunting Scraps, *his most vivid legacy.*

Against this background, James Cropper & Co.'s performance was fairly typical. "Trade is fairly good, there are plenty of orders", wrote Charles Cropper in 1903, summing up well the era as a whole, "but not much money making I regret to say".[62] It was an old and widespread observation. "In the last two years", reported the *Paper Maker's Monthly Journal* in 1883, "the amount of business done has been large, but profits not necessarily larger than periods in which trade has been small."[63] Three years earlier, John Evans of John Dickinson, the paper-maker and stationer, had found trade even worse. In 1880 he declared that the actual manufacture of paper was no longer profitable, and that his firm's profits were made in stationery rather than paper-making.[64]

Falling prices were chiefly to blame. From the mid-1870s into the early twentieth century paper prices fell again and again. Orange Laid paper made at

Burneside, for example, dropped from over 40s per cwt in 1875 to 20s by 1888 and 14s by 1910, and talk of price cuts dominates the business correspondence of the period.[65] Month after month, year after year, customers demanded price reductions. "Fleming says twenty shillings is too much for a Buff", reads a typical letter of the period, "and wants to see what we could now do at sixteen." And the company was usually compelled to accept the reduction or lose business, even if there was little profit in it.[66] "I fixed the M.G. Buff with Millingtons at 16/-", noted Charles Cropper in 1896, "and by economy and cheeseparing we must somehow manage to get something out of it."[67] On occasion Burneside's and Cowan Head's machines even ran at a loss. "I agreed the Cap order for Liverpool at 17/-", Charles informed Alfred Willink in 1898, referring to a McCorquodale & Co. order. "We shan't lose much".[68]

The news, however, was not all bad. Paper prices did at least partly reflect the falling cost of manufacture. Raw materials, for one, were cheaper than ever. Surat, for example, dropped from over ten shillings per cwt in 1880 to less than five by 1895, while the cost of chemical wood pulp, the firm's principal raw material by 1900, also fell. Furthermore, chemical costs were also on the wane. Aluminium sulphate, for example, which was used for sizing paper, halved in price between 1880 and 1895, falling from 6s to 3s per cwt.[69] Wage costs also fell owing to the greater use of wood pulp, which was less laborious to prepare than jute and surat.

The company also offset falling prices by improving productivity. In line with the British paper industry in general (the average annual output of British machines grew by six hundred percent between 1861 and 1912) the company managed to increase output dramatically without increasing the number of their machines. In the early 1890s, for example, when the company had five paper machines with a combined width of 324 inches, it produced an average 3,800 tons of paper per year, an average 11.7 tons per inch of width. By 1910-14, by which time the mills were turning out over 11,000 tons of paper per year, the company was making over twenty-nine tons per inch of width, an almost threefold increase in productivity.[70]

Such improvements were not, however, a choice so much as a necessity, owing to growing competition, a key feature of the industry after 1880, and one that demoralised paper-makers beyond measure. "The whole trade appears to be demoralised and utterly reckless", complained one paper-maker in 1887, and his view was shared by many, not least paper-makers in Lancashire. "The paper trade in Lancashire", reported the *Darwen News* in 1885, "has degenerated into a competition which is as fierce and deplorable as that existing in any of the staple trades of the country."[71] James Cropper & Co. would not have disagreed: the spectre of competition looms large in the company's business correspondence of the period.[72] Alfred Willink's meeting with Bemrose & Sons in October 1901 was typical. The prices he quoted for two papers "though reasonable compared with former contracts", were "quite out of it" in comparison with quotations received from other manufacturers.

For some firms the competition was too much. Between 1876 and 1900 the number of paper-mills at work in England in Wales fell from 300 to 221, a contraction that is largely attributable to the severity of competition.[73] Cumbria's paper industry followed the trend: numerous mills failed or changed hands between 1880 and 1914, including three in the vicinity of Ulverston, one of which was offered to James Cropper & Co. in 1905 but declined.[74] In 1894 and 1895 – perhaps the worst years of all for the British paper trade – the future of James Cropper & Co. itself was even questioned. Trading conditions so depressed Charles Cropper that he thought that his teenage son James Winstanley (known as Jem) might be better off pursuing a different career. "Charles is very low", wrote his sister Mary in 1894, "and wonders if it is fair to expect Jem to stick to the business."[75] James Cropper, who was consulted on the matter, thought similarly: "I confess that the actual prospects of our trade are not bright", he wrote in 1895 in a letter discussing his grandson's future, "the turnout is so large and the competition so great and so keen."[76]

In particular, the morale (and earnings) of paper manufacturers was being hit by competition from abroad. By 1880 the British paper industry's hold on home and foreign markets was no longer assured by a technological lead over the rest of the world, and several other nations, notably Germany and America, were beginning to compete on equal terms. Advances in ship-building technology – in particular the development of compound engines and better steel – made matters worse. They led to a new generation of bigger and faster steam-ships which eroded international trading boundaries just as the railways had dissolved provincial and national boundaries a generation before.[77]

The impact of foreign competition was made worse by Britain's prevailing economic policy – free trade – which gave foreigners free access to British home markets without securing admission to foreign markets for British producers in return. Since 1861, when import duties were abolished, paper manufacturers had argued that this was unfair, as most countries continued to have their paper industries protected by import taxes on paper. The United States, for example, charged a duty of £25 per ton duty on paper imports.[78] It was not, however, until the 1880s and 1890s that the situation really turned against them. It was then that Britain began to be flooded by cheap paper from abroad. Between 1875 and 1895 imports of paper rose from 41,000 to 543,000 tons, and by 1895 over half of the paper consumed in Britain came from abroad.[79]

In particular, Britain's open door was exploited by the German paper industry as a dumping ground for surpluses. By the 1890s almost half of German paper exports ended up in Britain, much of it at a discount to British prices.[80] Such paper perhaps did more than anything else to undermine British price levels. The price of imported printings and writings, for example, fell from £55 per ton in 1880 to £35 by 1890 and £10 by 1900. British paper manufacturers were understandably despondent. "We all agreed that it was the foreign stuff that spoilt our trade", wrote Alfred Willink after a large meeting of manufacturers in 1899, summing up the prevailing mood.[81]

For James Cropper & Co. foreign competition was by no means an idle threat. By the 1890s many of the firm's largest customers were buying paper from abroad and complaints about "the foreigner" (and at times the "wretched foreigner") are a conspicuous feature of the business correspondence of the period. "The foreigner is cutting under us in all directions", Charles Cropper wrote to Alfred Willink in 1894, when things were particularly bad. "I don't know if they are making it pay but I sadly fear they will cut us up until we cannot get our own out of it."[82] In another letter of the same period, in which was enclosed "a sample of what [Waterlows] are now buying from Bismarck's mill", Charles was even more pessimistic. "I fear if we don't make a terrible struggle to beat the foreigner", he informed Alfred, "we are going to be dished altogether."[83]

James Cropper & Co. was not, of course, "dished" by foreign competition, but it was brought to its knees in a more fundamental way, by disaster after disaster within the paper-mills themselves.[84] First and foremost, Burneside Mills was devastated by a series of fires. The first took place in 1882 when two large stacks of jute bales at Burneside station were ignited by sparks from a passing locomotive. The fire was contained by the combined effort of the whole workforce and four fire engines, two from Kendal and two the company's own, but a loss of £750 was nevertheless sustained.[85]

Four years later the company was not so lucky. On 4 July 1886 a far more intense fire destroyed much of Burneside Mills. Discovered in the No3 machine house in the early hours, this time it spread rapidly, fuelled by paper. By 10am, by which time the flames had been extinguished by fire engines from Bowston, Cowan Head and Kendal pumping water out of the River Kent, it was too late for much of the mill. Although no one was hurt and some parts of the mill such as the boiler house and warehouses were untouched, the core of the mill was gutted (Fig. 4.7 (i, ii). The upper and lower salles, the steam engine house and loft above, and Nos 1, 2 and 3 machine houses were all destroyed. "The appearance of the remains of the building is saddening", commented the *Kendal Mercury* in a long and detailed account of the disaster. "The strong front wall stands apparently firm, with its numerous windows, now bare empty gaps, open like sightless eyes in vacancy, while the large clock amid the impending ruin ceased to denote the flight

Fig. 4.7 (i-ii) – Burneside Mills after the great fire of 1886.

of time at twenty minutes to eight."[86] Inside the mill the machinery was also in a sorry state. Damaged by collapsing roofs and walls as well as the fire itself, much of it was beyond repair. "The intensity of the heat", reported the *Kendal Mercury* of one part of the building, "is evidenced by the broken and distorted condition of the machinery, some of it assuming strange shapes, while several iron shafts of three inches or so in diameter lie where they have fallen in warped shapes that give them the appearance of pliable water pipes."[87]

It was a catastrophe. Although the mills were insured and rebuilding began almost immediately, Burneside Mills did not operate at full capacity for over a year. While No2 machine was working by 6 September, it was not until June 1887 that No3 machine was running again, and No1 machine (which was entirely new, built by George and William Bertram of Edinburgh (Fig. 4.8)) did not start running until October 1887.[88] Even then it was an uphill struggle. Many customers had been forced to look elsewhere in the meantime, and reviving the lost sales was by no means a formality. "Owing to our fire", wrote Charles Cropper in December

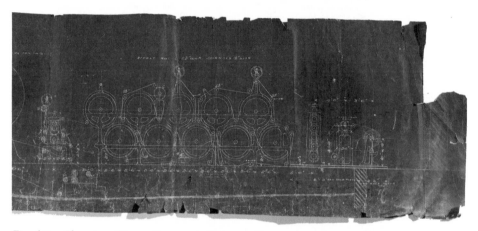

Fig. 4.8 – Blueprint of James Cropper & Co.'s new No1 machine, built by Bertram of Edinburgh following the 1886 fire.

1887, "we have lost ground considerably . . . during the rebuilding we have not been able to push trade as we could wish and it has fallen behind." In consequence, he and his partners decided to appoint an agent in London, J. M. Oldham, "to whom our customers may refer for their wants . . . as an occasional call is not sufficient to keep them together".[89] It was a longstanding appointment. The Oldham family continued to represent James Cropper & Co. until the 1970s, their agency proving to be an indispensable source of orders. "Your work has more direct effect on turnover", James W. Cropper wrote to Oldham in 1909, "than that of any other department of the concern."[90] Almost sixty years later this was still the case.[91]

The appointment did not, however, mark the end of the company's misfortunes. In November 1893 Cowan Head's chimney was blown down in a violent gale (Fig. 4.9), with tragic results. Three of the salle girls, Eleanor Winskill (aged twenty-six), Clara Clark (aged twenty-three), and Alice Sill (aged seventeen), were killed. They had been standing in the mill door waiting to be taken home.

Buried together in one grave at their parents' behest, their tombstone bears a simple message: "Watch therefore, for ye know not what hour the Lord doth come".

Fig. 4.9 – Cowan Head, following the collapse of the mill chimney in a gale, 1893; three girls lost their lives in the disaster. (Source: Margaret Duff collection)

As if such disasters were not enough, ten years later Burneside Mill was again devastated by fire. On 19 May 1903, a spark from an angle cutter ignited some paper shavings, and although hoses were rapidly brought in the fire had soon engulfed the whole of the salle, the registered letter department, No2 machine house roof, and stock rooms across the yard (Fig. 4.10 i, ii). This time, however, with the exception of some cutters and other auxiliary machinery the mill was largely undamaged. The steam engine survived the blaze intact and Nos1 & 3 machines were up and running again within a week. Furthermore, No2 machine, which had lost its roof, was making paper again only two weeks later. Nevertheless, it was some time before the mill was really back in order, as the numerous complaints from customers that followed suggests. One from George F. McCorquodale in September was typical: "Since the fire he says everything has been wrong", Charles Cropper informed Alfred Willink. "He makes his complaints as follows: Paper too thin and not to sample. Paper won't stand gum. Paper won't stand glue. Paper very dirty and full of spots. Worst of all – short supply."[92]

Fig. 4.10 (i, ii) – Burneside Mills after the fire of 1903.

In the face of such adversity Charles Cropper and his fellow directors can hardly be chastised for the lower returns generated by James Cropper & Co. after 1880. Far from it, records suggest that in spite of distractions such as hunting, the firm's managers were competent and hard-working. Alfred Willink, for one, was wholeheartedly dedicated to the survival and prosperity of the firm. By the 1890s his activities ranged from overseeing the day-to-day operations of the mills to recruiting personnel, and calculating costs and margins. He also took charge of matters relating to machinery (reflecting his genuine interest in all things mechanical) and spent much time engaged in statistical analysis, an occupation he enjoyed.[93]

Charles Cropper likewise gave much to his father's firm. Although he was frequently away from the mills on the hunting field (Fig. 4.11), he was wholeheartedly dedicated to paper-making, and had the energy and stamina to pursue both foxes and profits. For he was, in the end, an active and capable businessman, and as committed to the family firm as his father ever was.[94] Like Alfred, his activities within the business were diverse and numerous, ranging from purchasing materials to organising finance, keeping accounts and dealing with taxation. He also acted as the firm's chief salesman, making frequent trips to London and elsewhere to attend to customers or generate new business. And whatever he did, he was a talented organiser, who rarely rested until a job was completed or an issue resolved. This was particularly evident on the occasion of the 1903 fire, when Charles planned the clean-up and repair operation with military precision and worked day and night to see it through.[95]

Charles Cropper was also responsible for one the company's most enduring and profitable products. In 1878 the Post Office had launched a new product, the registered letter envelope, a new and expanding market for paper that the firm was keen to take advantage of.[96] There was, however, one problem: the Post Office required that the envelope be lined with linen scrim to give it strength, yet this was a laborious and expensive process. Charles, however, overcame the difficulty. In 1879 he patented a "new method of lining or coating Paper with Muslin or other similar material". This transformed the piecemeal task into a continual process by incorporating the lining stage into the paper-making machine, thin cloth being fed into the machine from rolls suspended above it.

It was an important and long-lasting innovation. James Cropper & Co. subsequently won the Post Office contract for registered envelopes, and remained Britain's leading manufacturer of cloth-lined paper (which was also later used for maps) for almost a hundred years. It was not only an enduring product, but also an extremely profitable one. In the early 1960s, for example, it was still yielding the company in excess of £100 of profits per ton, way above the returns generated by most grades, which rarely exceeded £40.[97] It helped that the way in which it was

Fig. 4.11 – Charles Cropper on Commando, painted by George Armour, 1907.

made was never successfully imitated. Until the end the manufacturing process remained a carefully safeguarded secret, helped by the fact that the production line was kept under wraps at Cowan Head mill, from which visitors were kept well away.[98]

Charles Cropper also understood that change and innovation in general were essential if the mills were to survive, a philosophy that he summarised in an address given to employees in 1882, which was reported in the local press. "There were some mills, which when they gone on prosperously, for a generation or so, begin to die down", he remarked. "Sometimes the master went to sleep, sometimes the men got old-fashioned and liked to do things the old way and resented the idea of any change which they thought might mean more work". He was thankful to say, however, that they had very few such men there, not least because he encouraged every level of the workforce, from the office to the shop-floor, to play a part in improving the paper-mills.[99]

He practised what he preached, not least by ensuring that the mills were kept up-to-date by a programme of continuous modernisation. The changes carried out are almost too numerous to list, although the greatest development of the period – the comprehensive reconstruction of Burneside Mills in the 1880s – was a direct result of the great fire of July 1886. Redevelopment, however, was already on the cards at the time: "The existing shape of the mill, having grown gradually is no longer advantageous or possible as a remunerative concern in these times", wrote Charles Cropper to his cousin William Wakefield on 7 July 1886, three days after

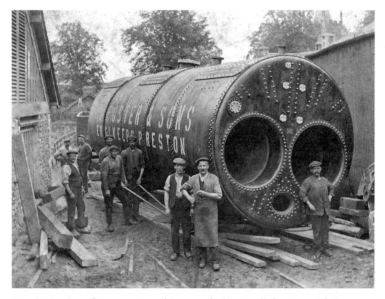

Fig. 4.12 – One of two new Lancashire steam boilers installed at Burneside in 1900.

the fire, "and a complete change has, as you know, been before us, in fact comprehensive plans have been prepared by us for Mills at Bowston."[100] In the event, however, it was decided to alter and enlarge Burneside instead, and by the time the rebuilding work was finished there was little left of the original cotton mill that had been converted into a paper-mill by Hudson, Nicholson & Foster in 1833. The reconstruction did not come cheaply: between 1886 and 1888 over £21,000 was spent on plant and machinery, only a tenth of which sum was covered by the insurance pay-out.[101]

The next major work took place in 1900, when two new steel Lancashire steam boilers were installed at Burneside at a cost of £1,800 (Fig. 4.12).[102] At the same time a new chimney was built at Burneside. This was notable for its design, which was produced by W. G. Collingwood, the gifted artist and antiquary who was John Ruskin's secretary. He was commissioned to bring back drawings of campaniles from Italy (Fig 4.13).[103] In due course a reconstruction of the bell-tower in Siena's Piazza del Campo soon rose up above Burneside and the surrounding area. The attempt at aesthetic enhancement was, however, sadly compromised by the squalid mess soon to be found at the foot of the edifice (Fig 4.14).*

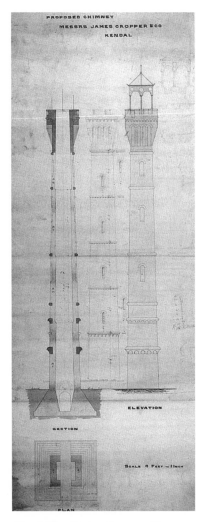

Fig. 4.13 – Design for new chimney at Burneside, 1900, from sketches by W. G. Collingwood.

---

* The merits of Collingwood's chimney were also compromised by the pollution that poured out of it. This was especially evident when James Cropper & Co. engaged in a "blow-out", cleaning the flue by blasting a jet of steam up it. "It was like the eruption of Vesuvius", recalls Robin Field, who explains that the practice was usually carried out at night owing to the amount of dirt that was expelled over the surrounding neighbourhood. These were especially unpopular with the local farmer. On one occasion he is reported to have entered the field adjacent to the mill on the day of the County Show to find that his flock (which had been specially groomed the previous day) was black with soot. James Cropper & Co., alas, had indulged in a blow-out the night before, and the wind had been blowing in the wrong direction.

Fig. 4.14 – A squalid mess: the scene that greeted all those who made it to the base of Burneside's fancy new chimney, 1900s. (Source: Margaret Duff collection)

In 1903, when Burneside Mills was again ravaged by fire, plans for reconstruction were again on the table. Indeed, building work was already underway, in preparation for the largest changes since the 1880s: the installation of a fourth paper-making machine (a 100" Fourdrinier machine made by Bertrams Limited of Edinburgh (Fig. 4.15) and a new gas-power generation plant. This time the fire did little to change the proposed plans, and after the three weeks of

Fig. 4.15 – Burneside's new No4 machine, completed in 1904. (Source: Margaret Duff collection)

rebuilding work, the teams of builders and other tradesmen who were already on site before the fire (one reason why the reconstruction was so quick) resumed their original tasks. Completed by May 1904, and in greatest part overseen by Alfred Willink, the work included new beaters, two steam engines and a calender made by Joseph Eck of Dusseldorf (evidence of the company's willingness to look beyond Britain in search of innovation) as well as the new gas plant and Fourdrinier machine.[104]

Such development was not cheap. By the time it was finished the 1903 extension to Burneside Mills cost over £41,000, and in total almost £150,000 was invested in the mills between 1886 and 1914, over four times the total sum spent between 1853 and 1886. Much of this sum came from the plough-back of profits, with further capital being provided by the company's bankers, the Kendal Bank (originally Wakefield & Crewdson). The bank largely financed the rebuilding of Burneside Mills in 1886 and remained an important source of funds into the twentieth century, not least by letting the company overdraw its account. By the 1900s the company was almost invariably overdrawn, and between 1907 and 1914 was only once briefly in the black, in 1912. The rest of the time it was overdrawn by an average of £12,000.[105]

From the mid-1890s, James Cropper & Co. also financed improvements by selling debentures, a form of fixed rate, fixed term loan that the company issued itself. In this way the firm raised £15,000 between 1894 and 1901 and a further £36,500 in 1903 and 1904. In return for their investment, those who bought them were given an official certificate and paid between four and four and a half percent interest per annum.[106]

The sudden growth in the company's borrowings owed much to a fundamental change in the structure of the business. In 1889 the private company of partners formed by James Cropper in 1852 was transferred into a limited liability company, and the capital of the concern into 760 shares of £100 each, £71 paid up. There were five major shareholders: Charles Cropper (who controlled almost twenty-five percent of the business) James Cropper, John Bryce and George McCorquodale (almost twenty percent each), and Alfred Willink (almost fifteen percent).[107]

The change to limited status was a logical move. First, it gave the company more power to raise funds, allowing it to issue debentures or more shares, or call up the unpaid capital on existing shares. Furthermore, it made holdings in the concern more easily transferable, which was an issue of some immediacy at the time, owing to the age of the two surviving partners from 1852. George McCorquodale was over seventy, and James Cropper was sixty-six.[108] Finally, and perhaps most importantly of all, incorporating the firm as a limited liability company safeguarded the personal assets of shareholders from seizure by creditors in the event of the business failing.

James Cropper & Co.'s principal shareholders were not, however, any less committed to the company. Indeed, while limited status reduced their personal liability their commitment to the paper-mills only increased. In the early days of the business James Cropper had been wary of long-term financial commitment to the business: he thought it wiser to be able to wind up the firm at any given moment. His successors, however, were forced to think differently. By the 1880s the cost of keeping the mills up-to-date (which was increasingly important as competition intensified) required them to run the firm from a longer-term perspective. "My father would never have approved the Mill extension", Charles Cropper remarked in 1904, soon after the fourth machine had been installed at Burneside, "but in that he would have been wrong. We said goodbye to his old idea of being able to wind up any day after the '86 fire."[109]

The greater commitment of Charles Cropper and others is further evident in the sums of money they invested in the company themselves. All of them bought the company's debentures, including the McCorquodale family, which represented a long-term commitment of resources. Even though debentures were a form of interest earning loan, the capital was not paid back for fifteen years at least.[110] The Cropper family invested even more in the firm, answering the call for additional funds on several occasions. Following Burneside Mill's disastrous fire of 1886, for example, Charles Cropper and his partners decided to purchase the freehold of the site from the Wakefield family, who still owned it.[111] There was just one problem: the company could not afford the £6,600 purchase fee subsequently decided upon, so James Cropper bought the freehold himself and leased it back to the firm.[112]

A few years later Charles Cropper again drew on family rather than company funds, this time to finance the construction of a new water supply. Between 1899 and 1902 he paid for (and supervised) the construction of a pipeline between the mills and a series of reservoirs perched on the fells above Burneside, a project that was designed to provide high-pressure water for power generation and cleaning as well as pure water for boilers. It cost him dearly: by the time the scheme was complete he had spent over £5,800.[113] It was not, however, a bad investment. The Cropper family still leases the water supply to the company today, and the pipeline continues to be used at Burneside Mills, supplying pure water for feeding the boilers and diluting chemicals, as well as high-pressure water for cleaning felts and wires.

Charles Cropper's decision to commit more capital to the paper-mills was perhaps underpinned by his son's readiness to enter the business. By 1900 it was clear that James Winstanley Cropper would follow in his father's and grandfather's footsteps. At his twenty-first birthday party in August of that year he made his intentions clear. "He indicated that he was going into the works to assist in the management there", reported the *Kendal Mercury* of the address he made to the assembled crowd of family, friends and company employees:

> . . . and expressed his gratification at being supported by such an excellent set of men, who he was sure would strive to make the business a success. In a business like theirs they must have their ups and downs, but he hoped they would all do their best and that they never would get into difficulties.[114]

Again the passage of James Cropper & Co. from one generation to the next was free from the problems of succession experienced by many family firms. This owed much to James W.'s attitude to his chosen employment. For him paper-making does not seem to have been so much a career choice as an inheritance. This in turn probably owed something to the good relationship he enjoyed with his father. "That complete trust between father and son", remarked Maisie Fletcher, his sister, "had been carried on unbroken into this second generation".[115] It also helped that he was an only son: "He hasn't been blessed with brothers, nor was I", Charles Cropper explained to his son's fiancée, Marjorie Bagot, on the eve of their wedding in 1910, "so we've been more like brothers than Father and Son."[116]

James W.'s loyalty to the Westmorland paper-making firm was also, like his father before him (and his son and grandson after him), assured by his affection for the area in general. For he not only loved the countryside (he was in later life Chairman of the Friends of the Lake District) but also, more importantly, the two small communities of Burneside and Cowan Head, in the main populated by paper-mill employees.[117] "I have no greater love than Burneside", he wrote to his father in 1916. "I think that to make a home, with all that it implies of affection and duty and love of a place is the happiest profession anyone can have."[118]

James W's allegiance to Burneside did not go unreturned. In 1899, for example, when he was bedridden with pleurisy in London, it not only worried his parents but also seems to have been a matter of some concern in the mills. "The enquiries after 'Mr Jem' & 'Young Mr. James' and 'Master Jim' are really most touching", Vin Jones wrote to him. "In fact I was suggesting that a daily bulletin should be posted in the mill".[119]

His coming of age ceremony in 1900 likewise bore witness to the good feeling that existed between him, his family, and the local community. "It was a function in which almost the whole of Burneside took part", reported the *Kendal Mercury* of the day of entertainment, which included performing dogs, a conjuror, and a firework display. "Social distinctions were cast to the winds, and all manner of men and women and boys and girls mingled in the common throng, and what is best of all, they seemed to and in reality did enjoy themselves". There was also a more formal side to the occasion. After tea a series of speakers addressed the gathering, including Richard Savage, the company secretary, who presented James

W. with an illustrated album containing a list of all 295 individuals employed in the mills and their length of service, as well as an illuminated address from the workforce (Fig. 4.16). "We wish to express", it reads, "the desire that you may long be spared to live amongst us, and we trust the same prosperity, progress, and good feeling may always abide and continue with us."[120]

Fig. 4.16 – Illuminated address presented to James W. Cropper by the paper-mill workforce, on the occasion of his twenty-first birthday, 1900.

At the time, however, and for many years previously, James W. was not living among the people of Burneside. Like his father he spent most of his youth away from home at school and university, first at a preparatory school in Berkshire – where he was sent in 1891, aged twelve – and then at public school (Eton this time) followed by Cambridge University. Again it was not the most fitting preparation for a career in industry, but James W. did not return home without any relevant experience.

Following his graduation he moved to London where he spent nearly a year working at Price Waterhouse, the accountancy firm. As a general introduction to business and accounting practices (which were increasingly important as profit margins narrowed) it was, according to his father, a worthwhile experience.[121] In addition, it suited his character well, as he proved to be very fond of figure-work. "I am essentially of a clerky, figuring type of worker", he commented on one occasion, and his love of figures is clearly evident in the numerous ledgers he kept in the course of his life, many of which seem to have been compiled for his personal interest and pleasure. In the long run Price Waterhouse also benefited from the opening it had offered to the young paper-maker. In 1906 James Cropper & Co. asked Price Waterhouse to audit its accounts, an appointment which has remained in place to this day.[122]

Fresh from this experience, James W. Cropper started working for James Cropper & Co. in October 1902. He was twenty-three years old. Like his father he first worked in the office at Cowan Head, where he soon became involved in the plans to extend Burneside Mills which were carried out in 1903 and 1904. "Very full of plans for No4 machine", he recorded in his diary for 1902, and in January 1903 he visited a number of paper-mills in Lancashire and Scotland with Alfred Willink and Daniel McNeill, probably to get ideas.[123]

The paper-mills were not yet, however, the only focus of his ambitions. While he could, he also desired to see something of the world, and in February 1903, less than four months after he began working at Cowan Head he left home on an eight-month journey around the world, travelling across Europe to the Far East – where he spent nearly three months in China and Japan – before returning via Canada and New York.[124] The tour did not entirely meet with his father's approval. Charles Cropper regretted that his son was not at home gaining experience from the extension of Burneside Mills, work on which began in the spring of 1903. "I am very sorry you can't be here this summer", Charles Cropper wrote to him in May, "as you would learn a lot and it is you who will have to run the place in the future when Alfred and I are done with."[125] James W.'s response was also tinged with regret. "You seem to be fearfully busy", he wrote back to his father from Japan, "and I feel a brute to be laying out here while you are hard put to it at home." He was not, however, without an excuse. "You know how I should like to be helping you and would come back at once if it was necessary. Only this is a chance of seeing the Wide World I shan't have again and with Japan before me I shouldn't like to have to go back."[126]

On his return, James W.'s progress through the company was characteristically rapid. In 1904 he began to take on a measure of his father's London work, which involved dealing with some of the company's most important customers such as Waterlow & Sons and McCorquodale & Co. Furthermore, on the death of the company secretary, Richard Savage, in 1905 he began to compile the company's fortnightly reports, an important and instructive job that he his father had carried out before him.[127] At the same time he was appointed a director.

James W.'s rapid assumption of responsibilities proved to be important. In June 1907 his father was asked to become a director of the London & Northern Western Railway, which required him to attend meetings in London for about a week and a half every month. Accepting the appointment, Charles decided to resign from James Cropper & Co. as a full-time director, and, although he continued to work in the paper mills as an honorary director whenever he was able, the break marked a turning point in his career. In the following years he began to shift his attention away from paper-making, in great part because he wanted to give his son more power and responsibility. "I hope as time goes on", he wrote to James W. shortly after his resignation, "to make more of my business interest over to you", and in 1907 he transferred a number of shares into his son's name, giving them both an equal twenty-one percent stake in the paper-mills.[128] He did, however, remain firmly committed to the mills: "I don't think I can ever clear out of paper-making", he commented in the same letter. "It has been my life so long that it has become part of my being and I couldn't if I tried cease to take a great interest".

Charles Cropper's desire to give his son a more substantial foothold in the family business in great part reflected the confidence he had in him. "You have more ability and more brains than either of us", he remarked in 1907, comparing James W. to himself and Alfred Willink. In another letter he was even more approving: "I admire the way you are doing your work at home and at the office, and it is a great pleasure to me to see the golden opinions you are winning from all kinds of people."[129] One such favourable report came from Daniel McNeill, the manager of Burneside Mills: "I am sorry that this will cause you to absent yourself from the Mill", he wrote to Charles Cropper on hearing of his appointment as a railway director, "but you are most fortunate in having such a capable son, he is so thorough and careful it is a pleasure to work for him."[130]

James W. was not, however, now solely in charge. Alfred Willink continued to work full-time in the mills as did Vincent Jones. An assistant director since 1901 and company secretary since Richard Savage's death in 1905, Vincent was appointed a full director following Charles' resignation. His contribution to the firm is largely undocumented, although if his pay is any indication, he was as important to the firm as anybody. By 1907 his salary and bonus was the same as James W.'s and Alfred's.[131] In part this reflected his sales work in Manchester and elsewhere, a role that he probably discharged well. For he was was outgoing and energetic, a gregarious extrovert like his cousin Charles Cropper.[132]

Vincent Jones was also very persuasive. In 1910 he asked Mary Bagot, youngest daughter of Sir Jocelyn and Lady Bagot of Levens Hall and a member of one of Westmorland's leading families, to marry him. She accepted his advances, although not, unfortunately, with her parent's approval. According to James W.'s sister, Lady

Bagot considered it "a quite unsatisfactory affiance . . . She refused to countenance the engagement if Vin remained at Burneside". In consequence, three days after their marriage at Heversham on 14 June 1910, Vin Jones and his bride left England for Newfoundland (Fig. 4.17) where he had accepted an offer to manage a new wood pulp and paper works at Grand Falls being set up by Lord Northcliffe, the publisher of the *Daily Mail* .

Fig. 4.17 – Vincent and Mary Jones on board the ship that took them from Liverpool to Newfoundland in June 1910.

His departure was both a huge loss for friends and family and for James Cropper & Co. Indeed, if his achievements abroad are any indication, the company lost a manager of immense capabilities. In Newfoundland he not only took care of a vast new manufacturing plant, but also an entirely new settlement that was soon seven thousand strong.[133] Moreover, he proved to be up to the job: "I think he has the confidence of everyone here, from Northcliffe to the humblest workman", James W. wrote to his father on a visit to Grand Falls in 1913, and in time he so excelled himself in Newfoundland that he was awarded a knighthood.[134]

Back at Burneside, the loss of Vin Jones was alleviated in a number of ways. First, there was another family relative in the paper-mills, Herman Willink, who had joined the business in November 1908 fresh from Cambridge University. In 1910 he was still a junior member of the firm with few responsibilities, but it was hoped that he would gradually rise up the ranks and eventually take his uncle

Alfred's place on the board. "If he made himself valuable here", Alfred explained to Herman's father in a letter setting out the terms of his engagement, "he would of course have every consideration and I hope would ultimately become a director."[135]

Second, for those whose spirits were depressed by Vin's departure, more joyful events were soon on the horizon. In September 1910 James W. Cropper married Mary Bagot's elder sister Marjorie at Heversham, near Levens. This time Lady Bagot had condescended to approve the match, perhaps owing to her respect for the groom's grandfather. Sir Jocelyn, however, was less than pleased to see a second daughter marrying into trade. "My daughters", he is reputed to have moaned, "are papier mâché."[136]

Following a honeymoon in the Austrian Tyrol James W. and his bride returned to Burneside where they were received in time-honoured fashion. On their arrival at Burneside, the horses were quickly released from their carriage, and ropes attached. A team of men then drew them up the hill to Ellergreen, just as Charles Cropper and his father before him had been drawn home many years before. On their arrival there, James W. stood up in the carriage alongside his bride and addressed the assembled crowd. "I thank you very much for pulling us up", he told them, "It is a splendid reception. If you all pull together like that in the future we shall make a big success of the old place."[137]

So far as Cowan Head was concerned his hopes did not prove unfounded. A one-machine mill since 1906, in 1910 the remaining machine was widened to seventy-two inches at a cost of £4,200, and the results were promising. Following the alterations the mill ran better than ever before, not least in 1912 when all the male employees working there were given a five percent bonus on their earnings for the year. Moreover, two years later the mill's performance was still a cause for contentment. "We see there", noted Charles Cropper in 1914, "a mill running without any cause for anxiety, and running to perfection."[138]

Elsewhere, however, there was not so much cause for satisfaction. Indeed, the years following the marriage of James W. in 1910 were less characterised by success than by a growing number of problems. In particular, the company was troubled by industrial unrest, an increasingly severe problem nationwide in the years leading up to the First World War. First, in March and April a national miners' strike, fought over the establishment of a national minimum wage, saw nearly a million miners stopping work for almost a month.[139] Coal prices soared, eating into paper-making margins, and for one week – when coal was either unavailable or prohibitively expensive – the paper-mills even ground to a halt.[140] Nevertheless, Burneside and Cowan Head fared better than most. In contrast with many mills they had alternative sources of power in gas and water, which helped them brave the worst of the crisis even if it did not keep them going all the time.

Around the same time, however, there were growing signs that dissatisfaction was spreading among employees at Burneside and Cowan Head. The directors began to be flooded by petitions. These ranged from a request for an annual summer excursion to more numerous and insistent calls for wage increases. "We the undersigned", read a typical petition of 1911, ". . . working in your employ as Shift workers having a good deal more work to do in consequence of the speeding up of machinery, hereby desire to ask you for an increase of wages."[141]

It is not clear if their wishes were met, although James Cropper & Co. was taking some steps to improve the welfare and earnings of its employees. First, in addition to housing provision, by 1909 (and probably for some years before) all employees were encouraged to be members of the Burneside, Bowston and Cowan Head Sick Society (Fig. 4.18). In return for a small deduction off their wages, ranging from 2d to 4d, each member could receive a benefit of up to 9s per week if they were sick for three days or more.[142] Offering them a measure of security in case of illness, the scheme notably anticipated government legislation: in 1911 the National Insurance Act made such cover obligatory for anybody in full-time employment.

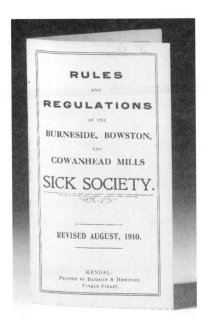

Fig. 4.18 – Burneside, Bowston and Cowan Head Sick Society card, 1910.

Secondly, the lot of some employees was improved by a bonus scheme. Introduced in 1898 to reward head machinemen and beatermen if the production of finished paper exceeded a certain amount each fortnight, in 1912 this was extended to include seventy-two more employees, including machine and beater assistants and those in charge of cutters, slitters, kollergangs (a form of macerator (Fig. 4.19)) and calenders (used to make paper smooth and shiny).[143] At the same time the directors also introduced a profits sharing savings scheme. This offered employees a chance to share in the profits of the company if they invested their own savings, and was, by the standards of its day, a pioneering venture. Most employers were still loathed to offer their workforce any share in a concern, but James W., who conceived and carried through the scheme, thought differently. "He felt that every worker should have an opportunity of becoming a shareholder", remarked Alfred Willink, "and thus receive a return on the investment of his or her savings".[144] Again it was an incentive-related scheme – it encouraged employees to take a more direct interest in the performance of the mills – although the rewards were generous enough. Those who deposited their savings could receive as much as ten percent interest per annum, which they almost did between 1915 and 1919.[145]

Fig. 4.19 – Kollergangs at Burneside, depicted by Herman Willink, circa 1910.

In the short term, however, the scheme did little to improve earnings. For those without disposable income to put aside for months at a time it was of little benefit, and at the outset it did not prove especially popular. Only twenty-seven employees had opened savings accounts by October 1915, together depositing £1,200.[146] More significantly, the scheme failed to satisfy those employees who felt they were being underpaid, who continued to overwhelm the directors with demands for wage increases. These increasingly took the form of formal negotiations conducted through Trade Unions. In 1913, for example, the Amalgamated Society of Engineers asked the company to observe their minimum rate of 37s shillings a week. They had found out that Burneside's and Cowan Head's engineers were currently being paid between 31s and 34s 8d for a fifty-six hour week. Their wishes were met.[147]

In 1914 it was the turn of the National Union of Paper Mill Workers to approach the firm, this time on behalf of Burneside's and Cowan Head's sorters, the female salle employees who sorted finished paper (Fig 4.20). Again pay was the dominant issue, and with good reason: the sorters had learnt that they were being paid nearly half the average rate for the district. According to the Union's general secretary, William Ross, they were receiving an average 11s a week. "It is little wonder that your employees are dissatisfied", he wrote to the company in March 1914, "when they realise how much better other firms pay their sorters . . . it is to be hoped that you will speedily and materially improve the remuneration of your sorters."[148]

Fig. 4.20 – The Burneside salle, c.1910. A relaxed scene, but tension was brewing owing to low wages; it also didn't help that the foreman Sylvester Clark, visible on the right, was tough on those in his employ.

The attitude of Sylvester Clark, the Burneside salle foreman who oversaw the sorters, perhaps did not help matters. If references to him in a contemporary letter Marjorie Cropper wrote to her husband are any indication, he was hard on those in his employ. She had recently visited a number of sick employees, including ". . . a very pretty girl called Nellie Bennett":

> . . . She is very anaemic and had been off work with bilious and eye troubles and said Sylvester kept sending her nasty messages so she'd go back to work. I think she is quite able for work now but I think Sylvester is a little hard on them, one or two mothers have said so to me. Of course it must be very difficult but I think they oughtn't to be bullied too much about being off when they're ill – it does affect their pockets so they probably wouldn't sham. . . .[149]

The sorters' demand for better pay was, however, neither quickly nor amicably resolved. The initial offer made by the directors was rejected and the dispute dragged on into the summer of 1914. Moreover, as time went on the sorters became more and more militant. In April they threatened to stop working overtime, and by the middle of May they were threatening to cease work altogether unless an agreement was drawn up soon. It was not an idle threat, as they had full union backing. Furthermore, their resolve was perhaps strengthened by the tide of feminism sweeping across Britain at the time. For it was the age of the suffragette, one of whose principal demands (alongside calling for universal suffrage) was equal pay for equal work.[150]

"We are threatened at the moment with trouble from our girls", James W. Cropper informed Alick McCorquodale on 16 May 1914. "They have joined the union and are desperately keen to make us kow-tow to their officials." He took their demands seriously, even admitting that owing to bad paper-making their wages had been lower "than can be justified in these days". He and his fellow directors were, however, sorely tested to reach an agreement with them. "We have offered them a revised scale equivalent to a twenty percent rise", he remarked in the same letter:

> . . . but they ask for forty and seem inclined to reject it. It seems strange to have trade union troubles and talks of strikes in Burneside. I always hoped it would be many years before that began here. But I hope we shall not have to put these grave matters to the proof. We have gone as far as we can . . .[151]

It was almost a month before the deadlock was broken, an agreement finally being reached on 13 June. The company had only narrowly escaped a strike: on 6 June the sorters had served notice that they would "cease work in fourteen days" if their demands were not granted, an ultimatum that proved effective.[152] In the end the company agreed to the offer proposed by the sorters in April, advancing wages for sorting and stacking paper as well as allowing them to stop work earlier on Saturday mornings.[153]

It was not, however, the end of James Cropper & Co.'s problems. Less than a week after it had resolved the dispute with its sorters, the earnings of its employees were again the subject of scrutiny. On 16 June Arthur Henderson, a leading Labour MP and future home and foreign secretary, had informed the House of Commons that James Cropper & Co. was one of several firms supplying the Stationery Office that were not observing the Fair Wages Clause.[154] This stipulated that all government contracts had to be worked by labour paid at current local trade union rates, and he intimated that James Cropper & Co. was paying its workers an average of 11s 6d a week, well below union levels.[155]

Henderson, however, was less than accurate. While some of James Cropper &

Co.'s younger employees were paid around that sum, the majority of workers received considerably more. Not surprisingly, James W. and his fellow directors were incensed. "We need scarcely point out", they wrote to Henderson on 19 June, "that a vague statement such as you made in the House of Commons is absolutely misleading, and apt to do us considerable and quite unmerited injury", and in order to counter it they invited the Comptroller of the Stationery Office to carry out a full investigation into their labour conditions.[156]

Although in the event Arthur Henderson's claims did not aggravate further unrest, they were the last thing that the directors needed. For by June 1914 their relationship with employees was only one of a number of sizeable problems troubling the firm. Not least, Burneside Mills was losing money. "We have done badly", James W. informed J. M. Oldham on 15 May, shortly after the company's accounts for the last six months had been finalised, "worse than ever before since we became a limited company, and we are actually showing a loss at Burneside Mill".[157]

In particular, the bad result was caused by problems with the quality and quantity of the paper being made.[158] James Cropper & Co.'s efforts to speed up the whole operation (which it did with some success, turnover doubling between 1900 and 1913) did not help matters. "Everything is so rushed", noted Charles Cropper in April 1914, "that if a paper starts wrong, it has to go on wrong".[159] In addition, finished paper also represented a mounting problem, as the company had let its stocks grow far too high. Indeed, they were so high by the summer of 1914 that it was suggested that the mills might have to stop working for a while. "The stock is so great", wrote Charles Cropper to Alfred Willink on 2 June, "that a weeks drop in orders might shut the mill down" (Fig. 4.21).[160]

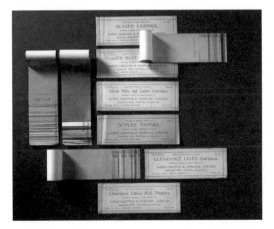

Fig. 4.21 – Pre-war sample brochures, including a number from the summer of 1914 advertising 'Clearance Lines', an attempt to cut down excessive stocks of paper.

James Cropper & Co.'s financial position was equally precarious. Throughout the first half of 1914 its overdraft with the Kendal Bank had exceeded £20,000, well above the £15,000 limit that their bankers authorised. It was likewise a source of danger. "The bank is so overdrawn", Charles Cropper informed Alfred Willink on 2 June, "that the shareholders are very near having to back the account."[161]

This time the company could blame neither disasters nor trading conditions for the difficulties. "I fear there is no genuine excuse for this bad result", James W. commented. "I don't think we can blame any great depression in trade. We have had no serious breakdown. In fact we have run more hours than usual."[162] In truth, poor management was to blame, as James W. acknowledged himself. "Burneside is the delinquent", he continued, "There is nothing for it but to admit that it has been thoroughly badly and slackly managed."[163]

In part the poor performance of the mill reflected the failings of its foremen. Daniel McNeill's nephew Frank Brown, for example, had not proved to be a very successful chief foreman at Burneside and was demoted shortly afterwards. Daniel McNeill, meanwhile, was also partly to blame. "I fear he has lost grasp of the mill", Charles Cropper noted in May 1914. "He has allowed the place to go to <u>chaos</u> . . . . He ought not to have allowed Donachie [another problematic foreman] to continue – He ought to have seen the awful condition that was coming in the mill far sooner than he did."[164]

The same, however, could also be said of James Cropper & Co.'s directors, who had likewise had failed to see trouble on the way and take decisive action. Nevertheless, Charles Cropper was hardly to blame. Since 1907 he had been frequently absent from the mills discharging his duties as a director of the London & North Western railway. James W., however, had more to answer for. He was frequently absent from the mills in the years leading up to the First World War, and not for reasons of business. Following in the footsteps of his father he hunted as often as two days a week in the winter months. And for much of the year he also spent a great deal of time shooting, often with the assistance of young paper-making apprentices, commandeered to flush out game in far flung corners of his growing estate.[165]

In 1913 James W.'s enthusiasm for field sports resulted in his absence from the mills for weeks. He was kicked on the head by a horse while hunting in North Yorkshire, and was forced to spend a month recuperating in a nursing home in Darlington following an operation on his skull. Furthermore, even following his return home he was incapable of work: "Jem is at home again", Alfred Willink informed Alick McCorquodale over a month after the accident. "He is improving, but slowly, very little talk or thought tires him, so we have not consulted him about anything."[166]

Moreover, following his recovery James W. did not return to work for long. In

June 1913 he set off on a four month tour of Canada and Japan with his wife. Whether or not the trip was undertaken for health reasons is not clear, although if his father's disapproval is any indication it was not: "I cannot help feeling", remarked Charles Cropper, "that the whole thing is a piece of unwarranted extravagance and a very great risk".[167]

Charles Cropper was similarly outspoken about the poor performance of Burneside in 1914. He did not, however, blame his son. The chief focus of his displeasure was Alfred Willink, who was largely responsible for the day-to-day running of the mill. In particular, he was annoyed by Alfred's failure to deal effectively with unsatisfactory foremen. "Ever since 1911", Charles informed him in a forthright and furious letter of 2 June, "Jem and I have been begging to get rid of Frank Brown. You wouldn't hear of it. . . . For two years Donachie was useless and you said so. Why did you let him stay?" Furthermore, Charles was incensed by Alfred's reluctance to admit Burneside's failings in general: "You say the mill has run well", Charles wrote to Alfred in the same letter. "My opinion is that the mill has run very badly and I could prove it up to the hilt. There is not a girl or a boy in the place who does not know this to be true. . . . You regard this affair as a calamity. I regard it as a piece of very gross mismanagement which must be stopped like a fire, or a disease."

He practised what he preached. By June 1914 Charles Cropper was back in the paper-mills taking a leading role in their management for the first time since 1907. Almost sixty-two years of age, it was forty years since he had joined James Cropper & Co. He was not, however, any less committed to the firm: "So long as it was plain sailing" he admitted to Alfred Willink, "I am afraid I let things go, but now that the pinch has come you cannot expect me to mince matters. . . . You say this business means more to you than to me, but it bears my name and the name of my father, and I am going to see it thro'."

His dedication proved important, as the mills were about to demand his input more than ever before. The tensions and troubles at Burneside were but an insignificant prelude to far greater and more devastating events. On 28 June 1914 Archduke Franz Ferdinand of Austria was assassinated in Sarajevo by a Bosnian student. A month later Austria invaded Serbia and a week after that Germany attacked Belgium. Finally, on 4 August Britain declared war on Germany and her allies, plunging the country into its first major conflict for almost a hundred years. It was James W. Cropper's thirty-fifth birthday, and a day he was unlikely to forget. "And then suddenly", remarked Maisie Fletcher, his sister, "the whole foundations of our life were shaken by a shot fired at Sarajevo . . . and the world as we knew it was never the same again".[168]

*Fig. 5.1 – Major James W. Cropper of the Westmorland &
Cumberland Yeomanry, 1915.*

5

Armageddon: 1914-18

"IT is odd to think and hard to realise", James W. Cropper wrote to his wife, Marjorie, in December 1915, "that we are plum in the middle of the Armageddon we always talked about in the old days as an awful possibility. I don't think anyone imagined it would be as beastly as it is."[1] He spoke from experience: stationed in France as a Captain in the Westmorland and Cumberland Yeomanry, he and his men had played an active role consolidating infantry positions at the Battle of Loos, where British casualties amounted to sixty thousand.[2] His most evocative account of the battlefields of France, however, predated the battle. Writing to his father in August 1915 he described the Western Front as he had seen it from the top of a slag heap, five miles distant: "The trees are half blown away", he reported of the trenches, surveying them through binoculars, "and there isn't a sign of a living thing. It's an absolute streak of hell, and there are four hundred miles of it running right across the map."[3]

By then the war had become a struggle in which the whole of the country was involved. In 1915 the British Army in France suffered 300,000 casualties, and as the immense cost of the war escalated, few escaped its effects at home. "For the first time", remarks one historian, "the industrial and commercial demands of modern warfare involved the entire nation in the conflict."[4]

James Cropper & Co. was no exception to the rule. The First World War affected paper-making from the start, leading almost immediately to uncertainties about raw material supplies. This prompted the company to withdraw its current prices and quotations and change its purchasing policies: within a week it was decided that the firm should buy as much pulp as possible. "It may cost us more and we may make less profit", Charles Cropper informed his son in the first of dozens of letters that give a vivid insight into the wartime operations of the mills. "But if we can keep this place going till next spring it will be everything and our stock will be cleared."[5] In due course orders for pulp were swiftly placed, and by the beginning of September the company had ordered sufficient quantities of the raw material to keep machines running until June 1915, provided it all arrived. In addition, lest the ordered pulp failed to reach British shores, the company also began to spin out existing pulp stocks by using more waste paper, a practice carried out in paper-mills across the nation during the war.[6]

In the event the precautionary measures proved premature. Pulp supplies did not dry up as soon as expected and the machines at Burneside and Cowan Head continued to run at full speed throughout the remaining months of 1914 and the whole of 1915, in which year output rose to a new high of 12,947 tons. Keeping the paper-mills going was not, however, without its difficulties. It was nothing like "business as usual" – a government slogan and universal catchword of the early war years – not least because raw materials, even when available, were increasingly expensive. "We are running these mills full time", Charles Cropper wrote to J. M. Oldham, the company's London agent, in December 1914, "but the margin owing to the increased price of pulp etc. is nothing at all and often the wrong way."[7]

A month later he was even more pessimistic about James Cropper & Co.'s wartime prospects, and with good reason. The company was not only being hit hard by the rising cost of material (dyes, for example, which had come from Germany before the war, rocketed in price) but also by labour shortages.[8] "I am not sanguine of any great profits while the war continues", he informed J. M. Oldham on 9 January 1915:

> All dyes are costing three to five times as much as they did, and soon there will be none to be had. Machine wires and clothing are much dearer. Rosin is very dear owing to high freights. Wages are going up, and worst of all we are in continual difficulties of keeping the mill running owing to enlistment. Ninety percent of our available men have gone and it is very hard to get others to replace them.[9]

Labour shortages owing to enlistment had troubled James Cropper & Co. since the earliest days of the war. Less than a week after the outbreak of hostilities thirty-six men had joined up, and by 1 September 1914, sixty-six employees had left their posts at Burneside and Cowan Head for the armed forces, the rush of recruitment probably a response to Lord Kitchener's call for volunteers, which had added 1,700,000 men to the ranks by May 1915.[10] Those who chose to enlist did so with the full backing of their employers – their places were kept open until their return and James Cropper & Co. paid them an allowance in the meantime – even though their departure took its toll on the company. Within a month the mills had lost over forty percent of their male employees of military age, the number drawn from every level and area of the workforce.[11] "We are doing badly at the mill", Charles Cropper regretfully informed James W. on 9 September 1914, "The exodus of all our good lads tells its tale." He was optimistic, nevertheless, that the paper-mills would keep going: "We shall settle down in a week or two but the machine men and every one are hard put to it just now. I mean to work my hardest at it."[12]

His personal contribution was increasingly necessary. James W. had been an enthusiastic soldier since his schooldays and a Captain in the Westmorland and Cumberland Yeomanry since 1911. He was called up as soon as war was declared. Alfred Willink, meanwhile, the only other remaining director, was not coping well with the strain of the war. It was playing havoc with his nerves: "Alfred is so jumpy", remarked Charles on 9 September, "that I don't think he can manage just now".

Forced to return to the fold, Charles Cropper was hopeful that his reappearance would only be temporary. Like many, he was reliably informed that the war would be over by Christmas: "News seems good", he wrote to Edith, his wife, on 29 October, "I met General Brocklehurst at Brooks', he is now Lord Ranksboro'. He was most hopeful . . . . He said 'It will all be over by Christmas. I shall be hunting in a red coat by New Year's day, we will meet at Holywell, and you *must* come'."[13]

Like many others, Charles's hopes were dashed, and his renewed involvement with James Cropper & Co. proved to be more permanent. As a result he was reappointed a full director in October 1915 (after eight years as an unpaid director) with a salary to be paid retrospectively from August 1914.[14] This was by no means money for nothing: as the conflict wore on he was compelled to play an increasingly central role in the mills. Herman Willink, Alfred's nephew, whom he had hoped would stay and gain experience and responsibility during the war, had joined up in December 1914, and in May 1915 Alfred himself was appointed commanding officer of an army base in Kendal. This was not a full time position, but took up much of his time until he was released from the position in 1918.[15] It was clearly a considerable distraction from paper-making: "Alfred's mind is full of military duties", Charles informed James W. in October 1916, increasingly weary of his fellow director's frequent absence from the paper-mills. "I am afraid I rather grudge Alfred's military job now", he wrote to his son soon afterwards. "There must be heaps of partially disabled officers who are dying to be of use, who could do his job at the drill hall, and I feel he is only blocking them out."[16]

Charles Cropper was not, however, weary of paper-making himself. Although demanding, he did not view his work in the paper-mills as a burden: "I find the Mills continually interesting", he remarked in the autumn of 1914, and his eagerness did not flag as the war dragged on. "I begin to dread the time when I have to clear out of management and directorship", he wrote to James W. in November 1916, "I really don't know how I could have got through these two years had I not had lots and lots of work."[17] In 1917 he was even more upbeat, apparently enjoying the constant challenges and uncertainties of wartime trading. "For me the duration of the war has been a happy time up to now", he wrote to James W. in August. "Life has been very full. Every day has brought some difficulty to be got over, and they have been got over."[18]

The difficulties were numerous. As the war progressed keeping the paper-mills going was becoming more and more challenging. Not least, James Cropper & Co. continued to be troubled by labour shortages: by October 1915 almost 120 male employees of military age had joined up – many of whom had been recruited since the beginning of the war – and although many of this number were replaced by older men there was still a great deficit of manpower. "We seem to be getting supplies of pulp", Charles Cropper informed Alick McCorquodale in September 1915, "but we may stop for want of men."[19]

Although the mills did not grind to a halt, labour shortages remained a problem until the end of the war. The introduction of conscription in May 1916 (to satisfy the acute demand for troops to replace those disabled or killed) did not help matters. Strictly governed by local boards, it soon led to the loss of even more employees, many of whom were difficult and costly to replace.[20] In addition, company resources were also tested by the increasing expense of labour in general. Wage costs rose dramatically throughout the war – doubling from £20,200 in 1914 to almost £41,000 in 1918 – not only driven up by the growing cost of new recruits but also by petitions from existing employees for pay rises to meet the rising cost of living.[21] These were particularly frequent in 1917, when inflation was at a height. A request for an advance of 6d a day from thirty-five employees in January 1917 was characteristic: ". . . owing to the continued increase of food and other necessaries of life", they informed their employers, "we find our present wages are quite inadequate".[22]

James Cropper & Co. did not allocate men's jobs to women as many firms did, although there was a noticeable influx of women into the company's offices. The number included Frances Cooper, who was appointed a clerk in September 1914. Initially recruited for the duration of the war only, by 1916 her employers had other ideas. "Our ledger clerk, Miss Cooper", Charles Cropper wrote to James W. towards the end of the year, "has pulled up the outstanding indebtedness of our customers by nearly £1,000 which does her great credit. We shan't want to lose her."[23] In due course her contract was extended: Frances Cooper continued to work for James Cropper & Co. until her death in 1941.[24]

By the end of 1916 the contribution of such recruits was increasingly important, as the strain of the war was beginning to take its toll on management. Daniel McNeill, the manager of Burneside Mills and second only to the directors in power and responsibility, was the first to falter. "His heart is amiss", Charles Cropper informed James W. on 30 November 1916, "and he may not hurry. I rather fear he will never be quite strong again. He nearly collapsed in the street in Manchester the other day and he is strictly ordered not to hurry any more . . . We must hope he will improve with treatment. He could be ill spared just now."[25]

Fortunately he did respond to treatment, but it was not long before another senior member of staff had joined the sick list. Gerard Walker, the head foreman of Burneside Mills, was laid off with bad legs in February 1917. According to Charles Cropper, who was a fierce advocate of physical exercise, his weight was to blame: "He is far too fat", he remarked, "if he kept himself decently fit with exercises he would be better".[26] Moreover, by the end of 1917, Herbert Corrie, the company secretary and another key figure in the firm, was also out of action for a while, prompting James W. Cropper to apply for a month's leave in order to help out at Burneside. "Our secretary", he informed his commanding officer, "has completely broken down from over-work."[27]

By 1917 personnel losses (temporary and otherwise) were not, however, the firm's most pressing problem. By then the greatest threat was a severe shortage of raw materials, in particular pulp. At first this was caused by an acute shortage of shipping, which by the beginning of 1916 had compelled the government to restrict the import of numerous goods and commodities, including pulp. Imports of the material were cut by a third in February 1916. Charles Cropper immediately protested to the government about the injurious effect the cuts would have on the paper industry, but his efforts were in vain. "I fear that such a bulky thing as pulp could not be overlooked", Walter Runciman of the Board of Trade wrote back to him. "We are having to make the best we can of a most difficult task, namely securing more space in the tonnage available to our ports."[28]

The subsequent restrictions did not, however, mark an end to Britain's shipping problems. By the end of 1916 the country was facing a far more severe shipping crisis, owing to the increasing number of ships being hit by German submarines. Between September and December 1916 sinkings rose to 160,000 tons monthly and even worse was to come. With unrestricted U-boat warfare from 1 February 1917, Allied sinkings reached 545,000 tons in April, the annual total amounting to 3,730,000 gross tons for British shipping alone. The losses, however, only tell half the story, for the submarine war also drove neutral shipping away from British ports and safety precautions slowed down the remaining merchant fleet.[29]

The new shipping crisis affected James Cropper & Co. as it did the economy and population of the British Isles in general. Pulp imports were cut from two-thirds to a half in November 1916, and in 1917 they dropped even more. "Germany's new submarine threats sound awful", Charles informed James W. on 6 February 1917. "I am amazed that we have no letters from any of our pulp agents as yet telling us that supplies of pulp will become more difficult." He did not have to wait long: "The blow has actually fallen on Burneside", Charles Cropper wrote to his wife a fortnight later. "Imports are cut down to half of 1916 which means that we shall have to close down a goodish bit of the works, almost at once."[30]

However, in spite of the scarcity of supplies from 1916 onwards and the ensuing cost of materials – the company's material costs grew fourfold from £97,000 in 1914 to £410,000 in 1918 – production levels remained high for the duration of the war. In 1916 output reached a new high of almost 14,000 tons, and in 1917 and 1918 it only decreased slightly to 12,250 and 12,500 tons (still above pre-war levels) where in many British paper-mills production fell by fifty percent or more.[31]

In great part this owed much to the company's choice of materials. Like many paper manufacturers it used more and more waste paper – by 1918 it was recycling over 4,500 tons of paper per year – but it also, more importantly, began to use jute. Last used in significant quantities in the 1890s this was used as a substitute for pulp from the spring of 1916 into 1918 and beyond.[32] Its use soon proved worthwhile, and played a big part in keeping the mills running. "Jute is a big factor now", Charles Cropper informed James W. in June 1916. "No1 and No2 use little else for strength and a very fair paper seems to be the result".[33] Jute was also, in James Cropper & Co.'s favour, more readily available than most materials. A sandbag shortage in 1915 led the government to undertake the buying of the whole of the jute crop from 1916.[34]

It was not the only way in which James Cropper & Co. was helped by the government in the final years of the war. In April 1917 the company was taken under government control, joining the increasing lists of firms and industries whose affairs were supervised by the Ministry of Munitions. Reflecting its manufacture of large quantities of paper for the government and the Post Office, it was one of the first paper manufacturers to come under control.[35] This owed much to a sudden change in the government's attitude towards paper. "Until a few weeks ago", Charles Cropper was informed by a Munitions man on 23 April, "the government had considered that paper was ridiculous useless trash. . . . Now suddenly they had discovered that they could not get on without paper and they at once proceeded to fix on a number of mills to be taken over and run."[36]

Becoming a controlled establishment helped James Cropper & Co. tremendously, for it largely ended its principal difficulties for the rest of the war. "We shall keep our men and get material", Charles Cropper wrote to James W. of the appointment. "The old struggle is over, for the last two years it has been on long struggle for material and men. . . . Now I suppose I shall have a busy time over interviews with 'Munitions' officials."[37]

Selling paper, in contrast, had not been a struggle. Throughout the war demand was greater than ever before, not least owing to the impact of the conflict on foreign competition, the bane of the British paper industry up to 1914. Although there are indications that Sweden continued to penetrate British markets during the war, paper imports from elsewhere almost ceased altogether, not least those from Germany, source of some of the most intense pre-war competition.* James Cropper & Co. profited from the change-around almost immediately. In September 1914 the company was contracted by De la Rue to manufacture 800 tons a year of Colonial Postcard for ten years. It was the largest order the firm had ever undertaken, and came as a direct result of the war. "The paper was made in Germany till the war", Charles Cropper wrote to his son at the time, "and the German mill had the contract for twelve years, two of which are passed."[38]

Demand for Cropper paper was further strengthened by slackening domestic competition and growing government requirements. Charles Cropper explained the situation in June 1916: "The paper trade is very small now", he wrote to James W., "and it is only the fact that government requirements are very high and that many mills are more than half shut for want of men and materials that keeps us so busy".[39] By 1916 over three-quarters of the paper made at Burneside and Cowan Head was being supplied directly and indirectly to the government, its uses including Inland Revenue Envelopes, Postal Wrappers, War Office Envelopes, Telegraph Envelopes, Registered Letter Envelopes, Active Service Envelopes, Inland Revenue forms and Colonial Postcards.[40]

The unprecedented and unnatural strength of demand for paper also led to meteoric rises in the price of paper. At Burneside and Cowan Head, paper prices rose from £13 per ton in 1914 to over £52 per ton by 1918.[41] In part such increases were necessary to cover costs: James Cropper & Co.'s total production costs rose from £150,000 in 1914 to almost £510,000 in 1918.[42] They also, however, reflected the company's efforts to try to control demand: "Orders coming in are so staggering", wrote Charles Cropper in one typical letter of the period, "that we shall have to raise prices." This led to spectacular rises in profit margins. After a slow start (the results for 1914 and 1915 were below pre-war levels) profits jumped to a record high of £22,800 in 1916, the best result since 1874. Even better was to come: in 1917 and 1918 profits leapt to £127,700 and £148,600, the massive increases largely reflecting the sky-high prices that Cropper paper was commanding.[43]

James Cropper & Co. was not, however, guilty of profiteering. Indeed, there is

---

* Contemporary evidence suggests that the Swedes were something of a thorn in the side of the British paper industry. During the war they exploited their neutrality and pushed up the price of British-made paper by restricting pulp exports to Britain. They then undercut the output of British paper-mills with their own paper. (JWC/58/b1, 18 Nov. 1916, Tolson MSS.) "The imports of paper from Sweden have been bigger than ever", wrote CJC in one wartime letter. "Sweden has stopped us getting Sulphite and has forced the price of Paper up to an abnormal figure and then undersells us in England with Paper. It does not seem fair that she should reap such a golden harvest when she has been of all neutrals the most unfriendly". (JWC/27, 24 Sept. 1916, Tolson MSS)

evidence that the directors cut prices where they could and objected to the meteoric prices that paper was commanding in the final years of the war.[44] Rather, the huge price increases of 1917 and 1918 were the result of government intervention. After the company came under control in April 1917 its paper prices were determined by the Ministry of Munitions. The spectacular profits that ensued, meanwhile, were largely returned to the government in the form of tax, principally Excess Profits Duty. Introduced in 1915 and levied on up to eighty

Fig. 5.2 – For many years, Remembrance Day poppies have been made from Cropper paper.

percent of the excess of profits enjoyed by a company above its average pre-war levels, it pushed up James Cropper & Co.'s tax bill from a negligible £430 (7.2 percent of profits) in 1914 to £131,500 (88.5 percent) in 1918.[45] Nevertheless, the company was not left empty handed. Shareholders received respectable dividends throughout the war and the bonuses paid to directors and staff were greater than ever before, rising from a pre-war average of £787 to over £4,500 by 1918.[46]

The war years were not, however, without severe loss. Twenty-three employees were killed in the conflict, including Herman Willink, who died of wounds in France on 7 November 1918, four days before the Armistice. The paper-mill continues to pay a tribute to their lives as the supplier of red paper for

Remembrance Day poppies (Fig 5.2), although today it is impossible to measure the impact of the death of so many young men on the small community of Burneside. The comments of George Walker, an employee who lost a son, nevertheless give some idea of the grief endured by many. "We have brought our lads up to help us and take our places at the Mill when we are gone", he wrote in 1919, "but this cruel war has taken them away from our side, and they are lying in a soldier's grave in France. No one knows the sorrow, only those that have lost them".[47]

Arranged by Beatrice Willink   Sketched from memory by Charles Cropper

BURNESIDE, JULY 26 1919

Fig. 6.1 – Peace celebrations at Burneside, 1919, depicted by Charles Cropper.

6

Renewal, Depression and Protectionism: 1918-39

ALTHOUGH a blessed relief for all sides, the end of the war in November 1918 was not greeted with universal optimism. Charles Cropper's outlook was characteristic. Like many he thought that peace would bring terrible times of hardship for all, paper-makers included. "I feel that the risk we run after the war is very great", he wrote to James W. a few months before the end of the conflict. "Prices must drop very much the moment peace is in sight and I expect we shall work at a loss for a while so we ought to keep some of our present income for the rainy day which is certain to come."[1] In consequence James Cropper & Co. began to build up greater reserves than ever before, including £45,000 invested in War Bonds in 1918.[2]

Initially, however, such prudence proved premature. As people scrambled for goods as they become available again, the war was followed by a worldwide boom. And far from collapsing, the price of paper made at Burneside and Cowan Head remained at wartime levels throughout 1919, and in 1920 even increased slightly to almost £55 a ton, helped by a world-wide shortage of the material.[3] "At the present time we have a record quantity of orders on the books," reported James W. Cropper at the company's Annual General Meeting in November 1919, "So that we can face the immediate future with hope and confidence."[4]

The company's results were also promising. In the year to October 1919 the paper-mills returned a profit of £128,000 in spite of a major problem with Burneside's main steam engine which caused output to fall to 11,900 tons, its lowest level since 1914. (On 1 March 1919 the engine's flywheel had shattered, curtailing output for two months and costing the company thousands in lost production and repair costs.)[5] In the following year results were even better. Production reached 13,360 tons – not far off the record output of 1916 – and profits jumped by almost fifty percent to a record high of £188,000. In the main this was attributable to the company's fortunate purchase of raw materials before prices shot up, which inflated profit margins dramatically and more than covered growing production expenses, in particular a marked advance in wage costs.[6]

In August 1919 the company introduced a three-shift system, reducing the hours worked by shift-workers per week from sixty-three to forty-four with no reduction in pay.[7] In line with a reduction in working hours in British industry in general – which in turn was a result of post-war trade union power and a response to studies in industrial fatigue – the change saw the company's wage costs rising from £47,000 in 1919 to £64,000 in 1920, while the number of employees exceeded five hundred for the first time.[8]

Profit margins were also inflated by falling taxation. At the end of the war Excess Profits Duty was cut from 80% to 40% in expectation of a slump, before being raised to 60% in 1920, a belated response to the post-war boom. In consequence the percentage of James Cropper & Co.'s profits consumed by tax fell from 88% in 1918 to 58% in 1919 and 64% in 1920, leaving the company with greater sums than ever to distribute: profits after tax grew from £17,100 in 1918 to £52,500 in 1919 and £66,900 in 1920.[9] It was an exceptionally prosperous two years for the paper-making company, suggesting that there was some truth in the declarations of Sir Lomin Gouin, the Prime Minister of Quebec: "Paper manufacture", he informed a Savoy luncheon in May 1920, "is nowadays as valuable as a goldmine".[10]

The profits of 1919 and 1920 did not, however, significantly increase the personal fortunes of James Cropper & Co.'s shareholders. Even though the company's three full-time directors, Alfred Willink, and Charles and James W. Cropper, together owned almost two-thirds of the share capital – the rest was shared between the McCorquodale family (24%) and various senior employees – they resisted distributing the bulk of the gains. Neither dividend nor bonus payments were excessive. Dividends, for example, totalled £10,600 in 1919 and £14,300 in 1920.[11]

The directors had good reason to keep a large proportion of profits in company coffers. Following the end of the war James Cropper & Co. had embarked upon one of the most extensive and expensive modernisation schemes to be undertaken in its history. Originally drawn up before war broke out in 1914, the plans centred upon the complete reconstruction of Burneside Mill's preparation facilities, including new buildings and additional machinery. At the same time the company decided to modernise the mill's power plant by installing a Parsons steam turbine. This was a much needed item: Burneside's main steam engine was unreliable and old (though much modified it dated back to 1873) and the other principal source of power, a 400 hp gas engine, was temperamental and unpopular. "We have hated her", noted Charles Cropper in 1919. "She made us white before our time."[12] The turbine also marked the beginning of a new age in energy terms: while it initially drove some machinery directly, it was principally designed to generate electricity and power all three of James Cropper & Co.'s mills through electric motors.

Such improvements did not come cheaply. By November 1920 it was estimated that the total cost of the work at Burneside would amount to at least £200,000.[13] This included £60,000 to be spent on a project not originally proposed. Encouraged by the unflagging strength of demand for paper and the continuing buoyancy of the economy, in March 1920 James Cropper & Co. had decided to invest in a fifth machine at Burneside. In due course a new 110-inch MG machine was ordered from Bertrams Ltd of Sciennes, Edinburgh, the principal contractors for the reconstruction work already underway.[14]

Unfortunately, the good times did not last. As a new and improved Burneside Mill rose up from the banks of the River Kent during 1920 (Fig. 6.2) the economy of Britain came crashing to the ground. Hastened by government efforts to control inflation and reduce debt, by the end of 1920 the post-war boom was rapidly turning to bust. Within a year industrial activity fell by almost twenty-five percent and prices dropped even more.[15] At the same time a coal strike from April to July 1921 pushed up costs while unemployment rose to record heights, jumping from two percent to a peak of twenty-three percent in May 1921.[16]

Fig. 6.2 – Burneside Mills, reconstruction of the preparation facilities, 1920-22.

James Cropper & Co. was affected by the changing economic climate from the start. It led to a dramatic and unexpected decline in demand for paper which – worsened by a sudden influx of foreign paper – soon made itself evident in the company's order books.[17] These had been "embarrassingly full" until July 1920, but by Christmas were so depleted that the company was forced to shut one machine and cut production on a further two.[18] The downturn in trade also compelled it to radically alter its ambitious reconstruction plans. Charles Cropper, no less shrewd for his advancing years, was the first to address the subject. "I fear that it is almost a certainty that if we do not cut down our ideas and schemes very severely, and even at great loss", he noted in a memorandum of 16 December, "we shall find ourselves in great financial stress within two years from now."[19] Backed up by financial forecasts drawn up by his son, he recommended that all work that was not absolutely necessary should be suspended. This included the installation of the fifth machine at Burneside, the output of which was no longer set to benefit the company so much as burden it. "We have been misguided in thinking there was a world shortage of paper", Charles Cropper explained, "and with that opinion we ordered No5 machine. . . . Now I believe we ought to scrap the whole No5 idea for the present at whatever cost. If I am right it must be done instantly."[20] His fellow directors agreed with him, and a week later the project was shelved.[21]

The quick and decisive response to the downturn in trade was soon vindicated. In 1921 trading conditions deteriorated still further, forcing James Cropper & Co. to curtail production dramatically. In the six months to April 1921 output fell to 5,440 tons, the lowest level since 1911.[22] Even worse was to come. In the next five months the company's problems were compounded by the long and bitter coal strike, and Burneside and Cowan Head almost ground to a halt owing to lack of fuel; production of paper fell to 2,220 tons.[23] "Our mills were shut practically throughout the coal strike", Herbert Corrie, the company secretary, informed the Inland Revenue in August, "and are at present shut for want of orders. Our stock of material is not moving at all."[24] This was a further problem. Throughout 1921 the value of the company's stocks was hit hard by the massive deflation that accompanied the slump in trade. Between March and August, for example, the value of its pulp stocks fell from £155,000 to £71,000, a capital loss it was unable to recover. The price of paper – if it was able to make and sell it – fell proportionately.[25] Not surprisingly, the company's balance sheet for the period bears witness to the ruinous affects of the crash. In the eleven months to September 1921 the value of paper made by the company (£454,700) was far exceeded by material costs and other charges (£547,000), leading to a loss of £93,300.[26] It was the first serious loss since 1853.

James Cropper & Co. was not, however, slow to recover. While a number of British paper-mills were bankrupted by the crash, the company was soon back in the black.[27] By April 1922 its finances had been largely resurrected by seven months of profitable trading – which cut its losses for eighteen months to £59,500 – and by an Excess Profits Duty refund of £68,900. There were even sufficient funds to pay out dividends totalling £11,400.[28] In the next twelve months the recovery continued, even though demand and production remained depressed. Even more importantly, the physical shape of the business continued to improve in leaps and bounds. With the exception of the fifth machine (the plans for which were never revived) the reconstruction of Burneside continued apace throughout the crash of 1921 and its aftermath. By the end of 1922 most of the work was complete, giving the directors confidence in the future in spite of the trading conditions: "We expect before the next meeting", they proudly reported at the Annual General Meeting in 1922, "to possess the best paper-mill in England."[29]

James Cropper & Co. had not, however, survived the crash unscathed. The sudden turnaround in its fortunes owed everything to the decision taken by the directors in the autumn of 1921 – at the prompting of Charles Cropper – to write down the value of its stocks.[30] The sums of money lost this way were huge: according to James W. Cropper over £190,000 had been written off the value of stocks by April 1922, the bulk of it drawn from reserves built up in previous years.[31] In consequence the company's borrowings shot up – by 1923 it was almost £27,000 overdrawn at the Kendal Bank – and it was also forced to make inroads into other investments.[32] In 1922 it cashed in £30,000 invested in War Loan stock to help pay for the alterations at Burneside, which were far from cheap: between 1920 and 1924 almost £180,000 was invested in the mill.[33]

The early 1920s were also expensive years for James Cropper & Co. in personnel terms. The company lost a number of its leading lights, starting with James Paterson, the chief engineer since 1903, who left Burneside for John Dickinson & Co. in March 1920.[34] His departure could not have come at a worse time – he was supervising much of the reconstruction work at Burneside – although his place was quickly filled. Within a month the company had recruited James Arnot, perpetuating the longstanding tradition of recruitment north of the border: he came from Springfield Mills, near Edinburgh.[35] His length of service – he remained chief engineer until 1950 – suggests he was a more than satisfactory replacement, as does James W. Cropper's reference to his character in 1933. "Work seems to be going on well", he wrote after a visit to Bertrams in Edinburgh to see a new cylinder being made. "They are thoroughly afraid of Arnot and won't let us down I feel for sure. I saw the cylinder . . . I asked Thomson if they would tell us how many pinholes they had to fill up, he said "No need to tell you – Mr Arnot will be all over it with a microscope."[36]

In 1922 Burneside Mills lost another senior member of staff, Daniel McNeill (Fig. 6.3). Manager of Burneside Mills since the turn of the century – and largely in charge of its day to day running – he was forced to retire owing to ill health. It was a great loss to the business, as Charles Cropper revealed. "We very deeply regret that you feel you cannot hold your post here", he wrote to McNeill in August 1922, ". . . We miss you dreadfully as a friend and as a fellow worker, and your lack of health is a grief to us all. We hope you may soon be better again, and that we may have you here to help us with your knowledge and experience."[37] His hopes, however, were in vain: Daniel McNeill never returned to work and died in December 1923, aged sixty-three.[38] Fortunately, however, his nephew, Robert

Fig. 6.3 – Daniel McNeill (far left) and a group of Burneside mill employees, circa 1910. He was in charge of the mill from 1889 until 1922, first as foreman and later as mill manager.

McNeill, agreed to take his place. A veteran of a number of British paper-mills like his uncle before him, he came to Burneside from the Devon paper-manufacturers, Reid & Smith, in July 1924.[39]

His arrival came soon after another notable departure. In May 1924 the company lost one of its brightest prospects for the future, Geoffrey Tower. Recruited in 1919 to take the place of Herman Willink (the directors failed to recruit their first choice, Jack Howson, a Cropper cousin) his credentials were excellent.[40] Educated at Eton and Cambridge and the recipient of a Military Cross in the First World War, he came to Burneside on the back of glowing references from Walter Fletcher, James W.'s brother-in-law.[41] His career there, however, was short-lived: a year after he was appointed an assistant director – which suggests that he was proving his worth – he resigned from the firm owing to problems with his "domestic affairs". The exact circumstances remain unclear, although the response of the directors to his application for reinstatement suggest that he had lost their confidence in some way. "As Chairman of the Directors", Charles Cropper wrote to him, "I have to convey to you that they cannot alter their decision as to your resignation."[42]

The directors' reluctance to reappoint Geoffrey Tower perhaps reflected the imminent arrival of Derek Willink, who joined James Cropper & Co. in August 1924 at the age of twenty-two. Fresh from Eton and two years at Cambridge, the opening in paper-making no doubt came from his Uncle Alfred, although his decision to accept it probably reflected events closer to home. By 1924 he had not only lost his childhood home in Liverpool, Dingle Bank (originally the Cropper family homestead), which was demolished to make way for petroleum tanks, but also his father William, a Liverpool architect, who died in March 1924.[43] It was probably this, above all else, that prompted him to cut short his university degree and start making his way in the world.[44]

Less than two months after Derek Willink had started work, the company experienced another major loss. On 6 October 1924 the company lost its chairman, Charles Cropper, who died a few days after an accident on the hunting field. He was seventy-two. Although sudden and unexpected, it was a fitting end. Charles's advancing years had done nothing to quell his enthusiasm for hunting, and in his final season he hunted for thirty-six days despite being laid up with gout for almost a month. Hunting was not, however, his only enduring interest, as Alfred Willink acknowledged in a tribute to his cousin and colleague of forty-five years. "The Mill was to him as to his father before him his great joy", he remarked at the 1925 AGM, "and none of us can forget the intense interest he had in planning anything and in seeing it carried out . . . He truly cared for these works and the place and the people."[45]

Following Charles Cropper's death the chairmanship of James Cropper & Co. passed unchallenged to James W, by then forty-five. The third generation of his family to hold the post, according to several sources he was more business minded that his father, particularly so far as finances were concerned. In particular, this is evident in the attention he paid to cost accounting – at the time a relatively unpractised branch of book-keeping – which allowed him to keep check of the fortunes of the firm week by week. Indeed, he even wrote a book on the subject which was circulated amongst members of the paper trade, and seems to have been well received.* He was respected by other paper-makers and was twice asked to be president of the industry's governing body, the Paper Makers' Association, although he never occupied the post.[46]

On the other side of the coin James W. was not the charismatic and commanding leader that his father had been. By his own admission he was a quiet and retiring man, and was, according to his sister Maisie, not fond of exercising authority. For this reason, in many people's eyes the real head of the mills following Charles's death in 1924 was Alfred Willink, the elder statesman of the

---

* In the pamphlet (entitled *Paper Mill Cost Accounts*) James W. observed that few British firms kept accurate cost accounts and that without them there was a dearth of accurate knowledge about where profits were being made or losses incurred. He concluded with a strong endorsement of James Cropper & Co.'s accounting practices: "From the results achieved in 10 years of working of our systems, we can claim that we are nearer knowing what kind of paper is the most profitable to make, and what is a fair price to quote for any orders that we have to compete for". (CA/18/11)

firm. By then almost sixty-five years of age, he was a noted disciplinarian and not unaccustomed to losing his temper, if necessary.[47]

According to many sources, however, Alfred was more passionate about music than paper-making. He and his wife Bee were the leading lights of Westmorland's annual Mary Wakefield music festival, and membership of his village choral society was reckoned by many to be the quickest route to promotion in the paper-mills. Nevertheless, he remained dedicated to the mills into his old age. Into his eighties he continued to cycle to work on a daily basis, more often than not wearing plus-fours and accompanied by Dumble, his slobbering Labrador. His staying power was formidable: on his death in 1947 at the age of eighty-seven he had worked for the company for sixty-seven years, only the final two of which were spent in semi-retirement.

A remarkably energetic and enthusiastic old man, Alfred's contribution to the firm did not wane in spite of his advancing years. During the Second World War, he was still monitoring the efficiency of the mills, a job he had carried out since the 1880s. He also remained innovative, as his development of a new product in 1934 suggests. "I've a new idea", he excitedly wrote to James W., who was away in London at the time. "We could paste manilla paper onto our present Reg. Shape paper, instead of Cloth Strips." The result was the strip-lined envelope, which began to be produced (and sell well) within a year.[48]

The enduring presence of Alfred Willink was not to say, however, that there was not another generation of management on the way. In addition to Derek Willink, by the mid-1930s two more family relations were being groomed to carry the firm forwards. First, on the last day of his life, Charles Cropper had arranged for his grandson, Geoffrey Acland, to join James Cropper & Co.[49] Son of Eleanor Cropper and Francis Acland, a Liberal MP and Devon landowner, Geoffrey was probably not party to the arrangement himself: he was only sixteen at the time and still a schoolboy at Rugby. He did not, however, oppose the idea as he grew older. "I have been offered a very interesting and pleasant job in life", he remarked to his father over two years later, "and I really do want to prepare to be useful."[50]

Geoffrey Acland's preparation for a career in paper-making initially marked something of a departure for James Cropper & Co. Rather than taking a degree at an élite British university, the customary route for someone of his upbringing, he was sent – at James W.'s behest – to a paper-making school in Grenoble to undertake three years of technical training. The decision to send him to France probably reflected the directors' recognition of the increasing importance of science and technology in paper-making – a feature of the industry in the inter-war years – although it was not entirely successful. Finding the technical side of the course, which demanded that he study maths, chemistry, physics and electricity, very challenging (and also, apparently, the skiing very distracting) he returned to England after a year in Grenoble and enrolled at Cambridge University. His paper-making career was not, however, cut short. On his return from France in 1927 he spent the summer working shifts in Burneside Mill – the first future director to work on the shop floor – and on completion of an engineering degree he joined the company for good in October 1930. In the coming years he took the customary route to a directorship: he was appointed an assistant director in 1933 and a full director in 1937, following the path taken by Derek Willink in 1926 and 1928.[51]

Charles Cropper also witnessed the early interest of another grandson in paper-making: James W.'s first and only son, Anthony. Born in 1912, as a child he was frequently in the paper-mills, not least when he was waiting with his sister Rachel to go home after day school in Burneside. "After lessons we ran across the village into the office and distracted Daddy", she recalls. "He would tell us to make ourselves scarce 'til he was ready and sometimes we'd go into the secretary's office, but we were just as likely to say come on, let's go into the mill. . . . We were in and out of the mills. We knew it backwards".[52] When he was even younger Anthony had also experienced the paper-mills with his grandfather. "Anthony has been down with me to see all these jobs", wrote Charles to James W. in 1916, "and has been much interested and very inquisitive, asking reasons for everything from all the men to their great delight. When we came in just now he said 'Haven't we had an interesting time Gran Gran?'. Dear little man, I wonder if he will boss it all some day. He is keen enough now".[53]

Charles would not have been disappointed. Anthony Cropper joined the firm in September 1935, eleven years after his death, and within two years had advanced – in the customary manner – to the position of assistant director, a preliminary step to becoming a full director of the concern.[54] His first experience of the business, however, was gained in 1931 when he spent six months working at Burneside after leaving school. This included shift work: "I remember him walking down to the mill in dungarees to start on the 6 am shift", his sister Dosia recalls, ". . . with a flask of cold tea and a biscuit tin."[55] At the same time he also began to learn something of the paper industry in general – in May 1931 he undertook a tour of British paper-mills with his father and Geoffrey Acland – and in the coming years his training continued. While at university he began accompanying his father on visits to customers in London, and after graduation he spent a year in Newcastle gaining accountancy experience with Price Waterhouse, the company's auditors.[56]

In greatest part, however, Anthony Cropper received the education of an English gentleman rather than the training of a future industrialist. Like his father and grandfather he was educated away from home at Eton and Cambridge, experiencing a life far removed from the hills and mills of his childhood. Nevertheless, there are no indications that he considered any career other than paper-making before joining the family firm.[57] Indeed, despite his evident enthusiasm for the diversions of his day – he drove fast cars (an open-top Bentley as an undergraduate), loved jazz music and was fanatical about dancing – his loyalties and aspirations remained simple. "I'm afraid Burneside Mill has got a very firm hold of me", he explained to his father on one occasion, "and I feel I am very lucky to be able to live my life in such a happy atmosphere. It's rather funny to feel sentimental about a business but somehow Burneside is so much more than just a business."[58]

His comments were not without foundation. James W., for one, always viewed the community in more than economic terms, and his family not only remained the chief employers in the village but also continued to play a leading part in its social life. Not least, this was evident at Anthony's twenty-first birthday celebrations in 1933, an affair that was almost identical to the party given on his grandfather's coming of age in 1873. Organised by the company secretary, Herbert Corrie (no doubt under the orders of James W.), over a thousand guests, in the main mill employees and their families, were present, and there was tea and cake for all, as well as games and a range of entertainment. This included the Kendal Borough Band, donkeys from Morecambe and even Miss Catherine Riddle's troupe of girl dancers all the way from Hawick in the Scottish borders. Last and not least there were also the customary presentations, which included the gift of a saddle to Anthony from mill employees, which was presented by Levi Keates, the head blacksmith and longest-serving employee (Fig. 6.4). The event was even reported in the *World's Paper Trade Review*.[59]

Fig. 6.4 – Levi Keates presents Anthony Cropper with a saddle on behalf of the Cropper workforce at a garden party held to celebrate his twenty-first birthday in 1933; around 1,000 people attended. Anthony's father, James W., is seated immediately to his left, next to Alfred Willink.

The extravagance of the celebrations was not, however, a measure of the prosperity of the paper-mills. While the event suggests that there was confidence in the future of the business so far as Anthony Cropper was concerned, trading conditions gave less cause for optimism. Indeed, the slump of 1921 only marked the beginning of what was to prove a notoriously difficult era for British industry. Although the economy picked up after 1924 the recovery was short-lived. It was soon interrupted by the General Strike of 1926 (which coincided with a lengthy and costly coal strike) and then cut short by the worldwide economic depression that followed the Wall Street crash of 1929. Moreover, as many of Britain's traditional industries – not least cotton – continued to decline throughout the inter-war years, the country continued to be plagued by mass unemployment and industrial unrest. Between 1921 and 1938 at least one out of every ten people of working age were out of work at all times. It was the scourge of the age: "The ordinary citizen", remarks one historian of the period, "may remember the inter-war years chiefly for the queues of the unemployed, the idle factories, yards and mines, the hunger marchers and the spiritual impoverishment and economic insecurity."[60]

Not surprisingly, James Cropper & Co.'s performance in the years leading up to the Second World War was less than spectacular. The coal strike of 1926 cost the company £8,000 in extra fuel, and the General Strike that followed led to over £3,500 of bad debts.[61] In addition, profits were severely hit by the Great Depression of the 1930s. They halved from £50,300 to £24,800 between 1929 and 1931 and took years to recover. Indeed, profits never returned to the levels of 1917 to 1920 throughout the late 1920s and 1930s. Moreover, the growth of output was similarly restrained. The record output of 1916 was only surpassed in 1935 – when 14,300 tons of paper were made at Burneside and Cowan Head – and by 1938 production stood at 15,800 tons, only twenty-five percent above the levels of the early 1920s, where in the same period the output of the British paper industry as a whole had almost doubled.[62]

James Cropper & Co. did not, however, in contrast with many British manufacturers, add to the growing ranks of the unemployed. There are no indications that any employees were laid off during the 1920s and 1930s, although many were, on occasion, forced to endure the hardships of short-time working.[*] Nor did the company need to shed labour. While profit and production figures were disappointing, the foundations of the business remained strong, reinforced by numerous changes and developments.

---

[*] Short-time was worked when there was insufficient demand to keep the machines running full time. There are indications that full pay was suspended at such times and that employees were granted access to their savings to compensate.

Fig. 6.5 – Sample brochures from the inter-war years, with a drawing of Burneside by Charles Cropper completed shortly before his death.

Not least, James Cropper & Co.'s resilience owed much to the range of papers it chose to manufacture, which were marketed through a series of sample brochures (Fig. 6.5). This included a number of grades the company had made for decades, such as cloth-lined paper for registered envelopes, and wrapping papers of various kinds and colours. The company also, however, began developing and making many new types of paper. In the 1920s it started producing several new types of cartridge paper, including waxing cartridge for wrapping bread and other foods, tea cartridge and even ribbed hosiery cartridge for packaging stockings.[63] In this way it benefited from the dramatic growth of retail grade in the inter-war years, which saw more and more chains of shops springing up nationwide (between 1923 and 1931 the number of Woolworth stores, for example, jumped from 100 to 494) and an explosion in the number of products which were packaged and sold under brand names.[64] By the 1930s Cropper paper was being used to package several well known brands, including Brooke Bond tea, for whom the company made a light green paper into the 1970s.[65]

The company also benefited from another important development of the era, the dramatic growth of the electrical industry. Britain was the first country in the world to possess a national grid, and the number of electricity consumers grew from 730,000 in 1920 to almost 9,000,000 in 1938.[66] This ensured a good demand for insulating paper – first made by the company in 1897 – which was made at Burneside into the 1920s and 1930s for the Pirelli General Cable Works in Southampton. There are indications, however, that the company had problems meeting the exacting technical specifications, not least because the grade was so different from anything else it made. "The real trouble is that we can't pretend to be makers of insulating papers at all", James W. explained to Alfred Willink in 1930, noting that Tullis Russell made a much better paper. "All the other cable makers tell Pirelli that they are fools to try and use our paper."[67] Nevertheless, the company persevered with the grade, and evidently with some success, as it continued to make insulating paper for various customers (including Pirelli) into the early 1960s.[68]

The most important product development in the inter-war years was not, however, related to individual grades. It involved a more fundamental shift in output, which saw the company beginning to forge itself a place in the British paper industry as a small, specialised manufacturer. In the 1920s the company began to steer away from the manufacture of lightweight commodity grades such as "Buff" (which was discontinued in 1927) towards the production of thicker, better quality papers which enjoyed better margins and were less vulnerable to competition.[69] These included old grades like duplex as well as many new ones such as pasted boards, postcards (1,000 tons a year of which was sold to the Indian post office in the 1920s and 1930s, the company's biggest order), ticket papers, manilla for filing and labels, and coloured and embossed cover papers.[70] Many of these grades are still made by the company in 2004.

James Cropper & Co.'s commitment to such papers is evident in its investment programme of the 1920s and 1930s. Much of the new machinery installed was geared towards the production of heavier, more specialised and expensive grades, including an embossing calender installed at Burneside in 1929, pasting machines at Cowan Head (1920 and 1929) and a second wire on Burneside's No4 machine (1936). Enabling the production of two-ply paper on the machine (which was much thicker, stronger, and better in quality) this was a major investment for the company, costing £15,600. It was also an important step historically, as the twin-wire process continues to suit the company's production requirements to this day, three out of four machines having two wires in 2004.[71] It was also a relatively pioneering project. The first twin-wire paper-making machine in the world was constructed in 1923 by Tullis Russell in Fife. That James Cropper & Co. should follow its lead was perhaps no coincidence as the two companies enjoyed a close relationship in the 1930s (more of which in a moment).[72]

The firm also sought to protect its margins in the inter-war years by improving the efficiency of the mills. In particular, this was achieved by cutting energy costs wherever possible, even if it demanded substantial investment. In 1926, for example, the company spent £5,000 on preheaters, which cut coal consumption to one ton per ton of paper by partially heating boiler water with exhaust gases. Ten years later the boiler plant itself was renewed at a cost of £30,000.[73] More importantly, however, the company saved running costs by continuing to electrify the mills. The switch to electricity, which had began with the installation of a steam turbine in 1922, continued into the late 1920s. Cowan Head was electrified in 1925, powered by electricity generated at Burneside, and in the following years electric motors were installed to power all four of Burneside's machines.[74] This not only led to savings in coal – by 1928 there were only three small steam engines left in the mill where there had been fifteen six years previously – but also in labour, light and oil. The company's yearly oil bill, for example, dropped from £950 in 1925 to under £450 by 1929.[75]

At the same time as it was phasing out steam engines, James Cropper & Co. also said goodbye to another archaic source of power: the horse. In 1927 the horse-drawn tramway connecting Burneside with Bowston and Cowan Head was replaced with a standard gauge railway. Built on rails seized in Palestine during the First World War, the new line saw horses being superseded by a petrol-driven locomotive named *Rachel* (Fig. 6.6) after James W.'s ten year old daughter. The new system, which cost almost £6,000 in total, led to considerable savings. It cost the company. in the region of £750 a year to run where the horse-drawn tramway had cost at least £1,500 and sometimes even more.[76] It was not, however, without its shortfalls: in 1932 the engine driver, Thomas Wray, a Cropper employee for

Fig. 6.6 – Rachel, which replaced horses on the company's private railway in 1927. She was retired to the Lakeside & Haverthwaite Railway in 1972.

over forty years, was killed after being crushed between two railway wagons at Cowan Head.[77]

It was not the only fatal accident to take place in the paper-mills in the inter-war years. In October 1929 Ronald Ellwood, a twenty-seven year old machine assistant, died from injuries sustained after his arm was caught in a machine at Burneside. He had slipped while padding out the diameter of a driving pulley with felt, a routine way of slowing down a section of the machine when changing from a thick to a thin paper. It was a common practice, the inquest was told, which could only be carried out when the machine was running. A verdict of accidental death was returned, but the coroner and others expressed the opinion that it was an unnecessarily dangerous job, and following the accident the few remaining drives where "bulking" (as it was called) was still in use were altered.[78]

In spite of such an improvement the paper-mills still remained a hazardous environment. Although the company warned its employees against dangerous practices, there was still a minimal culture of safety in the mills and coupled with the nature of much of the work – including handling chemicals, heavy loads and operating moving machinery – it is not surprising that accidents were numerous and severe. A slim volume in the company archives, "Compensation Claims" – a record of the sums of money paid to employees who were off work due to injuries sustained in the workplace – bears witness to this. In 1933, for example, an average year in the records, fourteen accidents are noted, including a fractured leg, dermatitis "produced by liquids", crushed toes and a number of cut or crushed fingers. Although nearly all injured employees did return to work, the book makes sobering reading, even more so because there are few signs of improvement between the opening of the book in 1915 and its close in 1964.

In other areas employees fared better. In particular, the company continued to offer its employees job security in an age more characterised by insecurity in the workplace. It was still normal for individuals to spend their whole working lives with the firm, often in excess of fifty years – Levi Keates, the head blacksmith, for example, retired in 1933 after sixty years – and the company continued to offer places to almost all local school-leavers who applied for a position.[79] Furthermore, in the 1920s and 1930s more and more employees began to benefit from the company's Profit Sharing Savings scheme which grew dramatically in popularity. By 1925 over two hundred employees had invested £26,400 in the venture, and by 1939 350 employees had deposited almost £57,000, perhaps drawn by the returns on offer: between 1919 and 1939 annual interest payments averaged just under ten percent, an attractive rate in the low inflationary climate of the era.[80]

The scheme was not, however, without its problems. While its runaway success increased James Cropper & Co.'s working capital it also increased its cash liabilities beyond reasonable levels. In consequence the company was twice forced to restrict the growth of the scheme, cutting the maximum sums that could be deposited by an individual to £1,000 in 1930 and £400 in 1939.[81] In spite of such restrictions the directors still felt it was a worthwhile scheme: "The way in which employees have supported the Profit Sharing Scheme", they commented in 1939, "has been most gratifying to the Directors and has done much to foster the friendly co-operation that so happily prevails in our enterprise."[82]

Good labour relations were also perhaps cultivated by the provision of housing. James Cropper & Co. provided rented accommodation for nearly all mill-workers and their families, and foremen were often provided with houses rent-free, often specially built for them, and usually with coal and light costs included. This was a good reason to work for the company if the experience of one employee who left the firm is any indication. "Great joy . . .", James W. wrote to his wife Marjorie in May 1939,

> . . . Joe Bradbury hated Cardiff when he got there and could see no prospect of getting a house for months, so wrote and asked if he could come back. He'll have to lose his promotion because he definitely gave notice and other people have been put into his place and it wouldn't be fair to shove them down again. But it will be good to have him back here and a bit of a puff for James Cropper and Co. that he found workpeople elsewhere weren't so well looked after".[83]

In due course Joe Bradbury returned to Burneside, where he continued to work in the paper-mills for another thirty-five years, twenty of which were spent as salle foreman.

The company had provided housing for mill-workers and their families since the earliest days of the business. When James Cropper bought the paper-mills in 1845 the purchase included thirty-one houses, and as the workforce grew in size more and more houses was built or purchased. By 1914 the company owned or had access to over 110 houses, including twenty-one in Bowston named Winstanley Row and Place, built in 1886 at a cost of £2,300 (Fig. 6.7), and six in Burneside built in the 1900s out of profits from the village pub, the Angler's Inn, which had been placed in trust by John Bryce and was administered by the company directors. At the same time his widow, Helen, added to the expanding village, building five houses at its southern end which she named Bourneville after Cadbury's pioneering development of the 1890s in Birmingham; these included baths, a notable luxury at the time.

The greatest period of housing development, however, came after the First World War. Between 1918 and 1926 James Cropper & Co. built or purchased nearly fifty houses, including Oakbank, Aikrigg Avenue and Kentrigg House, eighteen units outside Burneside bought in 1920, and Ivy Crescent, where eight houses were built in 1923 at a cost of £8,000.[84] In the same years the company also

Fig. 6.7 – Winstanley Row, Bowston, built in 1886; by 1930 the company had bought or built over 150 houses for employees.

became sizeable landlords for the first time: the number of freehold properties it owned rose from thirty-three in 1918 to 154 by 1930, the jump in great part reflecting its purchase of sixty-six freeholds from the Cropper family in 1923.[85] The post-war years also saw notable advances in housing conditions. All houses built after 1918 were provided with inside sanitation and baths, and in 1923 every home old and new was transformed by the installation of electric light and power, generated by Burneside's new steam turbine.[86] Householders were required to pay the company for this service until it was taken over by the Westmorland Electricity Co. in 1939 (Fig. 6.8).[87]

Such development was again not cheap. Bringing electricity into employees' homes cost James Cropper & Co. over £6,000, and in all the company spent at least £40,000 on buying, building and upgrading houses between 1918 and 1939, a significant proportion of the total capital invested in the business in the inter-war years. Furthermore, in contrast with investment in the paper-mills themselves, such expenditure offered little chance of a decent return, not only owing to the affordable rates at which houses were let but also due to maintenance costs. By the 1930s the company had built up a large team of labourers (known as the "outside gang") to look after its expanding property portfolio; this included slaters, wallers, joiners and painters.[88]

The directors did not, however, expect to make money from such investment. They envisaged a rather different type of return, as James W. explained at the

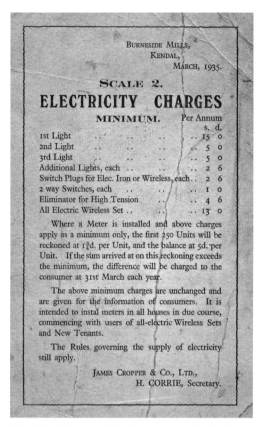

BURNESIDE MILLS,
KENDAL,
MARCH, 1935.

SCALE 2.
ELECTRICITY CHARGES

MINIMUM.	Per Annum	
	s.	d.
1st Light	15	0
2nd Light	5	0
3rd Light	5	0
Additional Lights, each	2	6
Switch Plugs for Elec. Iron or Wireless, each..	2	6
2 way Switches, each	1	0
Eliminator for High Tension ..	4	6
All Electric Wireless Set	13	0

Where a Meter is installed and above charges
apply as a minimum only, the first 250 Units will be
reckoned at 1¾d. per Unit, and the balance at 5d. per
Unit. If the sum arrived at on this reckoning exceeds
the minimum, the difference will be charged to the
consumer at 31st March each year.

The above minimum charges are unchanged and
are given for the information of consumers. It is
intended to instal meters in all houses in due course,
commencing with users of all-electric Wireless Sets
and New Tenants.

The Rules governing the supply of electricity
still apply.

JAMES CROPPER & CO., LTD.,
H. CORRIE, Secretary.

*Fig. 6.8 – Rates card for electricity supplied by James
Cropper & Co. to Burneside householders, 1930s.*

AGM in November 1919. "If fifty houses are built at a cost of £750 each, £37,500 is required", he noted in a discussion of the company's future housing plans. "Not more than half of this can be expected to be commercially sound expenditure. So that about £20,000 will have to be written off as expenditure on which the return will be health and comfort to our employees – and not in cash to our Shareholders."[89]

Such an attitude was characteristic of its day. In the aftermath of the First World War there was not only a pressing shortage of houses nationwide – estimated to have stood at over 800,000 in 1921 – but also a universal desire that the survivors of the war might return to "homes fit for heroes".[90] Edith Cropper addressed the subject in the midst of the war. "Everything our soldiers want they must have", she wrote to James W. in 1916. "It might easily wreck us at the end of the war and yet it is inevitable. I feel it myself every time one of the young men comes home."[91]

James W. had similar feelings. Although to some he appeared a rather formidable and superior employer – an aspect of his character perhaps exacerbated by his reticence – his private records reveal a man who genuinely cared for the well-being of those in his employ. The chief proponent of James Cropper & Co.'s post-war housing programme – one of his driving ambitions as chairman of the company was to house all his employees in Burneside – like his grandfather he not only saw himself as a businessman but also as the patriarch of a community whose welfare was his duty and responsibility. Profit was a secondary consideration, as his father revealed in 1920: "Jem is a very different person from me", Charles wrote to his wife Edith:

> . . . As you know we are spending a very large fortune on Burneside. I asked him "Why? What are you doing it for? Do you expect a fortune in return?". He said "No. We are spending it for the good of the place, for the people who work and live here, to give five hundred people happy lives".

Such an attitude is also evident in James W.'s construction of Charles Court in Burneside in 1926. Built in memory of his father at a cost of £7,000, he paid for the development out of his own pocket before selling it back to the company for £5,000. "I do not wish to own them when completed", he explained to Alfred Willink at the time. "I therefore propose to hand them over to the Company at a price that would make them a reasonable investment for the company."[92]

James W.'s concern for the welfare of others perhaps owed something to his wife Marjorie. A deeply religious woman like her husband's grandmother, Fanny Alison – with whom she was compared by the older people of the village – she acted as an unofficial welfare officer for the people of Burneside, Bowston and Cowan Head. She was not just another well-to-do lady doing her share of "good works". "She revolutionised our standards of kindness", remarked Maisie Fletcher, her sister-in-law. "She used to have sent to her every week from the office a list of people who had been absent through illness, and she visited their homes, and went to see them in Hospital, and took endless pains in caring for them."[93]

Such personal concern for employees – which was increasingly rare in an age less typified by family businesses than by joint-stock companies with anonymous shareholders and appointed boards – was not without its benefits.[94] While a growing number of British paper manufacturers (including John Dickinson & Co.) were troubled by bad labour relations, James Cropper & Co. were not, even though wages were increasingly dictated by unions.[95] There are no records of unrest in the mills throughout the 1920s and 1930s, even during the General Strike of 1926. Indeed, while almost every paper-mill in the country stopped production for the duration of the strike, the Cropper employees remained at work, maintaining full production at Burneside and Cowan Head. This not only saved the company money in the short term but also helped to generate future business. By keeping going through the strike, explained a grateful James W. a year later, "We won the confidence and goodwill of our customers, which has, I think, been reflected in our order books ever since".[96]

The firm also retained customers in a more fundamental way. Throughout the 1920s and 1930s demand for the company's output was not only assured by such factors as the service it offered customers and its choice of products. It was also, importantly, underpinned by government legislation. Dominated politically by the Conservatives, the inter-war years saw a large-scale shift away from the liberal policy of free trade towards protection, particularly after 1931 when a comprehensive range of duties was imposed on imports to safeguard British industry in the wake of the worldwide economic crisis. In consequence James Cropper & Co.'s output was protected from foreign competition throughout the 1930s by a variety of import duties on paper manufactured abroad, ranging from sixteen to fifty percent.[97] In addition, as much as three-quarters of the paper produced on the company's five machines (four at Burneside and one at Cowan Head) was protected in the 1920s by the Safeguarding of Industries Acts of 1921 and 1926. In 1926 this imposed import duties of sixteen percent on wrapping and packing grades including MG paper.[98]

While protective duties did not mark the end of foreign competition for British paper manufacturers (in 1938 thirty percent of paper consumed in the UK still came from abroad) they gave the industry a welcome boost, underpinning the dramatic expansion in the capacity of British paper-mills from 1,317,000 tonnes in 1924 to 2,541,000 tonnes in 1938.[99] In the same period imports grew at half the rate, and it is notable that negative references to "the foreigner" – a conspicuous feature of James Cropper & Co.'s pre-1914 business correspondence – are almost entirely absent from the company's records of the 1920s and 1930s.

Protection also helped James Cropper & Co. through the anti-competitive climate that it nurtured within British trade and industry. Sanctioned by the government and the Federation of British Industries and buttressed by price agreements and co-operation between competitors, by the end of the 1930s restrictive practices had permeated business life at all levels. The paper trade was no exception to the rule, as a contemporary source makes clear. "By close co-operation in nearly every section of the industry", the Paper Makers' Association observed in 1937, "mills have been able, generally speaking, to maintain paper and board prices . . . At present there are more price agreements in operation in the industry than at any previous time in its history."[100]

Records of James Cropper & Co.'s involvement in price-fixing are sketchy, but there is evidence that the company agreed to control the supply and price of cable insulating paper with three other paper manufacturers who made the grade.

Forged in 1937 between James Cropper & Co. and Tullis Russell, Cooke & Nuttall and R. & W. Watson, for a while the arrangement seems to have worked well. In 1938, however, Cooke & Nuttall breached the terms of the agreement in some way, and after a series of hastily convened meetings in Edinburgh the informal cartel collapsed.[101]

Fig. 7.1 – Anthony and Philippa Cropper on their wedding day, 1938.

7

A Controlled Establishment: 1939-45

THE outbreak of the Second World War on 3 September 1939 marked the beginning of a conflict very different in character from the Great War of 1914 to 1918. For one, it was not greeted with the fervent patriotism of August 1914. The culmination of years of tension with Hitler's Germany, this time the war was not expected to be a short and glorious affair, and expectations were more subdued. The military reaction to the declaration of war was similarly low-key: there was no immediate offensive, and the first few months of the war were characterised by peace more than bloodshed.[1]

Nevertheless, the reaction to the war was quick and decisive. Acting on elaborate war plans that the government had been drawing up for several years, during the autumn and winter of 1939 every aspect of life in Britain began to change. Starting with conscription and a national register of occupations – which were both introduced before war was declared – in the following months the government took steps to control the economy of the country at every point, including regulating output, prices, wages and the distribution of goods. By January 1940 they had even began to introduce rationing, a measure not resorted to until the final year of the First World War.[2]

At Burneside, as elsewhere, the impact of the war was sudden and profound. People's lives were changed with almost immediate effect, as many contemporary witnesses have recorded. This was especially true for my grandmother, Philippa Cropper (Fig. 7.1). Anthony's wife of a year and a half and mother of a nine month old baby boy (my father James), her life was turned upside down by the events of September 1939. On the first day of the month (the day Hitler invaded Poland) she not only witnessed the departure of her husband – who left home for a posting in Lancashire with the Duke of Lancaster's Yeomanry – but also prepared the family home, Tolson Hall, for the conditions of blackout, which were first enforced at sunset that day. The windows were covered with black Cropper paper, a product that was to find its way on many of the nation's windows during the war.* And as if that was not enough, a party of evacuees from Newcastle arrived, a group of young children with a teacher. "The children arrived last night", Philippa informed her mother on 2 September, "very weepy, but they are very sweet and quite clean."[3] The next day war was officially declared.

James Cropper & Co. was also swiftly affected by the outbreak of hostilities. All those employees who belonged to the territorial ranks – and many had been actively encouraged to join up before the war by their employers – were called up immediately, marking the beginning of a steady flow of labour out of the mills that continued into 1940 and beyond.[4] In addition, the company was also rapidly affected by government controls. Aware of the strategic importance of paper – whether for scientific purposes, writing, drawing, packaging or making munitions – the government set up the Paper Control on the 2 September. James Cropper & Co. themselves became a controlled establishment on 1 October and soon afterwards the Ministry of Supply took over the control and allocation of all stocks of pulp in the country.[5]

Henceforth the government not only regulated the supply and price of raw materials and finished paper but also imposed increasingly strict controls on consumption. Intent on preserving resources for essential needs (the Stationery Office, one of James Cropper & Co.'s largest customers, alone needed 80,000 tons per year) the size of everything from newspapers and menu cards to cheque books was reduced, and it became illegal to start a new paper or periodical of any kind, or publish new guide books or local directories.[6] The use of confetti at weddings was even prohibited, according to one source.[7]

At first, however, James Cropper & Co. was not unduly disrupted. Indeed, if anything the war actually improved trade, for it assured exceptional demand for paper and greater co-operation from customers and competitors. Complaints of faulty paper, for example, almost became a thing of the past. Furthermore, the war injected a new spirit of industriousness into the paper-mills, as James W. noted in May 1940: "Every man has been doing his best to win the war", he commented in the company's annual report, referring to the excellent results. In the first six months of the war stoppages had fallen to a record low – the company's five machines only stopped for thirty-eight hours against an average of 270 hours – and losses in process were smaller than ever. Output, meanwhile, which was yet to be hindered by raw material shortages, reached a record high of 8,000 tons, and

---

* James Cropper & Co. was – and still is – in a minority as a maker of black paper. Most paper-mills refused (and still do) to make black paper lest it contaminate their paler grades. By coincidence, during the war there was a weekly wireless programme called "Mr Cropper's Conscience", which ended with the topical ditty "Is your blackout really black? Can it be detected?".

profits were similarly buoyant. Much helped by the government's regulation of pulp and paper prices, profits jumped to £89,200 in the year to April 1940, the best result since 1920. Half of this sum, however, was returned to the government in the form of tax, principally Excess Profits Duty.[8]

The remaining profit was more than important. After bonuses and dividends had been paid out it was used to fund an extensive programme of modernisation. Two months before war broke out the directors had decided to implement a range of improvements, and with the exception of a second wire on Burneside's No2 machine (which was not installed until 1947) the various works continued in spite of the extreme uncertainties of wartime trading.[9] The salle at Cowan Head was updated in the first few months of the war (at a cost of £5,000), and at the same time new pre-dryers costing £3,000 were fitted on Burneside's No3 machine. Most important, however, were further alterations to Burneside's power plant. Carrying on from the installation of water tube boilers in 1938, in 1940 James Cropper & Co. invested in a new steam turbine, which allowed Cowan Head to be run directly from the switchboard at Burneside. Costing more than £31,000, it was started up in December 1940.[10]

By then the war was beginning to take its toll on the paper-mills, although not in the direct way that it devastated much of Britain during 1940. While bombs rained down on London and other major towns and cities James Cropper & Co. was hit by more mundane problems. By May 1941 the company had lost ninety-nine of its pre-war workforce of 450 to the armed forces and a number of valuable employees to munitions firms. This included several engineers, whose absence was sorely felt.[11] Furthermore, as the war went on and escalated in severity, replacements became harder to find and easier to lose: many were called up having only just finished their training.[12] "There is a constant changing of men", James W. commented in 1941, "and the work of maintaining an adequate staff is constantly more difficult."[13]

By the end of 1940 the ranks of the directors had also been depleted. In December 1940 Geoffrey Acland followed Anthony Cropper into the army, and although both of them spent much of the war on British soil (Anthony was the only one to see service abroad after 1943) neither of them returned to the mills until the end of the war.[14] Nevertheless, the war did not stretch the resources of the management as much it had from 1914 to 1918, when Charles Cropper ran the mills almost alone. This time three directors remained on site – James W., and Alfred and Derek Willink – as well as a full complement of senior managers, including Sam Lindsay, the Burneside Mill manager since 1931, and Herbert Corrie, company secretary since 1910. The company did, however, suffer the permanent loss of one leading figure during the war: Alick McCorquodale, an honorary director since 1896, died in 1941. His nephew Kenneth was appointed to fill his place, reflecting the sizeable holding that the McCorquodale family continued to have in the business.[15] This had diminished little over the years, and still stood at twenty percent in 1952, a hundred years after Kenneth's grandfather George had first joined James Cropper as a partner.[16]

As the war dragged on the company also suffered shortages of female labour. Largely stemming from the number of women drafted into nursing and the land army, this obliged James Cropper & Co. to recruit married women for the first time, breaking a longstanding tradition and unwritten rule that women leave the employ of the company on marriage. Most of those taken on in this way had worked in the mills already.[17]

For those who continued to work for the company during the war, working conditions were less than benign. Shortages of labour forced the firm to revert to twelve-hour shifts in nearly every department, even though the wartime workforce was less physically fit, principally being made up of old men and young boys. The work was also made harder by the materials the company was forced to use, many of which were dirty and unpleasant to handle.[18] Furthermore, as if things were not difficult enough already, the conditions of blackout made the mills gloomy and sunless by day and unbearably hot and stuffy by night.

The situation, however, would have been worse but for one significant development. In February 1942 James Cropper & Co. was appointed an "Essential Works" by the government, reflecting its manufacture of many products which were essential to the war effort, including paper for blacking out and the covers for ration books, the paper for which was impregnated with hairs in order to prevent forgeries.[19] The appointment not only permitted the firm to keep its most important men of military age – slowing down the exodus of men from the paper-mills – but also perhaps helped keep up morale. For employees were now not only serving their firm but also their country, as James W. acknowledged in 1945: "Paper was a necessity for carrying on the war", he wrote in a post-war tribute to the workforce, "and they have not failed their country or their firm."[20]

Essential Works status also gave the company access to a new source of labour. For the rest of the war it was assisted by Italian prisoners-of-war, about twenty of whom were brought in daily from a nearby prison camp. They were a welcome and useful addition to the workforce, despite the reservations of some employees that the Italians were better fed than they were. In 1943 they helped construct large concrete settling tanks at Bowston and Burneside – vital to the purification of effluent – and at other times they worked in the salle and yard at Burneside, sorting waste and finished paper. They were also, according to several sources, quite a hit with the girls. "There weren't many men about you see", one pensioner explains, "and they were Italians . . . they were very friendly". There were not, however, any scandals. "No, no . . . they were taken back to Bela [prison camp] at five o'clock in an open army lorry with a tarpaulin top".

James Cropper & Co.'s appointment as an Essential Works did not, however, solve its greatest difficulty, raw material shortages. This was a major problem from the spring of 1940, when the company's principal source of paper-making material – Scandinavian wood pulp – was cut off by Russia's seizure of Finland and the German invasion of Norway. The last shipment of Scandinavian pulp arrived at Burneside in April 1940, and following that all exports from the Baltic ceased completely.[21] For the rest of the war James Cropper & Co. was dependent on what pulp the Paper Control could secure from the United States and Canada. This did not amount to much: the company's pulp allocation fell from 13,000 tons in 1940 to 5,000 tons in 1941, 3,270 tons in 1942, 2,700 in 1943 and 2,600 in 1944.[22]

James Cropper & Co. attempted to make up the shortfall in a number of ways. First, like most British paper-makers it began to recycle as much waste paper as possible, using more of it than ever before.[23] In 1941 consumption jumped to 4,700 tons, and by 1942 it was a more abundant source of fibre than wood pulp. For the rest of the war the output of Burneside and Cowan Head was at least forty percent waste paper and less than thirty-five percent wood pulp.[24] Waste paper was not, however, always easy to get hold of. With less and less paper coming out of British paper-mills and demand for the material escalating, supplies were for a time very difficult to secure.[25] The situation improved markedly, however, with the formation of the Waste Paper Recovery Association in November 1941.[26] Accompanied by a national advertising campaign to salvage paper (Fig 7.2), waste paper collection rose to one million tons in 1942, and for the rest of the war supplies were more plentiful.[27]

Pulp shortages also compelled James Cropper & Co. to turn to more unusual sources of paper-making fibre. By 1942 the company was using large quantities of materials it had hardly touched in peacetime, including manilla ropes, sisal, and hessian.[28] It even, on one occasion, experimented with sawdust.[29] Above all, however, the company began using jute again, a familiar material to all those who had worked in the mills during the First World War and before. Readily available in the form of old sandbags, this was a key source of paper-making fibre from 1940 into 1945 and beyond.[30]

Jute did not, however, mark the end of James Cropper & Co.'s raw material problems. The output of the mills still fell dramatically during the war, from a pre-war average of almost 15,000 tons per year to 9,000 tons between 1941 and 1945.[31] In particular, the drop owed much to the time it took to process many of the materials the company was compelled to use in the absence of wood pulp. Jute and other such materials not only required cutting up – a job which was often carried out by hand using a large blade sticking out of a bench – but also boiling in caustic, pulping and making into half stuff on a paper machine before they were available for paper-making.[32] Some of this work was carried out at James Cropper

Fig. 7.2 – Wartime advertisement urging householders to recycle paper.

& Co.'s third mill, Bowston – a specialist preparation facility which had been rebuilt and re-equipped in 1930 – but it also used up valuable production time in the company's other mills.[33]

In part, the loss in productivity was covered by the growing value of paper. Fixed by the Paper Control, the price of paper jumped from £29 per ton in 1940 to £53 by 1943. Such increases, dramatic though they were, were not, however, sufficient to stop profits falling. During the early 1940s profit margins grew narrower and narrower, and wartime profits never reached the exceptional levels enjoyed by James Cropper & Co. during the First World War. After the initial heights of 1940 (when a profit of £89,200 was returned) they sank below pre-war levels, reaching a low of £36,000 in 1943-4. The downturn, however, was reversed in 1945 when profits jumped back up to £58,500. This was largely due to the company's purchase of a large quantity of cardboard ammunition containers in the autumn of 1944, which took the place of jute and low quality waste papers.[34] These containers proved to be much cheaper and quicker to process, and in the six months to April 1945 profits more than doubled to £39,000, bringing the wartime years to a more encouraging close.[35]

8

Prosperity and Adversity: 1945-67

A T Burneside, as elsewhere, the advent of peace in the summer of 1945 did not mark a sudden return to peacetime conditions. The Second World War left Britain heavily in debt, compelling the government to retain wartime controls over prices and consumption long after the end of hostilities. "The aftermath of five years of total war has left the world in a sorry state", James Cropper & Co.'s directors explained to their shareholders a year after the end of hostilities, "and it will be some years before the troubled world can hope to settle down to normal trading conditions."[1]

By the summer of 1946 the company was, however, beginning to see the end of labour shortages. By then over two-thirds of the 110 men who had served in the armed forces were back in the paper-mills, bringing to an end the practice of twelve-hour shifts. Amongst this number were Geoffrey Acland, who returned in February 1946, and Anthony Cropper, who was released from war duty in November 1945 and soon afterwards became a full director for the first time. Nine men, however, were never to return, having lost their lives in the war: William Cornthwaite, Frederick Renwick, Derek Snowdon, George Tallon, Douglas Swidenbank, William Hudson, John Knagg, William Metcalfe and Matthew Shepherd.

The Second World War also left an enduring mark on the firm in terms of raw materials. Although Scandinavian pulp (traditionally its chief source of paper-making fibre) began to find its way back into British paper-mills soon after the end of the war, the company continued to be troubled by shortages of material into the 1950s.[2] This was not, however, the result of a genuine scarcity of pulp so much as the consequence of government restrictions. Britain emerged from the war with a severe shortage of foreign currency and a chronic imbalance of payments, a situation that forced the government to limit imports and retain other controls for several years.[3]

Imports of pulp were not overlooked. They continued to be rationed by the

Paper Controller until 1950, and even then James Cropper & Co. was not entirely free to import the material. Although it was able to deal directly with overseas exporters after April 1950 (and Geoffrey Acland soon afterwards visited Scandinavia to make the necessary contacts) import licences were still required. More seriously, the company was still unable to buy as much pulp as it wished owing to currency restrictions.[4] Until the mid-1950s sterling for foreign purchases was allocated to firms by the government and such allocations often fell short of the sums required.[5]

The scarcity of pulp not only kept the output of the Cropper mills below pre-war levels until 1950 but also compelled the company to continue using a range of inferior substitutes. For years after the end of the war the company was forced to use large quantities of waste paper and jute ("which we sincerely hoped we had seen the last of", noted James W. in 1948). In addition, it made use of a number of materials left over from the war, regularly making paper from shell cases, army maps, and even on occasion camouflage netting, digested in boilers and pulped in kollergangs.[6] According to one source this produced such a foul stench that the crews who emptied the boilers were paid revulsion money.[7]

Britain's precarious financial position in the post-war world also limited the extent to which James Cropper & Co. could modernise the mills. Although it managed to upgrade its No2 machine in 1947 – when an additional wire was added at a cost of £24,000 – continuing restrictions prevented it from carrying out other repairs and improvements until the early 1950s.[8] Modernisation plans were, for instance, held back for several years by a pressing shortage of paper-making machinery. Owing to the shortage of foreign currency, the Board of Trade pressurised machinery manufacturers to concentrate on export sales, with the result that new machines for the home market were not readily available until the mid-1950s.[9]

Such shortages and restrictions were a considerable frustration for the directors, who frequently complained that "cramping control" was limiting the growth of their business.[10] The policies and controls that they criticised were not, however, without their benefits. Not least, they successfully prevented (as the government hoped they would) the slump that hit British trade and industry after the post-war boom of 1918-20.[11] Furthermore, if the experience of James Cropper & Co. is any indication, price controls – which remained in place on paper until 1950 – were a help rather than a hindrance. The price of paper made at Burneside and Cowan Head – which advanced from £50 per ton in 1945 to £60 in 1950 – left the company with a more than sufficient margin of profit. Profits jumped from £58,500 in 1945 to an average in excess of £100,000 between 1947 and 1950, in spite of the severe winter and coal crisis of 1947, which shut the mills for several weeks.[12] Indeed, this made scarcely any impact at all on the company's results. In

1947 the firm returned a profit of £106,000, the best result since 1920.

It was a foretaste of things to come. Throughout the 1950s British paper-makers enjoyed a seller's market of exceptional strength and duration, in part due to the benign economic climate.[13] Into the 1960s echoes of the trade cycle of boom and bust were faint, and although there were problems such as the imbalance of payments, for most people it was an age of dramatic advances in wealth and living standards.[14] The fortunes of the British paper industry were also assured by measures limiting domestic and foreign competition. First, within Britain the culture of restrictive practices, prevalent before the war, continued. Until the Restrictive Trade Practices Act was passed in 1956, price-fixing agreements remained in force throughout the industry, heartily endorsed by its governing body.[15] "Consumers and papermakers", the Paper Makers' Association noted in its 1954 Annual Report, "alike recognise the advantages of stability and the grave inconveniences that would result if freely rising and falling prices were to be relied upon to equate demand with supply."[16]

British paper-makers also enjoyed favourable trading conditions owing to measures which restricted foreign competition. Import controls on foreign-made paper (which were not relaxed until 1956) and protective tariffs (which remained in place into the 1960s) reduced imports to the lowest level in decades. Since the 1880s at least a third and sometimes half of the paper consumed in Britain had come from abroad, but from 1945 into the mid-1960s not more than a quarter was foreign-made, the lowest ratio since the 1870s (with the exception of the two World Wars).[17] In such a benign environment the British paper industry, not surprisingly, advanced considerably. Confident that demand was strong and prices stable, paper-makers invested huge sums of money in extra capacity as soon as the machinery was available in the 1950s.[18] Subsequently, the output of British mills rose dramatically, from 2.6m tons in 1950 to over 4.5 tons per year by the mid-1960s.[19]

James Cropper & Co.'s records tell the tale well. In the 1950s demand for its products was exceptionally strong – on occasion it was even forced to ration supplies to customers – while its results broke all previous records.[20] Output levels rose significantly for the first time in decades, from 15,600 tons in 1950 to over 23,000 by the mid-1960s, the most sustained period of growth since the 1900s and 1910s. Furthermore, with the exception of 1953, when the government briefly undermined paper prices by limiting the price of pulp, profits were also greater than ever.[21] Between 1954 and 1956 they averaged over £300,000, and although they fell back to average around £230,000 from 1957 to 1960, this still represented a return of more than twenty percent on the capital employed in the business, an excellent result by any standards.

The most exceptional returns, however, dated from the beginning of the decade. When war broke out in Korea in June 1950, the subsequent programme of rearmament sparked a boom that resulted in acute shortages of raw materials and primary commodities.[22] At Burneside the price of paper rocketed from £60 per ton to a height of £155, pushing up turnover from £943,000 in 1950 to a record £2,438,000 in the twelve months to April 1952. Profits grew even faster, in great part owing to the purchasing policy pursued by Anthony Cropper, who took care of pulp buying.[23] Anticipating that the price of pulp and paper would continue to rise, in 1951 and 1952 he filled the pulp sheds to the roof early in the year, exploiting the company's abundant reserves of cash. Although speculating on the future price of pulp and paper was not without its risks – as he and his fellow directors were well aware, keeping cash on reserve in case of falls – in the event the strategy paid off.[24] In both years prices rose considerably after the pulp had been bought, leading to dramatic increases in profits.[25] Between 1950 and 1952 James Cropper & Co.'s profits soared fourfold to more than £400,000, a level that was not surpassed until 1979.

The early 1950s were also notable years for James Cropper & Co. in terms of the company's status. In June 1951 the private company formed in 1889 was floated on the London Stock Exchange as a public company. "The main reason for this", explained Derek Willink at the time, "is that as a private company difficulty may be experienced in selling shares when they become available, especially in these days when savings by individuals are almost impossible."[26] At the time this was a pressing issue. Following the death of Alfred Willink in 1947, his executors wished to sell a fair share of his stake to cover bequests and death duties, but there were few takers within the firm.[27] Instead, they were sold a month after the company went public to a range of individuals and institutions including the Scottish Amicable and Friends Provident.[28]

Such investors would not have been disappointed with their new holding. Between 1951 and 1956 over £110,000 of bonus shares were issued to shareholders, a just reflection of the company's growing asset value, which jumped by fifty percent to more than £1.25m.[29] They did not, however, especially benefit from the exceptional profits of the era. Although it was in the self-interest of the directors to distribute a good share of the gains – between them the directors and their families still owned most of the shares – they resisted doing so, as they had many times before. Dividend payments remained modest throughout the 1950s, as did the bonuses they paid themselves, which were scarcely more than the sums paid out in the 1920s and 1930s.[30]

The directors had good reason to keep a good proportion of profits in company coffers. Between 1951 and 1957 James Cropper & Co. spent over £880,000 on one of the most extensive programmes of modernisation in decades, and almost three-quarters of this sum was taken directly out of profits. Originally drawn up in the late 1940s and overseen by the company's chief engineer James Hill (who was appointed on James Arnot's retirement in 1949) the plans centred upon the installation of new paper-making machines for the first time in fifty years.[31] In 1955 a new ninety-two inch MG machine made by Bertrams Ltd of Edinburgh was installed in the old cutter house at Burneside (Fig. 8.1). Costing over £150,000, it was a long overdue replacement for the company's ancient No3 machine, which dated back to 1871. Two years later Bertrams also replaced the company's No1 machine, which dated from 1887. In 1957 it was rebuilt, enlarged and converted into a seventy-two inch twin-wire Fourdrinier, a project that cost £225,000 by the time it was completed.

Fig. 8.1 – Delivery of the MG cyclinder for the new No3 machine installed at Burneside in 1955.

The work did not stop there. Other major improvements carried through in the 1950s include the reorganisation of Burneside's finishing end, the construction of a small machine at Bowston to make wrappers (out of old parts), and the installation of Bertram pulpers at Burneside, a more efficient and less laborious means of processing pulp.[32] At the same time Burneside's power plant was enlarged to cope with the increasing capacity of the mills.[33] Last and not least, by the mid-1950s the mills had been converted to run off AC electricity with individual electric drives fitted on all items of machinery. This was an expensive and time consuming project, but worthwhile all the same: at Burneside it enabled the company to scrap its main shaft and do away with a countless number of belts and rope drives, any one of which could stop a machine for a day if it broke.[34]

As the mills advanced in size and efficiency, the company also took steps to extend and improve the range of papers it made. New grades introduced during the 1950s included mottled papers for lining lever arch and box files, smooth water-finished papers (following the introduction of water doctors on No4 machine in 1958) and thinner and stronger kraft papers, which took the place of more old fashioned wrappings.[35] The 1960s, meanwhile, witnessed the launch of Bowston cover paper (a cheaper range designed to use up broke*), imitation book-cloth made for Winterbottom (the origin of the bookbinding range made for Winter & Co. today), and the introduction of acid-free papers (again, an important feature of the company's range today).[36] This owed everything to the launch of Aquapel, an alkaline sizing agent, the development of which in turn was tied to the advent of litho-printing, a process that worked better on acid-free paper, as the ink dried faster. Its introduction at Burneside, however, was driven by one of the company's biggest customers during the 1960s, Star Paper Mills.[37] Star stipulated that the smooth white "cast coating base" made on Burneside's No4 machine be acid-free, and helped the company introduce and perfect the process.†

In part the development of new grades reflected the demise of old lines. In the 1950s, for example, the company stopped making insulating paper (which it had made since the 1900s), while the next decade saw the decline of glazed casings for wrapping textiles, a product that had been made at Burneside and Cowan Head as long as the mills had existed.[38] On the whole, however, James Cropper & Co. continue to enjoy good markets for many of its traditional grades into the 1960s. This included MG envelope paper (made since the 1860s, and supplied to customers including John Dickinson, Butt Brothers & Cooke, and the Manchester Envelope Co.) and cloth-lined paper for registered envelopes, which had been supplied to the Post Office through McCorquodale & Co. since the 1880s.[39]‡ The company's most important products in the 1950s and 1960s, however, largely dated from the inter-war years. This included MG pasted board, green paper for Brooke Bond tea packets, coloured and embossed cover papers (Fig. 8.2), manilla

---

*   Broke is waste-paper produced within the mill which is then recycled.

†   Star Paper Mills coated the Cropper base with an extremely glossy finish, turning the grade into a product used for greeting cards, high quality cosmetic packaging and the covers of glossy magazines. Supplying a base of sufficient quality was something of a battle for James Cropper & Co., which was hampered by the age of the machine on which it was produced, and by the nature of Aquapel. If the paper was not dried absolutely right, the sizing on the paper would not cure properly. Furthermore, Aquapel released much more dirt from the machine into the paper than conventional size. (Interview: Nick Willink, John Larking)

‡   Cloth-lined paper was also made into Bartholomew maps and continued to be made at Cowan Head by the process patented by Charles Cropper in 1879. Remarkably, the process still remained a secret and continued to give James Cropper & Co. a competitive advantage over other makers of the grade.

Fig. 8.2 – Kendal Covers brochure, circa 1965, just after the firm
had adopted its Cropper pigeon logo.

made for HMSO (one of the company's largest and most enduring contracts) and
last and not least waxing cartridge for milk and ice cream cartons.[40] "It must be
regarded as one of our life lines", Geoffrey Acland noted of this grade in 1953.
"According to figures recently published we produce nearly two thirds of the
Waxing Cartridge made in the country".[41] At that time waxing cartridge was
keeping No4 machine going for nearly two weeks per month, and owing to
massive contracts with Mono Containers – who at one time even tried to persuade
James Cropper & Co. to build a new machine solely for its manufacture – it
remained a key product into the 1960s.[42]

The variety and endurance of James Cropper & Co.'s product range was not,
however, a cause for complacency, as the directors were well aware. "We have to
make papers cheaper and better", noted Geoffrey Acland in 1958, echoing
sentiments he had expressed the year before. "There is a general tightening of
standards required by customers", he informed the Mill Council (formed in 1947)
in March 1957. "Modern fast running machinery requires greater accuracy of
product and what was at one time considered a minor complaint could now be a
very serious one."[43] Anthony Cropper was even more forthright: "Unless we
produce good paper as efficiently as possible the future of these Mills and all who
work here may be in danger", he wrote in a circular letter sent to every employee
on 1 January 1957. He had only just become chairman on the death of his father
at the age of seventy-seven, and was keen to make his mark. In the open letter he
not only asked employees to keep machines in good order and running at full

speed, but also, importantly, emphasised the value of the product they handled every day. "Handle all paper in process with great care", he beseeched them

> . . . and remember all the time that a sheet of paper is a valuable thing – a Double Crown sheet of Medium Weight Cover Paper is worth 2^1/2d and if you tear or deface a sheet it is the same as throwing away a 2^1/2d postage stamp.[44]

Nurturing a culture of productivity, vigilance and low wastage could not, however, overcome one major problem. Paper-making at Burneside and Cowan Head was still a remarkably crude affair. Although the mills were full of massive and intricate machinery, in the 1950s paper-makers still depended almost wholly on their own judgement and experience to monitor and control the manufacture of paper. There were hardly any gauges on the machines, scarcely any scientific back-up, no charts nor formulae to refer to, and little in the way of formal training. Furthermore, given the value of experience, information was not readily shared. A machine-man might on occasion refer to a small note-book in his pocket – the fruits of years of experience – but seldom would he share the know-how therein with his assistants. "In those days the top men would never tell you anything", recalls Alf Whiteley, who started work on Burneside's No4 machine in the late 1940s. "They were frightened of losing their jobs, perhaps. You had to learn by watching."[45]

There was a lot to learn. Even though the machines were faster and more efficient than ever, the colour, consistency and weight of any given paper were still controlled by hand. The beater-man, for example, would decide whether or not

Fig. 8.3 – Beaters at Burneside Mills, 1955; their design had changed little in two centuries.

the stuff in his beaters was ready by a variety of crude tests, including pouring a diluted sample from one bowl to another.[46] The addition of colour and chemicals – all of which were added at the beating stage (Fig. 8.3), leaving little margin for error – was likewise left to the beater-man's judgement, carried out without reference to standardised charts or scientific recipes and using his personal collection of measuring vessels, mugs and cocoa tins included.[47] In this way beater-men numbered amongst the most skilled men in the mills. There was still, however, an inevitable margin of error. In 1963, for example, Derek Willink was forced to issue a memo to the beater-men after a spate of complaints about colour-matching (Fig 8.4).[48]

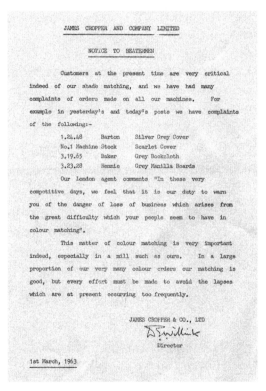

Fig. 8.4 – Notice issued to beater-men by Derek Willink, March 1963.

Testing the properties of a batch of paper was equally primitive. To check the shade of an MG paper, for example, the beater-man would rush to the other end of the mill and tear a small sample off the first reel of paper made, which he would then lick to see how the shade matched what he was preparing. This did not, however, always meet with the approval of the mill manager, Fred Craig.

On one occasion he ran into Billy Fawcett, the No3 beaterman, testing the shade of a new batch of paper. "That'll be all right", said Billy, licking a small sample. "Will it be all right Billy?" said Fred. "Are you going to lick all bloody six ton?"[49]

The men who tended the paper-making machines – who were responsible for controlling the thickness, flatness and moisture content of paper – also depended on their own judgement and experience. Everything had to be checked and adjusted by hand – including wires, felts, slices and the speed of the machine – and with a minimum of auxiliary equipment and controls. Altering the thickness of the sheet being made, for example, was achieved by minutely increasing or decreasing the volume of stuff flowing on to the wire, all the while bearing in mind the speed of the machine. Yet this was not carried out with one eye on a gauge and the other on a control calibrated and marked for fine adjustment. Instead, as many employees can remember, the lever on the stuff valve was knocked with a spanner.

Adjusting the flow of stuff onto the wire – to ensure that the paper was even across the sheet – was equally crude, especially in comparison with the precision of today's Voith head-boxes. Into the 1960s it was controlled with the aid of a building brick placed in the head-box, all of which were open at the time. This was then moved around to restrict or divert the flow in front of the slices.[50] Likewise, measuring the accuracy of the paper coming off the machine was also left to the judgement of machine-men, who would tear a piece of paper out of the web a few times every reel, and feel its thickness by hand.[51] "Machine-men could tell you the lbs Double Crown weight just by the feel of it", recalls Mike Wilkinson, who started work at Burneside in 1951, "and made paper virtually by the rule of thumb". It is a verdict reiterated by many, including Robin Field. "It was witchcraft rather than science", he remarks of the way James Cropper & Co. made paper when he joined the firm in 1962.

The days of paper-making as a craft were, however, numbered. By the early 1960s a programme of technical development was beginning to do away with traditional manufacturing methods, as Derek Willink suggested a year later. "Change" is a word very much in use at the present time", he told the Mill Council in April 1963, "and we are certainly very much involved . . . In the field of production methods we are trying to turn over from what could be called a craftsman approach to a more scientific approach".[52]

Although it was not until the early 1960s that the mills really began to change, the break with the past began in the 1950s. In 1952, for example, the company installed fluorescent lighting throughout the mills, one of the first paper manufacturers in the country to do so.[53] Costing £14,000 it allowed employees to prepare, make and sort paper more accurately than before (as well as at all times of day), especially in the beater house. "In no part of the mill is good lighting more desirable", the *Electrical Review* noted in an article describing the pioneering installation. "The colouring of the pulp which takes place at this stage is subject to many variables that may cause differences in depth or hue . . . In good daylight the differences are readily detected, but in poor daylight, or under tungsten light, they may pass unobserved."[54]

The next steps to improving the production of paper were more direct. In the course of the 1950s the company appointed paper testers to analyse the properties of every reel of paper coming off the machines – the first move towards a systematic monitoring of output – and invested in a new laboratory filled with up-to-date equipment.[55] More importantly, as the 1950s drew to a close James Cropper & Co. began investing in auxiliary equipment for the machines themselves. Bauer centri-cleaners, for example – which removed dirt from the stuff – were installed on all four machines at Burneside between 1957 and 1960, and in the same period measuring instruments were fitted to machines for the first time. In 1957 a Baldwin Automat (a basic weight gauge) and a De Zurick regulator (which controlled fibre consistency) were put on No4 machine.[56]

It was a foretaste of things to come. In the early 1960s the drive for improvement not only became more urgent, but also more wide-ranging. New incentive schemes were introduced, for example, on individual items of plant and machinery, with the hope that employees might be encouraged to work more efficiently.[57]* Efforts were also made to nurture a new culture of teamwork and knowledge-sharing, and overcome decades of secrecy and division between men of different ages and experience. "In the personnel field we are reviewing all our procedures", Derek Willink informed the Mill Council in 1963 –

> . . . and one of the factors that has come most to the fore is the great need to achieve successful team work. This requires all leading hands to realise that part of their job is to help, encourage and explain requirements to junior members.[58]

In addition, James Cropper & Co. began to offer a measure of formal training for the first time. In 1961 an educational scheme was started, offering employees the

---

* The new incentive schemes were introduced in conjunction with Associated Industrial Consultants, a London firm of a new breed of business adviser at the time, the management consultant. They had their benefits (particularly in the salle) but were – in the long run – of questionable value. Indeed, owing to the number of individual schemes that were set up (there was one for each department) and the difficulty of calculating where and when employees should be rewarded, they were themselves a source of inefficiency. A new "Work Study" department had to be set up to administer them (employing eleven individuals by 1966), lending weight to the view that the real beneficiaries were not James Cropper & Co. but the consultants, who billed the company thousands of pounds for their time and advice.

chance to study for a City & Guilds certificate in paper-making. Instigated and presided over by Geoffrey Acland's son, Oliver, and Derek Willink's son, Nick, who had both recently joined the company (and of whom more in Chapter Nine), it aimed to improve the practical skills of employees by giving them a basic grounding in the theory of paper-making. And there was, it seems, a thirst for such knowledge: of the sixty-five employees eligible for the course in 1961, thirty-seven agreed to take it.[59]

In the main, however, James Cropper & Co.'s quest for better paper-making in the 1960s continued to be forged through a programme of technical improvements. This became increasingly organised: in 1962 a special committee was formed to oversee technical development, and more actively seek and take advantage of new technologies as they became available.[60]

In part the drive for improvement was led from within, by such individuals as George Ferrier, the mill chemist since 1943, and the Burneside manager Fred Craig (who was a leading member of the Technical Section of the Paper Maker's Association and a keen advocate of innovation).[61] The firm's efforts to improve its paper-making capabilities also led them to recruit expertise from outside the firm. In 1962, for example, Robin Field joined the laboratory staff as an assistant chemist, while in 1963 an instrument engineer, Tony Blades, was taken on for the first time.[62] The most important arrival of all, however, was that of John Larking. Recruited to act as a technical advisor and improve technical controls on the machines, he joined James Cropper & Co. in January 1962, after eleven years working in a technical capacity for Whatman in Kent, manufacturers of specialist filter papers.[63]

Larking soon made his mark. Within a year and a half he had been promoted to the position of deputy manager of Burneside, not only responsible for technical controls on machines but also for production, new papers, trials and all errors of manufacture.[64] In the intervening period, meanwhile, he supervised the installation of a range of equipment that began to transform the manufacture of paper. Led by Nick Willink, the work was carried through by a newly created Technical Department (whose members included Maurice Crossley, Robin Field and Tony Blades). In 1963 they fitted moisture meters to Nos 1, 3 and 4 machines, the first steps towards forming a uniformly flat sheet of paper (and preventing the practice of over-drying). At the same time magnetic flow meters were attached to pipes, eliminating the need for guesswork when stuff valves were being opened and closed. Furthermore, in the beater house a small laboratory was set up, where hand sheets were made and tested before the contents of a beater was dispatched. This was John Larking's brainchild, as was the introduction of continuous sizing on all four of Burneside's machines. Completed in 1964, this involved automating the addition of rosin size and alum to the stuff as it approached the paper machine, rather than adding it in batches to beaters by the bucket-load, a sticky and inaccurate procedure. The project was initially viewed with great scepticism by many of John's superiors, but it soon proved its worth: it not only led to greater control, but also to savings in labour as well as size.[65]

Such changes were important. By the early 1960s paper-making was not the goldmine it had been in the previous decade, and any measures that protected profit margins or improved products were no longer a choice so much as a necessity. The first signs of tougher times to come had emerged in 1957, but it was not until the early 1960s that trading conditions really began to deteriorate, as Fred Craig indicated in July 1961.[66] "Up to last year, demand outstripped supply and during that year and early this year, customers continued to buy heavily for stock", he informed the Mill Council, "but by the beginning of this year, supply began to outstrip demand."[67] As a result James Cropper & Co. found orders harder to come by, and experienced great difficulty passing growing costs on to customers.[68] The company's results tell the tale well: in the twelve months to April 1962 profits fell to £171,100 – the worst result since 1950 – while the return of profit on sales fell below ten percent for the first time since 1944. Nor was there much in the way of a recovery in subsequent years. With the exception of 1967 – when James Cropper & Co. made £249,000 – profits remained below 1950s levels for the rest of the decade, even though turnover continued to increase year on year.

In part the harsher economic climate was to blame for the reversal of fortunes.[69] More significantly, however, the fortunes of paper-mills were hit by greater foreign competition, which in turn was fostered by the British government's decision, announced in 1959, to join a group of other European countries in the European Free Trade Association (EFTA).[70] The group's members included Sweden, Norway and latterly Finland, paper from which countries soon began landing on British shores in greater quantities than ever before. Such paper not only increased competition but also depressed prices, as most of it was sold at a discount to British-made paper, a reflection of the lower cost of production in Scandinavia's new integrated paper and pulp mills. Kraft paper made at Burneside, for example, fell dramatically in profitability owing to competition from Scandinavia (where it was a popular product). The profit it yielded the company fell from £12 per ton in 1959 to £3 by 1963.[71]

The immediate impact of EFTA was not, however, as disastrous as many paper-makers had feared. The reduction in tariffs was partially offset by other measures – including a temporary import surcharge of ten to fifteen percent, in force between 1964 and 1966 – and import penetration only grew gradually in the first few years of the agreement.[72] It was, however, the last thing that the company needed, as the same period that saw Britain joining EFTA was also an extremely testing time closer to home. For from 1957 into the early 1960s the prosperity – and indeed the survival – of the paper-mills were threatened by a problem that the company only had itself to blame for: pollution.

In 1957 James Cropper & Co. was taken to the high court in London by the Kent Angling Association, who obtained an injunction requiring the firm to stop polluting the river Kent (Fig 8.5). The event marked the beginning of years of conflict and anxiety for the company over pollution, but it was also the culmination of decades of disputes between the firm and local fisherman. The river Kent between Cowan Head and Burneside had long been popular with fisherman for its wild brown trout and runs of salmon and sea trout, a fact suggested by the long-established name of the local pub, the Anglers' Inn (now the Jolly Anglers').[73] For almost as long, however, fish stocks on this stretch of river had been depleted by pollution from the paper-mills. Records of pollution – which, it is worth noting, are to be found in old newspapers more than in company archives – can be found in almost every decade from the 1840s to the 1950s.[74]

On occasion the problem was confined to isolated incidents. In 1862, for example, the outflow from a burst pipe poisoned hundreds of fish at Burneside, an accident which led to the company's first confrontation with the recently formed Kent Angling Association, who were awarded £5 in damages at a tribunal in Kendal's Town Hall.* At other times, however, it was more sustained, as at Bowston Mill in the 1880s. Constructed in 1879 for the preparation of raw materials – which consumed large quantities of corrosive chemicals – for several

Fig. 8.5 – The river Kent at Burneside c.1900. The peaceful scene belies the damage the paper-mill was inflicting on the river, a dark episode in its history that persisted for many decades. (Source: Margaret Duff collection)

years fish stocks were poisoned by bleach seeping into the river from lime tanks. At the same time fibres from the washing of rags and jute made the river so filthy that fishing was impossible even if there was anything to catch. "The overflow from the tanks comes into the mill race and brings down jute", James Whitehead, a Kendal fishmonger explained at the time. "You cannot fish as your line and flies get covered with small fibres".[75]

In 1889 James Cropper & Co. was severely censured for such pollution at a meeting of the local River Pollution Committee, specially convened by the recently formed Westmorland County Council (whose chairman happened to be James Cropper).[76] The hearing did not, however, seem to improve matters very much. References to pollution from the paper-mills continue into the 1890s and beyond. In 1894, for example, the *Westmorland Gazette* reported that the river between Bowston and Burneside was almost completely devoid of natural life. "The bed of the river is bedded in fibrous dirt", the paper informed its readers, "and destitute of lesser fish such as bully-frogs and eel-roach, once abundant twenty-five years ago."[77]

At times the company did take steps to improve matters. In 1848, for example, the *Kendal Mercury* reported that James Cropper had announced that he would cease "emptying the contents of the dye-vats at his works into the river, a determination which will be hailed by lovers of angling".[78]† In addition, by the 1880s there were settling tanks at Bowston, which were further improved in 1889 with the installation of screens to filter out fibres. More often than not, however, the company continued to pollute the river. In part ignorance was to blame. In 1868, for example, it informed the Rivers Pollution Commission that it did not pollute the river, yet at the same time admitted that the "whole of the liquid refuse from washing, boiling of rags, and other processes of the manufacture flows direct into the stream".[79] It was, it seems, unaware that such discharge was harmful. Rags were boiled in caustic soda, an extremely corrosive chemical.

On other occasions the directors were well aware that effluent from the paper-mills could pollute the river, but failed to improve matters either out of general indifference or because they felt there was no satisfactory alternative. During the

---

* The newspaper report that refers to this incident notes: "About six years ago the fish had been poisoned in their thousands from Mr Cropper's works, but no association existed at that time. But on this occasion now charged against Mr Cropper hundreds of fish had been destroyed, and this fortunately came to the ears of the association [who] thought that the law should be appealed to, in order to show the importance of the matter to the public." (*Kendal Mercury*, 17 Jan. 1863)

† It is questionable, however, whether he kept to his word. In 1889 Thomas Hully of Burneside, a Water Bailiff, informed the River Pollution Committee of the Westmorland County Council that the tail race at Burneside was sometimes "of a yellow, blue, pink or red colour, according to the different makings of the paper". (CA/9/2)

First World War, for example, Charles Cropper justified polluting the river on purely practical grounds. "The refuse from [Burneside Mills] is colossal", he wrote to James W. in October 1916. "Alfred [Willink] takes the high moral tone and says it ought not to go into the river, but if I had not got rid of it down the river in floods, these two last winters, and a huge quantity already this October, the mills and place would have been absolutely bunged up."[80]

Following the end of the First World War James Cropper & Co. did begin to act more responsibly. In 1919 three new settling ponds and a pump house and drain were built at Burneside, and a year later Cowan Head's effluent treatment plant was also upgraded.[81] These facilities were further improved during the Second World War, when two more settling ponds were built at Burneside by Italian prisoners of war, and by the 1950s the company was also taking steps to improve their effectiveness by reducing water consumption.[82]

For a while such measures seem to have been effective. Between 1920 and 1950 records of pollution incidents fell to an all-time low. Only one is referred to in company archives for the period.[83] By the mid-1950s, however, the company was once again in trouble. In July 1955 a spillage of bleach at Bowston killed hundreds of fish, and although the matter was quickly settled with the Kent Angling Association (which was awarded £158 in damages, mainly for restocking), there were growing signs that its members would not tolerate such occurrences for much longer.[84] Soon after the incident they appointed a firm of London solicitors, Gerrish & Co., to advise and represent them, and commissioned an expert on fish pollution, Dr Ronald Killie of Edinburgh University, to examine the state of the river.

He found more than they (and indeed James Cropper & Co.) had bargained for. In addition to the damage inflicted by the bleach (which he estimated would affect the river for about a year) he discovered another form of pollution: a fine silt, up to three inches deep in places, which blanketed large parts of the river bed below Burneside Mills. This had first been noticed in 1937, but little attention had been paid to it in the intervening years, mainly owing to the fact that it was non-toxic and did not contravene the standards set by the Lancashire River Board. However, it was – reported Dr Killie – clearly harmful to fish life. He explained that the silt killed or prevented the natural propagation of fish food such as freshwater shrimps, snails and fly life, and that as long as it was there the river would not carry a normal population of fish.[85]

Alarmed by Dr Killie's report, the Kent Angling Association quickly convened the first ever official meeting with James Cropper & Co., which took place at Burneside in December 1955. There it informed the company's directors about the new findings and asked them to investigate the causes for the sediment, which it thought might emanate from untreated effluent leaking into the river.[86] The company does not, however, seem to have taken the request all that seriously.

Although it took some steps to prevent the overflow of raw effluent into the river Kent during 1956, the measures did not go far enough, especially in light of the extra waste produced by Burneside's two new machines, which started up in 1955 and 1957. "Unfortunately our engineering and paper-making staff were so occupied with the start up of these machines", Anthony Cropper later admitted, "that they did not sufficiently appreciate that these new machines would overload our existing effluent treatment plant".[87] As a result, the condition of the Kent actually worsened in 1956 and 1957, with crude effluent regularly escaping into the river, and a layer of fibres and other waste forming a layer of sediment on its bottom.[88]

Angered by the state of affairs, the Kent Angling Association's next attempt to tackle the ongoing pollution was more decisive. In October 1957, after repeated warnings communicated through Gerrish & Co., six members of the association (supported by the Anglers' Co-operative Society) instigated legal proceedings against James Cropper & Co.[89] This resulted in a hearing at the High Court in London, where a permanent injunction was served on the company, obliging it to stop polluting the river by the end of May 1958.[90]

Following the hearing James Cropper & Co. spent over £14,000 on improvements to its effluent treatment facilities, mostly at Burneside, where additional settling capacity, pumps and a fibre recovery unit were installed.[91] At first these measures worked. The layer of sediment on the riverbed seems to have disappeared, and the Kent Angling Association reported that fishing in the reach below the mills was satisfactory during the next two fishing seasons. Towards the end of 1959, however, George Ferrier, James Cropper & Co.'s chief chemist, began to notice that the purified effluent being discharged into the river was sometimes cloudy. Without delay he began to look into the cause of this, but by the time he discovered the root of the problem – which was tied to the company's recent use of large quantities of starch in the paper-making process – it was too late.*

Towards the end of March 1960 the Kent Angling Association discovered sewage fungus on the river bed below Burneside Mills, a fluffy grey deposit which was also related to the greater quantities of starch in James Cropper & Co.'s effluent. Its origin could be traced back to a pipe coming from the settling ponds,

---

* The company's use of Stadex, a brand of starch, had increased from 350cwt in the half year to April 1957 to 1800cwts in the half year to April 1960. George Ferrier found that when large amounts of it were being used in the mills, it held mineral substances such as clay, titanium and alum in suspension. These substances only precipitated from the effluent when it was discharged into the river, owing to a difference in pH levels between the river water and that in the settling ponds. As a result he decided to order equipment to control the pH level of the effluent, and in April 1960 made contact with the necessary suppliers. The court action commenced on 18 May. (CA/Court Action and Pollution Box)

and faced with such evidence, the anglers did not hesitate to pursue the matter at the highest level. On 18 May 1960 they applied to the High Court to confiscate James Cropper & Co.'s assets for breach of the 1957 injunction.

It was the most mortal threat the company had ever faced. If the court order was granted, the Kent Angling Association would be able to put the company out of business and almost six hundred people out of work.[92] In the subsequent court hearings, however, which took place in London in June and July 1960, James Cropper & Co. narrowly managed to escape disaster. Helped significantly by its solicitors, Richards, Butler & Co, it successfully fought off the action by swiftly carrying out a range of remedial measures.[93] By October it had invested over £38,000 trying to prevent the formation of sewage fungus in the river Kent, and by April 1961 had spent over £60,000 trying to put matters right.[94] Equipment installed included a plant to control the pH of the effluent automatically, and a pipeline and pumps to transfer the effluent to a marshy area where it was hoped the sewage fungus would grow instead of in the river.[95] This arrangement not only had the full backing of the Paper Industry Research Association (PIRA), but also of the presiding judge who finally drew the case to a close in December 1960, satisfied that the company had fulfilled its obligations.[96]

The work did not, however, mark the end of the problem. Although the Kent Anglers reported in 1963 that the river was cleaner than ever (for which they congratulated the firm) in truth the new treatment system never worked satisfactorily. While the sewage fungus grew well in the new ponds, it never grew sufficiently to have a significant effect on growths in the river, which continued to occur throughout the 1960s and 1970s when water levels were low.[97] As a result the threat of closure hung over the company long after the end of 1960 court case.

The Kent Angling Association's injunction remained fully binding and could have been invoked at any time given the ongoing pollution. In the event, however, the anglers never pressed charges against the firm. In part they perhaps feared putting so many people out of work, but they were also probably aware that James Cropper & Co. was doing everything in its power to overcome the ongoing pollution. Work on treatment facilities continued throughout the 1960s and 1970s, and from 1971 the firm participated in a number of research projects to establish the causes of sewage fungus and the best way of treating it. Carried out in conjunction with PIRA, the North West Water Authority and the Department of the Environment, these revealed that sewage fungus was in fact far more difficult to control that had previously been thought. It could grow in very low concentrations of glucose and other starch derivatives, and could only be effectively prevented if the effluent from the paper-mills was treated in conjunction with domestic effluent.[98]

Faced with these conclusions, James Cropper & Co. pursued the only option left open. In 1979 it decided (after two years of discussions with the North West Water Authority) to send all its effluent through a sewer to the Kendal Sewage Treatment Works, which was due to be rebuilt. It was an expensive solution: by the time the work was finished in 1982 it cost the company over £300,000, and processing the effluent in this way has incurred the company over £150,000 in extra costs per year ever since (equivalent to £5 per ton of paper made in 1982).[99] The project was, however, vitally necessary, for it finally brought the issue of pollution to a close. "If we are to protect the local environment and at the same time continue in business", explained James Cropper in the company's 1982 Annual Report, "then these costs have to be met".[100]

Looking beyond pollution, the late 1950s and early 1960s were also bad times for James Cropper & Co. in terms of accidents. Incidents of injuries in the workplace were more frequent than ever, with more than forty accidents per year reported between 1956 and 1964, well above the levels of previous decades. Some were relatively minor and the affected employees soon returned to work, but a great number were more severe. Most employees who sustained injuries were off work for weeks rather than days, and the list of injuries they sustained provides an appalling testament to the persisting hazards of paper-mill work and the lack of sufficient safeguards. Hand injuries, for example, were still commonplace, reflecting the manual nature of much of the work, which included feeding and unblocking machines by hand while they were moving. Company records detail numerous occasions on which fingers or hands were cut, bruised, crushed or fractured, and some employees even lost fingers.[101] Other common injuries included crushed toes and strained backs and shoulders, owing to the fact that many heavy items (including reels of paper and broke) were still lifted by hand.

Amongst those who sustained the most severe injuries were R. E. Hutchinson (head injuries, 1957), Leslie Dixon (fractured and lacerated arm, 1959), Thomas Woof (head and wrist injuries, 1959), and Thomas Bainbridge (head injuries and fractured right clavicle, 1961).[102] All were off work for months, but did eventually return to work. The worst accidents of all were fatal. In June 1958 Angus Carruthers, a member of the firm's building maintenance team, died after falling through an asbestos roof at Bowston Mill. The inquest heard that he was about to repair a wall when the accident occurred, and was not meant to be on the roof. Nevertheless, the company was severely censured for failing to post warning notices about the fragile state of the asbestos, and for failing to supply suitable ladders or crawling boards.[103]

It was not the only fatal accident to take place in the Cropper mills in the course of the 1950s and 1960s. In November 1965 Ronald Walker, a fitter's mate who had worked for the company for fourteen years, was killed at Burneside when an eight foot air compressor he and others were moving crushed him against a wall.[104] He was thirty-five years old. Standing on three legs, the compressor had suddenly swung round as he unhitched it from the block and tackle being used to winch it up. The inquest was told that the fitter in charge, Alan Brockbank, had warned him to stand back as he removed the block and tackle, but the tank had trapped him against a wall. A verdict of accidental death was returned.[105]

In spite of such accidents James Cropper & Co. was taking more steps than ever to make the mills safer to work in. In the late 1940s, for example, the company began to offer employees First Aid training for the first time, and in 1950 a more general drive to improve safety was initiated.[106] Progress, however, was slow. The introduction of safety footwear, for example, which was first proposed in 1950, was still in its early stages in 1958.[107] Furthermore, while there is evidence that the company began to try to reduce dangerous practices and dangerous places in the mills, there was no wholesale change in the culture of safety in the mills for many years.[108] One campaign for employees to be more careful – which was expressed in a "Take Care" notice posted throughout the mills in 1964 – illustrates this well. It seems to have been totally ignored: within a month and a half of the campaign being launched over forty (mostly minor) accidents had occurred.[109]

James Cropper & Co.'s next attempt to improve safety was more decisive. In September 1964 it decided to appoint a full-time safety officer for the first time, recruiting Sam Jenkins to fill the post.[110] Thereafter the drive for greater safety was more sustained and systematic. The results were not, however, instantaneous. As Sam Jenkins discovered, most accidents were not the fault of the company but the result of the carelessness of individuals. "Carelessness, indifference and a complete disregard for the safety of themselves or others, all these attitudes have contributed", he noted in 1966, referring to figures that indicated that ninety percent of recent accidents were the "faults of persons".[111] In this way, improving safety involved changing the outlook of every member of the company's six hundred strong workforce, a process that (inevitably) took time, effort and training.

The post-war years also saw James Cropper & Co. beginning to improve the working environment in other ways. In 1948 the company appointed its first welfare officer (promoting Harold Snowdon to fill the role) and in the next two decades various measures gradually changed working conditions for the better.[112] In 1951, for example, an extra six days holiday was granted to all (taking the total to eighteen including six bank holidays) and in 1955 a new pension scheme was set up.[113] It was, however, only open to members of staff, and it was not until the late 1970s that pensions were offered to all company employees.[114] In 1960, meanwhile, a shorter working week was introduced without any reductions in pay, resulting in a forty-two hour week for shift-workers (down from forty-four) and a forty-three hour week for day workers (down from forty-five).[115]

Other sundry improvements carried through in the 1950s and 1960s included the installation of indoor sanitation in company housing, the introduction of "Music while you work" in Burneside salle in 1953 (broadcast through loudspeakers), and the construction of a vast new canteen at Burneside in 1956.[116] Here employees were served with hot food at subsidised rates, cooked up by a team of newly appointed dinner ladies. In the past they had been expected to cater for themselves (although hot water and the occasional cake was provided), and the change did away with a number of traditions.[117] Before the advent of the canteen one of the duties of machine assistants was to cook up breakfast for their superiors using rudimentary facilities in a shed at the back of the mill.[118] Lunch, meanwhile, was sometimes fetched by assistants or brought in by wives, children, and even – if one story is to be believed – a dog. According to one source, Abe Aplin, one-time No4 beater-man, sometimes had his lunch delivered to him by his collie, Punch, who brought it in a basket all the way from Hollins Row, a quarter of a mile away.[119]

The gradual improvement in working conditions was in great part driven by the growing say that employees had in such matters. In the late 1940s the mills were officially linked up with the unions for the first time, the majority of employees joining the National Union of Printing, Bookbinding and Paper Workers, who were represented in the mills by John Storey and Harry Wilson. Thereafter the company largely deferred to national agreements between the Union and the Paper-Makers Federation (representing employers) on important issues such as wages and holidays.*

Around the same time, company employees gained further representation through the Mill Council, which was formed in 1947. Every department of the mill was represented by an employee elected by their peers, and the council met once a month to discuss issues such as wages, housing and the general working environment. Designed to improve communication between management and workers, the actual powers of the council were limited to making recommendations. Nevertheless, most of the proposals it made were accepted, and in the course of its thirty-year history (it was eventually disbanded in 1977), it put forward and pushed through hundreds of incremental improvements. However, like many committees it had an appetite for the trivial at times. At a meeting in March 1968, for example, the issue of "Rind on bacon in sandwiches" was discussed, following a recent investigation into whether or not the rind could be removed. The minutes record the outcome: "Our supplier is not prepared to remove the rind because of the price we pay for the bacon, and also because a side

---

* James Cropper & Co. had joined the Employers' Federation of Paper Makers in 1918. At that time there are indications that the National Union of Printing and Paper Workers tried (unsuccessfully) to persuade Cropper employees to join the union.

of bacon is very difficult to slice when the rind has been taken off. It is too big a job for the Canteen Staff to remove the rind from each separate rasher of bacon."[120]

Bacon rind aside, it was in the interest of directors to act on the recommendations of the Mill Council. By the early 1960s there was a pressing need to make the working environment of the mills more attractive, owing to the fact that recruiting new labour was proving increasingly difficult, especially so far as school-leavers were concerned. Indeed, where they had once queued up to work in the mills (recruitment simply being a matter of seeing who was next on the waiting list, sons following fathers as a matter of course), by 1960 the company's supply of fresh talent was drying up. Moreover, the firm was even beginning to have problems keeping the younger workers that it did manage to recruit.[121]

In part the problem stemmed from the low level of unemployment. Between 1945 and 1975 the number of people out of work in Britain never (with the exception of a few weeks) rose above one million, where in previous decades it had never fallen below this figure.[122] Closer to home even fewer people were un-employed. "Kendal and district have the lowest level of unemployment throughout the Country", noted Geoffrey Acland in 1962, referring to the labour problems. "Competition for the young and better class of worker is very keen."[123]

James Cropper & Co.'s inability to attract fresh talent also perhaps reflected the back-breaking nature of much of the work that junior employees were expected to undertake. In the 1960s the era of the forklift truck and other hydraulic lifting equipment was only just dawning, and tasks such as carrying huge bundles of waste paper upstairs or heaving rolls of paper onto bogies (Fig. 8.6) were still everyday occurrences. At the same time the allure of a career in the mills was perhaps compromised by the company's rigid and archaic system of promotion. Advancing up the ranks was, as several retired employees have remarked, simply a matter of "waiting for dead men's shoes", and the company's system of pay rises

Fig. 8.6 – Bogies such as this were still used for carting around rolls of paper and other heavy items into the 1960s.

was similarly inflexible. Although wages did advance in accordance with union agreements throughout the 1960s, the size of pay packets was still determined by age and length of service rather than merit. Even managers had to abide by such rules. On his appointment as Cowan Head foreman, for example, Harry Wilson's request for the same salary as his predecessor Jim Daws was rejected by Anthony Cropper on the grounds that he had not served for so long.[124]

The failure to attract new recruits led to a prolonged period of labour shortages. By 1961 this had resulted in the introduction of twelve-hour shifts on some machines, a practice that continued for several years in spite of a number of remedial measures.[125] These included the employment of prisoners from Bela River Prison from the early 1960s into the 1970s, most of whom worked in the yard or salle at Burneside.[126] In 1963, meanwhile, the company's third mill, Bowston (where wrappers were made and materials prepared) was closed so that its workforce could help out at Burneside and Cowan Head.[127] This was intended to be a temporary measure, but in the event the closure proved to be permanent, even though the mill had only recently been upgraded. Even then the company's labour problems were not over. In 1965 the labour situation was still noted to be "exceedingly difficult" in spite of a recent advertising campaign (Fig. 8.7), and it was not until the 1970s that things really began to improve.[128]

Fig. 8.7 – Advertisement in the Westmorland Gazette for new recruits, July 1964.

By the mid-1960s James Cropper & Co. was also beginning to encounter problems higher up the ranks. Before then changes in management were infrequent and usually planned well in advance, making little impact on the structure and stability of the firm. The exodus of a whole generation of senior figures in 1949-50, for example, including Herbert Corrie (company secretary since 1910), Joseph Shepherd (chief salesman) and James Arnot (chief engineer) passed without incident. They had all been scheduled to retire for some time, and their places were filled without a hitch. Herbert Corrie's place, for example, was filled by Ronnie Reddish, the first fully qualified accountant to work for James Cropper & Co. in the company's history.*

The death of James W. Cropper in 1956 potentially represented a greater problem for the firm. Rather than opting for retirement, he remained in office to the end and had only recently celebrated his fiftieth anniversary as a director (Fig. 8.8). However, in the event the succession of the chairmanship passed smoothly. His duties were quickly assumed by his son Anthony, who was unanimously elected head of the firm in his place. It perhaps helped that his responsibilities were no longer very extensive. Although James W. continued to come into the office until the last weeks of his life he had long ceased to play an active part in the day-to-day running of the mills. Instead, much of his time was taken up by local appointments, including the position of Lord Lieutenant of Westmorland, which was conferred on him in 1945.

Fig. 8.8 – James W. Cropper's fiftieth anniversary as a director was celebrated with a party at Burneside's Bryce Institute in 1955. He is pictured standing on the right.

---

* The same period also saw the retirement of John Parsons, the chief cashier, Sam Lindsay, Burneside Mills manager, and William Dawson, outside foreman. Joseph Shepherd and Herbert Corrie had both worked for the company for fifty-five years, serving four generations of the Cropper family. Other employees who retired in the 1950s and 1960s had worked for the company for even longer: H. Davis and M. H. Gaskell, for example, had both completed 57 years on their retirement in 1965. As for the oldest employee, this record was probably set by C. Swannack, who retired at the age of eighty in 1958, after 58 years with the company. (AR 1950, CA/MC2, 3 Mar. 1958, CA/MC3, 22 Nov. 1965, 4 Mar. 1968)

Fig. 8.9 – Geoffrey Acland, 1908-64.

The next major changes in management were not so orderly. First, in December 1963 John Larking, deputy manager at Burneside, announced that he was leaving the firm to take up the position of Technical Manager at Oxford's Wolvercote paper-mill. It was not welcome news. Although he had only been with the firm for two years, he had been a powerful force for change (particularly on the technical side of paper-making) and had taken control of several areas of production, the management of which the directors were hastily forced to reorganise.[129] To make matters worse he was also due to play a leading role in a new foreman training scheme as well as take on many of the responsibilities of Fred Craig (Burneside mill manager since 1943), who was about to retire.

In the event Fred Craig did not leave the company until May 1965, several months after his scheduled retirement. By then, however, the senior ranks of the firm had been still further depleted, this time in more tragic circumstances. In September 1964 Geoffrey Acland (Fig. 8.9) collapsed and died a week after a minor operation for the removal of an abscess. A director for almost thirty years, his death at the age of fifty-five was totally unexpected and a great loss for all members of the firm, directors and workers alike. He was the most vocal of the directors in promoting the welfare of employees, and it was at his instigation and under his leadership that many advances were made on the personnel side, including the formation of the Mill Council and the improvement of safety. Indeed, only a matter of days before his death he had been responsible for the appointment of the company's first safety officer, Sam Jenkins.[130] He was also, importantly, supportive of unionisation, and it was probably due to him that there was so little friction between management and workers when the mills were unionised in the late 1940s.[131]

In the tradition of company directors, Geoffrey Acland also played a significant role in the public life of Kendal and south Westmorland. He was a local councillor, school governor and, most importantly, leader of the Liberal party in Westmorland. A former chairman of the Liberal party executive, on his death he was just completing plans to contest the Westmorland constituency in the forthcoming general election.[132]

The loss of Geoffrey Acland was not the only death to shake James Cropper & Co. in the 1960s. In May 1967 Anthony Cropper (Fig. 8.10) died from a heart attack, the second he had suffered in the space of a few weeks. It was a devastating blow for the firm, which not only lost its chairman and figurehead but also – by all accounts – its chief driving force, its leader on the shop-floor as well as in the boardroom.[133] As with previous Cropper chairmen, the survival and prosperity of the company were always amongst Anthony's greatest concerns, and the mills played a central part in his life until the end. Not least, this was evident at his funeral, where Joe Bradbury, the salle foreman, read one of the lessons, and his coffin was borne by representatives from different departments.

His place in the annals of the mills had not always been so prominent. During his early years with the company in the 1930s, he does not seem to have gained much of a foothold in the concern, and on occasion even contemplated alternative careers, including politics.[134] During the Second World War, however, when he spent several years away from Burneside as a captain in the Duke of Lancaster's Yeomanry, he became more determined to make his mark as a paper manufacturer. "I rather feel I would like a job in the mill which I could get my teeth into a bit more and which would of necessity tie me down a bit", he wrote to his father shortly before his return. "In fact I would like to be the official secretary of the firm and really honestly earn my living to a slightly larger extent."[135]

Although he was never appointed secretary, Anthony Cropper's growing commitment was soon reflected by his position in the firm. In 1946 he was appointed a full director, and on the death of his father ten years later he became chairman, the fourth generation of his family to hold the post. His appointment was no doubt in part assured by his name, but according to several sources he was his father's natural successor, the most dynamic of the directors and the most

Fig. 8.10 – Anthony Cropper, 1912-67.

knowledgeable about paper-making. In particular, he was keen to modernise the mills where he could and made several visits to foreign paper-mills, picking up ideas which were later adopted at Burneside (such as pulpers).[136]

Like Geoffrey Acland, Anthony Cropper also dedicated much time to duties outside the firm, playing a significant part in the public life of Kendal and south Westmorland. At various times he was a magistrate, school governor, district and county councillor, and chairman of the Westmorland Agricultural Executive. Further from home his appointments included lay member of the Church Assembly, the governing body of the Church of England, and board-member of the Independent Television Authority, which controlled the recently founded independent television network.[137] For relaxation, meanwhile, he inherited his family's passion for field sports such as hunting and shooting.

Inside the mills his style was different from that of his predecessors. As a leader he was much more of a delegator, passing many of the tasks carried out by his forebears onto those below him.[138] Much of the book-keeping work that his father had done, for example, was passed on to the company secretary, Ronnie Reddish. He was also more authoritative than his father was. "He was very much the boss", recalls Harry Wilson, Cowan Head foreman at the time, and his view is backed up by several others: he was a decisive and energetic leader, who inspired confidence. A measure of this was the level of despondency on his death. "There was a death wish in the place", Nick Willink recalls. "Everybody felt that the mill could and would not survive without him, and at first it was very difficult to persuade people that life could go on."[139]

Raising morale was not straightforward. By 1967 there was a growing tide of gloom in the British paper industry in general, not only brought on by the faltering economic climate, which depressed demand for paper, but also by cuts in duties which had protected the industry from foreign competition.[140] On 31 December 1966 all duties on imports from countries in the European Free Trade Area (EFTA) were scrapped, three years ahead of schedule. This came soon after the removal of the temporary surcharge on imports, which had been introduced in 1964 in response to Britain's chronic imbalance of payments.[141]

The curtailment of duties had a profound impact on the industry. Foreign competition, which was already stronger than it had been for decades, increased even more, particularly with EFTA members Norway, Sweden and Finland, home to a growing number of highly productive integrated paper and pulp mills. Between 1965 and 1970 imports jumped by forty-five percent to 2.5 million tonnes, growing five times faster than domestic output, which peaked at 4.9 million tonnes in 1969.[142]

Against a background of slackening demand for paper, the growth of imports pressurised margins and pushed many mills out of business. During the late 1960s around twenty-five British paper-mills closed for good, including several independent mills, which were becoming increasingly uncommon as widespread rationalisation changed the size and structure of the industry.[143] By 1966 it was estimated that two-thirds of total UK production was in the hands of eight groups owning sixty-six mills.[144] Typical of these was the Reed Group, which bought up a number of independent paper-mills during the 1960s, including Alexander Cowan & Sons and Spicers Ltd, both which had long histories of independent ownership and family involvement.[145]

James Cropper & Co.'s results bear witness to the trading conditions that sparked such changes. In the late 1960s output remained static around the 23,000 tonne mark, while profits became increasingly unstable, fluctuating from £249,000 in 1967 (the best result since 1961) to £150,000 in 1968 (the worst result since 1950). Perhaps the most telling measure of the changing economic environment, however, was the deterioration of profit margins. In the 1950s (and for many years before) returns of profits on sales had almost always exceeded ten percent, and typically fifteen percent in the best years. During the 1960s, in contrast, they entered a period of sustained decline, falling from eleven percent in 1961 to less than five percent in 1969, when a profit of £136,000 was made on a turnover of £2.83 million. Making a profit had not been so difficult since the 1890s and 1900s, perhaps the last time that foreign competition was so intense.

Fig. 9.1 – The retirement of Derek Willink, 1971. Left to right: John Larking, Oliver Acland, Reggie Oldham, Derek Willink, Joan Willink, Nick Willink, Jim Hill, James Cropper, Ronnie Reddish.

9

Provincial Mill to World Class Specialist: 1967-2003

FOR many firms the loss of key figures or a prolonged downturn in trading conditions has been the beginning of the end – a prelude to drastic restructuring, change of ownership, or even closure. Yet for all the problems experienced by James Cropper & Co. in the 1960s, the future of the company was never in doubt. By the mid-1960s a new generation of young and enthusiastic directors were ready to take control of the paper-mills, and – perhaps by virtue of their family connections – all of them were determined that the business would survive. Failure was out of the question.

By the time of Anthony Cropper's death in 1967 three directors' sons were working for James Cropper & Co., (hereafter referred to as a *plc*, a nominal change in suffix that took place in the late 1970s). Geoffrey Acland's son Oliver was the first to join, beginning work at Burneside in 1958 after completing a history degree at Cambridge University.[1] He had decided to follow in his father Geoffrey's footsteps several years before. "It seemed like a good idea", he recalls. "Dad used to take us into the mill quite a lot, and it seemed exciting and interesting. When it was offered I said yes."

For Derek Willink's son Nick, who joined the company in 1959, a paper-making career had been on the cards for even longer. "I was brought up to expect it", he says, adding that owing to ill health in childhood his parents thought that a position at Burneside was a safe option. To a certain extent this conflicted with his own ambitions (which included harnessing tidal power as a marine engineer) although he was, by the time he joined the firm, well qualified to pursue a career in paper-making, having completed a degree in engineering at Cambridge University. Importantly the subject was not only interesting to him but also – as he is keen to point out – very relevant to paper-making. He even addressed it in a university thesis, *The Physical Properties of Pulp and Paper*.

On joining Oliver and Nick received extensive training. They started out by working in nearly every department of the mill – often on shift – and both also gained outside experience. In preparation for an envisaged sales role Oliver spent time with the company's largest customer, Mono Containers, as well as one of its oldest, McCorquodales.[2] A few years later, by which time he was preparing to work in production, he spent a month as a machine operative at Alexander Cowan & Sons near Edinburgh, following in the footsteps of the company's founder, who had spent time there learning the rudiments of paper-making management in 1845. In a similar vein Nick spent several weeks with another Scottish paper-making firm, Tullis Russell, as well as time working for a number of the company's engineering suppliers, where he was dispatched by Jim Hill, the chief engineer. Added to this, in 1960 the pair was sent by Anthony Cropper on a three week tour of Canadian pulp and paper-mills organised by the Technical Section of the British Paper and Board Makers' Association. "It was a formative trip", recalls Nick, "enabling us to see many different styles of equipment. Our training allowed us to see Croppers in the context of the industry", he reflects, "on a national and international basis."

Responsibility followed quickly. Foreshadowing much of his later work, in 1961 Oliver introduced a pioneering educational scheme (see Chapter 8), and from 1962 both he and Nick took seats on a new Technical Development Committee.[3] Two years later both were appointed directors, by which time Nick was responsible for technical developments (following the departure of John Larking), while Oliver was preparing to step into the shoes of Fred Craig, the Burneside general manager, who retired in 1965. At his own behest, his training for this included operating a paper machine, the first and only director ever to have done so.

James Cropper, who joined the company in February 1966, followed a rather different route to the board. Like his forebears a paper-making career was not so much a career choice as a duty, an inheritance that he was always expected to take on. "I always presumed I would work in the mill", he says, "and I never wanted anything other than to be involved with Croppers". His education also followed family tradition. Like his father and grandfather, Eton and Cambridge University (where he studied law) were followed by Price Waterhouse, the company's auditors since 1906. This time, however, rather than spending a few months learning the rudiments of accountancy, he completed a full three years training with the firm, returning to Burneside as a fully fledged Chartered Accountant.*

---

* James Cropper's life was entwined with the mills from the earliest moments of his life. Only a day after his birth he was mentioned at a mill meeting, where – the minutes tell us – "the Staff and Mill Workers rejoice the birth of a Son in the Fifth Generation of Croppers". (CA/NS/15, Extracts from Fortnightly Meetings, 23 Dec. 1938). The sense that he was destined for a position in the mills is reinforced by his father Anthony, who presumed that his son would become Chairman of the company long before he joined the firm. Oliver Acland and Nick Willink, it appears, were not even considered for the role. (ACC Future Management Plans, CA/3/23)

In contrast with Oliver and Nick, on his return James received almost nothing in the way of training. "I was simply put to work", he recalls, ". . . to put my accountancy skills to use". Rather than working on shift or passing through all the different departments, he was given clerical work, at first in the Costings Department and then in the Work Study Department, which handled the company's increasingly complex range of incentive schemes. His promotion was similarly abrupt. On his father's sudden death in May 1967 he was appointed a director, and took over many key responsibilities, including dealing with finance and banking.[4]

The loss of Anthony Cropper led to a number of other changes in management. Derek Willink, a director since 1928, was appointed chairman, agreeing to postpone his retirement to lend the board some age and experience. Further stability was lent by the appointment of a non-executive director, Reggie Oldham, the company's London sales agent for forty-five years. Neither appointment, however, was long-lived: Derek Willink retired in 1971 (Fig. 9.1) relinquishing the position of chairman to James Cropper, the fifth generation of his family to hold the post. Reggie Oldham died in 1972.

By then the board had been strengthened by a more enduring appointment. Sensing the need to recruit outside talent (and finding himself with too many inherited responsibilities) in 1970 Oliver Acland visited John Larking out of the blue, offering him a directorship if he was willing to return to Burneside. Since leaving the Cropper mills in 1964, John had been general manager at Wolvercote paper-mill, which was owned by the Oxford University Press, and as it happened, Oliver's surprise visit was welcome. The timing was good – there was talk that the university might dispose of the mill – and John duly accepted the position. He became only the second full-time director in the company's history who was not a Cropper relative.[5]

The early 1970s was also a period of significant change in terms of management structure. For the first time in the company's history, directors were allocated defined roles, bringing to an end a system and culture of management in place since the earliest days of the firm. The directors had previously chosen responsibilities as they pleased, "a free-for-all" situation, comments John Larking. Geoffrey Acland, for example, had looked after two unrelated areas, personnel and the collection and use of waste paper. Derek Willink's remit, which included chairing meetings and looking after the provision of housing for employees, was even more vague. The lack of definition also filtered down the ranks. Neither Oliver Acland nor Nick Willink was given specific responsibilities during the first few years of their careers, and there was little structure to their training. Indeed, at first Nick was given nothing more than an office, not even a job or a title.

The reasons for the loose management structure are clear enough. Since the earliest days of the firm, the day-to-day running of the mills had been largely left to the mill manager and foremen. The directors only interfered when and where they chose, most frequently at the company's fortnightly meeting, a review of production and sales held every two weeks.* Beyond this their responsibilities were, at least in comparison with today, not particularly onerous. Issues were only dealt with as they arose, and not within the context of any strategic framework. Besides that, the focus of directors was narrow. Production was the key function; in an age of moderate competition the company would survive so long as it made paper. Other areas were secondary considerations.

Selling paper, for example, was almost taken for granted. The company had a long list of loyal clients, and failing that it could rely on sales agents such as J. M. Oldham, which was still selling a large proportion of output in the late 1960s.[6] "The attitude towards selling was very low key", recalls Alan Sutton, who worked in the company's Manchester sales office from 1959. "Generating new business, for example, was generally non-existent." Similarly, for much of the company's history recruitment and other personnel issues only demanded occasional input from directors. There was (at least until the early 1960s), a ready source of labour in the local community, and dissent was rare. "You did as you were told", one pensioner explains. "It was the way you were brought up."†

In this context a hands-off system of management was not out of place. However, by the 1970s, as this chapter will examine, the situation was very different. There was a pressing need for leadership and strategy in production, selling, personnel and many other areas, compelling John Larking and his fellow directors to assign themselves individual roles and responsibilities for the first time. Thereafter James Cropper took charge of finances, Oliver Acland of personnel and Nick Willink of engineering and paper-making. Meanwhile, John Larking became responsible for sales and all areas of production with customer contact, namely finishing, dispatch and transport. In the following years further changes followed. On Derek Willink's retirement in 1971 James Cropper added chairman to his list of duties, and in 1972 John Larking was appointed sales director. It was not until

---

* The fortnightly meeting had governed the routine of mill life since the earliest days of the firm. It centred upon the contents of a large black volume, the fortnightly book, which contained all the necessary details of production and sales. This was viewed by many as the firm's very own bible, and there was also a sacred quality to the accounting procedure used within, which had changed little since the 1850s.

† The respect for authority was, she adds, enforced by religious doctrine. Prior to confirmation in the Church of England, everyone of her generation and many before was required to learn a catechism in the prayer book. It demanded that all those who learnt it should ". . . labour truly to get mine own living, and to do my duty in that state of life unto which it shall please God to call me".

1974, however, when Peter Charlton was appointed chief engineer on the retirement of Jim Hill, that the reorganisation of management was truly complete. He brought years of paper-making engineering experience with him, and in recognition of his contribution to the firm was promoted to the board as engineering director in 1977.

The creation of an organised and determined management team was of critical importance, as the downturn in trading conditions in the late 1960s proved to be just a foretaste of things to come. The early 1970s to early 1980s were bleak years for British trade and industry, and the paper industry was no exception, suffering the most dramatic decline in its history. In just over a decade production of paper and board fell by more than a third, from a high of 4.9 million tonnes in 1969 to under 3.2 million tonnes in 1982. The number of paper-mills fell by a similar proportion, from around 165 in 1970 to less than 90 by 1983, and many well known and long established companies disappeared or were taken over. The decline in employment was equally brutal. Thousands of paper-mill workers lost their jobs, as a 1975 pamphlet highlighting the crisis made clear (Fig. 9.2).

Fig. 9.2 – Save our Industry! A 1975 Pamphlet produced by paper industry union SOGAT.

There were many reasons for the catastrophic decline, not least the poor performance of the British economy. This depressed demand for goods such as paper, consumption of which fell from a record high of 7.2 million tonnes in 1970 to less than 6.8 million tonnes in 1980. Paper-makers were also hit by rising

energy costs resulting from the two oil crises of 1973 and 1979, which were
themselves responsible for much of the economic instability. Added to this, the
poor state of labour relations also took its toll on the industry. Although paper-
mills themselves were rarely prone to industrial action, there was plenty of fall-out
from the wave of strikes in other sectors.[7] A postal strike in 1971, for example,
resulted in £81,000 of bad debts for James Cropper plc, and a seven-week miners'
strike in 1971-2 had a similar impact.[8] Production at Burneside stopped for two
weeks and the price of coal soared, causing the company to incur £50,000 in extra
costs, a significant proportion of that year's profit of £171,000.[9]

Foreign competition had an even greater impact on British paper-mills.
Throughout the 1970s paper imports rose rapidly, and by the early 1980s almost
sixty percent of the paper consumed in the United Kingdom came from abroad.[10]
Paper manufacturers had hoped that entry into the European Economic
Community in 1973 would curb foreign competition, as imports from EFTA
countries such as Norway and Sweden would be subject to the EEC's common
external tariff.[11] However, in the event the tariff did little to control imports from
Scandinavia, which continued to land on British shores in record volumes.[12]
Moreover, paper-makers also found themselves under attack on a new front, from
West Germany, France and other Common Market producers, which were home
to new and rising paper industries of their own. In the mid-1960s paper
production was higher in Britain than any of the six Common Market nations. By
1974 the rankings were very different: Britain was in fourth place, behind West
Germany, France and Italy. Added to that, by investing in new capacity EEC
competitors such as France (where production almost doubled from 1962 to
1974) had more modern and productive mills.[13]

The decline in British paper-making came to a head in the early 1980s, a
disastrous time for trade and industry in general, not only owing to an
international recession but also very high interest rates, which themselves were a
response to record inflation. Manufacturing output fell more than it had in the
Great Depression of 1929 to 1931, and in 1980 to 1982 over 1.5 million jobs
were shed in British industry.[14] In paper-making employment fell by forty percent
in four years, from 60,000 to 36,000, reflecting the closure of almost forty mills.
In the same period paper and board production plummeted from 4.2 million to
3.2 million tonnes.[15] "The announcement of yet another mill closure is a regular
and depressing feature of the news from the paper industry at present",
commented James Cropper in the *Westmorland Gazette* in March 1982.[16] A year
later the situation was even worse. "In the first month of 1983 there have been
industry job losses of 1,900 people, which is not far short of the total for the
whole of 1982", he reported. "This includes the closure of three paper-mills in the
North West."[17]

For James Cropper plc the 1970s and early 1980s were one of the most difficult periods of trading in its history. Margins were tighter than ever, and owing to slack demand, output was well below capacity for nine out of thirteen years. The notable exception was 1974, when a shortage of pulp and waste paper led to panic-buying of paper. "It was madness", recalls Nick Willink. "Customers were begging for anything, whatever the quality. It was actually a cause of concern." One client, Swindon Letter File, even promised to pay the company a £100 premium for every tonne it diverted from export. The boom, however, was short-lived. In December 1974 the mills shut down for Christmas with full order books, but as soon as they started up again orders began to be cancelled, and by mid-January they were running at seventy percent capacity. Prices also crashed, marking the beginning of a prolonged slump in demand which brought many paper-makers to their knees. By August 1975 there were even rumours that James Cropper plc would shortly close or be taken over. In the event the company survived the recession, as James Cropper assured employees it would, but it struggled to break even for two and a half years.[18] In 1976 it posted a loss of £202,000, the first since 1922, and in 1977 it only just scraped into the black, generating £44,000 profit on sales of £8,246,000, a shocking return by any standards.*

The downturn also forced the company to shelve ambitious expansion plans, which involved doubling the output of its five machines to 55,000 tonnes. "There are now insufficient markets for so much paper, and insufficient profit to move forward on such a scale", commented Oliver Acland in March 1976, who instead proposed a programme of rationalisation.[19] This led to the closure of the company's small machine at Cowan Head in January 1977 (Fig. 9.3), the tonnage of which was transferred to No3 machine at Burneside, which was enlarged for the purpose with the addition of a wider 16 foot MG cylinder.

The rationalisation paid off. The early 1980s proved to be an equally tough time for the firm, with margins dropping to less than two percent. Weak paper prices were partly to blame but of greater concern were energy costs. Between 1981 and 1983 the cost of powering the mills accounted for twelve percent of turnover, double the level of a few years before, and over three times the level of today (2004). As a result the company was forced to implement radical cost reductions. There were several rounds of voluntary redundancies or early

---

* The company was not only hit by the drastic slump in demand but also by huge stocks of overpriced pulp. In Autumn 1974 it ordered as much pulp as it could, confident that pulp shortages would continue for some time to come. "There was a great shortage of pulp at the time", explains Nick Willink, who was responsible for pulp buying, "and deliveries from suppliers were very slow". Unfortunately, the pulp began arriving just as demand and prices crashed, and by April 1975 the company had two to three times its normal stock of pulp, all of it at inflated prices.

Fig. 9.3 – The last reel of paper made at Cowan Head, 1977. Left to right: Frank Thompson, Robert Johnson and Maurice Crossley, the mill manager.

retirements, and Cowan Head, where paper continued to be converted on a new laminating machine, was closed altogether in 1981.* At one point James Cropper even called for all heating systems to be run at the lowest temperature possible in the name of cutting overheads.[20] Even then there are clear indications that the company was running close to the bone. Company archives reveal that in October 1981 James Cropper was looking at temporarily shutting down some machines altogether, and a year later the firm was very close to implementing a "contingency plan", which included shutting machines and effecting compulsory redundancies.[21]

Compared to other paper-makers, however, the firm's performance in the face of adversity was impressive. As well as staying in the black on many occasions when its competitors did not (and surviving where many did not), the 1970s and early 1980s was a period of remarkable growth for the firm. Between 1970 and 1984 turnover grew from £3.0 million to £21.5 million per year, well in excess of inflation. Output also rose, from 22,500 tonnes to 35,800 tonnes, while export tonnage jumped from three percent of production to twenty percent. Productivity shot up from 37 tonnes to almost 90 tonnes of paper per head. In great part this reflected a sharp decline in employee numbers from 606 in 1970 to 414 in 1984. Remarkably, this was almost entirely achieved through natural wastage, voluntary redundancy or early retirement, in line with the company's "unwritten but well quoted policy" of no compulsory redundancies. In spite of the closure of Cowan

---

* The site was sold off in 1984, after a protracted battle with the planning authorities for permission to convert it to residential use. Nothing now remains of the mill, which was bulldozed by its eventual buyer, Bentley, to make way for several blocks of luxury flats. (AR 1981, 1983)

Head, and the disappearance of positions throughout the mills, the policy was only broken on one occasion in 1975, when seven jobs were shed.[22]

Summarising how the company made such advances during some of the toughest times in the history of the British paper industry is not an easy task. In the first place, however, its survival was perhaps assured by the fact that it had stronger foundations than most. Its traditional range of products, for instance, was not as susceptible to foreign competition as those of many British paper-makers, particularly manufacturers of commodity grades such as newsprint. Moreover, in physical terms the firm was better equipped than most to survive the shocks of the 1970s. Where many British paper-makers had failed to modernise in the comfortable trading climate that followed the war – and paid the price when the tables turned – James Cropper & Co. had never stood still.[23] During the 1950s it had undertaken one of the most extensive modernisation programmes in decades, and thereafter the drive for improvement only intensified, unchecked by the dramatic downturn in trading conditions after 1966.

In the late 1960s, for example, the company became the first paper-manufacturer in the country to automate the addition of rosin size, alum and

clay, the three main chemical additives used in paper-making. The work was completed in 1969 with the installation of an automatic china clay handling plant at Burneside, designed in-house. The process had previously been carried out by hand (Fig. 9.4). This resulted in substantial savings in manpower and improvements in control, as well as cutting the cost of clay by nearly £4 per tonne, owing to the way it was transported following the change.[24] Best of all, however, automating the production and addition of clay encouraged the company to use more of the material, which not only saved money but also improved the quality of its paper. "China clay imparts flatness, smoothness, opacity and gloss to paper", explained an internal newsletter at the time, "as well as increasing profits by substantially reducing furnish costs."[25]*

Fig. 9.4 – Clay, one of the main chemical additives used in paper-making was added by hand until 1969.

---

* The furnish consists of the blend of pulp mixed with various other materials to define the final characteristics of the paper. Various chemicals are added depending on the particular specifications of the paper to be made. For example, fillers such as clay and calcium carbonate (chalk) are added for opacity, brightness and smoothness; dyes are added for shade control; optical brighteners are added for whiteness and sizing agents are added to control liquid penetration.

Investment in labour-saving equipment has been a recurring theme in the modern history of James Cropper plc. Examples range from the introduction of machines for counting paper in the late 1960s (before which paper was still counted by hand) to the installation of a Japanese-made ream wrapping machine in 1998 (Fig. 9.5). Until then the firm continued to pack all sheeted paper by hand, one of the last paper-makers to do so. "We are continuing to reduce employment costs by designing jobs out of the business", James Cropper noted on the change, a comment that continues to apply to this day.[26]

Fig. 9.5 – The Japanese-made Maruishi ream wrapping machine installed in 1998.

His remark could be equally applied to dozens of other projects, not least the automation of Burneside's raw material preparation facilities, which began in the late 1960s. In 1967 a whole range of machinery and processes began to be replaced, marking the greatest change at this end of the mills in the company's history. It was a formidable task: each of Burneside's four machines had their own separate preparation facilities, and ripping them out and installing the new machinery (which included pulpers, blending chests and refiners) took seven years. However, by the time the work was finished the company not only had one of the most modern preparation plants in the country, but had also cut its labour costs dramatically. The number of people working in this end of the mill was halved. The flow of production from raw materials into finished products was also radically improved, making the mill both more productive and more versatile, as it became easier and quicker to change the colour and types of paper being made. "We are now completely flexible in the use of pulp, waste papers and chemicals", remarked James Cropper at the time, "and can make to whatever furnish is required."[27]

The new system did away with a range of piecemeal processes, many of which dated back to the earliest days of the firm. Waste pulpers, for example, replaced equipment that would not have been out of place in a museum. Previously, waste paper had been loaded by hand into spherical digesters in the mill's top loft, huge rotating cauldrons that had changed little since the days they were used to boil rags, over a century before. These were then emptied onto the floor, and the steaming heap of material shovelled into kollergangs (Fig. 9.6). The kollergangs (which were as medieval looking as the name suggests), were then drained into little trucks, which in turn were emptied into the beaters. By the mid-1960s forklift trucks were used at this stage, tipping the material into the beaters, but had only recently superseded the use of forks and shovels.

Fig. 9.6 – The row of kollergangs at Burneside Mills, 1955.

Keeping the old plant clean was also labour-intensive. Each of Burneside's sixteen beaters, for example, had to be raked out by hand every time they were used, and scrubbed with caustic whenever the colour of the paper being made changed.[28] Another unpleasant chore was cleaning out the digesters, which involved climbing inside them only a few moments after they had been emptied. "It was like something out of Faust", described Oliver Acland, who gained direct experience of the job during his first week with the company in 1958. "You had to get in as soon as possible . . . Take off the lid with its eight or so huge nuts after letting the steam out. Empty the digester by revolving it . . . Wait half an hour and put a ladder down and then climb in. The wet heat hits you from the feet up and by jove, it's a free Turkish bath!"

Another major break with the past that took place in the early 1970s was the end of railway haulage, which was abandoned in favour of road transport. The firm's private railway to Cowan Head (one of the very last of its kind in the country) was closed in 1965, and by 1970 the firm was making nearly all of its deliveries using a new fleet of articulated lorries (Fig. 9.7).[29] In great part the change was tied to the revolution in transport taking place in Britain at this time, namely the construction of the motorway network, which reached Westmorland in 1970. It was not, however, until 1972, when British Rail announced that it planned to stop all commercial traffic on the branch-line that passed through Burneside, that the firm's association with railways was finally drawn to a close. Until then coal was still delivered to Burneside station by rail, and hauled into the mill by the firm's own petrol locomotives, along a four hundred yard line that cut through the centre of the village. These were subsequently scrapped, as were the bogies and railway tracks still being used for carting waste paper and pulp within the mill, which were abandoned in favour of fork-lift trucks.[30]

Fig. 9.7 – James Cropper & Co.'s new fleet of lorries, 1970.

The final closure of the railway coincided with another major development at Burneside. With coal no longer coming by rail, in 1972 the company installed four new boilers that could run off gas, available from a recently installed pipeline through Burneside. It was an expensive change, but the total cost of £350,000 was more than justified as gas was cheaper and the new plant was more efficient and cheaper to run. Furthermore, during the 1974 miners' strike it allowed the company to continue production while much of British industry ground to a halt, and in subsequent years it significantly lessened the impact of soaring energy costs.

The new boiler plant was the last project to be completed by Jim Hill, who officially opened it on his retirement in June 1974. The mills had changed enormously during his thirty-five years as chief engineer, but his legacy was not without its shortcomings. Indeed, in spite of the company's record of improvement and some notable advances, much of the plant and machinery at Burneside and Cowan Head was desperately out of date.[31] The engineering shop, to take one example, was full of ancient tools and machines, despite being moved to a new building only a few years before. "I had never seen such antediluvian machinery – it came out of a museum", recalls Peter Charlton, Hill's successor, who came from Reed Board Mills in Kent. "The stuff was frightful, the lathes were ancient . . . everything was out of true."

The greatest problem, however, was not the age so much as the design of the machines, particularly the paper-making machines themselves. The small machine at Cowan Head, for example, had been built only three years prior to Peter Charlton's arrival, yet it included a wet-end and press section based on identical designs to the company's No4 machine, which had been constructed in 1904.[32] "It was an old machine in new metal", says John Larking, who recalls his horror on discovering that it did not include any of the improvements that he and his fellow directors had recommended. Unfortunately for the firm, the same was true of all its other machines. Burneside's No1 and No3, which were both rebuilt in the late 1950s, and the second wires added to No4 and No2 in 1936 and 1947, were all extensively modelled on turn of the century designs.[33]

In part the antiquated design of the machines reflected the inertia of the manufacturer that had made them all, Bertrams Ltd. of Edinburgh. James Cropper plc's connection with the firm dated back to 1887, and it remained the company's preferred supplier until Jim Hill's departure, even though there were better suppliers elsewhere. Without doubt the relationship was perpetuated by Hill himself. He had served his apprenticeship in Bertrams' Edinburgh foundry, and stayed close to his *alma mater* throughout his career, sending orders its way whenever possible. The preference for old designs also, however, reflects badly on the directors of the time, who were ultimately responsible as they sanctioned Hill's choices.

The company's response to the situation facing it in the mid-1970s was altogether more impressive. Against a background of unprecedented decline and decay in British industry, Peter Charlton and his fellow directors spent their way out of trouble, initiating a remarkable programme of investment that was to continue into the early 1990s, during which time Burneside was transformed from a small provincial mill into one of the most advanced paper-making operations of its size in the world. Led by Peter Charlton and Nick Willink, who worked together on all major engineering projects, it was a sensational transformation, not least for the sums of money that were sunk into the business. In the year following Peter's arrival in 1974, capital expenditure jumped from £174,000 to £420,000, and by 1983 over £7.8 million had been spent, despite the paper industry passing through two of the most severe recessions in its history. Thereafter the investment programme only intensified. By 1991 almost £46 million had been invested. It is little wonder that paper-making is widely known as a capital-intensive industry.

The lion's share of the money was spent on the paper-making machines, starting with the modernisation and enlargement of the dry end of No3 machine at a cost of £720,000 in 1976. The catalyst for the project was the discovery that the machine's existing MG cylinder was porous and needed to be urgently replaced, but as the plans took shape it became clear that other benefits could be derived. By installing a larger 16ft cylinder (made by Beloit Walmsley), the company created sufficient extra capacity to close its small MG machine at Cowan Head, which generated savings that more than justified the necessary investment. This ceased production in January 1977 (less than six years after it had been rebuilt) and the tonnage was transferred to Burneside. It marked the end of over two centuries of paper-making at the small mill, the appearance of which had changed little since its construction by Thomas Ashburner in the 1750s. Even its inside looked ancient, in spite of the recent upgrade (Fig. 9.8).

The enlargement of No3 was the catalyst for a great deal of change. "A surge of adrenalin followed its successful completion", says Nick Willink, who recalls how it gave the directors the confidence to think about more ambitious projects, not least the reconstruction of the company's largest machine, No4, a twin-wire Fourdrinier which had originally been built in 1904. Plans to rebuild the existing machine were first drafted in 1978, and within a few months had become even more ambitious, the directors deciding to replace it completely, and increase capacity from 10,000 to 18,000 tonnes. The work was carried through in stages, starting with the installation of a new press section in July 1979, followed by top and bottom wires in December and a new dry end and waste preparation plant in July 1980 (Fig. 9.9).

Remarkably, only three weeks of production were lost on the machine during the whole process, a tribute to the organisation of chief engineer Peter Charlton, and the team of planners, engineers and contractors that worked under him. The project did not, however, run as seamlessly as intended. From the outset the new machine encountered commissioning problems, severely hitting profits in 1981 and forcing the company to make modifications in the following years.[34] The principal cause of the problems was the new headboxes, which Peter Charlton and Nick Willink had decided to design and build in-house. Unfortunately, they failed to work as intended and within a few months of their construction it proved necessary to replace them, the company electing for headboxes made by the German company Voith, a world-leader in the field. It was a costly mistake: the Voith headboxes, which were installed in July 1982, cost £470,000, helping to

Fig. 9.8 – The small paper-making machine at Cowan Head, early 1970s.

push the total cost of the new No4 to more than £3.7 million, far above the original estimate of £2.5 million.

The early 1980s were also expensive times for James Cropper plc owing to the cost of sending its effluent to Kendal's new sewage treatment plant, a final and vital solution to years of problems with pollution, previously discussed in Chapter Eight. In spite of such extra costs, however, the modernisation programme only gathered pace. As the new No4 approached completion the firm began to improve its much smaller No1 machine, which dated from 1957. Around £1 million was spent on it from 1981 to 1984, starting with the installation of a new calender stack in 1981 and finishing with new Voith headboxes in 1984. The core of the rebuild, however, took place in 1982, when the bottom wire was reversed and a new press section and dandy rolls installed at a cost of £505,000. The press section

Fig. 9.9 – Installation of the new No4 machine at Burneside, 1980.

was designed and built in the company's own engineering workshop with some help from firms in Kendal, a tribute to the skill and dexterity of the company's engineers and the faith that Peter Charlton continued to have in his team despite the recent problems with No4 machine.[35]

The modernisation programme continued at full pace into the early 1990s, by which time hardly a corner of Burneside Mills was left untouched. Many developments will be discussed later in this chapter, but one key feature that attracts attention is that the company did not only modernise its paper-making equipment. It also sought, wherever possible, to improve the efficiency of the whole operation. In 1987, for example, it spent almost £3 million on a combined heat and power plant – the second most expensive project it undertook in the 1980s – which incorporated a six megawatt gas turbine.[36] At the time it was an extremely ambitious scheme – one of the first of its kind in the country – and there were some teething troubles, but the benefits were clear. As well as providing all the company's electricity and steam requirements, the new plant cut energy costs from over nine percent to less than four percent of sales (which equated to several hundred thousand pounds per year), a saving that not only paid for the investment but gave vital protection to margins.

James Cropper plc's reconstruction programme not only demanded the dedication of Peter Charlton and his engineering department, but also the commitment of almost every other department of the firm, not to mention suppliers and contractors. The machine crews, for example, were required to learn totally new modes of operation, while at the other end of the business the sales team had an equally important role finding orders to fill the extra capacity. That all managed to work together (often to very tight schedules) without severely disrupting production or cash flow was a remarkable achievement.

Another key to the company's dramatic modernisation programme was finance. Reconstructing Burneside demanded huge capital investment. In the fifteen years from 1976 to 1991 – in which time the company rebuilt or replaced all of its four remaining machines (in one case twice) – James Cropper plc spent almost £43 million, over three times the accumulated profit for the period, which totalled £14.7 million. Not surprisingly, much of the sum was financed by borrowings, which rose to record levels. The company's annual interest bill rose accordingly, from £53,000 in 1975 to £508,000 in 1983 and a peak of £2 million in 1991, at which point gearing reached a high of 110 percent.

It need hardly be said that investing at such a rate was fraught with risk, not least owing to interest rates, which were at a record high level from the mid-1970s onwards. Furthermore, the risk that the company might fail to repay its borrowings was increased by its habit of investing when trading conditions were at their worst. The decision to rebuild No3 machine in 1976, for example, coincided with the company posting its first loss for fifty-five years, a result of the worst recession in paper-making in living memory.[37] The same thing happened again with No4 and No1 in the early 1980s and No3 in 1990; in both cases paper-making profits were squeezed by major recessions just as the company was borrowing more money than ever before.

In 1991, when borrowings peaked at £21 million and gearing at 110 percent, this led to James Cropper plc's first and only major problem with a bank when it breached the lending conditions imposed by Hill Samuel, which had provided a £3 million loan. Its relationship with the bank subsequently became very strained, Hill Samuel demanding repayment if its wishes were not met. In response the board were forced to instigate a major cost-cutting exercise (notably managing to avoid compulsory redundancies), and initiate a consultant-led programme to remodel the culture within the mills.* Even then the bank was still a thorn in the company's side for some time, and the issue was only truly laid to rest when the directors managed to refinance the loans with other borrowers in 1993.

In spite of the evident risks (and the close escape) there were, nevertheless, sound reasons for investing at the bottom of the cycle. "The best time to invest in new capacity is towards the bottom rather than at the top, so that the capacity is there when the market moves up", noted James Cropper in 1977, explaining a strategy that continued to be pursued for many years thereafter. At the same time he took pains to explain why the company needed to spend as much as it did:

> It is easy for a very long established company to not plan ahead with an eye on changing demand or technology. These changes mean that customers either no longer require traditional grades or can get them manufactured cheaper elsewhere. The investment required to change gear to meet new requirements can, for a period, exceed the money that the company generates internally. The gap becomes larger, however, with every year a decision to change is delayed, the eventual result being that the company goes out of business.

On paper such a policy sounds sensible enough, but to enact it in the real world – and at times when the future of British paper-making seemed in doubt –

---

* The cost-cutting exercise was carried through as "The Burneside Challenge". Aiming for annual savings of £2 million to offset falling profits and record interest payments, every opportunity to save money was exploited, however minor, from reducing subscriptions to trade journals to cutting the time taken to change from making one paper to another. With the help of ER Consultants, the company's efforts to change the culture within the mills evolved into a concerted drive to adopt the principles of "Total Quality Management". Noted at the time to be "a major step in the development of the company", this sought to install a sense of unity amongst the workforce and focus efforts on meeting customer needs. Some of the activity TQM initiated – such as problem-solving teams – has fizzled out but it laid the foundation for much work that still continues today.

demanded genuine courage. Indeed, the outlay on new plant and machinery was often greeted with disbelief by others within the industry.

The company's ability to spend as much as it did can be attributed to a number of factors. First and foremost, it reflected the genuine faith of James Cropper and his fellow directors, not only in the future of the firm and paper-making in general, but also in each other. "The team worked very well together", comments John Larking, "and by working closely together we were able to take leaps and be adventurous in a way not possible at other mills." Although each director had his own part to play, the team's success ultimately owed much to James Cropper, not only in his capacity as chairman – in which he was very successful at ensuring consensus on major decisions – but also as the firm's finance director.[38] "He was never afraid of finding the money", comments Peter Charlton. "If Nick, John and I were convinced that something would work, James would go for it."

Another important asset was the company's independence. In contrast with many paper-makers, James Cropper plc has never been beholden to higher powers, which at best might have required the directors to draft convoluted justifications for their actions, and at worst could have abandoned the business, a fate suffered by many British paper-mills.* This is no coincidence. It has been a longstanding belief of the board that the interests of the company are best met by remaining independent. "Cropper maintains that its ownership position serves its interests well, including employees, customers and the community at large", commented a paper trade journal in the 1980s, and it is an accurate summary of the company's position both then and now.[39]

Remaining independent has not only been assured by the sizeable shareholdings that still belong to the Cropper and Willink families, but also by the company's reluctance to link up with other enterprises, numerous advances from which have been received since the early 1970s. Some have been interested in buying a stake in Cropper, others in a merger or taking it over altogether.[40] Still more paper-making firms, however, have approached James Cropper plc with the opposite in mind. The company has been offered dozens of businesses in the last thirty years and the list says much about the contraction of the industry in recent times. Many mills, having failed to find a new owner, were subsequently closed.

Paper-mills offered to James Cropper plc range from the North Wales Paper Mill in 1968 to the East Lancashire Paper Mill (where James Cropper was a non-executive director in the 1980s) in 1996.[41] Most offers have been rejected almost

---

* One example of this was the closure of Oakenclough paper-mill in Lancashire, even though its future had seem assured by the installation of new machine. In 1971 it was closed by its parent, British Tissues, much to the shock of its 385 employees who were informed that their workplace was no longer an economic prospect. (*Lancashire Evening Post*, 31 Mar. 1971)

immediately, but a few have been considered in more detail, including the possibility, in 1981, of buying Kentmere, a Lake District manufacturer of photographic paper, the potential purchase of which was eventually turned down by its directors. Another interesting offer came in 1989, when DRG (Dickinson Robinson Group, formerly John Dickinson) proposed that it transfer the tonnage from its Nash Mill to Burneside in the wake of a hostile takeover bid from an investment firm.[42] It was a sign of the times that one of the oldest and most famous members of the British paper industry was knocking on James Cropper plc's door for help, and the offer was taken seriously at Burneside, even being allocated its own codename, "Project Eagle". However, owing to DRG's request for a substantial stake in exchange, the directors eventually rejected it, deciding that remaining independent was more important.*

Another feature of James Cropper plc's interaction with other paper firms has been the growing international dimension. Indicative of the growing globalisation of the paper industry – which has seen the number of UK paper companies in wholly British ownership rapidly contract in the last thirty years – the company has received a growing number of offers from abroad in recent years.[43] In 1988, for example, it was offered Papierfabrik Weissenstein, a German manufacturer of special papers and card. The prospect excited the directors, but was subsequently rejected owing to insufficient funds.[44] However, with European economic integration on the horizon the company continued to look for opportunities on the Continent, and a year later spent £738,000 buying a thirty-five percent stake in Pacofa, a French company specialising in coating, printing and embossing paper, board and synthetic materials. It was and remains the firm's first and only acquisition in a century and a half of trading. "This agreement will form part of our strategy for Europe", James Cropper commented on the purchase. "Pacofa's products complement our own, and the company could also form a distribution base for our products in Europe". At first the purchase yielded good results: Pacofa's profits doubled in 1990, and continued to be respectable until 1995. Since then, however, the acquisition has been a disappointment. Pacofa never became the European distribution base for Cropper products and in recent years the French firm's performance has been poor, a state of affairs that eventually led the directors to write down the value of its stake by £300,000 in 1999.

Remaining independent may have given James Cropper plc the freedom to spend money, but it does not explain how the company raised the necessary finance, which is a story in itself. This was not straightforward, especially in

---

* DRG was subsequently broken up and many of its mills closed. Nash, however, survived and is now one of a number of British paper-mills owned by the large South African paper-making group, Sappi, which bought the mill in 1990, ending 180 years of single company ownership.

comparison with earlier periods when capital requirements were, by and large, met by the cash generated by the business. Spending over £40 million in a decade and a half, however, demanded both a more involved and inventive approach to finance, requiring James Cropper to act as much like an entrepreneur as an accountant in his role as finance director. Persuading people to lend money in the first place was often a challenge, and his task was complicated by the fact that rights issues – perhaps the safest and easiest form of finance available – were not an option, as they would have diluted the firm's precious independence.[45]

Banks, on the other hand, were prevailed upon as much as possible. Before the mid-1960s one bank had sufficed: the company's comparatively modest requirements were all met by the Liverpool banking firm Martin's, which was soon afterwards taken over by Barclays, still the firm's day-to-day banker today. Thereafter, however, as borrowing requirements grew the company approached other banks for longer term finance. Many arrangements – which ranged in size from £100,000 to several million – were made by James Cropper himself, but a good number were also facilitated by John Sclater, a non-executive director of the firm since 1972.[46] For more than thirty years, during which time he has enjoyed a very successful career in the City, he has been an indispensable source of financial advice and contacts. Indeed, he introduced James Cropper plc to a number of banks where he worked, including Glyn Mills (account opened in 1969), Guinness Mahon (1986) and Hill Samuel (1991), one of several firms where he has been chairman. His position and influence did not, however, prevent the relationship with Hill Samuel turning sour in the early 1990s, as previously mentioned.

Banks were, however, only part of the equation. "There were limits to how much they were prepared to lend, and how much was sensible to borrow", says James Cropper, "and as we weren't making enough profit to pay up front for re-equipping the mills as fast as we wanted to, we had to find money elsewhere." One key alternative was leasing, where the cost of equipment was paid for by a leasing firm and then leased back to the firm over a specified period, usually five to ten years. It is a common enough form of finance today, but the company first took advantage of it when it was in its infancy. In 1969 it paid for a new high speed Masson Scott cutter by leasing it through Astley Industrial Trust, a pioneer in the field. It was a ground-breaking move at the time ("way out" comments John Larking) but nevertheless made sound economic sense. Leasing finance was not only easier to secure than bank loans, but also allowed the company to borrow more money than it could otherwise have done. Until the 1980s (by which time the accountancy profession had grown wise) the company was not required to show its leased assets on its balance sheet. This kept the visible level of debt down and made the company's return on assets look better, which helped its relationship with banks and shareholders.

Leasing finance was subsequently used on many occasions. It paid for a whole range of new finishing equipment, including winders, embossers and several cutters, the most expensive of which (made by the Spanish company Pasaban) was installed at a cost of almost £1 million in 1986. Leasing also facilitated the final and most expensive project in the company's modernisation programme, the installation of a new No3 machine in 1990, which cost more than £10 million. Over £7 million of this sum was financed by leases from Crédit Lyonnais and the Banque National de Paris, without which the scheme could never have gone ahead. Even finding this money was a challenge. "Nearly all of the UK leasing companies we approached wouldn't touch it as they thought the risk was too high", recalls James Cropper. "Even these two companies only agreed to the deal after considerable persuasion from the leasing broker we appointed."[47]

Another very important source of funding (and, crucially, one that did not require repayment) was the government. Many British paper-makers felt that the government betrayed the industry by entering EFTA and subsequently the EEC, but James Cropper plc's experience tells a very different tale. The firm was helped enormously by several government schemes, not least regional development grants, which were introduced in 1967. These aimed to promote investment in certain areas, including Westmorland, and the sums paid out were substantial. Between 1967 and 1971 forty to forty-five percent of the cost of new plant and machinery at Burneside and Cowan Head was financed in this way, and from 1972 to 1980 (after which Westmorland was removed from the catchment area) twenty percent of the cost of capital projects was paid for. Over the whole period the company received regional development grants exceeding £1.8 million.

The importance of such funding cannot be overestimated. "Government grants were a key to our survival", comments James Cropper. "Without them we could never have invested at the rate we did and might not have modernised quickly enough to survive." In particular, they played a central part in the replacement of the firm's No4 machine in 1980, a third of the cost of which was paid for by the Treasury, not only in the form of a regional development grant (£625,000), but also through a special grant of £480,000 from the Department of Industry, which administered a scheme to encourage greater use of waste paper. The Department of Industry also led the company to the remainder of the finance for the project, as one of the conditions of its grant was that James Cropper plc take a loan from the European Investment Bank. The exact reasons for this remain unclear, but James Cropper seized the opportunity, borrowing £1.4 million from the bank. He had good reason to do so: the interest on the loan was fixed for seven years at the extremely preferential rate of 8.5 percent, almost half the base rate of interest in the UK at the time.

In retrospect such finance seems almost too good to be true, yet government assistance did not stop there. During the 1970s and 1980s the company also benefited from generous tax allowances, which allowed it to write off capital expenditure against profits. In place between 1970 and 1986, for much of this period the company was able to offset one hundred percent of the cost of new plant and machinery and between forty and seventy-five percent of the cost of new buildings against profits. As a result it paid no mainstream corporation tax on its profits and hardly any tax at all for more than fifteen years. Much to James Cropper's regret, however, the allowances were cut by the Chancellor in 1984 and then phased out altogether in 1986. "I hope the government will reconsider this disincentive to invest", he commented in 1987, when the firm began paying tax on its profits for the first time since 1970. "Otherwise increasing amounts of profit will have to be reserved for tax, despite the continuing need to generate internal funds to finance our future investment". Needless to say, however, his viewpoint was unheeded, and today thirty percent of the company's profits are consumed by the taxman. It is only fortunate that since the early 1990s the company's capital requirements have been much lower than they were in the 1970s and 1980s, when tax bills of this size would have crippled the business.

The final source of funds made use of by James Cropper as finance director was altogether closer to home. Since the mid-1970s the company has raised considerable sums by the periodic sale of houses built or bought since its foundation in 1845. A few houses had been sold in the past, but it was not until 1976 that the directors decided to starting selling its houses in Burneside and nearby. The decision marked the end of an era in terms of the firm's close relationship with the local community, but it was not taken for solely commercial reasons. It was also socially a sign of the times: demand for accommodation from employees was declining, not only because growing numbers were choosing to buy rather than rent, but also because more lived further away and came to work by car. In addition, there were plenty of council houses available, including fifty built in the early 1970s on the Hall Park Estate adjacent to Burneside Mills.

Nevertheless, there was a compelling economic case for selling houses, as the value of property was growing enormously. In 1966 the company's 180 houses were estimated to stand the company at £99,000 – only a few hundred pounds each – yet in the course of the next thirty years yielded more than £4 million for the firm, a very useful, if unusual, source of money. Furthermore, even though James Cropper plc was gradually divesting itself of the asset, housing was also a useful form of security. On many occasions houses were used to secure borrowings, although not any more. The 79 remaining houses in its ownership were sold in 1999 for £1.8 million, 68 of them to a housing association.

Impressive though they are, James Cropper's skills at raising and spending money are only one facet of the reshaping of the firm in recent times. As the modernisation of Burneside Mills gathered steam from the mid-1970s, the directors were equally busy ensuring the success and survival of the business in other less tangible ways. In 1974, for example, they overhauled the firm's accounting procedures by introducing a new system and appointing the company's first chief accountant, David Carey. Thereafter the company was able to set annual budgets for the first time and keep a more accurate check on its performance, a critical change in an age of narrowing margins. This had not always been possible before, when production and sales were reviewed on a fortnightly basis. "The results didn't tally with the estimates", explains David Carey, "so the company did not actually know whether it was losing or making money. It could lose money when it thought it was profitable." The new system is still in use today, and David remains chief accountant as well as company secretary, a position he has held since 1997.

From the mid-1970s there were also many changes on the personnel side, affecting how the firm's employees were paid, trained, protected and represented. It is difficult to summarise many of these, influenced as they were by such diverse factors as changing legislation, unions and union representatives (key figures here include Ian Huck), not to mention individuals such as Les Buckle – personnel manager from 1974 to 1998 – and Oliver Acland, in charge of personnel issues for over thirty years until his retirement in 1997. Nor is it easy to appreciate the delicate balance that the company has had to maintain between creating a desirable workplace and motivated workforce – a pressing issue in the early 1970s when labour shortages were still a problem – and keeping employment costs under control, a problem in the 1980s and 1990s. It has not been an easy balance to strike, but over the years Burneside Mills has become a more financially rewarding, fairer, safer and less strenuous workplace.

Such changes were as important, in their own way, as the physical reconstruction of the mills. "The company is not a machine", explains Oliver Acland. "Its heart is its labour force and modernising this has been equally important." Key developments he oversaw included the introduction of a contributory works pension scheme in 1978 (pushed through in great part by the unions), and a growing emphasis on creating a skilled and knowledgeable workforce through training. Indeed, this was a major focus for Oliver throughout his career. Instigator of the firm's first educational scheme in 1961, thereafter he led many advances in this field, including the appointment of the firm's first training officer in 1971 (Jack Webb), the launch of youth training in the 1980s (pushed through with Webb's successor, Ian Valentine), and the introduction of City & Guilds courses for all process operators (also in the 1980s). Indeed, his enthusiasm for education and training took him far beyond Burneside. From the early 1970s he took the lead in the British paper industry as a whole, initially as chairman of the Employers' Federation Education & Training Committee, and from 1982 as chairman of the UK Paper Federation's Education & Training Council, in recognition of which he was presented with the Paper Industry Gold Medal in 1995, the industry's highest award.[48]

Oliver Acland also played a central role in the harmonisation of pay and conditions across the company.[49] Involving all manner of changes from the early 1970s, this issue was only finally laid to rest five years after he retired, with a new remuneration agreement which came into effect in 2002-3, carefully designed to remove all artificial and historic barriers between salaried staff and hourly-paid status. For many years there had been considerable friction between the two parties, both wanting the best of each other's perks and agreements. "The aim was to remove a deeply engrained culture of 'them and us' between various groups of employees which had not served the company and its employees well", explains James Cropper. "The culture represented a significant barrier to change and prosperity over many years and had to be removed to enable the company to survive." As a result, all jobs are now graded and evaluated through the same process and all employees paid in the same way, on a monthly basis.

One element of the harmonisation that had been dealt with many years before related to the payment of bonuses. Before the late 1970s staff were paid a certain percentage of profits as bonus (the exact amount in proportion to their salary), while hourly-paid workers had various incentive schemes, which were tied to meeting productivity targets. First introduced in the 1950s, these became increasingly complex and costly to administer and were eventually superseded in the early 1980s by a single-profit related pay scheme for all employees. "In retrospect this was one of the most important moves that we ever made", notes Oliver Acland, not only as it simplified the matter enormously but also because it saved the company money; the staff bonus scheme, in particular, had become very expensive with as much as twenty percent of the company's profit paid out in some years. For several years the new scheme paid employees a bonus the moment the company made a profit, but in 1999 a threshold was set (currently £2 million) in order to reduce employment costs, which at that time were accounting for over a quarter of turnover.

As one delves further and further into the various factors that have underpinned the development of James Cropper plc since the early 1970s, it is easy to lose sight of the ultimate source of the firm's prosperity and survival: the profitable manufacture and sale of paper. Over 40,000 tonnes of paper and board are now produced at Burneside every year, and since 1970 the company has sold over 1.25 million tonnes of the material. Producing and selling such quantities has, of course, been enabled by the company's reconstruction programme, which doubled capacity and ensured that the whole operation remained competitive by dramatically improving productivity and efficiency. Moreover, it gave the company the technical capability to make new grades, and ensured that output met the growing quality requirements of customers.

Keeping the machines rolling has also, however, been ensured by James Cropper plc's sales and marketing strategy. Another area of sweeping change in the period covered by this chapter, this chiefly developed in reaction to growing competition, particularly from overseas countries with vast forestry resources. "With EFTA and the rise of combined paper and pulp mills we said we can't compete with these people, and never will – we will therefore make the things they can't make", explains Nick Willink. "This led to a completely different marketing strategy. We began to ask 'What do you want, and can we make it for you?'"

The results of the change in outlook were profound, leading the company to transform itself from a relatively unknown provincial manufacturer of strong but crude papers into a world-class producer of coloured and specialised grades, with a vision statement to match: "Our vision is to be THE company which excels in coloured and other specialist paper . . . for a worldwide market".[50] Along the way this has involved a sustained movement away from commodity grades to exclusive products with higher margins that are less vulnerable to competition. Time and time again lower margin papers have been dropped, ranging from a plethora of products in the early 1970s (including glazed casings, tea cartridge and insulating paper) to general printing and writing grades in the 1990s. "Much of the improvement in our performance has resulted from the continuing evolution of our products mix out of commodity papers into more complex areas", noted James Cropper in 1997, referring to that year's record profit of £5 million.

The key break in the transition to higher margin products, however, was the company's withdrawal from MG (machine-glazed) paper-making in 1990. The market for MG grades (by that time mainly brown envelopes and white poster paper) had first begun to look fragile in the 1970s, mainly due to competition from substantial new capacity installed in Scandinavia. By the mid-1980s it was even worse despite the closure of a number of British competitors, so when the directors decided to replace its ancient No2 MG machine in 1986 (Fig. 9.10), it made sense to opt for a small twin-wire Fourdrinier machine instead. Designed and constructed in-house with help from local firms at a cost of £3 million, this enabled the company to make more of its trademark coloured paper, a shift in output that soon paid off. "The decision has been amply justified as the market we left deteriorated further", noted James Cropper in 1991, "and the paper made on the new machine has been much more profitable."[51]

By 1989 the success of the new No2 machine had encouraged the directors to

Fig. 9.10 – Detail of the ancient No2 machine which was replaced in 1986, 123 years after it began making paper at Burneside. Although much modified, some of its parts were still wooden, as shown here.

abandon MG paper-making altogether, by replacing its remaining MG machine (No3, last upgraded in 1976) with a large single-wire Fourdrinier, designed to make higher value-added papers. This, however, was a much bigger leap, not only historically – it ended almost 130 years of MG paper-making at Burneside – but also financially. By the time the work was completed in 1990 the total project costs (which included a new cutter and warehouse extension) had soared way over budget to more than £10 million, easily the most expensive project the company has ever undertaken. The machine alone, which was designed and constructed by Holder Pamac, cost £8.8 million. It was also a very challenging project commercially, as it meant doing away with many existing grades (MG lines were still fairly large in volume) and finding a considerable amount of new business to fill the capacity, which was double that of the machine's predecessor. The logistics were also daunting: "This was no green-field site that could be worked on while the mill ran smoothly", noted Nick Willink in the 1991 Annual Report. "This was a development taking place in the heart of the mill with a very short timescale." In total eighty-two different contractors were involved, supervised by Peter Charlton (Fig. 9.11). It was the last project he led as the firm's engineering director before retiring in 1991, and a fitting climax for it marked the end of the transformation of Burneside Mills that he had led since joining James Cropper plc in the mid-1970s.

The sustained move towards more specialised, higher margin papers was facilitated by many factors. Not least, although it was not its cardinal attribute, it helped that the company had a long history of specialisation. As early as the 1860s James Cropper & Co. was an acknowledged specialist in the production of coloured paper – an association that has been exploited to the full in recent times – and by the 1870s had begun to venture into higher margin technical grades with the manufacture of cloth-lined paper by the process invented and patented by Charles Cropper. By the early twentieth century the value of such specialisation was clearly recognised. "Our great hope seems to be in specialities", Charles remarked to his son James W. in 1916, and this was perhaps the basis for the firm's move away from lightweight commodity grades such as 'buff' to thicker, better quality papers in the 1920s.

Fig. 9.11 – Peter Charlton, James Cropper plc's engineering director, pictured in the No3 machine house prior to the installation of the new machine, 1990.

Meeting customer requirements, another important element of the company's evolution into 'speciality' manufacturers, also drew upon an enduring strength, flexibility. The Cropper mills had always been more flexible than most, making a diverse range of papers on machines of varying type and size, an attribute that has been exploited to the full in recent times. As new plant was installed, flexibility was quite literally built into the fabric of the mills. The firm's No1 machine, for instance, was rebuilt to the same specification as the much larger No4 so that both could produce the same papers but in very different quantities. Flexibility also played a part in the selection of individual components. Voith headboxes, for example, were chosen as they were rapidly adjustable, allowing quick changes in the weight of papers. Furthermore, the machines were designed to allow for very quick changes in colour, and state-of-the-art computer controls installed so that the specification of different grades could be tightly controlled even when small batches were being made. This was particularly important given the company's emphasis on quality.* "Computer measurement and control enabled us to become fine paper-makers", comments James Cropper. "Before it was almost impossible to make paper to any defined specification".

The results are clear. Today there are few paper-makers in the world who can make such a wide range of fine, coloured paper (Fig. 9.12) and even fewer that are prepared to make black papers on the same machines that they use for their cleanest whites. Indeed, most paper-makers still refuse to make black papers, a situation that the company has exploited to the full as a market leader in this field.[52] There are also few paper-makers that can handle such a variety of order sizes. Indeed, despite annual output doubling to more than 40,000 tonnes, the company can still handle orders of less than two tonnes, which can be made in under an hour. Most paper-mills would not dream of making paper in such small batches, not only due to the logistics but also the losses in process, which are correspondingly high. Indeed, it has been an ongoing battle at Burneside to minimise wastage between colour and weight changes.

Fig. 9.12 – Left: *Fan of colours made on one machine in just one month, as good an example as any of the wide range of coloured paper made at Burneside. Fig. 9.13* – Right: *One of many examples of packaging using Cropper materials, in this case liqueur boxes made from paper merchant G. F. Smith's Colorflute range.*

---

* On No.1 machine changing the basis weight of papers is further enabled by the installation of a high frequency dryer, one of only four in the world ever built and the only one still in operation. This concentrates the drying energy on places where the moisture is, creating a more even sheet. (Interview, Nick Willink)

James Cropper plc's evolution into a specialised paper-maker was also hastened by changes in the market place. This is particularly evident in the realm of retail packaging materials, a market that the company has supplied since its earliest days. Historically, this was predominantly a market for the company's cheap plain grades such as MG Kraft, which were still commonly used for wrapping goods at the point of sale in the 1960s. Thereafter, however, it quickly became a market for high quality, expensive papers in a spectrum of colours, reflecting the fact that packaging had become, in many cases, as important as the product itself (Fig. 9.13). Arising from the switch to self-service retailing in the 1960s (which called for goods to be pre-packaged), James Cropper plc exploited the new demand to the full. Indeed, high grade packaging soon became (and remains) a key market for paper made at Burneside. Since the mid-1990s in particular, Cropper paper has been used to package all manner of branded goods such as perfume and whisky (names supplied here include Jean Paul Gaultier and Glenmorangie) as well as other luxury products. In the late 1990s, for example, Gucci carrier bags were all made from a ribbed grey paper produced at Burneside (Fig. 9.14).[53]

Fig. 9.14 – Left: *Gucci carrier bags made from Cropper paper.* Right: *in recent years packaging for perfumes and other cosmetics has become an important market for paper made at Burneside.*

Another area where the company has benefited from the growing vogue for presentation is corporate communications. Annual reports, for example, which are now a medium for marketing as much as for presenting results, have become an excellent market for the company's cover papers, an area in which it is dominant today. Not least, this is evident in James Cropper plc's own reports, which evolved from thin bland publications in the early 1970s (akin to school exercise books in quality and excitement) into carefully designed and illustrated brochures showcasing an array of its papers by the 1990s, several of which subsequently won awards as the best of their kind.[54]

Opportunities to specialise were also created by the contraction of British paper-making in the 1970s. In particular, the closure of one Scottish mill in 1971, Robert Craig, by then part of Associated Paper, had long-lasting repercussions at Burneside. First, it brought new business in bookbinding grades – thin, durable embossed papers that were beginning to supersede cloth on the covers of hardback books. The company had first made imitation bookcloth in 1964, but following the demise of Craig (a competing producer), became European market leaders in this specialised field, latterly through its association with the Swiss-owned Winter & Company, with which it has enjoyed a fruitful relationship for many years. Indeed the mill closure even helped in physical terms, as the company subsequently acquired one of Craig's embossers, which is still being used to produce bookbinding papers today.

More significantly, the closure of Craig had a dramatic impact on James Cropper plc's standing in the field of cover papers. It brought the firm two of its most important customers in the last thirty years, the specialist merchant G. F. Smith and the paper group Wiggins Teape, which sold cover paper under the brand-name Keays. Both came to Burneside looking for a new supplier of cover paper and within a few years were accounting for a significant chunk of turnover. Furthermore, the new customers, in particular G. F. Smith, took James Cropper plc into the premium end of the market for the first time. Before this, it had been reluctant to quote for contracts with very high specifications – in 1970, for instance, it had declined to tender for a contract to supply the covers for British telephone directories. However, with a pledge of support from G. F. Smith, the company agreed to try its hand at higher quality papers, and success soon followed.

In retrospect, the move to better grades of paper was a vital moment in the move towards specialisation. "More than anything else", comments James Cropper, "this marked the birth of Croppers as fine coloured paper-makers." Indeed, not long afterwards the previously ignored contract for telephone directory covers was won, and by the mid-1970s the company was pre-eminent in cover papers, a position it has maintained to this day, not least owing to its close and long-lasting relationship with G. F. Smith, whose Colorplan range is made at Burneside (and used in the end-papers of this book).[55] For many years this has been one of the most successful ranges of cover papers in Europe. The relationship with Wiggins Teape (latterly Arjo Wiggins) was equally important for many years, but not so enduring: it came to an end in the early 1990s when it decided to make all of the cover papers it sold at its own Stoneywood paper-mill near Aberdeen.[56]

The transformation of James Cropper plc into a specialised paper manufacturer gained further momentum owing to the direct impact of foreign competition, particularly from the Nordic bloc. Scandinavian mills not only pushed the company out of MG papers, but also out of several other grades. For instance,

Cropper's dominance in waxing cartridge – a lifeline in the 1950s – was effectively destroyed in the late 1960s when the Norwegian manufacturer Borregaard introduced a much cheaper equivalent it could not match on price. The same happened soon afterwards when Billerud, a Swedish paper manufacturer, introduced a new filing board: the Scandinavian-made product was so cheap it took a significant share of the market for MG pasted boards made at Burneside, a staple source of revenue since the 1920s.[57]

In the long term, however, the loss of such products benefited the company. The market in waxing cartridge (which was used in food packaging) was beginning to be mortally damaged by the rise of plastics, while the demise of pasted boards, production of which stopped fairly quickly, also worked to its advantage.[58] Soon afterwards the company replaced it with a new filing product – a water finished manilla – specially developed in response to the competition. Used in files, folders, document wallets and suspension files (Fig. 9.15), this was the foundation of a range that proved to be more resilient to foreign competition. Indeed, manillas have generated a large share of income and profits ever since. By

Fig. 9.15 – Filing grades made by James Cropper plc, c.1995. The Guildhall brand belongs to Tollitt & Harvey, one of the firm's most longstanding customers.

the 1980s James Cropper plc was producing half the UK output of manilla paper, and it still accounts for a large percentage of turnover in 2004, even though the market has become more competitive. The new manilla also brought the company some of its most important customers, including Swindon Letter File (taken over by Avery International in the 1980s), which was a major customer until 2002, and Tollitt & Harvey, manufacturers and distributors of office products.[59] The latter firm has been a key customer since the mid-1970s, and its Cropper-based products (which include document wallets and notepads) are available through many outlets on the high street, including W. H. Smith.[60]

The way James Cropper plc went about meeting customers' specifications was also transformed by its sales strategy. Prior to the early 1970s this had changed little in decades, the firm following the same practices and routines that it had since the late nineteenth century. There was no leadership from directors, and little more from the sales manager, whose chief task was making routine visits to existing clients. Similarly, though there was a sales team at Burneside, its task was not to generate new business but to process orders as they came in. The stagnating state of affairs was perpetuated by the way paper was sold in Britain in general, which until the 1960s had changed very little since the dawn of a national paper trade in the mid-nineteenth century. Most paper was still sold indirectly to customers through small merchants and agents, the majority of which were concentrated in a small area of London around Fleet Street. James Cropper & Co. followed the general trend, continuing to sell a large proportion of output through small merchants and its two agents, Thomas Ross in Scotland (appointed in 1898), and the London firm of J. M. Oldham (appointed in 1888). Indeed, Oldham was still considered such an important asset in the late 1960s that Reggie Oldham (in charge since the early 1920s) was appointed a non-executive director on Anthony Cropper's death in 1967. "A very large proportion of our production is sold through them", commented Derek Willink at the time, "and undoubtedly Mr Oldham's experience will give great strength to the Board in its overall sales policy."[61]*

Within a few years, however, the situation had changed dramatically. The 1970s saw the end of the firm's age-old association with agents, including J. M. Oldham, which became its London sales office not long after Reggie Oldham's death in 1972. In 1974 even more dramatic changes followed: the London and Manchester sales offices were both closed, and the sales force completely reorganised with everybody based at Burneside. At the same time the company took steps to terminate arrangements with its Scottish and Irish agents.[62]

In part the transformation was a consequence of the changing structure of the British paper trade. In the early 1970s the historic dominance of the Fleet Street area began to wane – prefiguring dramatic changes in printing and publishing in the same area – and smaller paper merchants and agents began to disappear nationwide just as many paper-mills closed their doors for the last time. The whole process of change was accelerated by improvements in communications, in

---

* With Oldham representing James Cropper & Co. in London, it was rare for anyone from the firm to venture into the capital. Indeed, Philip Huck, regional salesman for many years, recalls the interest when he turned up in the Old London, a pub in Ludgate Hill where many paper merchants plied their trade. It had been so long since any of them had met anybody from Burneside that he was the centre of attention. "The message went round", he recalls, "'there's somebody live from Croppers!' . . . and everybody gathered round, keen to know what was happening".

particular roads. Indeed, just as railways transformed the paper industry in the nineteenth century – a topic covered extensively in Chapter Three – the development of the British motorway network also had significant repercussions. By switching deliveries to road rather than rail, it became much easier for paper-makers to supply customers directly or, failing that, through a new network of large national merchants such as Robert Horne. The same applied to selling. Helped by better roads and motorcars a small sales team at Burneside could service customers throughout Britain. Agents were no longer necessary.

For James Cropper plc there were, of course, other strategic reasons for direct selling. Bringing the sales team back to Burneside helped the firm build closer relationships with customers – a key consideration as competition intensified, particularly as its policy was to win business through quality and service rather than price. The change in sales organisation was also driven by the need to seek business actively, another significant break with the past that became increasingly apparent during the 1970s. "In the past year the need to sell, as opposed to visiting customers or waiting for new business to arrive by enquiry", a mid-1970s company memo comments, "has become more and more obvious."[63] This became even more necessary as new capacity came on line. Indeed, when the new No4 machine came into use in 1980 it required the Cropper sales team to sell an extra 200 tonnes per week, a challenge that pushed them to the limit owing to the severe recession in British paper-making at the time.

The need to solicit business actively was made all the more urgent by the demise of many long-established customers, including McCorquodale & Co. Major shareholders since 1853 and purchasers of cloth-lined paper since 1879, by the 1970s the relationship was fast approaching the end of its life. The production of cloth-lined ceased with the closure of Cowan Head in 1977, and with the McCorquodale shareholding in steep decline, it was only a matter of time before the family gave up its long-held non-executive position on the board. This came in 1978, with the resignation of Alastair McCorquodale, the fourth generation of his family to be associated with the firm.

Another element of the company's new sales strategy, but one that experienced a more gradual evolution, was marketing. In a market where it could no longer expect orders without actively pursuing them, the company had to pay much more attention to its reputation and prominence, necessitating a shift in focus that can clearly be seen in its attention to branding, which began with its pigeon logo, first introduced in 1964 (Fig. 9.16). Since the mid-1970s it has also launched more branded lines alongside the established Kendal range, including Portfolio in 1990 and Accent in 1995, a collection of super-smooth text and cover papers created with G. F. Smith.[64]

Fig. 9.16 – The evolution of James Cropper plc's pigeon logo, first introduced in 1964. It was based upon the Cropper species of pigeon, notable for its proud chest.

The chief driving force behind the rapid modernisation of James Cropper plc's sales and marketing strategy was John Larking. Stepping sideways out of production to become the firm's first designated sales director in 1972, without him it is doubtful that the firm would have been so quick to react to changing circumstances or so shrewd in its reaction. For he was not only a fount of new ideas but a powerful and uncompromising manager with the drive and nerve (and temper) to make sweeping changes even when business was at its most precarious. It was at his behest, for example, that the company's London and Manchester sales offices were closed, and he was also behind the company exploring new products and new customers. Moreover, he did much to improve the efficiency of the mills by harmonising sales and production. Until the early 1970s most orders (with the exception of a handful of standard lines) were made to a unique specification, based on laboratory analysis of samples sent to them by customers, and which were often so small that they were stapled to the corner of a letter. It was, it need hardly be said, a far from ideal procedure, especially as the analysis usually dictated the price quoted for the job. "Almost everything was made on a bespoke basis, and the whole thing had a very dodgy scientific and technical basis", comments John Larking. "The poor production people had hundreds and hundreds of specs to work to." What he did instead was at once obvious, but revolutionary. Grades were grouped together so they could be made from the same blends of pulps and other materials, whittling down the number of possible variations to a limited list of standard furnishes.

John Larking was also a driving force in the field of exports. In the 1960s and before exports of Cropper paper had been negligible, accounting for less than three percent of turnover at most, nearly all of which was dispatched through Crown agents to Commonwealth countries outside Europe, such as India, Pakistan, Australia and New Zealand.[65] Under his supervision, however, selling paper abroad became a key source of revenue for the company. Helped by figures such as Alan

Sutton, Alan Bobbett and Nigel Read (appointed export manager in 1983), he improved the company's export performance dramatically in the 1970s and 1980s, the value of exports jumping from £138,000 in 1970 to almost £4.8 million by 1985. Since then the trend has only continued. In the last decade almost a third of turnover, equating to revenues of almost £20 million per year, has been sold overseas. In that time Cropper paper has been delivered to more than fifty different countries in almost every corner of the globe.

The dramatic growth of exports began in Europe. In the early 1970s many perceived that entry into the European Economic Community in 1973 would spell the end of the British paper industry, which was already in decline at home. "Many paper-makers said it would be death – 'it will be hell, we'll all go down'," recalls Nick Willink. At Burneside, however, it was greeted as an opportunity. "John [Larking] said 'Rubbish – it's a market, we'll go and sell in it'." Which is exactly what he did: on the back of a scheduled trip to Germany in January 1973 he spent a few extra days visiting potential customers in Germany and Holland.

It was the company's first ever attempt to generate business abroad, and the results were promising. Orders were won in Holland, and within a year 750 tonnes of paper had been shipped to Germany.[66] A good proportion of this was made into telephone directory covers in the Hanover district, an achievement that the company were rightly proud of, even reproducing the cover in its 1974 Annual Report. Thereafter the export drive went from strength to strength: agents were appointed in most EEC member states, market research was commissioned and more overseas visits made. By 1975 Alan Sutton had been to the Far East and John Larking to Africa, where significant quantities of paper were subsequently sold in Nigeria, an excellent market until oil revenues declined a few years later. By 1980, by which time the company could even boast it was selling paper to Sweden, home to many competing products, around 5,000 tonnes of paper was being sold outside the UK each year.

The growth has continued in more recent times. Between 1987 and 1991, for example, the number of export customers jumped from 187 to 318, and in Europe from 73 to 183, following a concerted sales drive. This, and more recent growth, has been underpinned by the appointment of agents in more and more countries, and by exhibiting at trade fairs.[67] The company's Taiwanese agent, for example, was appointed after a chance encounter at the DRUPA print and paper exhibition in 1992, where James Cropper plc was exhibiting for the first time. Within three years he was bringing the company £500,000 of business per year. In terms of volume, however, Europe continues to dominate: since the mid-1990s it has accounted for sixty to seventy percent of export business.

James Cropper plc's export record is in many respects the ultimate expression of the company's achievement in recent times. For it has not only managed to survive in a British market dominated by large international firms, but also to forge a place for itself as a global player, a world-leader in its specialised area of fine coloured papers. Given the fate of many British paper-mills and the fact that the firm remains in independent British ownership, it is a remarkable achievement that James Cropper and his fellow directors should be proud of. It is also one that they have had just cause to celebrate a number of times, not least the company's 150th anniversary, which was marked with four days of celebrations at Burneside in the summer of 1995.

The occasion would be a good note to conclude on, but there is a catch in the tale. For despite all the best efforts of everybody at Burneside, James Cropper plc has not been able to control every factor influencing its fate. To its credit the company has survived and is, today, on a steady footing with a great reputation, modern operation, desirable products, and low borrowings. On the downside, however, the profitability of paper-making in the small Lake District village is still a cause for concern. There have been some good times in the last twenty years, and the size of profits and turnover have grown dramatically, underpinned by the massive investment in new capacity. Furthermore, with the exception of 2001, when a small loss was sustained, the company has stayed in the black every year since 1976. Equally importantly, it has managed to pay back huge borrowings. Profit margins, however, perhaps a better indication of performance, have remained as low as they were in the early 1970s, rarely exceeding five percent. Indeed, for much of the last decade and a half margins have struggled to reach this mark.

Remarkably, it was a situation that the company's founder knew well. "My business is pretty brisk", noted James Cropper in 1847, just two years into his paper-making career, "but it is not very profitable. Until you know by experience, it is almost impossible to conceive the many points which affect the profit in this trade." More than a century and half later, his great-great grandson and namesake can identify with his frustration, although the failure to generate decent returns is not attributable to inexperience so much as a reflection of trading conditions.

In common with much of British industry, the rapid growth of international trade has had mixed blessings for James Cropper plc. For although it has brought new opportunities, it has exposed the company to economic pressures outside its control more than ever before. The strength of sterling in recent years, for instance, has often given foreign mills a competitive edge, both within the UK and abroad. At the same time margins have also been regularly eroded by global fluctuations in energy costs.

The most pressing problem, however, and an enduring thorn in the side of James Cropper plc and many other paper-makers, has been the volatility of pulp prices. As the trade and production of pulp has globalised – regions such as China and South-East Asia joining established producers such as Sweden and the USA – the material has become more and more entrenched as a commodity subject to price fluctuations that are volatile and hard to predict. The pulp cycle is a well charted phenomenon, and one that refuses to go away. Indeed, if anything it has become more frequent: whereas in the 1970s a full cycle typically covered a span of a few years, today the swing from peak to trough and back again can take as little time as a few months.[68]

The effect of such fluctuations on James Cropper plc's profits can be clearly charted. A sudden dip in profits in 1985, for example, following a record year in 1984, exactly corresponded with a thirty percent rise in the cost of wood-pulp, which was sparked by a strike in Canadian pulp-mills and made worse by the strengthening dollar. In the following year, meanwhile, when pulp costs had eased off, profits jumped to a new high. Since then the pattern has recurred again and again. In 1996, for example, when profits dropped from £2.5 million to £1.8 million, pulp prices were again the chief problem. "Never in my working lifetime have I experienced such a rapid movement in the price of pulp in such a short period", commented James Cropper. "Bleached Kraft [a common type of pulp] started at $750, was almost $1,000 by Christmas, then down to $550 by the end of March."[69]

Assuring consistent returns in the face of such fluctuations has proved very difficult. In theory, the company could make use of the global trade in pulp and buy in the cheapest market regardless of quality, but as a manufacturer of high quality paper and card this carries significant risks. Alternatively, pulp price increases could be passed onto customers by raising paper prices, but again this has often proved undesirable: on many occasions James Cropper plc has resisted passing price increases onto customers, in order to nurture long-term stable relationships, even if this has meant lower profit figures at times. At other times, passing on pulp costs has been impossible: sometimes the market will not support the required paper price.

For many years, however, the company has been nurturing a long-term solution to the enduring problem. Indeed, the directors recognised the problem long before it became so serious, and their reaction was characteristically quick and shrewd. The result is that since the early 1980s James Cropper plc has been pursuing a strategy, as yet unmentioned, that has done much to shelter it from the worst excesses of the pulp cycle, and much else besides. Rather than depending solely on paper-making for its success and survival, it has built other legs for the business to stand upon through one basic policy: Diversification.

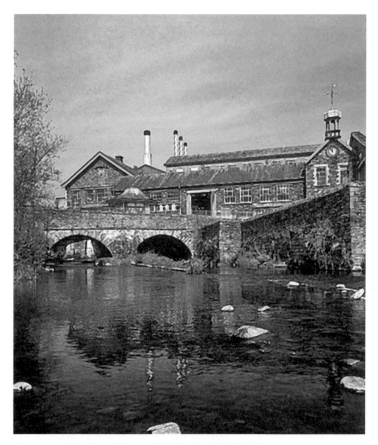

Fig. 10.1 – The view of Burneside Mills across the river Kent.

Postscript

A diversified concern: 2004

"Throughout the course of this century, James Cropper has reinvented itself many times – from a three into a one site mill; out of wrappers and kraft papers and MG paper making into more specialist grades; and more recently from pure paper making into paper converting and specialty high performance materials. Each of these changes has required a tremendous ability to adapt and in many cases a leap of faith into the unknown". (James Cropper, December 1999)

LIKE any history, the story of the Cropper paper-mills and the generations that have worked inside them is a record of constant change, and this final postscript – an adjunct to Chapter Nine in subject-matter as well as time – is no exception. Yet even as the company approaches its 160th anniversary, there are still strong threads of continuity in this tale. Production, for instance, remains on the same site at Burneside where James Cropper began trading in 1845, the firm refusing to give up its roots in the beautiful surroundings of the English Lake District. Every ton of paper the company sells is still produced in the small village on the banks of the river Kent, which also remains the workplace of nearly all of its employees.

Burneside's paper-mill also looks the same, at least from the outside (Fig. 10.1). Indeed, if the generations of men and women buried in the village churchyard were to look across the river from their final resting place, a stone's throw from the mill, they would see much that was reassuringly familiar. The same bridge pictured in an oil painting of the 1820s still crosses the river, while the clock-tower built after the catastrophic fire of 1886 stands firm. The lofty chimney modelled on an Italian bell-tower has gone, replaced by a row of smaller stainless steel flues in the 1970s, but the elegant night-watchman's cabin remains, a relic of the late nineteenth century, and much else has changed little since the 1920s.

It is in relation to people, however, that there is the greatest sense of continuity. Although James Cropper plc draws in a skilled workforce from a wider catchment area than ever before, its employee registers are still home to many familiar names, foremost amongst them Daws, Huck, Lightley, Palmer, Robinson, Thornbarrow, Walker and Wilson. Of these the Lightley and Robinson families deserve a special mention, for both have been earning their living at Burneside for seven generations, an association with paper-making that stretches back beyond the Croppers to the very earliest days of paper-making at the mill. There is also strong continuity at the head of the firm. Few companies can boast a succession of four generations of directors, the achievement of the Willink family, and even fewer have been presided over by five generations of chairmen from the same family, the accomplishment of the Croppers.

There is perhaps no greater link with the past, however, than my father James. It is not just that he bears an uncanny resemblance to his ancestors, including his great-great grandfather and namesake, nor that he has lived in the same place, even the same house. What is most remarkable, especially given the passage of time, is how similar his life has been to his forebears. He has been the cornerstone of capital and management at Burneside over the course of a life-long career that is now approaching forty years. Furthermore, like his great-great grandfather and all the generations in between, his life has not only been characterised by unwavering loyalty to the family firm but also to the community, a dual inheritance that he has never neglected. For he has never just been a paper manufacturer, but at various times also a councillor, farmer, school governor, member of a water authority, and many other things besides, not least President of the UK Paper Federation from 1987-9 (the first Cropper to hold the post), and Lord Lieutenant of Cumbria, a position he has occupied since 1994. Notably, in all these fields he has acted with a sense of duty and spirit that his forebears would not only recognise but also, no doubt, be proud of.

Much as James Cropper represents the strong thread of continuity that persists at Burneside, there are, of course, many differences between the company that he presides over today and the one that he joined in 1966. Most of these have been described in detail in Chapter Nine, a catalogue of the dramatic reinvention of the paper-making firm since the late 1960s, but there are a few notable exceptions. First, although he remains chairman, a position he has occupied since 1971, today he leads a very different team from the one that surrounded him for much of his career (Fig. 10.2). Oliver Acland, Peter Charlton, John Larking and Nick Willink all retired in the course of the 1990s, making way for a new generation of management headed by Alun Lewis, appointed chief executive in 2001 after fifteen years at Burneside, where he began work as finishing manager in 1986. Four other new names also appear on today's board of executive directors: John Denman (finance director), George Quayle (division director), Nigel Read (sales director) and Patrick Willink, operations director and the fourth generation of his family to work at Burneside. In addition, the firm can also rely on the advice and guidance of two new non-executive directors, Peter Herring (appointed in 1997)

Fig. 10.2 – James Cropper plc's board of directors, 2004. Left to right: *Nigel Read, George Quayle, David Wilkes*, Alun Lewis, John Sclater*, James Cropper*, Patrick Willink, Peter Herring*, John Southwell* (retired 2004), John Denman. (*denotes non-executive)*

and David Wilkes (appointed in 2004 on the retirement of John Southwell).

Another key distinction between the company that James Cropper joined in the 1960s and the firm today is the mill at Burneside itself, for although it looks much the same from the front, from the air a very different picture can be seen (Fig. 10.3). Beyond its entrance, the footprint of the site has almost doubled in the last two decades, along the way consuming the village football pitch, as well as a sizeable patch of local farmland. Some of the expansion has been new warehousing for paper, but in greatest part it has been undertaken with new enterprises in mind. Therein lies the greatest difference between James Cropper plc in the twenty-first century and the firm that my father joined almost forty years ago. It is no longer one company but four: James Cropper Specialty Papers, James Cropper Converting, The Paper Mill Shop, and Technical Fibre Products.

In legal terms, the four have only been separate enterprises since 2003, but the history of diversification goes back many years. The firm first moved beyond basic paper-making as early as the 1860s, by which time envelopes were being made at Burneside. It was not until the early 1980s, however, that diversifying into new areas became a key element of its strategy for the future, discussed and implemented at board level with one goal in mind: to protect the company from the fluctuations in demand and profitability associated with the pulp and paper cycle. "We decided we should have more legs to stand on", comments James Cropper, who says that the idea was pushed forward by the company's non-

Fig. 10.3 – Burneside Mills from the air. Top: *the view in 1970.* Bottom: *the view by 2000.*

executive directors, including John Southwell of Laing & Cruickshank, the firm's stockbrokers, who was appointed in 1984 and retired at the 2004 AGM. A year after he joined the board James Cropper plc announced for the first time a policy to develop businesses "complimentary to paper-making but not dependent on the pulp and paper cycle".

In 2004 James Cropper plc's core activity, paper-making, is undertaken by James Cropper Specialty Papers, which is presided over by Alun Lewis as managing director, with Nigel Read in charge of sales and marketing and Patrick Willink in charge of operations. The first extra leg, and the largest in terms of turnover after this, exists around 'converting' paper, producing more valuable, higher margin products through additional processes, not least laminating sheets of paper together to produce board. Based upon a product line first developed in the 1970s, converting became a separate division in 1987 and latterly a stand-alone business as James Cropper Converting (JCC), and for the last ten years has occupied its own 55,000 square foot building at Burneside. Constructed in 1994 at a cost of £3.5 million, after a protracted battle for planning permission, the dedicated facility has more than paid for itself. Turnover grew dramatically in the course of the 1990s and in recent years has exceeded £11 million per year, generated from three main streams of activity.

Fig. 10.4 – Adrian Dolan (left) and Geoff Leech testing the superior fire resistance of the flame-retardant display board Pyrogard, 1993.

The first is the production of display board, a market that has grown through long-term collaboration with a number of paper merchants, especially Robert Horne. In particular, the merchant has helped JCC become the largest UK manufacturer of display board for point of sale advertising. Notably, the range includes fire retardant grades, initially developed at the behest of London Underground in the wake of the King's Cross fire (Fig. 10.4). Marketed under the Pyrogard brand-name, these continue to be used in Underground trains and stations and a multitude of other places where European safety legislation requires fire-proof materials.

The second line of activity is the production of high quality mount board for picture framing, a field in which the company has benefited from a long term relationship with Arqadia (previously known as Arquati), a subsidiary of Larson

Juhl, the world's largest art material distributor. JCC has worked with the company for nearly thirty years, in which time the range it has made has grown from twenty colours to almost 250 colours and textures. Finally, JCC has also carved out a valuable niche for itself as a provider of contract converting services for other members of the paper industry. The business began in the late 1970s with a contract for laminating and sheeting from Tullis Russell, another great survivor in British paper-making history, and today extends to embossing, impregnating, solid colour flexo-printing, varnishing, guillotining, and packing and labelling.

In the seventeen years since it became a separate division, James Cropper Converting has established a strong track record with regard to profits. After an initial operating loss of £30,000 in 1987, profits grew spectacularly in the first few years of the business, topping £800,000 by 1994. Thereafter they fell back to a low of £326,000 in 1996 as the business absorbed the costs of its new building, before climbing steadily to a new high of £1.06 million in 2002. Since then profits have taken another downturn, dropping to less than £400,000 in 2004 owing to a number of factors, not least fierce competition in the display board market. Nevertheless, the business has more than matched up to its task of supporting the company when paper-making margins are thin. As early as 1993 its strong performance lessened the impact of falling paper-making profits, and in 2001 a profit of £961,000 considerably softened the blow of the £1.7 million loss generated by the paper-making division. Furthermore, even in bad years margins have been better than in paper-making.

In 2004 James Cropper Converting is led by Martin Thompson. Much of its success, however, must be attributed to the leadership of Alun Lewis, who only relinquished direct responsibility for the business in 2003, two years after his appointment as chief executive. General manager from 1989, he not only oversaw the dynamic growth of the business from a small offshoot into a significant source of revenue and profit, but also the major investment in new premises in 1994. That the construction and subsequent move went so smoothly must in part be credited to his systematic outlook and attention to detail. "How do we get it right first time?", he asked at the time. "Plan, plan and plan again".

The key figure in the history of JCC is not, however, Alun Lewis so much as John Larking. He was the chief driving force behind the business until his retirement in 1991, and it was also largely his creation. Together with Nick Willink, it was his decision to invest in a laminator capable of producing four-ply boards in the mid-1970s that first enabled the company to produce display board and mount board. Furthermore, he was responsible for generating the sales that got converting off the ground. He won the first order for display board, for instance, on a sales trip to South Africa in 1975, responding to the requirements of a supermarket even though the company had never made the product before. Around the same time, and accompanied by Alan Sutton, another key figure in the early history of JCC, he also forged the long-lasting relationship with Arquati, seeing the potential in a company whose first order was initially turned down as being too small. Most importantly, however, it was his brainchild that the laminator and other equipment (such as embossing machines) that were already installed at Burneside could be used to create valuable products using paper from other mills, an approach which led directly to the formation of a separate division in 1987 and subsequently to a thriving independent business.

John Larking was also the brains behind the second leg of James Cropper plc as a diversified concern: Technical Fibre Products (TFP). Without question, TFP represents the greatest departure for the company in its long history, not only in terms of technology but also products and markets. In recent years the business has generated a turnover of over £6 million, with significant potential for future growth from its production of high performance non-woven materials for a wide range of industrial markets, including fire protection, composite structures, aerospace, thermal insulation, and fuel cells. It all started, however, as a simple idea that occurred to John Larking one day in 1982. As he read his newspaper, he came across a report about a company called RK Textiles, which had set up a plant in Scotland to produce carbon fibres and was interested to hear from organisations who might wish to use them. It set him thinking. Can we make paper from carbon fibre? How can we make it into a sheet?

Fortunately for James Cropper plc, he knew that it was possible. Before coming to Burneside for the first time in 1962 he had spent eleven years working as a technician for Whatman, the Kent based manufacturers of specialist filter papers, during which time the firm was approached by the Farnborough Royal Air Force Research Establishment. It wanted to know if carbon fibres (which had just been produced commercially for the first time) could be used in aerospace projects, and gave Whatman some samples to see if they could be made into a useful material. In the event the Airforce did not pursue the matter much further, but not before Whatman had successfully made a few sheets by hand, using basic paper-making technology.

Over twenty years later it was not, however, a simple matter of reviving the Whatman process. Although its success gave John Larking confidence, he had not been directly involved in the research and it was not an easy task to get carbon fibres to form a sheet in the same way that cellulose fibres bond in conventional paper. Nevertheless, he was very excited about the prospects and was careful to keep his idea under wraps, in the first instance only telling fellow director Nick Willink, a trained engineer with an abiding interest in the science and technology of paper-making. Together they began a clandestine trial. "We didn't tell a soul",

Nick recalls, "not even James [Cropper]". The laboratory technician Nigel Walker, who subsequently played a major part in the development of TFP, was also privy to their efforts, as John and Nick only went into the company's laboratory after dark, when everybody had gone home. They were also very careful to cover their tracks. "We washed everything up", adds Nick. "Nobody knew we'd ever been there".

Using the lab's hand-sheet paper-making equipment, after a lengthy series of experiments they eventually managed to make a carbon-fibre sheet, which was then promptly dispatched to the materials science department at Durham University for testing. The results were not disappointing. "The university reported back that the properties of material were amazing", says Nick Willink, and shortly afterwards he and John Larking decided it was time to reveal their covert experiments to others in the firm.

Thereafter the formation of a business rapidly gathered pace. By 1983 research had been transferred to the Department of Paper Science at the University of Manchester Institute of Science and Technology, and widened to cover other non-cellulose materials including glass, polyethylene and aramid fibres. In a matter of months production technology was also scaled up with the construction of a hand-sheet making facility based on traditional hand made paper-making techniques, which could produce large enough sheets for customer evaluation. The development was partly covered by a £50,000 grant from the Department of Trade and Industry secured in 1983, which also contributed towards the salaries of John Larking and Nigel Walker, who joined the project to lead technical development, a responsibility that remains his to this day.

In 1984 there was even more progress. A separate division called Fibertec was formed, commercial uses for the technology explored in the UK and the USA (which remains a key market), and a range of products exhibited at an industrial fair in Frankfurt. At the same time continuous production technology was rapidly developed. Combining aspects of Fourdrinier and vat paper-making machines with a tunnel drying oven, this led to the commissioning of the first production line in 1985. By this time the business was also making impressive progress in commercial terms. In 1985 a proposed merger with Whatman Reeve Angel tied to combining expertise in battery separator paper was abortive, but it was a measure of how seriously the business was viewed by established competitors, and there was plenty of other interest besides. In particular, there was strong demand for basalt fibre insulation paper from two sources, Lancashire Glass Fibre and Deutsche Basaltseinwolle (DBW). By 1986 this was generating sufficient volume for production to become a twenty-four hour, three shift operation. The year also witnessed success in other areas, including a distribution agreement with US company Dexter Corporation, one of the world's leading makers of wet laid nonwovens, and the introduction of two new products, ceramic fibre paper and rockwool papers. The business also became a separate limited company called Technical Fibre Products (TFP).

Fig. 10.5 – Technical Fibre Products' new premises under construction, 1987.

Remarkably, the new concern returned a profit in its first six months of trading, a considerable achievement for such a young enterprise, and in subsequent years there has been no shortage of developments that merit attention. In 1987 a joint venture, Fasertec, was created with DBW leading to the installation of TFP technology in northern Germany to produce basalt insulating paper for automotive exhausts. At the same time a new building was constructed at Burneside costing almost £800,000 (Fig. 10.5), shortly followed by a second machine installed at a cost of £480,000 in 1988. The 1990s also saw many achievements, amongst them a move into significant profitability, returns jumping from a small loss of £52,000 in 1992 to an operating profit of more than £500,000 by 1995. Not least, results were boosted by collaboration in the field of thermal insulation materials with Thermal Ceramics Inc, a division of Morgan Crucible; this led to TFP technology being installed under license in the USA, and latterly to a contract to manufacture Thermal Ceramics insulation products at Burneside.

The 1990s also saw TFP materials being used in a number of high profile areas. For instance, the unique ability of its carbon fibre materials to absorb electromagnetic interference, which was first recognised in the Durham University analysis, led to its use in two seminal consumer products of the 1990s: the Dodge Viper, the all-American muscle car launched in 1993, and the first IBM Thinkpad, a pioneering product in the history of the laptop computer launched in 1994. Furthermore, as if that was not enough, TFP materials (exactly what remains classified) were also used in another famous icon of the 1990s, the Northrop B2 Stealth Bomber.

Exciting as such uses are, an overall review of the development of Technical Fibre Products over the course of its twenty year history strikes a more disappointing note. For although hardly a year has gone by without a new development of some kind, the business has not found it easy to find its feet. Indeed, neither profits nor turnover – though they are respectable – have grown as fast as expected, and in recent years the growth of the business has stalled, turnover only having advanced slightly from roughly £5 million in the mid-1990s to £6 million in 2004. Given that TFP is the one leg of James Cropper plc where the most growth is expected, the results are not encouraging, but it would be unfair to lay blame on its management. If anything, it has been a lesson that there are as many perils associated with operating in immature, high-tech markets as there are in mature markets such as paper-making. Like many other companies before it, TFP has learnt that although the potential might be huge, new technologies can be very difficult to get off the ground. Indeed, in order to compete against existing technologies, a new product must not only offer better performance or lower cost (and preferably both), but also be accepted by customers and meet applicable codes and standards, which can often require slow and tedious trials. New technologies might also require government support if their most important benefits are not (at least in the short-term) commercial.

Technical Fibre Products has had to face all of these hurdles, and more. New materials can be dropped as readily as they are picked up, as it experienced with its Fasertec joint venture, set up in 1987 to produce thermal insulation for automotive exhausts. Despite being a significant source of revenue for several years, the machine was closed in 1996 as exhaust technology had changed and no long used fibrous insulation. A similar thing happened with IBM on a shorter timescale. A year after it began production of the Thinkpad, which resulted in TFP's largest ever order for carbon fibre, the computer manufacturer decided to make its computer cases from an injection moulded product based on different materials that TFP could not supply.

Another problem that TFP has experienced is the competitive climate that can develop when a new product does finally begin to sell in high volume. In particular, this was the case with battery separator paper made from glass micro-fibres. Like much of TFP's range, the paper took years to be qualified, five years passing between the date it was first marketed (1984) and the start of sales in any volume (1989), a frustrating hiatus that occurred in spite of strong support from its first customer, Chloride Industrial Batteries. In subsequent years TFP was, nevertheless, compensated for its efforts as battery separator paper became a key product, in part due to sales to US battery manufacturers but more importantly owing to a three-year contract signed in 1994 with the Hawker Battery group, which had recently acquired Chloride. However, when the contract came up for renewal in 1997 in a new form (which no longer just covered the UK but the whole world), the competition to win it was so intense and the required volume so large that TFP declined to tender. Furthermore, owing to the very aggressive sales policy being pursued by Hollingsworth & Vose, a competing manufacturer, it was not long before it decided to abandon battery separator paper altogether and steer the business back towards "low volume, high margin products".

Since then TFP has yet to strike gold in any of its target markets, but with a profit of £646,000 in 2003 and £474,000 in 2004 it is still proving to be a valuable part of James Cropper plc as a diversified group. Furthermore, whatever the disappointments of the past, it is hard not to feel excited about the future that beckons for the business. Not least, it has strong leadership in the form of George Quayle, who joined the business from Whatman Specialty Products in 1992 and became general manager in 1996 following the resignation of Jim Oakley, who took control of TFP on John Larking's retirement in 1991. His persistence, energy and foresight has led the company into many markets where success would spell significant growth in turnover and profits, not least fuel cells, in which field he forged an exclusive agreement with Johnson Matthey in 2000 for the development and supply of carbon fibre electrode substrate materials. The collaboration continues in 2004 (most recently through a programme funded by the UK Department of Trade and Industry), and although timing remains a vexed issue, it will assure the company a foothold in what could be one of the most significant industrial developments of the twenty-first century.

George Quayle has also built strong foundations for TFP in composite structures and the use of metal-coated carbon fibre materials, the marketing of which is being pursued through Electro Fiber Technologies, a joint venture formed with US company Thermion International in 2003. Perhaps the most promising development he has overseen, however, is the introduction of intumescent products for use in fire protection. Engineered to expand as many as fifteen times on exposure to heat (Fig. 10.6), these could play a major part in fire protection in buildings by forming a pressurised seal around doors and air ducts that prevents fire spreading. Sales are also likely to accelerate rapidly in the next few years owing

Fig. 10.6 – TFP's line of intumescent products for use in fire protection expand as many as fifteen times on exposure to heat.

to the implementation of new building codes, a process that is already underway in the USA. Indeed, in this market TFP is already well on the way to commercial sales having completed qualification programmes with eight major US door manufacturers, a milestone that was announced in James Cropper plc's 2004 annual report.

Emphasising as it does the future, the story of Technical Fibre Products provides a more than fitting postscript to this story, and until recently would have marked the end of this history. There is now, however, another venture to tell of. A few years ago the discarded portakabin selling surplus paper in a corner of Burneside Mill would hardly have merited a mention (Fig. 10.7). An extension of the company's supply of paper to local schools, on its opening in 1996 it sold an insignificant amount of paper that was only notable for the slight inroads it was making into the large quantities of second grade 'broke' generated in the mill.

In 2004 The Paper Mill Shop, as it became known, presents a very different picture. In the eight years that have passed since its humble beginnings at Burneside, it has become a national retail chain of fourteen stores and counting (Fig. 10.8), a dramatic transformation that is matched by the growth of turnover from £52,000 in the first year of trading to £3 million in 2004. The success of the business is even more notable as it has been quite unexpected. On the opening of the first retail shop outside the mill – at the Rheged visitor centre near Penrith in 2000 – James Cropper plc's directors were not at all sure if the concept would work beyond the shop at Burneside. Indeed, it was only owing to the persistence of Rheged's developer John Dunning, who offered to provide the necessary staff, that they agreed to take some space in the new centre, a fortuitous decision that

Fig. 10.7 – The Paper Mill Shop began life in a Portakabin within Burneside Mills.

continues to pay dividends. The performance of the outlet, and all those that have followed, exceeded expectations and there is still no sign that expansion is slowing down. In 2004 three new stores have been opened, at Ashford, Belfast and Spalding, and warehousing and distribution activities have been relocated to a much larger facility to cope with growth.

The success of the business can be attributed to several factors, not least its

Fig. 10.8 – The Paper Mill Shop at Bridgend, Somerset. It is one of fourteen stores in the UK.

small and dynamic management team. Overseen by Nigel Read, the director in charge, its commercial side is run by Gill Murray and its operational side by Andy Tomlinson. Both started work for The Paper Mill Shop in its early days in addition to existing roles (in Gill's case as Nigel's PA), subsequently assuming full-time positions as their efforts paid off. The growth of the business can also be attributed to the appetite of the British public for factory outlet stores. Many of The Paper Mill Shop's fourteen shops are based in factory outlet centres such as McArthurGlen, the growing number of which have provided an easy way for James Cropper plc to extend the chain and tap into the buoyant consumer sector.

The popularity of The Paper Mill Shop has also, however, had much to do with the way in which paper is sold. Its unique Pick 'n Mix approach allows customers to fill standard-priced boxes with A4 and A5 paper and board from a range of around a hundred different colours and finishes. In addition to this core offering, sales are supported by a number of other paper products such as coloured envelopes (supplied by the company's long term customer, G. F. Smith), and other specially developed items such as jotters and artists pads. The shop also offers a wide range of craft accessories for customers making cards as a hobby, a significant source of business. The shops are still, however, underpinned by the same concept. The paper and card sold in them is the result of excess production or is second grade material, enabling James Cropper plc to convert scrap into a profitable sale.

As the latest in a long line of innovations that have ensured James Cropper plc's survival for almost 160 years, The Paper Mill Shop provides a more than fitting conclusion to this history. For it is, in many respects, the ultimate complementary business for a specialist paper manufacturer. Not least, compared to running an enormous, expensive, and technically very complex paper-mill, the business is reassuringly simple. The format can be rolled out in any suitable location in a relatively short space of time, and the necessary investment and overheads are low. Furthermore, by selling direct to consumers, it gives James Cropper plc an outlet for paper that is free from many of the hazards associated with the modern trading environment, amongst them foreign competition and the endless cycle of global commodity prices. Escaping these would in many respects represent a new beginning for James Cropper plc, ensuring that this is not a story with an ending, but one that will long continue to unfold.

Bibliography

Unpublished Sources

Alexander Cowan & Sons records, Scottish Record Office, Edinburgh.

Cropper family archives, Tolson MSS.

Cropper family archives, Liverpool Maritime Museum (LMM).

Cumbria Record Office, Kendal (KRO).

James Cropper plc, Company Archives (CA).

Cropper, Anne (ed.) *Extracts from letters of the late James Cropper* (privately printed, c.1860).

Diary of Charles Cowan, 1842-6, Edinburgh City Library.

Fletcher, M. *Ellergreen and the Croppers 1848 to 1956* (Typescript, 1967).

Gavin, J. *Papermaking and printing in Cumbria 1600-1900* (MPhil thesis, University of Lancaster, 1990).

Laybourn, K. *Study of two industrial communities in Westmorland* (MA thesis, University of Lancaster, 1969).

Willink, A. *John and Anne Cropper of Dingle Bank, Liverpool* (Typescript, 1935).

Paper-making history

Bertrams Ltd., *Within a Mile of Edinburgh Town, The History of Bertrams Limited 1821-1955* (Bertrams Ltd, Edinburgh, 1955).

Carter, H. *Wolvercote Mill A Study in Paper-Making in Oxford* (Oxford University Press, Oxford, 1975).

Chater, M. *Family business: a history of Grosvenor Chater 1690-1977* (Privately printed, St. Alban's, 1977).

Clapperton, R. H. and Henderson, W. *Modern Paper-making* (Basil Blackwell, Oxford, 1947).

Clapperton, G. *Practical Paper-Making* (Crosby Lockwood & Sons, London, 1894).

Clapperton, R. H. *The Paper-making Machine* (Pergamon Press, Oxford, 1967).

Coleman, D. C. *The British Paper Industry 1495-1860: a study in industrial growth* (Clarendon Press, Oxford, 1958).

Dykes Spicer, A. *The Paper Trade: A Descriptive and Historical Survey of the Paper Trade from the Commencement of the Nineteenth Century* (Methuen and Co, London, 1907).

Evans, J. *The Endless Web, John Dickinson and Company Ltd 1804-1954* (Jonathan Cape, London, 1955).

Forbes Royle, J. *Lecture on Indian Fibres Fit for Textile Fabrics, or for Rope and Paper-making* (Read at the 18th Ordinary Meeting of the Society of Arts, 12 April 1854).

Funnell, K. J. *Snodland Paper Mill. C. Townsend Hook and Company from 1854* (C. Townsend Hook, Snodland, 1980).

Gavin, J. *Some Notes on Papermaking in Cumbria* (History of the Book Trade in the North, Newcastle-upon-Tyne, 1988).

Hampson, C. G. *150th Anniversary of Robert Fletcher & Son Ltd* (Robert Fletcher & Son, Manchester, 1973).

Harris, C. *Stowford Paper Mill and the Industrial Heritage of the Erme Valley* (Halsgrove, Tiverton, 1999).

Herring, R. *Paper and Paper Making Ancient and Modern* (Longman, Brown, Green & Longman, London, 1855).

Hills, R. L. *Papermaking in Britain 1488-1988: a short history* (Athlone Press, London, 1988).

Horne, K. *Somebody Said That It Couldn't be Done* (Paper Publications Ltd, Hertfordshire, 1995).

Hunter, D. *Papermaking: the history and technique of an ancient craft* (Alfred A. Knopf, New York, 1947).

Ketelbey, C. D. M. *The History of R. Tullis and Company and Tullis Russell and Co Ltd 1809-1959* (Tullis Russell and Co Ltd, Markinch, 1967).

Labarre, E. J. *Dictionary and Encyclopaedia of Paper and Paper-Making* (Swets & Zeitlinger, Amsterdam, 1952).

Laker, B. G. *Mill 364: Paper Making at St. Cuthbert's* (St. Cuthbert's Paper Mill, Wells, 1991).

Leif, I. *An International Sourcebook of Paper History* (Dawson, Folkestone, 1978).

McGaw, J. *Most Wonderful Machine, Mechanization and social change in Berkshire Paper making, 1801-1885* (Princeton University Press, Princeton NJ, 1987).

Magee, G. B. *Productivity and Performance in the paper industry: Labour, capital, and technology in Britain and America, 1860-1914* (Cambridge University Press, Cambridge, 1997).

Mandl, G. *Three Hundred Years in Paper* (Clifton Hill, London, 1985).

Muir, A. *The British Paper and Board Makers Association 1872-1972* (Privately printed, London, 1972).

Munsell, J. *Chronology of the Origin and Process of Paper and Paper-Making* (5th ed., J. Munsell, Albany, 1876).

Pilkington, A. *Frogmore and the First Fourdrinier* (The British Paper Company, Hemel Hempstead, 1990).

Reader, W. J. *Bowater: a history* (Cambridge University Press, Cambridge 1981).

Robertson, J. *Fifty Years' Experience in Paper-Making* (Reid & Co, Newcastle upon

Tyne, 1897).

Shorter, A. H. *Paper-making in the British Isles, An historical and geographical study* (David & Charles, Newton Abbot, 1971).

Sindall, R. W. *Paper Technology, An Elementary Manual* (Charles Griffin & Co., 1906).

Thomson, A. G. *The Paper Industry in Scotland 1590-1861* (Scottish Academic Press, Edinburgh, 1974).

Tillmanns, M. *Bridge Hall Mills* (Compton Press, Bury, 1978).

Watson, N. *The Last Mill on the Esk* (Scottish Academic Press, Edinburgh, 1987).

Weatherill, L. *One Hundred Years of Papermaking: an illustrated history of Guard Bridge paper company 1873-1973* (Guard Bridge Paper Co Ltd, Guardbridge, Fife, 1974).

Wray, M. *The British Paper Industry: A Study in Structural and Technological Change* (The British Paper and Board Industry Federation, London, 1979).

Anon. *Henry Cooke, Papermaker 1773-1973 a short history to celebrate his bi-centenary* (Lund Humphries, London, 1973).

Anon. *Carrongrove, 200 Years of Papermaking* (Argyll Publishing, Glendaruel, 2000).

Other Sources

Albion, R. G. *Square Riggers on Schedule. The New York Sailing Packets to England, France, and the Cotton Ports* (Princeton Univesity Press, Princeton NJ, 1938).

Anstey, R. & Hair, P. E. H. *Liverpool, the African Slave Trade and Abolition: essays to illustrate current knowledge and research* (Historic Society of Lancashire and Cheshire, Liverpool, 1989).

Ashton, T. S. *The Industrial Revolution 1760-1830* (Oxford University Press, 1996).

Aspin, C. *The First Industrial Society Lancashire 1750-1850* (Carnegie Publishing, Preston, 1995).

Baines, T. *History of the Commerce and Town of Liverpool* (Thomas Baines, Liverpool, 1852).

Besse, J. *A Collection of the Sufferings of the People called Quakers* (Luke Hinde, London, 1753).

Bicknell, P. *The Picturesque Scenery of the Lake District 1752-1855, A Bibliographical Study* (St Paul's Bibliographies, Winchester, Detroit, 1990).

Bingham, R. K. *Kendal, A Social History* (Cicerone Press, Milnthorpe, 1995).

Boon, J. *Under Six Reigns: being some account of 114 years of progress and development of the House of Waterlow* (Waterlow & Sons, London, 1925).

Booth, H. *An Account of the Liverpool and Manchester Railway* (Wales & Baine, Liverpool, 1831).

Brice, A. C. *Indian Cotton Supply: The only effectual and permanent measure for relief in Lancashire* (Smith, Elder & Co., London, 1863).

Briggs, A. *Victorian People* (Penguin, London, 1990).

Brown, A. T. *Some Account of The Royal Institution School, Liverpool, with a Roll of Masters and Boys (1819-92)* (University of Liverpool Press, Liverpool, 1924).

Bryce, J. *Their Words and His . . . Articles and Letters relating to the late John Bryce, J. P.* (Edward Gill, Kendal, 1898).

Cairncross, A. *The British Economy since 1945* (Blackwell, Cambridge MA, 1995).

Carlson, R. E. *The Liverpool & Manchester Railway Project 1821-31* (David & Charles, Newton Abbot, 1969).

Chandler, G. *Four Centuries of Banking as Illustrated by the Bankers, Customers and Staff Associated with the Constituent Banks of Martins Bank Limited* Vol 2 *The Northern Constituent Banks* (B. T. Batsford, London, 1968).

Chapman, S. D. *The Cotton Industry in the Industrial Revolution* (Macmillan Education, Basingstoke, 1987).

Charlton, K. James Cropper and Liverpool's contribution to the anti-slavery movement, *Transactions of the Historic Society of Lancashire and Cheshire*, Vol. 123, 1972.

Charlton, K. James Cropper (1773-1840) and agricultural improvement in the early nineteenth century, *Transactions of the Historic Society of Lancashire and Cheshire*, Vol. 112, 1960.

Charlton, K. "Liverpool and the East India Trade", In: *Northern History*, Volume VII 1974.

Charlton, K. The state of Ireland in the 1820s: James Cropper's plan, *Irish Historical Studies*, Vol. XVII, 1971.

Chorley, H. F. *Autobiography, Memoir and Letters* (R. Bentley & Sons, London, 1873).

Cockin, R. Jenkins J. *et al. Pen Pictures of London Yearly Meetings, 1789-1833* (Friends Historical Society, London, 1930).

Coleman, D. C. Gentlemen and players, *Economic History Review*, 26, 1 February 1973.

Conybeare, F. A. *Dingle Bank, The Home of the Croppers* (W. Heffer & Sons, Cambridge, 1925).

Cropper, James *Letters addressed to William Wilberforce, M.P. recommending the encouragement of the Cultivation of Sugar in our Dominions in the East Indies . . .* (Longman, Hurst & Co., London, 1822).

Cropper, James *Relief for West-Indian Distress shewing the Inefficiency of Protecting Duties on East-India Sugar* (Ellerton & Henderson, London, 1823).

Cropper, James *The Support of Slavery Investigated* (Hatchard & Son, London, 1824).

Cropper, James *The Present State of Ireland, with a Plan for Improving the Position of the People* (George Smith, Liverpool, 1825).

Cropper, James *Outline of a Plan for an Agricultural School and for the Employment of Agricultural Labourers by Spade Cultivation at Fearnhead near Warrington* (Egerton Smith & Co., Liverpool, 1834).

Cropper, James *Some Account of an Agricultural School for Orphans at Fearnhead near Warrington, Lancashire, in a Letter to a Friend* (Thomas Hurst, Warrington, 1839).

Cropper, James & Gladstone, John *The Correspondence between John Gladstone Esq M.P.*

and James Cropper Esq on the Present State of Slavery in the British West Indies and the United States of America (West India Association, Liverpool, 1824).

Cropper, James *Notes and Memories* (Bateman & Hewitson, Kendal, 1900).

Curwen, J. F. *Kirkbie-Kendall* (Titus Wilson, Kendal, 1900).

Davis, D. B. *Slavery and Human Progress* (Oxford University Press, New York and Oxford, 1984).

Dennis, M. *Dennis's Extracts of East India Journals . . . To Which is Added A Supplement . . . Containing Vessels that have sailed to India from Liverpool, since the passing of the Act* (M. Dennis, London, 1819).

Eddershaw, M. *Grand Fashionable Nights: Kendal Theatre 1575-1985* (University of Lancaster Occasional Paper No. 17, 1989).

Eglin, G. T. *A Plain Statement of Facts on the Dangers of Partnership* (J. Bosworth, London, 1846).

Emden, P. H. *Quakers in Commerce A Record of Business Achievement* (Sampson Low, Marston & Co., London, 1940).

Ensor, R. C. K. *England 1870-1914* (Oxford University Press, Oxford, 1992).

Evans, R. J. *The Victorian Age 1815-1914* (Edward Arnold, London, 1968).

Farmer, J. H. & Routledge, J. *Local Chronology: being notes of the principal events published in the Kendal newspapers since their establishment* (Hamilton, Adams & Co., London; Thomas Atkinson, Kendal, 1865).

Farnie, D. A. *The English Cotton Industry and the World Market 1815-1896* (Clarendon Press, Oxford, 1979).

Farrer, W. *Records Relating to the Barony of Kendale* (John F. Curwen, ed) (Titus Wilson, Kendal, 1923).

Feather, J. *The Provincial Book Trade* (Cambridge University Press, Cambridge 1985).

Ffinch, M. *Kendal and the Kent Valley* (Robert Hale, London, 1983).

Floud, R. & McCloskey, D. (eds) *The Economic History of Britain Since 1700* Vol. 3: *1939-1992* (Cambridge University Press, Cambridge, 1994).

Hackett, D. *The History of the Future The Bemrose Corporation 1826-1976* (Scolar Press, London, 1976).

Hobsbawm, E. *The Age of Capital* (Abacus, London, 1998).

Hobsbawm, E. *Industry and Empire* (Penguin Books, London, 1999).

Hobsbawm, E. *The Age of Extremes* (Michael Joseph, London, 1994).

Holland, Margaret, Viscountess Knutsford *Life and Letters of Zachary Macaulay* (Edward Arnold, London, 1900).

Huggins, A. K. *British Postal Stationery* (Great Britain Philatelic Society, 1970).

Hyde, F. E. *Liverpool and the Mersey. An Economic History of a Port 1700-1970* (David & Charles, Newton Abbot, 1971).

Isaac, P. The provincial book trade from the end of the Printing Act to 1800 (Working Paper, History Of The Book Trade In The North, Newcastle-upon-Tyne, 1987).

Jones, E. *True and Fair, A History of Price Waterhouse* (Hamish Hamilton, London, 1995).

Jones, T., & Willink, A. *James Cropper & Co. Ltd. and Memories of Burneside 1845-1945* (*Westmorland Gazette*, Kendal, 1945).

Kay, B. (ed.) *The Dundee Book: an anthology of living in the city* (Mainstream, Edinburgh, 1990).

Lane, J. H. *A History of Newton-Le-Willows* (P. & D. Riley, Warrington, 1992).

Lee, C. E. *The Centenary of "Bradshaw"* (*Railway Gazette*, London, 1940).

Lloyd, A. *Quaker Social History* (Longman, London, 1950).

Malchow, H. L. *Gentlemen Capitalists: The Social and Political World of the Victorian Businessman* (Macmillan, London, 1991).

Marshall, J. D. Kendal 1661-1801, *Transactions of the Cumberland and Westmorland Antiquarian and Archaeological Society*, Vol. LXXV, 1975.

Marshall, J. D. *Old Lakeland. Some Cumbrian Social History* (David & Charles, Newton Abbot, 1971).

Marshall, J. D. & Walton, J. K . *The Lake Counties from 1830 to the Mid-twentieth Century. A Study in Regional Change.* (Manchester University Press, 1981).

Mathias, P. *The First Industrial Nation. An Economic History of Britain 1700-1914* (Routledge, London, 1995).

McCord, N. *British History, 1815-1906* (Oxford University Press, Oxford, 1991).

Mellentin, J. *The Kendal and Windermere Railway* (Dalesman Books, London, 1980).

Milligan, E. H. *Quakers and Railways* (Sessions Book Trust, York, 1992).

Mordaunt Crook, J. *The Rise of the Nouveaux Riches* (John Murray, London, 1999).

Newsome, D. *The Victorian World Picture* (John Murray, London, 1997).

Nicholson, C. *A Well-spent Life – a memoir of Cornelius Nicholson* (Titus Wilson, Kendal, 1890).

Nicholson, C. *Annals of Kendal* (2nd edition, Whitaker & Co., London, 1861).

Nottingham, L. *Rathbone Brothers: 1742-1992* (Rathbone Brothers, London, 1992).

Orchard, B. G. *Liverpool's Legion of Honour* (Published privately, Birkenhead, 1893).

Owen, G. *From Empire to Europe: The Decline and Revival of British Industry Since the Second World War* (Harper Collins, London, 1999).

Parkinson, C. N. (ed) *The Trade Winds A Study of British Overseas Trade during the French Wars 1793-1815* (George Allen, London, 1948).

Parkinson, C. N. *The Rise of the Port of Liverpool* (Liverpool University Press, Liverpool, 1952).

Pollard, S. *The Development of the British Economy 1914-1967* (Edward Arnold, London, 1976).

Pratt, D. H. *English Quakers and the First Industrial Revolution*, (Garland Publishing Inc., New York, 1985).

Raistrick, A. *Quakers in Science and Industry* (Sessions Book Trust, York, 1993).

Read, D. *The Age of Urban Democracy: England 1868-1914* (Longman, London, 1994).

Reed, M. C. (ed) *Railways in the Victorian Economy* (David and Charles, Newton Abbot, 1969).

Royde Smith, G. *The History of Bradshaw* (Henry Blacklock & Co Ltd, London & Manchester, 1939).

Somervell, J. *Water Powered Mills of South Westmorland* (Titus Wilson, Kendal, 1930).

Spicer family *Albert Spicer 1847-1934. A Man of his Time by One of his Family* (Simpkin Marshall, London, 1938).

Taylor, M. W. *The Old Manorial Halls of Westmorland and Cumberland* (Titus Wilson, Kendal, 1892).

Taylor, S. J. *The Great Outsiders. Northcliffe, Rothermere and the Daily Mail*, (Weidenfeld & Nicolson, London, 1996).

Thomas, R. G. *The Liverpool & Manchester Railway* (B. T. Batsford, London, 1980).

Thomson, D. *England in the Nineteenth Century* (Pelican Books, London, 1991).

Thomson, D. *England in the Twentieth Century* (Penguin Books, London, 1991).

Tomlinson, C. *The Useful Arts and Manufactures of Great Britain* (Christian Knowledge Society, London, 1861).

Trevelyan, G. M. *Illustrated English Social History*, Vol. IV, *The Nineteenth Century* (Longmans, Green & Co., London, 1952).

Wake, J. *Kleinwort Benson: The history of two families in banking* (Oxford University Press, Oxford 1997).

Waterhouse, N. *Memorials of the Families of Cropper, Cubham and Wolsey of Bickerstaffe* (Privately printed, Liverpool, 1864).

Whatley, C. A. *The Life and Times of Dundee* (John Donald, Edinburgh, 1993).

Whellan, W. *The History and Topography of Cumberland and Westmorland* (William Whellan & Co, Pontefract, 1860).

Wiener, M. J. *English Culture and the Decline of the Industrial Spirit 1850-1980* (Penguin, London, 1992).

Williams, G. *History of the Liverpool Privateers and Letters of Marque* (Heinemann, London, 1897).

Wilson, F. *Crusader in Crinoline: The Life of Harriet Beecher Stowe* (J. P. Lippincott Company, Philadelphia, 1941).

Wilson, P. Kendal reservoirs, *Transactions of the Cumberland & Westmorland Antiquarian & Archaeological Society*, Vol. LXXIII, 1973.

Wood, A. *Nineteenth Century Britain 1815-1914* (Longman, London, 1982).

Contemporary Sources

Gore's Liverpool Directory.

Mannex, P. J. *History, Topography, and Directory of Westmorland, and Lonsdale North of the Sands* . . . .

Paper Mills Directory compiled by the editor of, and reprinted from *The Stationer,*
    1860.
Post Office Directory of Stationers, Printers, Booksellers, Publishers and Paper Makers,
    1872.

Periodicals
Gentleman's Magazine (1824).
Macniven and Cameron's Paper Trade Review.
The Quarterly (Journal of the British Association of Paper Historians).
Kendal Mercury.
Kendal Mercury and Times.
Kendal Weekly Mercury.
Paper Maker and British Paper Trade Journal.
Paper Maker's Circular.
Paper Maker's Monthly Journal.
Paper Record (1886-8).
Paper Trades' News (1860-1).
Paper Trade Review.
Westmorland Gazette.
Transactions of the Cumberland and Westmorland Antiquarian & Archaeological Society
    (CWAAS).

Appendix I:
Directors and other key personnel

James Cropper operated as a Sole Trader from 1845-52, before forming a Partnership with William Blacklock and George McCorquodale that ran until 1889, when a limited company, James Cropper & Co. Ltd was formed. Public limited status was attained in 1950 with the flotation of the company on the London Stock Exchange.

Directors

1845-1900	James Cropper	Chairman 1889-1900
1852-1895	George McCorquodale	
1852-1870	William Blacklock	
1859-1896	John Bryce	
1870-1924	Charles Cropper	Chairman 1900-24
1884-1947	Alfred Willink	
1895-1925	Alick McCorquodale	Honorary director
1900-1910	Vincent Jones	
1905-1956	James W Cropper	Chairman 1924-56
1925-1942	Harold McCorquodale	Honorary director
1928-1971	Derek Willink	Chairman 1967-71
1933-1964	(Arthur) Geoffrey Acland	
1938-1967	Anthony Cropper	Chairman 1956-67
1942-1960	Kenneth McCorquodale	Honorary Director
1960-1978	Alastair McCorquodale	Non Executive
1964-1997	Oliver Acland	
1964-1998	Nicholas Willink	
1967-present day	James A Cropper	Chairman since 1971
1967-1971	Reginald Oldham	Non Executive
1972-present day	John Sclater	Non Executive
1970-1991	John Larking	
1977-1991	Peter Charlton	
1984-2004	John Southwell	Non Executive
1991-1996	James Oakley	

Directors *(continued)*

1995 -present day	John Denman	
1997-present day	Peter Herring	Non Executive
1998-present day	Alun Lewis	Chief Executive since 2001
1998-present day	Nigel Read	
1998-present day	Patrick Willink	
1998-present day	George Quayle	
2004-present day	David Wilks	Non Executive

Company Secretary

John Bryce	1852-1896
Richard Savage	1896-1905
Vincent Jones	1905-1907
Herbert Corrie	1907-1949
Ronnie Reddish	1949-1978
Oliver Acland	1978-1996
David Carey	1996-present day

Burneside Mill – Foremen and Managers

(Post discontinued, 1965)

John Dewar	1854-1887
G. Porteas	1887-1889
Daniel McNeill	1889-1922
Robert McNeill	1924-1931
Sam Lindsay	1931-1951
Fred Craig	1951-1965

Cowanhead Mill – Foremen

(Paper-making ceased at Cowan Head in 1977)

James Robinson	1845-1850
Mark Birkhead	1850-1862
A. K. Wood	1862-1868
Jonathan Harrison	1868-1891
W. John Lever	1891-1894
George Clapperton	1894-1901
Gerard Walker	1901-1914
H. S. Reed	1914-1933
James Daws	1933-1958
Harry Wilson	1958-1976
Maurice Crossley	1976-1977

Chief Engineer

(Post discontinued, 2001)

James Savage	1854-1887
Andrew Robertson	1887-1898
John Watson	1898-1903
James Paterson	1903-1920
James Arnot	1920-1949
Jim Hill	1949-1974
Peter Charlton	1974-1991
Jim Oakley	1991-1996
Richard Duffell	1996-2001

Appendix II:
Financial and Production Figures

Year	Output (tons)	Turnover (£)	Profit (£)
1853			(-405)
1854	380		1,274
1855	293		659
1856	458		1,959
1857	476		1,475
1858	471		2,053
1859	457		3,294
1860	609		4,648
1861	671		4,601
1862	806		3,854
1863	858		2,807
1864	950		4,102
1865	925		6,799
1866	1,142		7,992
1867	1,180		4,322
1868	1,220		3,674
1869	1,254		5,074
1870	1,280		4,544
1871	1,441		4,563
1872	1,720		9,422
1873	1,846		15,485
1874	1,884		16,736
1875	1,771		16,343
1876	1,770		14,457
1877	1,991		13,378
1878	2,021		9,177
1879	2,017		9,437
1880	2,249		9,409
1881	2,411		3,328
1882	1,882		6,984

Year	Output (tons)	Turnover (£)	Profit (£)
1883	2,637		10,864
1884	1,730		9,329
1885	2,795		4,952
1886	N/A[1]		2,141
1887	1,887		1,278
1888	3,187		3,062
1889	2,622		1,833[2]
1890	3,749		7,755
1891	3,928		9,786
1892	3,797		9,020
1893	3,738		7,015
1894	3,787		4,170
1895	4,049		4,995
1896	4,451		8,825
1897	4,847		11,333
1898	5,196		7,985
1899	5,544		9,556
1900	6,123		11,011
1901	6,510		4,123
1902	6,633		9,361
1903	6,700		7,601
1904	6,928		7,364
1905	7,744		3,864
1906	8,646	121,445	7,451
1907	9,388	128,053	7,967
1908	9,787	132,318	7,996
1909	9,213	124,711	5,664
1910	10,066	134,771	7,166
1911	10,575	141,515	7,195
1912	11,234	150,134	9,237
1913	12,146	162,899	10,223
1914	11,822	158,974	6,074
1915	12,947	184,807	7,490
1916	13,892	319,982	22,853
1917	12,250	512,398	127,699
1918	12,536	662,125	148,591
1919	11,881	633,514	128,093
1920	13,360	730,420	188,284
1921	7,642	–	–
1922	5,418	635,904	(89,467)[3]
1923	11,065	302,291	35,098
1924	11,538	306,707	18,027
1925	12,016	315,446	26,642

Year	Output (tons)	Turnover (£)	Profit (£)
1926	12,625	325,680	25,888
1927	13,191	342,692	30,552
1928	13,018	335,128	35,044
1929	13,447	340,001	50,326
1930	13,704	335,357	39,485
1931	12,381	293,574	24,804
1932	13,125	283,045	30,038
1933	12,535	257,578	28,669
1934	13,736	261,475	28,919
1935	14,304	277,754	37,237
1936	14,281	280,275	38,144
1937	15,061	301,855	38,245
1938	15,844	380,060	65,311
1939	13,858	345,695	41,048
1940	15,768	427,465	89,208
1941	11,111	470,113	66,701
1942	9,370	450,309	45,832
1943	7,867	408,986	36,078
1944	8,081	431,578	36,876
1945	8,588	454,876	58,525
1946	9,641	517,083	79,044
1947	11,422	598,691	106,617
1948	12,002	759,099	108,585
1949	12,974	902,829	92,281
1950	15,678	943,000	99,237
1951	16,557	1,331,000	271,200
1952	16,860	2,438,000	393,800
1953	14,355	1,686,200	175,200
1954	16,470	1,619,300	294,600
1955	17,653	1,834,300	301,600
1956	18,683	2,002,000	316,800
1957	17,752	1,958,500	238,600
1958	18,702	2,034,500	234,500
1959	18,071	1,936,300	194,100
1960	20,670	2,131,300	230,900
1961	21,145	2,213,300	253,300
1962	21,022	2,221,900	171,100
1963	21,023	2,137,900	169,600
1964	21,450	2,274,800	195,900
1965	23,468	2,564,900	216,400
1966	23,240	2,636,800	194,800
1967	22,928	2,630,700	249,000
1968	22,952	2,644,700	150,193

Year	Output (tons)	Turnover (£)	Profit (£)
1969	22,960	2,831,100	136,311
1970	22,560	3,030,200	203,444
1971	22,585	3,333,400	216,000
1972	21,000	3,329,000	171,000
1973	22,995	3,847,500	213,500
1974	23,795	4,734,100	325,000
1975	25,099	6,794,000	310,000
1976	18,530	6,197,000	(-202,000)
1977	19,741	8,246,000	44,000
1978	21,521	9,553,000	380,000
1979	24,471	10,998,000	576,000
1980	26,646	13,716,000	887,000
1981	26,841	15,022,000	100,000
1982	28,706	16,975,000	304,000
1983	29,648	17,573,000	341,000
1984	35,810	21,567,000	1,333,000
1985	37,248	25,138,000	763,000
1986	38,712	27,482,000	1,820,000
1987	39,145	29,109,000	1,680,000
1988	40,836	32,707,000	2,060,000
1989	42,350	35,268,000	1,949,000
1990	42,564	39,148,000	1,024,000
1991	43,955	39,374,000	1,476,000
1992	46,191	40,297,000	1,060,000
1993	43,792	40,302,000	1,243,000
1994	48,677	45,726,000	2,562,000
1995	49,854	49,736,000	2,566,000
1996	51,315	57,591,000	1,852,000
1997	52,725	69,271,000	5,003,000
1998	51,612	54,685,000	2,406,000
1999	50,407	53,078,000	2,498,000
2000	50,363	53,365,000	3,060,000
2001	49,135	54,427,000	(-779,000)
2002	48,256	54,451,000	1,526,000
2003	45,923[4]	55,010,000	1,867,000
2004	45,475	56,565,000	785,000

[1] Burneside mill burnt down, 4 July 1886.
[2] Results for 9 months.
[3] Results for 18 months.
[4] Internal sales and mountboard 'middles' excluded from tonnage for first time.

Appendix III: Pedigrees

1. Early Croppers

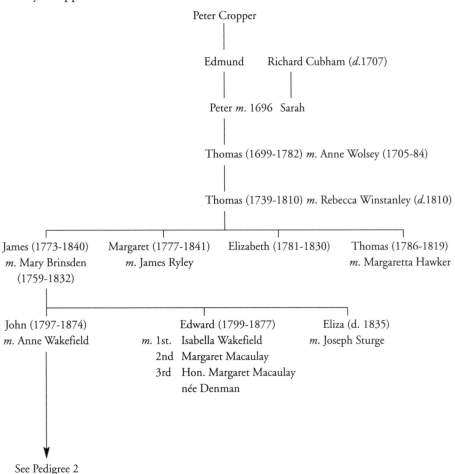

Peter Cropper

Edmund   Richard Cubham (*d.*1707)

Peter *m.* 1696 Sarah

Thomas (1699-1782) *m.* Anne Wolsey (1705-84)

Thomas (1739-1810) *m.* Rebecca Winstanley (*d.*1810)

James (1773-1840)   Margaret (1777-1841)   Elizabeth (1781-1830)   Thomas (1786-1819)
m. Mary Brinsden   *m.* James Ryley   *m.* Margaretta Hawker
(1759-1832)

John (1797-1874)   Edward (1799-1877)   Eliza (d. 1835)
m. Anne Wakefield   *m.* 1st. Isabella Wakefield   *m.* Joseph Sturge
                                        2nd Margaret Macaulay
                                        3rd Hon. Margaret Macaulay
                                                née Denman

See Pedigree 2

2. Cropper Family
Names in **Bold** have all worked for James Cropper & Co./plc.

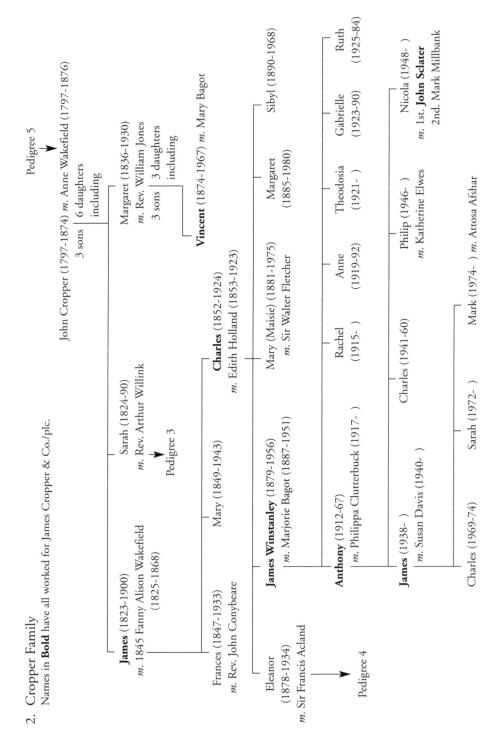

3. Willink Family

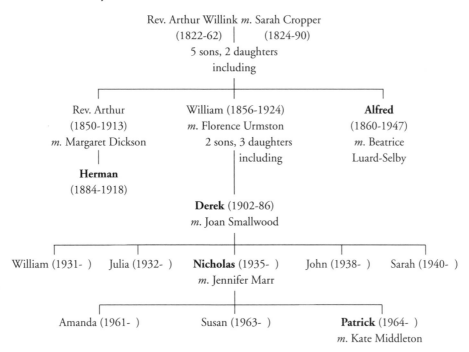

Rev. Arthur Willink *m.* Sarah Cropper
(1822-62)   (1824-90)
5 sons, 2 daughters
including

Rev. Arthur	William (1856-1924)	**Alfred**
(1850-1913)	*m.* Florence Urmston	(1860-1947)
m. Margaret Dickson	2 sons, 3 daughters	*m.* Beatrice
	including	Luard-Selby
Herman		
(1884-1918)		

Derek (1902-86)
m. Joan Smallwood

William (1931-)   Julia (1932-)   **Nicholas** (1935-)   John (1938-)   Sarah (1940-)
m. Jennifer Marr

Amanda (1961-)   Susan (1963-)   **Patrick** (1964-)
m. Kate Middleton

4. Acland Family

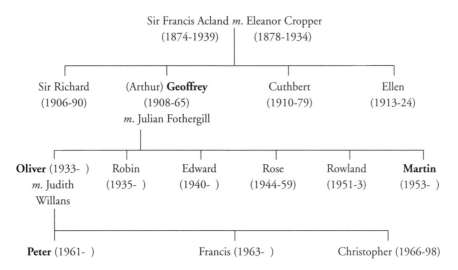

Sir Francis Acland *m.* Eleanor Cropper
(1874-1939)   (1878-1934)

Sir Richard   (Arthur) **Geoffrey**   Cuthbert   Ellen
(1906-90)   (1908-65)   (1910-79)   (1913-24)
                   m. Julian Fothergill

Oliver (1933-)   Robin   Edward   Rose   Rowland   **Martin**
m. Judith   (1935-)   (1940-)   (1944-59)   (1951-3)   (1953-)
Willans

Peter (1961-)   Francis (1963-)   Christopher (1966-98)

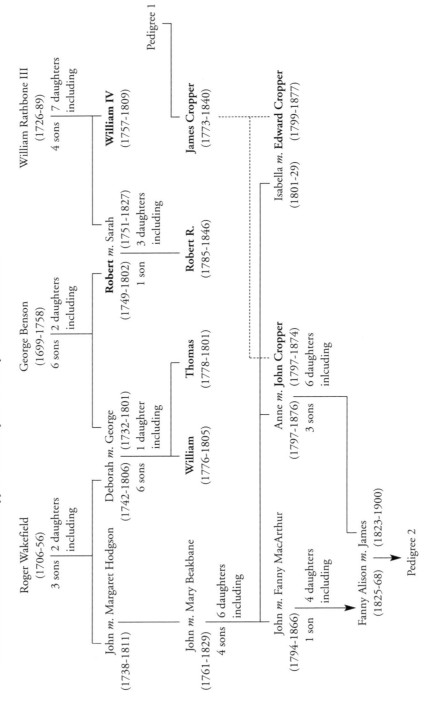

5. Quaker Connections: Bensons, Rathbones, Wakefields and Croppers
Names in **Bold** were involved in Cropper, Benson or previous Liverpool merchant houses.

References

CHAPTER 1

1 Farrer, 1923, p.277.

2 Somervell, pp.xi-xii.

3 *Ibid.* p.xii.

4 KRO WD/L acc. 724.

5 M. Davies-Shiel, Cowan Head notes. Will of Thomas Ashburner, 7 December 1776, KRO, WDX/577/4/10.

6 Gavin, 1990, p.114, 231. In 1730 Thomas Scarisbrick left "fulling, wood and paper mills" to his eldest son Henry. Handbill in KRO, WD/TE.

7 Cowan Head and the land around it was sold to Dame Dorothy Fleming of Rydal Hall in April 1746, who immediately sold the mill to Thomas Ashburner. (Feoffment, 17 May 1746, KRO, WDX/577/4/1).

8 Release of mortgage, 19 May 1749, KRO, WDX/577/4/2.

9 Gavin, 1990, "Gazetteer of Cumbrian Paper Mills".

10 Gavin, 1990, p.136, "Cumbrian Paper Mill Valuations". Insurance policy, 24 June 1769, KRO, WDX/577/4/4-5.

11 Hills, 1988, pp.18-20.

12 Gavin, 1990, p.84.

13 Hills, 1988, p.57.

14 KRO, WDB 63 Accession 1474, Abraham Dent.

15 Marshall, "Kendal 1661-1801", 1975, p.189. Thomas Ashburner himself applauded the construction of the area's first turnpike road in his *Agreeable Miscellany*. Bingham, 1995, p.101.

16 Shorter, 1971, p.63, identifies a geographical correlation between press or glazed paper-making and the woollen industry, and mentions the Kendal-Milnthorpe district of Westmorland as one area where the association is particularly marked.

17 A list of books for sale at the "Printing Office" in Kendal (KRO, WD/TE) lists over two hundred titles. *Kendal Weekly Mercury*, 17 Jan. 1735, "printed by Thomas Ashburner in the Fish market, who gives *Ready Money*, and *Books* in exchange for libraries". From *Local Chronology*, p.48. In 1762 Thomas Ashburner advertised for sale the library of the late Thos. Shepherd. KRO, WD/TE, 27/12.

18 English Short Title Catalogue (ESTC).

19 Curwen, 1900, p.319. Eddershaw, 1989, p.5.

20 Copy of poem in CA/4/8.

21 Wordsworth Trust, Dove Cottage.

22 Thomas Ashburner's Will, dated 7 Dec. 1776. KRO WDX/577/4/10.

23 Coleman, 1958, p.142.

24 Gavin, 1990, pp.148-50.

25 *Bailey's Northern Directory*, 1781, 1784.

26 *Universal British Directory*, 1790.

27 Apprenticeship details from Gavin, 1990, p.145.

28 Gavin, 1990, p.228.

29 In 1781 James Ashburner also published Thomas Dixon's *A Description of the Environs of Ingleborough and Principal Places on the Banks of the River Wenning*.

30 KRO WD/TE Box 27/17.

31 Cark Parish Registers record the baptism of the son of Edward Branthwaite of Cark, paper-maker, on 18 Jun. 1729.

32 1787 plan, KRO WD/Rig/7. 1854 plan, KRO WDX/577/4/21.

33 Jones & Willink, 1945, p.17.

34 Shirley Thomas, "Thomas Bewick: A study of his purchase and use of paper *c.*1787-1826". *The Quarterly* (Journal of the British Association of Paper Historians), no. 28.

35 Gavin, 1990, p.150.

36 CWAAS, Vol XIV, old series, 1897, p.79.

37 *Ibid*, p.78.

38 Curwen, 1900, p.372.

39 KRO, WD/W Box 1, Bundle 3, Accounts (1763-1810).

40 Jones & Willink, 1945, p.16. Chris Aspin, notes on John Wakefield's "Adventure into cotton".

41 Wake, 1997, p.25.

42 Chandler, 1968, p.85.

43 M. Davies-Shiel, Burneside notes. Thomas Jones was manufacturing wool at Burneside in 1823.

44 *Ibid*. p.3.

45 Curwen, 1900, p.109. Nicholson, 1861, p.280. The Institute was founded on the principle of Dr Birkbeck's London Institute, which Nicholson had read about (Nicholson, 1890, pp.153-9).

46 Nicholson, 1861, p.279.

47 Nicholson, 1890, p.5.

48 Pigot's Directory, and Parson and White's *A History, Directory and Gazetteer of Cumberland and Westmorland*, 1829.

49 Curwen, 1890, pp.76-7.

50 He was son of William Pennington (1745-1815), Thomas Ashburner's apprentice.

51 Advertisement, Jan. 1828. Gavin, 1990, p.168.

52 Gavin, 1990, pp.167, 229. The 1828 Deed of Co-partnership, KRO WD/mm Box 41, decrees the partners' responsibilities. H & N's rag warehouse is referred to in *Local Chronology*, Sept 26, 1829.

53 Gavin, 1990, p.170, from *London Gazette* 12 Oct. 1832.

54 Coleman, 1858, p.196. John Dickinson's cylinder machine, dating from 1809, was as yet unavailable.

55 Shorter, 1971, p.109.

56 Shorter, 1971, pp.103, 124.

57 Nicholson, 1890, p.5.

58 Shorter, 1971, p.101.

59 It is known that John Roberts was against mechanisation a few years later. Eglin, 1846.

60 Nicholson, 1890, p.5.

61 Jones & Willink, 1945, p.34.

62 On the whole mechanisation within the paper industry was conducted peacefully, with the exception of the anti-machine riots of 1830 in the High Wycombe district. Shorter, 1971, p.106.

63 CA, KRO WDX 577/4/12.

64 Cowan Head paper-mill was registered in his name only from 1816. Gavin, 1990, p.171.

65 Lease for twenty-one years, 1 October 1834. KRO, WDX/577/4/12.

66 *Westmorland Gazette*, 8 April 1835.

67 Bankrupt in 1839, an incensed Eglin protested his innocence and blamed Roberts, a man of "imbecile mind", for his misfortune in a pamphlet. Eglin, 1846.

68 Gavin, 1990, *Gazetteer of Cumbrian paper mills, 1600-1900*, p.217.

69 Machines could also be run day and night where the hours worked by vatmen and their teams was restricted by the hours of daylight they needed.

70 Nicholson, 1890, p.8.

71 *Ibid.*, p.8.

72 *Kendal Mercury*, 12 Aug. 1843.

73 *Westmorland Gazette*, 24 Nov. 1860, 2 Oct 1937. *The Whitehaven News*, undated article from J. H. Palmer collection, has article on the "Wonderful Walker", *c.*1900.

74 Bicknell, 1990, pp.115-8, 148-50.

75 KRO/WDX/577/4/15.

76 Nicholson, 1890, p.11. Nicholson became a life member of the British Association for the advancement of Science in 1835.

77 *Westmorland Gazette*, 24 August 1844. Wilson, 1973.

78 *Kendal Mercury*, 16 Dec. 1837.

79 Nicholson, 1890, p.16-17. John Wakefield was deputy chairman of the line. *Kendal Mercury*, 9 Dec. 1843.

80 *Kendal Mercury, Westmorland Gazette*, 24 August 1844.

81 Nicholson, 1890, p.71.

82 In later years he was for a time managing director of the Great Indian Peninsula Railway. Nicholson, 1890, pp.60, 88.

83 *Kendal Mercury*, 19 Jul. 1845.

CHAPTER 2

1 James Cropper's apprenticeship indenture, Cropper MSS, LMM, D/CR/2/1.

2 Waterhouse, 1864, p.16.

3 *Ibid.* p.15.

4 *Ibid.* p.9.

5 *Ibid.* p.22.

6 *Ibid.* p.62. Lloyd, 1950, p.166.

7 Anne Cropper, p.2.

8 Anne Cropper, pp.11-12.

9 Waterhouse, 1864, p.63.

10 Williams, 1897, pp.187-9.

11 Rebecca Cropper to James Cropper (JC), 14 June 1790. Anne Cropper, p.5.

12 Charlton, 1972, p.57.

13 Baines, 1852, p.492.

14 Wake, 1997, p.28.

15 Wake, 1997, pp.27-8.

16 Wake, 1997, p.16. Nottingham, 1992, pp.9-22. Nottingham, p.20, mentions that Thomas Thornely recalled that "whilst still a young man, William Rathbone IV had reorganised the American trade with Liverpool".

17 Chorley, 1873, vol. ii, pp.270-1.

18 Wake, 1997, p.36.

19 Anne Cropper, p.12.

20 Anne Cropper, pp.338-9.

21 Anne Cropper, p.12.

22 Wake, 1997, p.34.

23 Wake, 1997, p.31.

24 Nottingham, 1992, p.24. Dissolution of partnership deed, LMM, CR/2/3.

25 Conybeare, 1925, p.6.

26 Wake, 1997, p.34.

27 Hyde, 1971, p.108

28 Partnership deed of 1 September 1799, LMM/CR/2/2.

29 Parkinson, 1948, pp.204-5.

30 American Chamber of Commerce of the Port of Liverpool, Minute Books, 1801-1908. Liverpool Record Office, Accession No. 380 ANE.

31 Wake, 1997, p.35.

32 Anne Cropper, p.19.

33 Thomas Cropper to Robert R. Benson, 23 July 1807, Benson family papers, private collection.

34 Thomas Cropper to Robert Benson, 23 July 1813, Judd MSS, 514/26, Friends House Library, London.

35 Wake, 1997, p.38

36 *Ibid.* p.38.

37 *Ibid.* p.38.

38 *Ibid.* p.39.

39 Dennis, 1819. The *Bengal* arrived back in May 1816. Baines, 1852, p.573.

40 Dennis, 1819.

41 Wake, 1997, pp.41-2.

42 *James Cropper* was brought into service in 1822 and wrecked in 1832. Albion, 1938, pp.276-7.

43 Wake, 1997, p.28.

44 Conybeare, 1925, p.24.

45 Chapman, 1987, p.38.

46 Booth, 1831, p.8. Carlson, 1969, p.20.

47 Wake, 1997, p.41.

48 Ashton, 1996, p.61.

49 Carlson, 1969, pp.20-1. "Increasing Prosperity of Liverpool", *Gentleman's Magazine*, XCIV (1824) Pt I, p.75. Farnie, 1979, p.12.

50 Farnie, 1979, p.9.

51 Wake, 1997, p.41.

52 They also speculated in corn, importing grain from America, Ireland, and the Baltic for sale in Britain for many years. Wake, 1997, p.45.

53 Wake, 1997, p.44.

54 Wake, 1997, p.46.

55 *Ibid.* 1997, p.46.

56 Booth, 1831, p.6.

57 Wake, 1997, p.47.

58 *Ibid.* 1997, p.48. JC to Eliza Cropper, 9 August 1831. Cropper MSS, LMM, D/CR/10/58.

59 Mathias, 1995, pp.256-7.

60 Wake, 1997, p.48.

61 JC to Eliza Cropper, 10 August 1831. Cropper MSS, LMM, D/CR/16/5.

62 Anne Cropper, p.337.

63 Holland, 1900, p.428.

64 Davis, 1984, p.180.

65 He was assistant clerk of the Hardshaw Meeting in 1798, and its clerk from 1799 to 1801. Charlton, 1971. Cockin, Jenkins *et al.*, 1930, records that James Cropper was present at the Yearly Meeting in 1826 and 1827.

66 Memories of James Cropper (1823-1900), Tolson MSS, MCH/49. Pratt, 1985, p.24.

67 *Ibid.*

68 Wake, 1997, p.41.

69 Anne Cropper, p.18.

70 *Ibid.* p.18.

71 *Ibid.* p.16.

72 John Cropper's Book of Years, Tolson MSS, CH/7.

73 Anstey & Hair, 1989, p.198.

74 Parkinson, 1952, p.141.

75 JC to Joseph Sturge, 14 July 1827. Anne Cropper, p.123.

76 *Ibid.*

77 Davis, 1984, p.181.

78 JC to Joseph Sturge, various letters summer 1825. Anne Cropper, p.108 ff.

79 Anne Cropper, pp.338-9.

80 JC to Margaret Cropper, 24 May 1831. Anne Cropper, p.153.

81 *Ibid.* p.153.

82 *Ibid.* p.27. Charlton, 1960, p.69. James Cropper also described the project himself in two pamphlets published in 1834 and 1839.

83 JC to Anne Cropper, 19 November 1836. Anne Cropper, p.264.

84 JC to John and Edward Cropper, 27 April 1830. Anne Cropper, p.137.

85 Edward Cropper was more inclined to act the part of the parvenu, living an extra-vagant lifestyle in London and elsewhere.

86 Wake, 1997, p.50.

87 *Ibid.* pp.51, 53.

88 Cropper, 1900, p.ii. *Gore's Liverpool Directory* indicates that the Cropper family had a Duke Street residence from the early 1800s.

89 Conybeare, 1925, p.2.

90 John Cropper, *Journal*, 29 Apr. 1842. Tolson MSS, CH/15.

91 Willink, 1935, p.12.

92 Eliza Conybeare, Memories of Anne Cropper, Tolson MSS.

93 Anne Cropper, Journal of James Cropper's conduct as a child, 1829-32. Tolson MSS, 8/9.

94 *Ibid.*

95 *Ibid.*

96 Conybeare, 1925, p.57.

97 JC to John Cropper, 20 September 1839. Anne Cropper, p.318.

98 JC to Joseph Sturge, 9 April 1836. LMM, D/CR/8/21.

99 Brown, 1924. James Cropper enrolled in February 1838.

100 JC to John Cropper, 20 September 1839. Anne Cropper, p.318.

101 John Cropper's *Journal*, Tolson MSS, CH/15.

102 1851 Census, Strickland Roger and Strickland Ketel census districts. Sixty-one individuals – twenty-nine men and boys and thirty-two women and girls – are readily identifiable as paper-mill employees. "James Cropper is with us", noted Charles Cowan, the firm's head, on 1 May 1845, "having come on Tuesday night, to learn his business for a while". Diary 1842-6. Edinburgh City Library, Accession no. YDA1820C87 X64035.

103 James to Charles Cropper, 13 Dec. 1882. Tolson MSS CJC/35.

104 The trip is noted in Cowan's diary, and took place on 26 March 1845. The pair travelled up from Liverpool together and stayed the night with Cornelius Nicholson at Cowan Head. Diary 1842-6. Edinburgh City Lib-

rary, Accession no. YDA1820C87 X64035.

105 Coleman, 1958, p.239. Charles Cowan invented a stuff regulator and the fixed deckle, both patented in 1846, and a way of watermarking paper with the first or second drying cylinder rather than a dandy roll. Clapperton, 1967, pp.177-8.

CHAPTER 3

1 Memories of James Cropper (1823-1900) Tolson MSS, MCH/49.

2 *Ibid.*

3 *Kendal Mercury*, 29 Nov. 1845.

4 *Kendal Mercury*, 20 Dec. 1845.

5 John Long of Cowan Head to James Cropper, 26 Nov. 1845. Tolson MSS, CJC/16.

6 Memories of James Cropper (1823-1900) Tolson MSS, MCH/49.

7 Maisie Fletcher, p.7.

8 Kendal Record Office, "Purchase of Paper Mills Summary". WDX/577/4/T14.

9 John Cropper, Book of Years, Tolson MSS CH/7.

10 James Cropper (JCII) to Charles Cropper (CJC), 13 Dec. 1882. Tolson MSS CJC/35.

11 John Cropper, Book of Years, Tolson MSS CH/7.

12 JCII to W. H. Wakefield, 7 Sept. 1847. Tolson MSS.

13 JCII to CJC, 13 Dec. 1882. Tolson MSS CJC/35.

14 Cropper, 1900, pp.v-vi.

15 JCII to George McCorquodale, 16 June 1852. CA/1/1.

16 Jones & Willink, 1945, p.17.

17 The Kendal Reservoirs Act (which included Kentmere) received the royal assent on 21 July 1845. Wilson, 1973, p.325.

18 Cropper, 1900, pp.v-vi.

19 Improvement Account, Burneside. CA/4/2.

20 Fortnight Record Book, 1853. CA/FB1.

21 Chronology of business by ACC & JAC, CA/NS15.

22 1855 Cowan Head Improvement account, CA/4/2.

23 *Westmorland Gazette*, 24 Nov. 1855.

24 Improvement account, CA/4/2.

25 Orchard, 1893, p.486.

26 Royde Smith, 1939, p. 12, 18.

27 *Gore's Liverpool Directory*, 1800. No McCorquodales are listed in the 1796 directory. John Cropper corresponded with Helen McCorquodale, 1839-40. Cropper MSS, LMM, D/CR/7/ items 13, 14. The business links between the Cowans and McCorquodales are clearly to be seen in the records of Alexander Cowan & Sons in the Scottish Record Office, Edinburgh.

28 Charles Cowan's Diary. Edinburgh City Library, YDA1820C87.

29 Obituary, W. T. Blacklock, *Salford Weekly News*, 2 July 1870.

30 Jones & Willink, 1945, p.52.

31 The history of Valleyfield Mills is detailed in the *World Paper Trade Review*, 12 Jul. 1912.

32 Jones & Willink, 1945, p.49.

33 Jones & Willink, 1945, p.49. James Savage's death was reported in the *Kendal Mercury*, 4 February 1887.

34 Wage Book, Bank Mill. Alexander Cowan & Sons company records, Scottish Record Office, Edinburgh.

35 Jones & Willink, 1945, p.52. In the 1851 census John Bryce is noted to be a clerk apprentice. CA/NS13/John Bryce file.

36 Obituaries, *Kendal Mercury and Times*, 27 Mar. 1896, and the *Westmorland Gazette* 28 Mar. 1896.

37 Chronology of business by ACC & JAC, CA/NS15.

38 *Ibid.*

39 CA, Partnership Ledger, pp.48-49.

40 Statistics of Business, CA/4/2.

41 *Kendal Times*, 25 February 1865. "Manufacture of Kendal and the Neighbourhood No. VII The Paper Manufacture". This gives a lengthy description of Burneside Mill. Chronology of Business by ACC & JAC, CA/NS15.

42 *Ibid.*

43 Briggs, 1990, p.23. The poet was Martin Tupper.

44 Hobsbawm, 1997, p.49.

45 *Ibid.* p.45.

46 Evans, 1968, p.154. Thomson, *England in the Nineteenth Century*, pp.100-1.

47 Coleman, 1958, p.200, p.211.

48 Hills, 1988, p.126. Coleman, pp.203-4.

49 Hills, 1988, p.126.

50 Coleman, 1958, p.204. In 1872 Macarthur & Co. of Belfast, to give one more direct example, ordered Glazed Casing in 31 different sizes, all wanted in varying quantities of reams, from 10-150!

51 Coleman, 1948, pp.203-4.

52 Coleman, 1958, p.318.

53 Hobsbawm, 1998, pp.51-3.

54 Fortnight books, CA/FB3-4. Comparison of papers made before and after 31 October 1861.

55 Herring, 1855, p.107, p.110.

56 Jones & Willink, 1945, p.17.

57 CA/CH order book, 1872-4, p.61. Regarding other papers see Labarre, 1952, p.39, p.237, p.243. Sugar was commonly wrapped in blue or purple paper. In *The Paper Mills Directory*, from 1864 into 1870s, manufacture of "small hands" – a generic term for wrapping papers, which probably included shops and caps (Labarre, p.274) – is noted to be one of principal specialities of Burneside and Cowan Head Mills.

58 CA Fortnight books. Mauve is first mentioned in April 1871 and was also made for the Stationery Office in 1872. For more information on William Perkin, mauve and the synthetic dyes industry, see Simon Garfield, *Mauve* (Faber & Faber, 2000).

59 CA/CH Order Book, 1872-74. "Double Crown" sheets were 20 by 30 inches. Labarre, 1952, p.255.

60 Hills, 1988, p.122. Wood, 1982, p.98.

61 Hills, 1998, p.123. *The Paper Maker and British Paper Trade Journal*, 26 Jan. 1891.

62 *Encyclopaedia Britannica*, Thirteenth Edition, 1926.

63 Hills, 1988, p.123.

64 *The Paper Mills Directory*, 1872 and 1874, notes that "Envelope Papers" are one of Burneside's chief specialities.

65 Hills, 1988, pp.200-201. Labarre, p.90, p.244.

66 *Kendal Times*, 25 February, 1865, 'Manufacture of Kendal and the Neighbourhood No VII, The Paper Manufacture'.

67 *Ibid.* A sample of Orange Laid MG paper (smooth one side, rough the other) survives dated December 1869 and marked "Telegraph Envelope Paper", above which is written "Approved". CA/17/1A.

68 Wakefield & Crewdson Bank Book, 5/2/1873. Barclays Bank Group Archives Accession 25/334 (3)

69 Mathias, 1995, p.257, p.263.

70 Newsome, 1997, p.36. Trevelyan, 1952, p.68.

71 Nicholson, 1890, p.60, p.88.

72 Milligan, 1992, p.6.

73 Tolson MSS, Private Ledger 1844-1877. Edward Cropper, noted a parliamentary report of 1845, had put his name down for £118,400 worth of shares in railways then under consideration, the fifty-first biggest subscriber in the country. *Westmorland Gazette*, 5 July 1845.

74 James Cropper sold almost £5,000 of railway shares in the months leading up to the purchase of the mills in July 1845. Private Ledger, 1844-1875, Tolson MSS.

75 Conybeare, 1925, p.26, records that James Cropper was given £15,000 on his 15th birthday in 1838.

76 William Blacklock Memorial Tract, Manchester Record Office T590/2.

77 See Royde Smith, 1939, and Lee, 1940. G. McC. was a trustee of *Bradshaw's Guide* for a long time (Orchard, 1893, p.486)

78 J. H. Lane, *A history of Newton-Le-Willows*, P & D Riley, 1992.

79 Boon, 1925.

80 Hackett, 1976, pp.23-26, p.31.

81 JC & Co to McC. & Co, 20 Nov. 1869. JC & Co. to Wiggins Teape, 14 Jun. 1875. CA/L23/1.

82 Wood, 1982, pp.98–99.

83 *Encyclopaedia Britannica*, 13th Edition, 1926. Telegraph section.

84 Marshall & Walton, 1981, p.25.

85 *Ibid.*, 1981, p.18.

86 Maisie Fletcher, p.13.

87 Jones & Willink, 1945, p.17.

88 It opened all the way to Carlisle on 15 Dec. 1846. *Kendal Mercury*.

89 *Kendal Mercury*, 19 Jul. 1845.

90 Marshall & Walton, 1981, pp.180-4.

91 JCII was elected director of the K & W Railway in 1846 (*Kendal Mercury*, 12 Sept. 1846). He was a director of the L & C by 1854 (*Kendal Mercury*, 2 Sept. 1854).

92 Ordnance Survey, 1st Edition, 1858, shows a single siding at Burneside, passing through a goods shed.

93 The tram-line was only extended to Cowan Head when James Cropper had managed to purchase all the land connecting the two mills. Jones & Willink, 1945, p.57. Tolson MSS, JWC's Estate Capital Account Ledger.

94 Shorter, 1971, p.129, p.157.

95 CA Cowan Head Order Book, 1870-1872.

96 "Send a wagon weekly till further notice of from four to five tons". JC & Co. to Muspratt Bros. & Hindley, 16 Jan. 1871. CA/L23/1.

97 *The Paper Mills Directory*, 1860-1874 gives a clear picture of specialisation within the industry.

98 *Westmorland Gazette*, 5 Apr. 1835.

99 *The Paper Mills Directory* "compiled by the editor of and reprinted from *The Stationer*," 1860, 1862, 1864, 1865-72, 1874.

100 Magee, 1997, p.105.

101 *Ibid*, p.114.

102 *Ibid*, p.113.

103 Coleman, 1958, p.196. Hills, 1988, p.136.

104 Magee, 1997, p.113.

105 John Evans of John Dickinson & Co. was the paper-maker. Coleman, 1958, p.344.

106 Fortnight books, 1853-4. CA/FB1.

107 Magee, 1997, pp.117-8. Coleman, 1958, pp.341-2.

108 Fortnight Book, 3 Dec. 1853. The company had started experimenting with straw in August 1853. CA/FB1.

109 CA, Fortnight Books, Chronology of business by ACC & JAC, CA/NS15.

110 CA, Fortnight Books.

111 CA, Fortnight Books, and Magee, 1997, p.105. Elsewhere, the average cost of rags used to make ordinary printing paper averaged 16s per cwt in the same period.

112 CA, Fortnight Books, Chronology of business by ACC & JAC, CA/NS15.

113 Brice, 1863, p.38.

114 Evans, 1955, p.109 mentions that John Dickinson & Co. experimented with surat, but no date is given.

115 Brice, 1863, p.38.

116 Hills, 1988, p.140. Esparto first mentioned in company records, 4 Oct. 1862. CA/FB3.

117 Shorter, 1971, p.139.

118 Hills, 1988, p.141.

119 CA/FB3.

120 Whatley, 1993, p.69.

121 Dard Hunter, 1957, p.330. Shorter, 1971, p.114.

122 Clapperton, 1894, p.14.

123 *Ibid*. Preface indicates that at time of writing Clapperton was working at Penicuik.

124 Labarre, 1952, p.140.

125 Fortnight Books, 1863-4, CA/FB3-4.

126 Its price between 1863 and 1869, for example, averaged 9s 3d per cwt. "Jute Cuttings Average Cost in Liverpool", 1863-1873, CA/A1/6.

127 *Encyclopaedia Britannica*, 13th Edition, 1926. Kay, 1990, p.39.

128 Sindall, 1906, p.164. "Jute Cuttings Average Cost in Liverpool", CA/A1/6.

129 CA/A1/6.

130 *Barrow Almanack*, 1889, p.109 "The Flax and Jute Works". CA/A1/6.

131 Magee, 1997, p.117.

132 *Ibid.*, p.135. Hills, 1988, p.146.

133 CA, Fortnight Books.

134 Maisie Fletcher, p.2.

135 Cropper, 1900, p.vii.

136 Cropper, 1900, p.v.

137 James Cropper's Journal, 28 Apr. 1873. Tolson MSS, 8/11.

138 John Bryce's notebook, CA/23/2B, reveals that Burneside's No2 and No3 machines were operating 24 hours a day in 1877, but No1 was not. Thomson, *England in the Nineteenth Century*, 1991, p.47.

139 Strickland Roger, Strickland Ketel Census Records, 1841-1881.

140 JCII to Anne Cropper (AC), undated. Tolson MSS, CJC/54.

141 Jones & Willink, 1945, p.17. Apprentice wage details from CA/K21/IB. John Cunningham recorded in 1923 that up to the 1870s all the paper-makers belonged to the old Society of Paper-makers, but reckoned that all members ". . . must have tried to observe the motto on the clubmen's card: 'United to support and not combined to injure'." Jones & Willink, 1945, p.49.

142 Jones & Willink, 1945, p.25. James Cropper's wife Fanny referred to the event. "I am very very sorry about the mills being stopped", she wrote to her husband at the time "and hope thou wilt be as liberal as possible to the poorer part of the people". Fanny Alison Cropper (FAC) to JCII, 17 Jan. 1854, Tolson MSS, 8/1.

143 *Kendal Times*, 25 Feb. 1865.

144 James Robertson, a nineteenth century paper-maker in the north-east, recalled that "Rag boilers were open at one time . . . I have seen, when I have been emptying out the rags, the blood oozing out of every one of my fingers, as they were burnt with the lime and soda ash employed in boiling the rags." Robertson, 1897, p.4.

145 "Coroner's Inquest. Melancholy Death at Cowan Head". *Westmorland Gazette*, 10 Mar. 1866.

146 *Kendal Mercury*, 10 Apr. 1858.

147 *Kendal Mercury*, 12 & 19 Dec. 1868.

148 *Kendal Mercury*, 2 Dec. 1871.

149 Journal, 11 Aug 1875. Tolson MSS 8/11.

150 CA/K21/IB

151 JCII to Revd. W. Jones, open letter, *The Westmorland Gazette*, 1 Aug 1884.

152 Undated fragment, Tolson MSS, CJC/54.

153 Tolson MSS, 9/6.

154 Jones & Willink, 1945, p.46.

155 Jones & Willink, 1845, p.35.

156 James Cropper refers to taking classes himself in his Journal, 9 Oct. 1870. Tolson MSS 8/10. In 1860 it was noted that at Burneside "there is a school for girls and infants, partly supported by James Cropper Esq. and attended by about sixty children". Whellan, 1860, p.873.

157 Jones & Willink, 1945, p.35.

158 *Westmorland Gazette*, 7 Aug. 1875.

159 *Kendal Mercury*, 16 Feb. 1856.

160 *Kendal Mercury*, 4 May 1861.

161 *Westmorland Gazette*, 9 May 1861.

162 *Kendal Mercury*, 10 Aug. 1867.

163 Open letter from James Cropper, 4 Feb. 1868. Tolson MSS, 9/6.

164 Journal, 17 Jun. 1875. Tolson MSS, 8/11. Maisie Fletcher, p.66. JCII also wrote about being High Sheriff: "It is a curious position with so little position about it and no decisions to make except as to one's own amount of style and display . . .".

165 *Kendal Mercury*, 16 Dec. 1854. It was an occasion of "much cheering", the newspaper noted.

166 Cropper, 1900, pp. vi–vii.

167 JCII to AC. Tolson MSS, 8/6.

168 Journal, 30 Oct. 1870. Tolson MSS, 8/10.

169 *Ibid.*

170 Journal, 6 Nov. 1874. April 26, 1876. Tolson MSS, 8/11.

171 Journal, 7 Dec. 1878. Tolson MSS, 8/11.

172 *Westmorland Gazette*, 24 Dec. 1880.

173 Journal, 12 Dec. 1880. Tolson MSS, 8/11.

174 Journal, 26 April 1876. Tolson MSS, 8/11.

CHAPTER 4

1 Journal, 4 June 1876. Tolson MSS, 8/11.

2 Chronology of business by ACC & JAC, CA/NS15.

3 FAC to CJC, November 1867, Tolson MSS, 10/1.

4 Journal, 16 Mar. 1877. Tolson MSS, 8/11.

5 Mathias, 1995, p.390

6 JCII to CJC, 13 Dec. 1882. Tolson MSS, CJC/35.

7 JCII to AC, 21 Jul. *c*.1871. Tolson MSS, CJC/54.

8 CA, Cowan Head Order Book, 1872-1874. Scrap of paper inserted in p.55, perhaps in JCII's own hand, records "CJC's first entering of an order", 5 Aug. 1872.

9 Journal, 16 Sep. 1872. Tolson MSS, 8/11.

10 *Kendal Times*, 12 July 1873.

11 Journal, Tolson MSS, 8/11.

12 CA/FB5-7.

13 Journal, 24 Jan. 1875. Tolson MSS, 8/11.

14 *Ibid*, 9 Apr. 1876.

15 Maisie Fletcher, p.35.

16 *Ibid*. 28 Aug 1870. Maisie Fletcher, p.35.

17 Journal, 13 Aug 1871. Tolson MSS, 8/10.

18 Maisie Fletcher, p.73.

19 CJC to Edith Holland, undated, 1876. Tolson MSS, CJC/63.

20 Hampson, 1973, p.14.

21 Mordaunt Crook, 1999, p.87.

22 Maisie Fletcher, p.103.

23 *Kendal Times*, 2 Sept. 1876.

24 *Ibid*, 12 Sept. 1879.

25 *Ibid*.

26 *Westmorland Gazette*, 24 Dec. 1880.

27 Jones & Willink, 1945, p.49.

28 JCII lost contest for Westmorland by 263 votes out of an electorate of over five thousand. *Kendal Mercury*, 4 Dec. 1885.

29 "In Memoriam Daniel McNeill", CA/22/7A.

30 CJC to James Winstanley Cropper (JWC), 1917. Tolson MSS, JWC/27.

31 AHW lived at Dingle Bank from the age of six. H. G. Willink, *Memoir of William Williamson Willink* (Privately printed, 1936).

32 Maisie Fletcher, p.109.

33 JCII to Alfred Willink (AHW), 16 May 1881. Willink MSS.

34 CA/1/3, 1890s.

35 Census records 1841-81, CA/K21/2, Illustrated Album of Workpeople on JWC's coming of age, 1900.

36 Note listing "Material for One Year", Feb. 1900. CA/1/3. Henderson was the name of the pulp agent. Two-thirds of the wood pulp used by the company was sulphite pulp.

37 Magee, 1997, p.20.

38 Read, 1994, p.66. *Paper Maker and British Paper Trade Journal*, Jan. 1891.

39 Read, 1994, p.63.

40 CJC to AHW, 29 Jun. 1899. CA/1/3.

41 CJC to Waterlow & Sons, 10 Nov. 1897. CA/1/3.

42 Notes of Buff Sales delivered to McCorquodale and Co., CA/4/2. In 1895, for example (CA/1/3, 13 Aug. 1895), CJC asked G. F. McC. to arrange a meeting for him with Lewis Evans of John Dickinson & Co.

43 AHW to CJC, 19 Feb. 1902. CA/1/3.

44 CJC to AHW, 21 Mar. 1904. CA/1/3.

45 These papers are referred to in letters of 13 May 1901, 13 May 1902, and 21 June 1899.

46 CJC to AHW, 7 Jul. 1897. CA/1/3.

47 JCII to CJC, 24 Apr. 1895. Tolson MSS, CJC/35.

48 Evans, 1955, pp.39-40. CA/21/2.

49 CJC to AHW, 1 Nov. 1898, 10 Feb. 1899. CA/1/3. There is also a reference to AHW taking out patents on Duplex Paper circa 1913.

50 Profits peaked at £11,300 in 1897.

51 JCII to CJC, 1882, 1895. Tolson MSS, CJC/35.

52 Journal, 27 June 1875. Tolson MSS, 8/11.

53 CJC to EEH, CJC/63. CJC echoed view of T. H. Huxley, the Victorian scientist and essayist, who wrote in 1867: "If I intended my son for any branch of manufacture, I should not dream of sending him to university". Coleman, 1973, pp.98-100.

54 Journal, 4 June 1876. Tolson MSS, 8/11.

55 CJC was still, however, a sincerely religious man, although in a less vocal way than his parents. On the confirmation of his son in 1895 he wrote to him: "I humbly pray to God that you may learn to love Him, and that he may give you faith in Christ, and that you may be able to realise what Christ means, and what He has done for us". (Tolson MSS, CJC/44).

56 Journal, 16 Mar. 1877. Tolson MSS, 8/11.

57 Maisie Fletcher, p.62.

58 FAC to CJC, 31 Jan. 1868. Tolson MSS, 8/16.

59 Journal, 24 Dec. 1875. Tolson MSS 8/11.

60 Neil McKendrick, Introduction to *Hunting Scraps* (unpublished), p.9. Coleman, 1973, p.114.

61 The British price index fell by thirty-two percent between 1871-5 and 1891-5. Read, 1994, p.216.

62 CA/1/3, CJC to JWC, 17 May 1903.

63 *Paper-Maker's Monthly Journal*, February 1883.

64 Evans, 1955, p.132. In 1886 John Dickinson & Co. was formally incorporated as a limited company with a capitalisation of £500,000.

65 CA/Box 17/Item 1A.

66 CJC to AHW, 6 Nov. 1896. CA/1/5.

67 CJC to AHW, 18 Jun. 1896. CA/1/5.

68 CJC to AHW, 8 Jul. 1898. CA/1/3.

69 CA/1/6b.

70 Jones & Willink, 1945, p.41. Hills, 1988, p.158.

71 Evans, 1955, p.143.

72 *Paper-Makers' Monthly Journal*, 15 Jan. 1885, quoting the *Darwen News* of 3 Jan.

73 Shorter, 1971, p.146, 152.

74 James Cropper & Co. was offered Canalside. The other two mills that failed were Ellers Mill and Penny Bridge. Gavin, 1990, p.250. CJC to A.C.McC., 16 Oct. 1905. CA/DBLB.

75 Maisie Fletcher, p.144.

76 "I remember so well", his daughter Maisie recalled, "the shadow of that year on my childhood when my father's high spirits were brought low." Maisie Fletcher, p.145.

77 Ensor, 1992, pp.107-8.

78 Wray, 1979, p.33.

79 Magee, 1997, p.70.

80 *Ibid.*, pp.240-66. Muir, 1972, p.24.

81 Dykes Spicer, 1907, p.134. AHW to CJC, Nov. 1899, AHW to CJC. CA/1/3.

82 CJC to AHW, Jul. 1894. CA/1/3.

83 AHW to CJC, 24 Nov. 1899. CA/1/3.

84 Hills, 1988, p.186.

85 *Kendal Mercury*, 21 Jul. 1882.

86 *Kendal Mercury and Times*, 9 Jul. 1886.

87 *Ibid.*

88 Notes on the burning and restoration of Burneside Mill, written by CJC. CA/4/5.

89 CJC to J. M. Oldham (JMO), 9 Dec. 1887. CA/DBLB.

90 JWC to JMO, 25 Feb. 1909. CA/DBLB.

91 CA/MC3, 15 May 1967.

92 CJC to AHW, 17 Sep. 1903, CA/1/3.

93 Obituary, *Westmorland Gazette*, 27 Sept. 1947.

94 Tolson MSS, CJC/19.

95 CA/2/7. At the time CJC wrote to JWC, "I have never worked so hard for three weeks in my life but I've been very happy – tremendous pals with a lot of men who as a rule I never see."

96 Huggins, 1970, p.102.

97 CA/NS15/1.

98 Cloth-lining was actually transferred from Burneside to Cowan Head in 1911. Chronology of business by ACC & JAC, CA/NS15. Registered Envelopes proved especially popular during the Boer War when huge numbers were used by soldiers for sending money home. CJC to JC & Co., 18 Nov. 1902. CA/1/3A.

99 *Kendal Mercury and Times*, 20 Oct. 1882. "Treat to the Burneside Work-People".

100 CJC to William Wakefield, 7 Jul. 1886. CA/DBLB.

101 CA/JWC Ledger, Item 11, Property Account. CA/Chronology of business by ACC & JAC, CA/NS15.

102 CA/Bertrams' Valuation, 27 Mar 1901.

103 Building an ornamental chimney was by no means unprecedented in British industrial history. The chimney at the India Mill in Darwen, for example, was based on Venice's campanile, and was probably seen by James and Charles Cropper on their visit to the town in 1886. It was constructed in 1867. Aspin, 1995, p.4.

104 CA/Burneside Extension letters, 1903. CA/SLB1.

105 Old Balance Sheets, 1907-14. Company archives.

106 CA/JWC Ledger.

107 Chronology of business by ACC & JAC, CA/NS15. Division of holdings, 1889: CJC 188, JCII 149, G.McC 150, JB 150, AHW 113, Staff 4.

108 This ties in with JCII's notes in Tolson MSS dated spring 1888, CJC/35, which discusses the possibility that G. McC might pull out of the concern in a year.

109 CJC to Mary Wakefield Cropper (MWC), c.1905. Tolson MSS, CJC/44.

110 CA/Balance sheets, 1907-14. CA/JWC ledger.

111 CJC to W. H. Wakefield, 7 Jul. 1886. CA/DBLB.

112 The freehold remained in family hands until 1923. Deeds of Burneside Mills, KRO, WDX/577/5/T13.

113 Tolson MSS, JWC's Estate Capital Account Ledger. CJC to AHW, 21 Jun. 1900. CA/1/3. Letterbooks of CJC, 1900-1915, Tolson MSS, CJC/14. Somervell, 1930, notes that the Potter Fell pipeline provides about 100hp on a Pelton wheel, when there is plenty of water.

114 *Kendal Mercury*, 17 Aug. 1900.

115 Maisie Fletcher, p.219.

116 CJC to MCC, May 27, 1910. Tolson MSS, JWC/63.

117 JCII to JWC, 23 Jul. 1899, Tolson MSS, JWC/41/i.

118 JWC to CJC 22 Jun. 1916. Tolson MSS, CJC/17.

119 VSJ to JWC. Tolson MSS, JWC/41.

120 *Kendal Mercury*, 17 Aug. 1900.

121 JWC to EEC, 21 Aug. 1916. Tolson MSS, JWC/41/iv. CJC to AHW, 14 Jul. 1902. CA/1/3.

122 CA/Minute Book, 1889-1941. Annual General Meeting, 31 Oct. 1906. At the outset the appointment was perhaps not only underpinned by James W.'s time with the accountancy firm, during which he worked alongside Nicholas Waterhouse, a future senior partner who was almost the same age, but also by family connections: Nicholas's father Edwin, one of the founding partners, was son of a Quaker merchant in Liverpool, and a distant relative of the Cropper family.

123 Tolson MSS, JWC/29, Diary 1902-3. Paper-mills they visited included Guard Bridge, Valleyfield, Star, Spring Vale and New Mills.

124 Tolson MSS, JWC/29, Diary, 1903.

125 CJC to JWC, 17 May 1903. CA/1/3.

126 JWC to CJC 17 Jun. 1903. Tolson MSS, JWC/26.

127 Jones & Willink, 1945, p.65. At first JWC did not exactly make a success of his Fortnight Book work: "We cannot make his figures tally with the result", CJC regretfully informed Alick McCorquodale on October 16, 1905 (CA/DBLB, p.365). CA/Fortnight Books.

128 CJC to JWC, 5 Aug. 1907. Tolson MSS, ACC file. CA/JWC Ledger, Summary of holdings of Ordinary Shares.

129 CJC to JWC, 5 Aug. 1906. Tolson MSS, CJC/44.

130 Daniel McNeill to CJC, June 1907. Tolson MSS, MCH/50.

131 Appointed director Nov. 6 1907, DMB, 1897-1922). By 1901 VSJ had 72 shares in JC & Co., almost 9.5% of issued capital.

132 Maisie Fletcher, p.202.

133 VSJ to JWC, 8 Oct. 1911. Obituary, *Westmorland Gazette*, 5 May 1967.

134 JWC to CJC, 19 Sep. 1913. Tolson MSS, JWC/30. JWC adds: "This summer [Vin] was threatened with a strike. The men sent for the head man of the American

Papermakers Union and met him at the station three hundred strong. Vin treated him as an equal – told him the truth – and the boss told the men they had nothing whatever to grumble about and went away, only two men seeing him off." VSJ was made a KBE in 1941. More details about Vin and Mary Jones in Newfoundland is given in Taylor, 1996.

135 AHW to Revd Arthur Willink, 21 May 1903. CA/DBLB. CA/1/3, 11 Dec. 1908.

136 Interview: Philippa Cropper (PGMC).

137 *Westmorland Gazette*, October 1910. There was also a large parish party after the return of JWC and his bride, described by CJC in a letter to 'Mink', 9 Oct. 1910, Tolson MSS, JWC/41/v. 860 guests attended and were entertained in the usual way, with games, tea, a bonfire, music and dancing.

138 CJC to AHW 29 Apr. 1914. CA/1/3.

139 Pollard, 1976, p.32.

140 CA/FB10, first week of April, 1912. "Standing still for Coal Strike".

141 CA/K22/6.

142 CA/K22/6A.

143 CA/K21/3A. "Tonnage for Shift Workers and Others".

144 Jones & Willink, 1945, p.43.

145 CA/JWC Ledger, item 19.

146 *Ibid.*

147 CA/K22/6.

148 *Ibid.*

149 Marjorie Constance Cropper (MCC) to JWC, *c.*1911. Tolson MSS, JWC/16.

150 Read, 1994, p.490. In the event it was not until 1975 that women received equal pay.

151 JWC to A.C.McC., May 1914. CA/DBLB.

152 W. Ross of National Union of Paper Mill Workers to JC & Co. Ltd, 6 Jun. 1914. CA/K22/6.

153 W. Ross of NUPMW to JC & Co., 13 Jun. 1914. CA/K22/6.

154 Pollard, 1976, p.38.

155 *Daily Citizen*, 17 Jun. 1914.

156 JWC to Arthur Henderson MP, 19 Jun. 1914, CA/DBLB.

157 JWC to JMO, 16 May, 1914. CA/DBLB

158 *Ibid.*

159 Memo by CJC, 1914, CA/2/11.

160 CJC to AHW, 2 Jun 1914. CA/3/11.

161 *Ibid.*

162 JWC to A.C.McC., May 1914. CA/DBLB.

163 *Ibid.*

164 CA/3/11.

165 Bernard Airey, who joined James Cropper & Co. in 1952 recalls spending many afternoons as an apprentice up at Ratherheath, flushing game out of the woods and scrub.

166 AHW to A.C.McC, 29 Apr. 1913. CA/DBLB.

167 CJC to Edith Cropper (EEC), 20 May 1913. Tolson MSS, CJC/57.

168 Maisie Fletcher, p.230.

CHAPTER 5

1 JWC to MCC, 1 Dec. 1915. Tolson MSS, JWC/41/5.

2 David Thomson, *England in the Twentieth Century*, 1991, p.39.

3 JWC to CJC, Tolson MSS, JWC/48/3. This letter was later published in *The Westmorland Gazette*.

4 Jones, 1995, p.105. Thomson, 1991, pp.38–9.

5 CJC to JWC, 9 Aug. 1914. Tolson MSS, JWC/27.

6 CJC to JWC, 2 Sept. 1914. Tolson MSS, JWC/27.

7 CJC to JMO, 21 Dec. 1914. CA/DBLB.

8 Muir, 1972, p.26.

9 CJC to JMO, 9 Jan. 1915. CA/DBLB.

10 CA/K21/5. List of men on Active Service, August 10 and September 1. *Everyman's Encyclopaedia*.

11 Notices in CA/K22/6 and CA/K21/5.

12 CJC to JWC, 12 Sept. 1914. Tolson MSS, JWC/27.

13 CJC to EEC, 29 Oct. 1914. Tolson MSS, CJC/44.

14 CA/JWC Ledger, Directors' Remuneration.

15 Hermann Willink was mobilised December

1914. CA/NS17/JWC Staff Salaries Ledger.

16 CJC to JWC, 16 Oct. & 30 Nov. 1916. Tolson MSS, JWC/58/1.

17 *Ibid.*

18 CJC to JWC, 2 Aug. 1917. Tolson MSS, JWC/21.

19 CJC to A. C. McC., 9 Sept. 1915. CA/DBLB

20 At the beginning of 1917, for example, engineers were particularly in short supply and had to be recruited at rates of pay far above peacetime levels. CJC to JWC, 1 Jan. 1917. Tolson MSS, JWC/27.

21 CA/JWC Ledger.

22 CA/K22/6.

23 CA/SLB1, 7 Sept. 1914. CJC to JWC, 2 Nov. 1916. Tolson MSS, JWC/58/b1.

24 CA/NS17/JWC Staff Salaries Ledger.

25 CJC to JWC, 30 Nov. 1916. Tolson MSS, JWC/58/b1.

26 CJC to JWC, 15 Feb. 1917. Tolson MSS, JWC/58/b2.

27 Tolson MSS, JWC/27, application for demobilisation, towards end of 1917.

28 Walter Runciman to CJC, 5 Feb. 1916. CA/DBLB.

29 Pollard, 1976, pp.48-9.

30 CJC to EEC, 22 Feb. 1917. Tolson MSS, CJC/44.

31 Muir, 1972, p.27. At St. Cuthbert's, Somerset, for example, turnover dropped by over sixty percent between 1915 and 1918, from 3,131 to 1,178 tons. Laker, 1991, p.35.

32 CJC to F. Atterbury, HMSO, 25 May 1916. CA/SLB.

33 CJC to JWC, 4 Jun. 1916. Tolson MSS, JWC/27.

34 Pollard, 1976, p.43.

35 Although a Royal Commission was set up in 1916 to supervise the import of paper-making materials and the supply of paper for wartime needs (Hills, 1988, p.187), a Paper Controller was not appointed until March 1918 (Muir, 1972, p.26).

36 CJC to JWC, 23 Apr. 1917. Tolson MSS, JWC/27.

37 *Ibid.*

38 CJC to JWC, undated, Autumn 1914. Tolson MSS, JWC/27.

39 CJC to JWC, 4 Jun. 1916. Tolson MSS, JWC/27.

40 CJC to Walter Runciman, 29 Jan. 1916. CA/DBLB.

41 CA/JWC Ledger. A good example of the exceptional inflation of prices was discussed by CJC in a letter to JWC in 1917, in which he enclosed a piece of card made from boiled jute. "In ordinary times it could not compete with straw board at £5", he wrote, "but now people are tumbling over each other to buy it at £28 – We made the trial on Tuesday and we already know of 150 orders by Thursday morning." CJC to JWC, 2 Aug. 1917. Tolson MSS, JWC/27.

42 CA/JWC Ledger.

43 *Ibid.*

44 "I am so glad you are protesting against the ridiculous prices of paper", James W. wrote to his father in October 1916, "I can't get over the idea that it's awful to be making money out of this war." JWC to CJC, 22 Oct. 1916. Tolson MSS, CJC/17. In November 1916 James Cropper & Co. reduced prices by over £4 per ton. CJC to JWC, 30 Nov. 1916. Tolson MSS, JWC/58/1.

45 Pollard, 1976, p.64. CA/JWC Ledger.

46 CA/JWC Ledger.

47 Jones & Willink, 1945, p.46.

CHAPTER 6

1 CJC to JWC, 16 May 1917. Tolson MSS, JWC/27.

2 CA/JWC Ledger.

3 CA/JWC Ledger. (*The Times*, 11 May 1920, notes a "World Shortage of Paper").

4 CA/Minute Book, AGM, 27 Nov. 1919.

5 CA/2/14.

6 CA/Minute Book, AGM, 24 Nov. 1920.

7 CA/Minute Book, AGM, 27 Nov. 1919.

8 Pollard, 1976, p.91. There were 510 employees in 1920. CA/SLB2, 7 Oct. 1925. Numbers fell back below 500 in 1921–5.

9 Pollard, 1976, p.64. *Encyclopaedia Britannica*, Thirteenth Edition, Vol. 29, p.1085. CA/JWC Ledger.

10 *The Times*, 12 May 1920. Gouin was trying to encourage British investment in papermaking in Quebec.

11 The jump in dividend payments in these years reflected an increase in capital. In 1919 James Cropper & Co. were told by the Paper Makers' Association "that the proportion our dividends bore to our wages was one of the lowest in the trade – so that we can feel that we have not been underpaying our Employees or overpaying ourselves as shareholders." 1919 AGM minutes, 27 Nov. 1919, CA/Minute Book.

12 CA/2/14. Harry Wilson recalls how his wife's father (surname Simpson) used to beat the gas engine with a stick to try to get it to work.

13 CA/Minute Book, AGM, 24 Nov. 1920.

14 CA/DMB, 8 Nov. 1918, 8 Mar. 1920. A vast cache of letters survives between JC & Co. and Bertrams relating to the work carried out from 1919 to 1921. CA/ Extension letters.

15 Pollard, 1976, pp.216-7.

16 Thomson, *England in the Twentieth Century*, 1991, p.69.

17 Influx of foreign imports mentioned CA/MB, AGM, 24 Nov. 1920.

18 CA/2/15, notes by CJC, 16 Dec. 1920.

19 *Ibid.*

20 CA/DMB, CA/2/15. "We had it preached to us, again and again, that there was a world shortage of paper", commented CJC. "The world shortage does not exist . . . We have been misguided in thinking that there is a world shortage, and with that opinion we ordered No5 machine, for which I fear there is no need, and demand for its output will have to be bought on very expensive terms."

21 CA/DMB, Dec. 1920.

22 CA/PL1, BS and CH Revenue Accounts.

23 CA/MB, 22 Feb. 1922. "For the first time in the history of these mills, machines have been standing for long periods for lack of orders and also lack of fuel during the coal strike."

24 H. Corrie to Inland Revenue, 4 Aug. 1921. CA/SLB2. JC & Co. tried to lessen the impact of the coal strike by fitting up two boilers to run off diesel (details in CA/7/3), on the lines of the Lots Road power station, London, which worked well on such fuel. The scheme did not, however, work.

25 Herbert Corrie to Price Waterhouse, 12 Dec. 1921. CA/SLB2. The value of paper made at Burneside fell from £63 per ton (average up to March 1921) to under £45 (in the months up to September 1921). It then fell to £32 in the seven months to April 1922. Muir, 1972, p.33, notes that bleached sulphite wood pulp was £120 a ton at end of 1920. Eight months later it was £20 a ton, yet many mills were forced to pay the former price as deliveries arrived.

26 CA/PL1, p.139.

27 Muir, 1972, p.33.

28 CA/JWC Ledger.

29 CA/MB, 22 Jan. 1922.

30 CA/2/15, CJC Memo, undated but probably Autumn 1921.

31 Note by JWC in CA/JWC Ledger, Revenue Accounts.

32 CA/SLB2, p.313. Details on capital of company, 1914-24. CA/JWC Ledger, Revenue Accounts.

33 CA/MB, AGM, 10 May 1923. A further £15,000 was raised by issuing debentures in 1923-4. (CA/SLB, p.313). The company also cashed in £10,000 in War Loan stock in 1923-4. CA/PL2, Balance Sheets.

34 Paterson went to Dickinson's Croxley Mills.

35 CA/DBrLB, 6 April 1920. Arnot started on £500 a year, with house, light and coals free.

36 CA/2/16, Journey Letters, 29 May 1933.

37 CA/DBrLB, 31 Aug. 1922. In the same letter CJC asks McNeill to accept £250 per year "in recognition of the past and in hope of the future".

38 *Westmorland Gazette*, obituary 15 Dec. 1923.

39 CA/NS17/Staff Salaries. R. McNeill started on £700 with house, light and coal free.

40 CJC's mind turned to Jack Howson as soon as the war ended, but doubted that he would come. CJC to EEC, 12 Nov. 1918. Tolson MSS, CJC/44. CA/DBrLB, notes by JWC, 30 Dec. 18, outlines a five-year proposal made to Jack Howson for five years. Maisie Fletcher, p.241.

41 Walter Fletcher to JWC, 1 Jun. 1919. Tolson MSS, JWC/28.

42 A cache of letters in CA/DBrLB relates to the affair. It suggests that there were problems with his wife's health, although more probably there was trouble with their relationship.

43 Conybeare, 1925, p.64. Dingle Bank was more recently the site of the Liverpool International Garden Exhibition.

44 Interview: Bill Willink.

45 Minute Book, AGM, 13/5/1925.

46 In 1932 he accepted the Presidency but was forced (for unknown reasons) to stand down at the last moment when Captain Nuttall (of Cooke & Nuttall) was put forward for the position. In 1942 he was asked to be President again but refused on account of his age (sixty-three years old).

47 Interview: Ronnie Reddish. "If he said do something", Ronnie recalled, "you *did it*. With the other directors, you did it, but not so willingly." Harold Snowdon recalled that AHW would run the village choral society like a military operation. Any members who missed practices were swiftly brought into line and usually summoned to his house to go over what they had missed.

48 AHW to JWC, 4 July 1934. CA/2/16. CA/23/2/A, AHW's note book. Dates from 1887 to 1945. Strip-lined was still being

made in 1947, CA/19/21, letter of 7 Jul. 1947.

49 Maisie Fletcher, p.264.

50 Tolson MSS, JWC/25.

51 Tolson MSS, JWC's Personnel Ledger and diary. CA/2/17.

52 Interview with Neil McKendrick, 1995.

53 CJC to JWC, 25 Dec. 1916. Tolson MSS, JWC/58/b2.

54 CA/DMB2, 10 Nov. 1937.

55 Anthony Cropper (ACC) worked in every department of the mill between school and university. *Westmorland Gazette*, 24 Jun. 1933.

56 JWC to AHW, undated letter, 1934. CA/2/16.

57 PGMC corroborates this.

58 Tolson MSS, ACC file.

59 CA/3/17 has all details of the arrangements. Another entertainer was W. Tallis Manley, "Royal Punch and Judy Entertainer with the Celebrated Dog 'Toby'". Total costs, including four marquees, came to £194 16/11.

60 Pollard, 1976, p.92. Floud & McCloskey, 1992, p.360.

61 CA/JWC ledger, Bad Debts reserve account.

62 Hills, 1998, p.186.

63 CA/No.4 machine records, 1929-1933.

64 Jeremy, 1998, p.352.

65 Brooke Bond are mentioned in CA/Journal 1912-1973 (Transfers to Credit of Debit Ledger), from 1930 onwards.

66 Pollard, 1976, p.100.

67 JWC to AHW, 6 Feb. 1930. CA/2/16.

68 Interview: Mike Wilkinson.

69 CA/2/16, journey letters. JWC called Harold McCorquodale on 28 Nov. 1927, who "regretted the passing of 'Cropper's Buff'". Several annual reports refer to the company's efforts to improve the quality of output. In 1935, for example, it was noted that the satisfactory results were "due to the larger quantity of specialities which we have been able to manufacture."

70 CA/No4 machine records 1929-33 indicates

that Indian postcards kept No4 running for days on end. In 1927 JC & Co. made 1,000 tons of Indian postcards. Pasted MG papers noted to one of company's principal specialities, JWC to G. Tower, CA/DBrLB, 13 Jun. 1924. A pasting machine was installed at CH in 1920.

71 Chronology of business by ACC & JAC, CA/NS15.

72 Hills, 1988, p.197, Hughes, 2000, p.55. Labarre, 1952, p.312.

73 John Thompson water boilers were installed. CA/8/7.

74 Chronology of business by ACC & JAC, CA/NS15.

75 1929 Annual Report.

76 1927 Annual Report. CA/PL1, Burneside and Cowan Head Revenue Accounts.

77 *Westmorland Gazette*, 5 & 12 November 1932. Thomas Wray joined James Cropper & Co. in 1891. A verdict of accidental death was recorded at the inquest, which heard that the accident was caused by Edwin Huck easing back one wagon into another, while Wray was passing in between. It was also noted that there were regulations posted in the factory highlighting the danger of passing between wagons.

78 Another serious but non-fatal accident occurred in 1925, when Raymond Clark had his arms burned and crushed while feeding the pasting machine.

79 Levi Keates died in 1953 aged ninety. He began work as a half-timer for a wage of 2s 6d. a week aged nine in 1872, when his family moved to Burneside from Dorset. *Westmorland Gazette*, 7 Nov. 1953.

80 CA/PL1, Profit Sharing Savings Account.

81 Any money held in excess of these sums was returned to the investor in cash, debentures, or, in 1939, in 5% Preferences Shares. Documents relating to Profit Sharing Savings Scheme in CA/3/19 and CA/21/5A.

82 CA/3/19, Proposals for Employees' Savings Accounts, 29 Sept. 1939.

83 JWC to MCC, 21 May 1939. Tolson MSS, JWC/41/5.

84 The total cost was actually £10,080. £2,080 was paid by way of government subsidy. CA/DBrLB, 16 Dec. 1918.

85 CA/JWC Ledger, Property Account.

86 Burneside Women's Institute, "Description of the most significant changes in village life over the last fifty years", 1969. Kendal Record Office. Older houses continued to have bucket closets into the 1950s.

87 CA/JWC Ledger, Electric Light Capital Account.

88 The "outside gang" remained a peculiar feature of James Cropper & Co.'s workforce into the 1980s.

89 CA/DMB, 29 Nov. 1919

90 Burnett, 1986, p.217. Pollard, 1976, pp.87-8.

91 Tolson MSS, JWC/27.

92 CA/4/16. JWC to AHW, 22 Apr. 1926. CA/DBrLB

93 Maisie Fletcher, pp.271-3. Interview: Ronnie Reddish.

94 Pollard, 1976, p.163.

95 Evans, 1955, p.197, notes that one of John Dickinson & Co.'s biggest problems post-war was labour relations. Evidence of Union and Federation wage agreements is found in many places, including CA/NS14.

96 CA/MB, AGM, 2 Apr. 1927.

97 Wray, 1979, p.43.

98 In the 1930s import duties were less benign. Ramsay Macdonald's National Government signed treaties with Scand-inavian countries which reduced British import duties on certain types of wrapping and other papers in exchange for which these countries agreed to buy large quantities of British coal. As a result, "British mills found themselves no longer able to produce, at economic prices, a range of paper that included kraft, sulphite, grease-proof, tissue, and certain kinds of coated papers and boards". Muir, 1972, pp.41-2.

99 Hills, 1988, p.186. Protection was undoubtedly welcomed by James W., who had argued in favour of a system of protective tariffs for years, much to the annoyance of his brother-in-law Francis Acland, a Liberal MP. Tolson MSS, JWC/19.

100 Wray, 1979, p.49. Pollard, 1976, p.168, p.171.

101 CA/2/16.

CHAPTER 7

1 David Thomson, *England in the Twentieth Century*, Penguin, 1991, p.190.

2 Jones, 1995, p.187. Pollard, 1976, p.297.

3 Barbary Crag MSS, PGMC to her mother, 30 Aug. to 2 Sept. 1939.

4 JWC to MCC, 30 April 1939: "We have been busy trying to get people into the Territorials". Tolson MSS, JWC/41/v.

5 Wray, 1979, p.54.

6 Evidence of HMSO's importance in CA/No4 machine records, 1929–33.

7 Muir, 1972, p.50.

8 CA/JWC Ledger, Profit and Loss Account, 1940.

9 CA/DMB2, 26 Jul. 1939.

10 CA/JWC Ledger, Development Reserve Account. CA/8/7,8.

11 1941, 1943 Annual Reports.

12 1943 Annual Report.

13 1941, 1943 Annual Reports.

14 JWC Personnel Ledger, CA/NS/17. Oliver Acland (OGDA) says Geoffrey Acland (AGDA) was stationed in Lancaster for most of war training people to use anti-aircraft guns. He was demobbed in February 1946. CA/NS17, JWC Personnel Ledger.

15 JWC to Hugh McCorquodale, 3 June 1942. CA/DBrLB.

16 CA/JWC Ledger.

17 CA/New Employees Started Book.

18 1945 Annual Report.

19 Interview: Alf Whiteley.

20 1945 Annual Report.

21 This included £3,000 of pulp already paid for by the company, which was written off as a bad debt until the sum was recovered in 1944 CA/JWC Ledger Profit & Loss Account. 1940 Annual Report. CA/JWC Ledger Bad Debts reserve.

22 Annual Reports *passim*.

23 1942 Annual Report.

24 By 1943 waste papers provided half of all the company's raw materials, even though the mills were only consuming 16% more than they did in peacetime. Annual Reports *passim*.

25 1941 Annual Report.

26 Muir, 1972, p.51.

27 Shorter, 1971, p.164. "Waste papers were for much the time very difficult to get hold of", noted James W. in May 1942 (Annual Report), "but the recent Press Campaign has improved the position and they are now more plentiful".

28 The consumption of jute and other fibres rose from 140 tons (1%) pre-war to 1600 tons in 1941 (14%), 2430 (26%) in 1942, 2,100 (25%) in 1943. Annual Reports 1941-3.

29 Interview: Alf Whiteley. The company notably steered clear of straw, the most popular source of paper-making fibre after waste paper during the war years, particularly for Britain's numerous esparto mills. Shorter, 1971, p.164.

30 1941 Annual Report. Frank Thompson (who worked at Cowan Head) recalled that in wartime they used to make paper out of old sandbags. He remembers cutting up sacks manually with a big knife sticking out of a bench, the way rags had been cut up for centuries.

31 The drop in output was in line with the British paper industry as a whole: national production dropped from 2.5 million tons in 1938 to 1.3 million tons in 1945.

32 Frank Thompson interview, 4 May 1991. Company Archives.

33 Chronology of business by ACC & JAC,

CA/NS15. Bowston was rebuilt in 1930 with a new water-turbine (started up by ACC), chopper, duster and bleach plant. At the same time it was electrified.

34 Interview: David Penn, Small Firearms expert at the Imperial War Museum, who confirmed that they were made of low quality cardboard.

35 1945 Annual Report.

CHAPTER 8

1 1946, Annual Report.

2 *Ibid.*

3 Cairncross, 1992, p.48.

4 Notes of AGDA's visit to Scandinavia, CA/3/20. Wray, 1979, p.56. CA/MC1, 7 July 1950, notes that purchases of pulp had been arranged.

5 CA/MC2, 4 Jul. 1952. CA/MC2, 12 Nov. 1953. CA/MC2, 31 May 1954. CA/MC2, 5 Apr. 1955.
CA/MC2, 10 Nov. 1955.

6 CA/MC1, 6 Mar. 1948. CA/Fortnightly Agendas, November 1950 and elsewhere. Interview: Philip Huck. AR, 1948.

7 Interview: OGDA.

8 Annual Reports, 1946-9. In spite of the restrictions around twenty cottages were built during the late 1940s and early 1950s, named Churchill Court.

9 Wray, 1979, pp.56-7.

10 ACC, New Year message, 1957, CA/3/25, notes that the first five years of peace were a period of "control and frustration".

11 Cairncross, 1992, p.8, p.55.

12 Annual Report, 1947.

13 Owen, 1999, p.156.

14 Hobsbawm, 1999, p.245.

15 Owen, 1999, p.156.

16 Wray, 1979, p.61.

17 Hills, 1988, p.186.

18 Wray, 1979, p.62.

19 Hills, 1988, p.186.

20 CA/MC1, 1 Sept., 3 Nov. 1950. CA/MC2,

26 April 1954. AR 1955.

21 CA/MC2, 7 March, 4 April 1952. AR 1953.

22 Cairncross, 1992, p.55, p.90.

23 Interviews: James Anthony Cropper (JAC), Oliver Acland (OGDA), Nick Willink (NWW).

24 Annual Report 1951. CA/MC1, 7 July 1950.

25 Annual Reports 1951, 1952. Both mention that much of the profit was due to fortunate purchases of pulp.

26 CA/MC1, 5 May 1951.

27 Interview: Bill Willink. 18,300 ordinary shares belonging to AHW's executors were sold to outside investors soon after the company went public. On his death AHW held almost 16 percent of ordinary share capital and over 13 percent of preference capital (CA/JWC ledger).

28 CA/DMB2, 31 Jul., 15 Aug. 1951.

29 CA/JWC Ledger, Ordinary & Preference Share Capital Accounts, Balance Sheets.

30 Balance sheets in JWC/Ledger show that dividends averaged £12,400 from 1950-5, and around £18,500 from 1956-9. JWC Ledger Profit & Loss Accounts reveal that director's bonuses averaged £9,700 from 1951-5, and did not rise above this sum until 1966. Salaries and bonus combined averaged just over £15,000 throughout the period 1950-65. CA/JWC Ledger, Directors' Remuneration.

31 James Hill was appointed on a salary of £800, plus free house, car allowance and bonus based on profits of about £300. CA/SLB4, 5 Aug. 1949.

32 CA/Property Register 1942-60. Pulpers installed 1953-7 on three machines, Nos 1, 3 & 4.

33 AR 1954. ACC's New Year message, 1957. CA/3/25. CA/MC2, 10 Sept. 1956. In 1954 the company invested £45,000 in a second 3,000kW steam turbine and also bought an additional water tube boiler (£50,000). CA/Property Register, 1942-1960.

34 CA/3/24. JAC's notes on retirement of Mr Hill, 1974. AR 1954.

35 CA/MC2, 15 Jan. 1954. Chronology of business by ACC & JAC, CA/NS15. CA/MC3, 18/2/1963.

36 CA/NS17 has sample booklet of first range of bookbinding paper ever produced for Winterbottom, 1964.

37 OGDA reckons that Star bought *c*.2,000 to 3,000 tons a year of its white cast-coating base.

38 CA/MC2, 18 Nov. 1957. CA/MC2, 7 Mar. 1955. Interviews: OGDA, Mike Wilkinson. The demise of glazed casings was perhaps tied to the decline of Britain's textile industry, the output of which fell by 35 percent between 1950 and 1965. Owen, 1999, p.65.

39 CA/MC2, 6 Dec. 1954. Another of company's biggest contracts in this period was for labels supplied to the Post Office through Fisher Clark. Interview: NWW. CA/NS15, Messages for Notice Boards Folder, 26 Nov. 1962. McCorquodale & Co. and JC & Co. correspondence, 1940s-1967, CA/17/7B.

40 HMSO: CA/MC1, 1 Sept. 1950, CA/MC2, 9 Feb. 1959. CA/MC2, 8 Jun. 1959. CA/MC3, 15 Jan. 1962, CA/MC3 in general. CA/MC3, 18 Feb. 1963. Interviews: OGDA, NWW, JAC, Alf Whiteley. CA/MC3, 15 Jun. 1961. Brooke Bond: CA/MC3, 20 Feb. 1967 notes that No3 largely kept going by Pasted Boards and Brooke Bond's Green.

41 CA/MC2, 18 Dec. 1953.

42 Interview: NWW. CA/MC2, 5 Apr. 55, 18 Nov. 1957, 8 Jun. 59. CA/MC3, 4 Apr. 1960.

43 CA/MC2, 18 Aug. 1958, 11 Mar. 1957.

44 "New Year Message", 1957, CA/3/25.

45 Interview: Alf Whiteley.

46 Interview: John Larking (JHL).

47 Interview: Tommy Pinch.

48 CA/NS15, Messages for Notice Boards Folder.

49 Interview: Maurice Crossley.

50 *Ibid.*

51 Interview: Alf Whiteley.

52 CA/MC3, 24 Apr. 1963.

53 CA/3/24. J. F. Hill's retirement speech by JAC.

54 *Electrical Review*, 23 May 1952. CA/7/7.

55 CA/Property Register, 1942-1960. Laboratory staff also increased at this point, with Brian Postlethwaite and Alan Stables joining George Ferrier in 1951.

56 *Ibid.*

57 CA/NS14/AGDA notes. CA/NS17, correspondence between ACC and AIC. The link between the incentive scheme and its proposed benefits is explicit in an announcement relating to its introduction on No4 machine in 1962. "We hope that this machine will now be operating at a new level of efficiency." CA/Notice Board folder, 13 Jun. 1962.

58 CA/MC3, 24 Apr. 1963.

59 CA/MC3, 23 Oct. 1961.

60 Interview: NWW

61 CA/DMB3, 5 Dec. 1962.

62 CA/MC3, 19 Aug. 1963.

63 CA/MC3, 4 Dec. 1961.

64 CA/NS14/AGDA notes. 10 Sept. 1963 memo. CA/DMB3, 16 Sept. 63.

65 Interviews: NWW, JHL.

66 CA/MC2, 18 Nov. 1957. AR 1959.

67 CA/MC3, 24 Jul. 1961.

68 AR 1962, 1963.

69 Muir, 1972, p.64.

70 Owen, 1999, p.156-7.

71 CA/NS15/1. CA/MC3, 18 Jul. 1960.

72 Owen, 1999, p.157.

73 The inn existed on a property called Chapel Field in 1786. Known as the Anglers' Inn by the mid-nineteenth century. Parson and White's *History, Directory and Gazetteer of Cumberland and Westmorland*, 1829, refers to The Fisherman at Burneside, Thomas Taylor, victualler. Mannex, 1848, also refers to The Fisherman, Mary Taylor, victualler.

74 *Kendal Mercury*, Aug.-Sept. 1843, 13 Sept. 1845, 13 Dec. 1862, 17 Jan. 1863, 29 Jun.

1878, 22 Jun. 1888, 12 Jul. 1889, 4 Mar. 1898. *Westmorland Gazette*, Mar. 31 1894, 16 Oct. 1897, 9 Mar. 1912. Records in CA/9 point to pollution incidents at Bowston in 1886-9. In 1903 £30 was given to the Kent Angling Association for restocking the river with brown trout. CA/DBLB, 2 Nov. 1903.

75 *Kendal Mercury*, Jul. 12 1889.

76 Published typescript of proceedings, 7 Nov. 1889, CA/9/2.

77 *Westmorland Gazette*, Mar. 31 1894.

78 *Kendal Mercury*, 13 May 1848.

79 Extract from Vol. 2 of evidence given to the Rivers Pollution Commission by James Cropper & Co., published in 1872. CA/NS8.

80 CJC to JWC, 26 Oct. 1916. Tolson MSS, JWC/58/b2. Such pollution did not go unnoticed. CJC to JWC, 24 Jul. 1917, referring to *Westmorland Gazette*. "[The editor] says they have kept out any amount of letters, and that the feeling is very sore about the present state of the river." Tolson MSS, JWC/27. CJC to Pollitt, 30 Jun. 1918. CA/DBrLB.

81 CA/Property Register, 1901-21.

82 CA/MC2, 2 May 1952.

83 Extracts from Fortnightly Meetings, 11 May 1938. CA/NS15.

84 Gerrish & Co. to James Cropper & Co., 25 Jan. 1956. CA/1961 Court Action and Pollution trial box.

85 The results of Dr Killie's report are outlined in an address given by the Kent Angling Association to James W. Cropper in December 1955. CA/9/9.

86 *Ibid.*

87 ACC Affadavit, 13 Jun. 1960. CA/Court Action and Pollution box.

88 Affidavit from J. G. Sherratt of the Public Analysts Laboratory. CA/Court Action and Pollution box, 1960.

89 The proceedings were instigated by Warriners & Others (being Thomas Warriner, Kenneth Wiper Wilkinson, Herbert Bland, Douglas Todd, and Robert and John Atkinson).

90 Richards, Butler & Co. to JC & Co., 6 Jan. 1958. CA/Court Action and Pollution box.

91 ACC Affadavit, 13 Jun. 1960. CA/Court Action and Pollution box.

92 *Westmorland Gazette*, 3 Jun. 1960.

93 Interview: NWW.

94 J. H. Hill affadavit, 13 Oct. 1960. CA/Court Action and Pollution box. Annual Report 1961.

95 Project to Divert Company's Trade Effluent to the North West Water Authority's Sewerage Treatment Works at Kendal, Memo from JAC to all directors, 1982. CA/NS6A.

96 CA/MC3, 5 Dec. 1960.

97 *Westmorland Gazette*, 13 Dec. 1963. AR 1982. CA/NS6A/Trade Effluent to Sewer notes, NWW, 12 May 1982. CA/MC3, 18 Feb. 1963.

98 CA/NS6A/Trade Effluent to Sewer notes, NWW, 12 May 1982. Project to Divert Company's Trade Effluent to the North West Water Authority's Sewerage Treatment Works at Kendal, Memo from JAC to all directors, 1982. CA/NS6A.

99 CA/NS9/3. Article written by JAC for the *Westmorland Gazette*, March 1982.

100 Annual Report 1982.

101 Ian Gibson had his right middle finger amputated in 1957. CA/Compensation Claims, 1915-1964.

102 CA/Compensation Claims. Leslie Dixon's accident was reported in the *Westmorland Gazette*, 20 Mar. 1959.

103 CA/MC2, 16 Jun. 1958. CA/NS17.

104 *Westmorland Gazette*, 5 Nov. 1965. CA/MC3, 22 Nov. 1965.

105 *Westmorland Gazette*, 19 Nov. 1965. Interview: Maurice Crossley.

106 CA/MC1, 4 Oct. 1947. CA/MC1, 3 Feb. 1950.

107 In 1958 the company posted a notice board in the mills requesting employees to purchase safety boots and shoes by means of weekly deductions off wages. CA/Notice Board folder.

108 CA/MC2, 16 Jun. 1957.

109 CA/MC3, Jul. 1964.

110 CA/MC3, 18 Sept. 1964. CA/DMB3, 16 Sept. 1964.

111 CA/MC3, 19 May 1966.

112 Harold Snowdon was appointed welfare officer in 1948 (CA/DMB2, 29 Sept. 1948), starting on a salary of £370 on his return from training at college, which included learning about industrial law, labour relations and psychology. He was, in effect, the company's first personnel officer, by which title he was later known.

113 Six days consecutive holiday were granted in 1939, on top of six bank holidays. CA/SLB4, 19 Jul. 1939.

114 CA/MC2, 19 Nov. 1955. In 1949 proposals were put forward for a new pension scheme for all employees, but these were later shelved owing to the largest costs that the company would have to incur. CA/DMB2, 21 Nov. 1949.

115 CA/NS15, Notice Board folder, 31 Mar. 1960.

116 CA/MC2, 6 Feb. 1953. CA/MC2, 13 Jun. 1955. A uniform system of meal breaks was introduced for the first time in 1954. Meal Breaks, General Notice, 15 Mar. 1954, CA/NS15.

117 Interview: Alf Whiteley.

118 Interview: Tommy Pinch, OGDA.

119 Interview: Philip Huck.

120 CA/MC3, 4 Mar. 1968.

121 CA/MC3, 16 January 1961.

122 Floud & McCloskey, 1992, p.27.

123 CA/MC3, 16 Jul. 1962. Owen, 1999, p.31, says lack of surplus of labour in post-war Britain was one reason its industry fell behind Europe.

124 Interview: Harry Wilson.

125 CA/NS15/Notice Board folder, 21 Dec. 1961.

126 Interview: Maurice Crossley.

127 Annual Report, 1963. CA/MC3, 24 Apr. 1963.

128 Westmorland Gazette, 23 Jul. 1964.

129 CA/MC3, 13 Jan. 1964.

130 CA/MC3, 28 Sept. 1964. Interview: OGDA.

131 Interview: Harry Wilson.

132 Westmorland Gazette, 14 Sept. 1964.

133 Interviews: JHL, Harry Wilson.

134 Interview: PMGC.

135 Tolson MSS, ACC file, ACC to JWC, 13 Aug. 1944.

136 Interviews: JHL, Maurice Crossley, Alan Sutton, Tommy Pinch, NWW.

137 Obituary, Westmorland Gazette, 5 May 1967.

138 The company secretary Ronnie Reddish, for example, was asked to represent the directors in dealings with stockbrokers and solicitors in London.

139 Interview: NWW.

140 Wray, 1979, p.86.

141 Wray, 1979, p.62. Under the terms of the 1960 EFTA treaty, the countries involved were to have their imports admitted with a yearly 10% reduction in duties until 1970, when all duties would be ended. In the event, the process was accelerated.

142 UK Paper Federation. Hills, 1988, p.186. Wray, 1979, p.67, p.72.

143 Shorter, 1971, p.176. In 1967 a Financial Times editorial on the paper industry predicted that there would be a "reshuffling" of the paper industry in response to the changing marketplace, "into a small number of large groups each able to offer a full range of products . . . This process has already gone some way, and a number of mergers have already taken place". Financial Times, 28 Feb. 1967.

144 Shorter, 1971, p.182. "Difficult Times for Paper and Board Makers", Financial Times, Annual Review XXVI, 15 July 1968.

145 Shorter, 1971, p.176. Spicers was founded in 1796.

CHAPTER 9

1 OGDA started work on a salary of £750, plus a profits bonus of about £50 per year. He was also allowed a company car in the 8-10 horsepower range. ACC to AGDA, 18 August 1958, CA/NS18.

2 "It has already been agreed that [Oliver's] central 'theme' as an executive should be direction of 'Sales'." CA/DBrLB, Memo from AGDA to James Cropper & Co. directors, 1958.

3 CA/DMB3, 5 Dec. 1962.

4 NWW took on another of ACC's responsibilities, pulp buying.

5 The only other director without family connections was John Bryce, who was a partner from 1859 and a director from 1889, when the firm became a limited liability company.

6 CA/MC3, 15 May 1967. J. M. Oldham handled some of the company's largest accounts.

7 Wray, 1979, p.157.

8 CA/MC3, 22 February, 19 March 1971. Annual Report, 1971.

9 CA/MC3, 10 Apr. 1972.

10 Figures from the UK Confederation of Paper Industries.

11 Owen, 1999, p.157

12 Wray, 1979, p.75.

13 Wray, 1979, p.185.

14 Cairncross, 1995, p.244, p.231.

15 Figures from the UK Confederation of Paper Industries.

16 Article by JAC for the *Westmorland Gazette* Industrial Supplement, March 1982. CA/NS9/3.

17 Article by JAC for the *Westmorland Gazette* Industrial Supplement, March 1983. CA/NS9/3.

18 CA/MC3, 20 Aug. 1975.

19 CA/NS18, Statement to Sogat, 19 Mar. 1973. Ten year strategy plan by OGDA.

20 JAC Memo, 9 Sept. 1980, CA/NS12.

21 CA/NS12, Directors' Conference, Nov. 1981. CA/DMB3, 16 October 1981.

22 CA/NS34, Report for directors by OGDA, 8 Aug. 1974, p.15.

23 Wray, 1979, p.60. Owen, 1999, p.3.

24 The new system allowed clay to be delivered in bulk by lorry direct from Cornwall, where previously it had been delivered in bags by sea to Preston docks.

25 CA/News-sheets, April 1969.

26 Annual Report, 1999.

27 CA/Property Register shows £180,000 of expenditure on waste paper and pulp scheme from 1967-70. Blending chests put in from 1972-4.

28 Interview: Maurice Crossley. There was nothing in the way of protective clothing.

29 With the railway closed, Cowan Head was converted to run off oil. *Lancashire Evening Post*, 31 Nov. 1965.

30 Railway and Bogies were scrapped in 1972. CA/Property Register, 1960-1980s. The company operated two locomotives. *Rachel*, named after James W. Cropper's daughter, notched up nearly fifty years service for the firm, and was retired to Haverthwaite.

31 Interview: Peter Charlton.

32 £75,000 was spent on the machine in 1971 and £50,000 on a pulper scheme in 1972-4. Annual Report 1972 says £87,000 spent.

33 No4 and No2 machines were also based on the 1904 designs, despite being upgraded in the 1930s.

34 JAC Memo, 9 Sept. 1980, CA/NS12. Annual Report, 1981.

35 JAC, article for *Westmorland Gazette* Industrial Supplement, March 1983. CA/NS9/3.

36 Annual reports, 1987, 1988. Hills, 1988, p.64. The first gas turbine in a UK paper-mill was installed in a Birmingham mill in 1985, by which time JC plc's plans were well advanced.

37 The situation stretched cash resources so much that the firm was forced to secure a borrowing facility of £1.2 million from its bankers, Barclays.

38 "He is an amazing chairman", comments NWW. "He senses the vibes in a group of people like nobody else I know." Interview with Neil McKendrick, 30 Aug. 1994.

39 European paper magazine, CA/NS28/JAC.

40 Talks regarding a possible merger with Swindon Letter File, the firms' principal manilla customer, took place in 1978. A. G. Thompson of J. Bibby & Sons to JAC, 16 Jan. 1980. CA/NS1/1.

41 Annual Report, 1968. North Wales Paper Mill was owned by McCorquodale & Co. CA/NS5 has details on the approach from East Lancashire Paper Mill.

42 CA/NS26, related correspondence from June to July 1989.

43 By the late 1990s only three of the largest fourteen UK paper companies were wholly British-owned, whereas thirty years earlier all had been in British ownership. Owen, 1999, p.164

44 CA/NS5 has various papers relating to this. "We feel we do not have sufficient financial resources to cover our own needs and make this investment", commented James Cropper in June 1988.

45 In 1978 the directors resisted the advice of their bankers to make a rights issue for this reason. CA/NS12, Directors' meetings, Feb.-Apr. 1978. Tens years later its acquisition policy was still the same. "The company must retain its control over the equity for as long as possible and must resist temptations to dilute as and when the opportunity arose. Therefore cash should be used for acquisition and not shares". (6 May 1988, CA/DMB3)

46 JAC arranged the following facilities himself: Samuel Montagu (from 1978), Barclays Merchant Bank (1979); Société Générale (1987); Scandinavian Bank (1987); Singer & Friedlander and Nord Land Bank (1993). CA/DMB3.

47 £5 million from Credit Lyonnais, £2.2 million from Banque National de Paris, securing through a leasing broker, Olympic. In the 1980s the company also paid for much of its power-plant improvements through a £3.5 million lease with the Forward Trust.

48 The Paper Industry Gold Medal is awarded annually to one individual who is deemed to have made an outstanding contribution to the UK paper industry. OGDA was also a member of UMIST Paper Science Steering Committee 1984-97.

49 CA/NS18/6

50 First stated in the 1992 annual report.

51 Annual Report, 1991.

52 Annual Report, 1991. Article in DPW magazine, 1991, CA/NS28/JAC. "Cropper claims to be the largest producer of black paper in Europe".

53 Like many changes, it was a mix of good fortune and foresight that led JC plc into new packaging products. The company's dominance in the prestige packaging sector can be traced back to its efforts to find tonnage, whatever the profit, for its new No4 machine in the early 1980s. A sales agent introduced the firm to the corrugated board industry, in particular Blackburn Corrugated, which made coloured corrugated for the perfume industry. At first the contributions from this sector were low, but in time the association established JC plc as a leading supplier in the packaging of perfume and alcohol, such as whisky.

54 The production of annual reports was overseen by OGDA for many years.

55 Colorplan is first mentioned in company records in 1977. Report on Sales Policy 1977/8, 30 May 1977, CA/NS3/1.

56 CA/NS21/1990-6 plans.

57 Interview: NWW.

58 CA/NS3/JAC Correspondence 1975-1979. Sales Report Nov. 1975.

59 Sales analysis, 1976/7, CA/NS3/1.

60 CA/NS3/JAC correspondence 1975-1989; CA/NS9/1.

61 CA/MC3, 15 May 1967.

62 The catalyst for the closure of the London office was the expiry of the Oldham lease

in 1974. And with the London sales office closed, JHL thought "why not Manchester too?" CA/DMB3, 24 Sept. 1975.

63 A report on sales policy 1977/79. 30 May 1977, CA/NS3/1.

64 Annual Report, 1995.

65 *Lancashire Evening Post*, 13 Nov. 1965.

66 CA/NS3/JAC correspondence, 1975-1989, Sales Report, Nov. 1975.

67 JC plc's network of agents meet at Burneside every two years.

68 Richard Cockram, "What future for the market pulp sector?", *Pulp & Paper International*, October 1998.

69 Annual Report, 1996.

Index